A Chameleon *from the* Land *of the* Quagga

— AN IMMIGRANT'S STORY —

From Your Appreciative Chameleon Author

EX-LIBRIS

A Chameleon *from the* Land *of the* Quagga

— AN IMMIGRANT'S STORY —

Joan Bismillah

 FriesenPress

Suite 300 - 990 Fort St
Victoria, BC, V8V 3K2
Canada

www.friesenpress.com

Copyright © 2019 by Joan Bismillah
First Edition — 2019

All rights reserved.

No part of this publication may be reproduced in any form, or by any means, electronic or mechanical, including photocopying, recording, or any information browsing, storage, or retrieval system, without permission in writing from FriesenPress.

Photo Credit: Photo of Author Joan Bismillah by Liora Kogan.

Artist Credit: Deep appreciation for permission to use part of Artist Beth Restrick's Glimpses of Africa Collection for Cover.

These are the recollections of a 90 year old who has recreated events, locales, and conversations as best she can from her memory. Some of the incidents and names have been changed and combined in order to illustrate the torment people lived with, to protect relatives from reliving these incidents again and to protect the identity of certain individuals. While actual people, places, and events are presented in the context of the author's experience, individuals' recollections of those same people, places and events may very well diverge, all in good faith. The author and the publisher do not intend to harm and regret any unintentional harm that may nonetheless result or be inferred through these recollections.

ISBN
978-1-5255-3176-7 (Hardcover)
978-1-5255-3177-4 (Paperback)
978-1-5255-3178-1 (eBook)

1. *Biography & Autobiography, Cultural Heritage*

Distributed to the trade by The Ingram Book Company

DEDICATION

This memoir is dedicated to the memory of Bis—forever in my heart and mind. Written for our four children: Enver, Nadya, Nisha, and Sigi.

TABLE OF CONTENTS

Part One		**1**
Chapter 1	Under the Sign of Pisces	3
Chapter 2	Milestones	9
Chapter 3	Recollections of the Past	20
Chapter 4	A Victorian Grandmother	24
Chapter 5	Life at the Convent	32
Chapter 6	Curious and Curiouser!	38
Chapter 7	Art College and Interior Design	44
Chapter 8	Only Fools Pay for Experience: Drama in the Labour Ward	48
Chapter 9	Falling in Love	60
Chapter 10	Holy Unction	66
Chapter 11	A Surprise Gift	69
Chapter 12	Against All Odds	72
Chapter 13	The Madding Crowd	80
Chapter 14	Chinese Interns	88
Chapter 15	African Residents	91
Chapter 16	A Forbidden Tryst	94
Chapter 17	Trauma in the Labour Ward	102
Chapter 18	The Hospital Board Inquiry	110
Chapter 19	Remembrance of Things Past	114
Chapter 20	Dangerous Moonlight at the Zoo Lake	121

Chapter 21	Sighting the New Moon	127
Chapter 22	A Marriage Proposal	133
Chapter 23	Secret Nuptial	137
Chapter 24	Hide and Seek	145
Chapter 25	A Marriage Licence and a Passport	151
Chapter 26	Aboard the Blue Train	153
Chapter 27	A Sea Voyage	160
Chapter 28	A Lonely Heart through Error Forlorn	168
Chapter 29	A Stateless Baby	181
Chapter 30	Down the Rabbit Hole	190
Chapter 31	Bis sets up a Medical Clinic	197
Chapter 32	Potchefstroom – A Muslim Family	201
Chapter 33	Owning a Home in Potchefstroom	206
Chapter 34	The Importance of Colour	213
Chapter 35	The Inquisition	218
Chapter 36	Trouble in the Rabbit Hutch	225
Chapter 37	The Group Areas Act	230
Chapter 38	Lion Country, a Farewell	233
Chapter 39	Reminiscence: The London Years	239
Chapter 40	A Highland Fling	256

Part Two		**265**
Chapter 41	Woodlawn Memorial Garden Cemetery	267
Chapter 42	Life in Fergus	280
Chapter 43	Guelph University 1966–1970	288
Chapter 44	A Canadian Education	300
Chapter 45	Fergus Medical Centre	306
Chapter 46	Bigotry	310
Chapter 47	Menopause	315
Chapter 48	The Farm at Ennotville	319
Chapter 49	Our Home in Ennottville	332
Chapter 50	A Return to Johannesburg 1982	340
Chapter 51	Secrets	348
Chapter 52	A Routine Check-Up 1997	350
Chapter 53	Life as a Widow	363
Chapter 54	News from Zimbabwe	367
Chapter 55	Requiem for a Departed Sister	370
Chapter 56	Tribute to Peggy	373
Chapter 57	Verity Remembrance	376

Acknowledgements   385

Part One

CHAPTER 1
Under the Sign of Pisces

I WAS BORN UNDER THE SIGN OF PISCES IN 1928—THE YEAR OF THE dragon, in the city of Johannesburg, South Africa. My father was Italian. My mother was of Scottish and Anglo-Indian descent (and who knew what else), and into this genetic cauldron I made my first appearance. We were European in a country that was racially divided into European and non-European, which simply meant white or non-white. The South Africa I knew was not a homogenous nation, rather it was a cosmopolitan combination of European explorers and immigrants, the Bantu tribes, the indigenous San, and the indentured Indians who worked the sugar-cane plantations. Thus, the population was multi-coloured, ranging from white through all shades of pinks, tans, browns, and black skin tones. It is not surprising then the importance and impact of race in my eventful journey or that the emphasis on colour played such a major role in our daily lives. I was influenced by religion and folklore, my horoscope, and superstition inherited from a maternal grandmother, a disciple of Madam Blavatsky. It all helped to shape my thinking. My earliest recollection growing up was how I learnt to adapt in that unstable, racially-conscious environment.

This multi-hued society should have adopted the quagga, that extinct beast with its varicoloured body, as an emblem for the country. It was neither horse nor zebra, but its features resembled both animals. The distinctive irregular black, brown, and white stripes circled the head and mane. The tawny torso and hindquarters faded gradually to cream at the under-belly, and white legs supported the unusually coloured animal.

It was the eve of my eighty-fifth birthday and I lay in bed listening to the howling March wind, which was accompanied by the intermittent sound of crackling ice that ricocheted and descended in salvos, breaking tree branches and landing on hydro lines. The lights flickered, then utter darkness. An eerie silence permeated the isolated, rambling farm house that was shrouded in gloom. All was still. Any communication with the outside world was severed and I wondered what the future held. My husband had been dead for ten years. I was alone and still overcome with grief. A lingering sadness persisted that was exacerbated by the long, black night ahead. The ice storm continued. Sleep evaded me, and in the darkness, I ruminated. My birthday, as usual, triggered memories of the momentous events that had shaped my life, dating back to my landmark seventh birthday. Reminiscing played havoc with my emotions. I was a voyeur peeping into a kaleidoscope of miniature, overlapping scenes that reflected my life and the many milestones I had passed along the way. Pictures of places and people, both living and dead, tumbled like acrobats across the screen of my mind, but with the slightest tilt they slid out of focus. My thoughts were awash in the past and they continued to intrude.

Deprived of sleep, I got up and lit a candle and checked my horoscope. One line caught my fancy: *Your mind really does create your world. So, create a world you can love.* Nothing very exciting, but instinctively I realised it was a signal that I had to continue to live and not merely exist.

In my present state, the prediction was encouraging advice, particularly as I was on my own. I acknowledged that time was fleeting. I decided that my story needed to be told before the dreaded executioner of memory, Alzheimer's, lurking in a recess of my brain, threatened to distort my recollections to a deconstructed, Picasso-like abstraction. Unlike Scheherazade, who needed a thousand-and-one tales to survive, my time was limited and my story was exigent for posterity before all was lost. I determined to cloak my discomfort and my insecurity with feigned bravado. Vanity had caused me to postpone the task, for I was sensitive to criticism and dreaded being made to feel a fool like poor Quasimodo, or worse, an idiot like Punchinello.

Part One

George Bernard Shaw's *St. Joan* made its debut in Johannesburg in 1928, at a small concert hall where amateur groups tried out new plays. My story began in that auspicious year. Lily, my young mother, an aspiring actress, had been cast as an understudy for the leading role, and she named me after the martyred protagonist. My mother, an avid theatre buff, hoped that one day I too would become a bona fide member of the illustrious thespian world.

Alas, that was not to be, for invariably when adults asked my name, and I answered "Joan." They raised their eyebrows. "Ah, Joan of Arc!" This made me feel strange. I became self-conscious and sensed that somehow I was different, a dislocation particularly felt when a corpulent uncle pinched my cheek and waving his fat finger said, "Ah ha! The one that was burnt at the stake!"

I had no answer, for I felt uncomfortable in the presence of this grownup, who made me feel odd by singling me out because of my name. I did not understand what he meant, but I worried whether he was predicting some future punishment. Thus began my childhood aversion to that sanctified name and to my loathsome uncle.

Matters were not helped when I overheard my grandmother tell my mother, "You will rue the day you named her after that witch."

"Which witch?" my mother had asked innocently.

My grandmother, a devotee of the Ouija Board, was not impressed and warned my mother repeatedly that acting was hardly a fit profession for genteel women.

Any discussion about my name further convinced me I was indeed different. To cover my embarrassment, I would talk at length in an attempt to divert the conversation, and I drove adults to distraction with my endless questions. I paid little heed to their replies, thereby earning me the hated moniker of "Chatterbox." Since listening was an essential part of acting, any gene I might have inherited was stunted, a flaw that prevented me from becoming talented like my mother or Shirley Temple, the famous child star of the time.

My boundless curiosity led me into all sorts of problems. Grandmother especially took issue with my antics, which escalated once she became my guardian in the absence of my mother. I was constantly scolded or upbraided: "Joan, sit up straight. Take your elbows off the table. Look people in the eye when speaking or being spoken to." Worst of all, "Children should be seen and not heard."

How could one become an actor, which my mother had so ardently wished for, if I was not allowed to use the tools of the trade—*words*?

In retrospect, Gran, as we called her, was an adherent of rigid Victorian morality; she tried to instil good manners. Her reprimands were a personal affront. Thus, it became necessary to retaliate against what Grandmother tried to inculcate.

Gran was a pious woman. She insisted on morning and evening prayer and grace before and after meals. I began the rebellion by not shutting my eyes and slouching during prayers, for which I received a sharp poke in the ribs. "God is watching," she intoned in her most reverential voice. "Show Him respect."

I was on shaky ground. Should I continue to slouch and open my eyes during grace, I most certainly would be punished and sent straight to Hell, where the fires burned brightly, ready to incinerate all miscreants, including a disobedient child named Joan. I was terrified and I felt beyond salvation. To atone for my misdeeds, I would have to apologize and improve my manners, but would it be sufficient penance even saying countless Hail Marys?

What should I do?

I doubled my prayers and asked for guidance. After all, if what I was told to be true, that God listened to all, even sinners, then surely I too fitted that category. Help was needed for how best to combat Grandmother's endless scolding, which now included my slothful habits: "Pull up your socks!" "Tuck in your blouse!" "Wipe your dirty shoes before entering the house." "Stop biting your nails!" "Don't talk with your mouth full!"

Gran's ire even extended to my playmates. "I don't like you playing with that unmannerly Michael," she scolded. Michael was our neighbours' son, and my brother Barney's bosom pal.

I became desperate and decided that in addition to prayers, morning and evening, I would recite the Angelus at noon and read *The Book of Common Prayer* during the deadly-dull sermon at Sunday mass, a time when I normally fidgeted and yawned and attracted disapproving stares. Incidentally, I discovered the most interesting part of the *Common Prayer* book was on the back pages, where it clearly listed whom a man could not marry. Here, at least, was gender equality, because it also stated whom a woman could not marry. For a long time, this puzzled me. Why would anyone want to marry any of their relatives?

Part One

That set me thinking: If Cain and Abel were the first people, where did they get their wives? Were their wives their sisters or where did they find them? Their marriages were in direct opposition to what the church dictated. I pondered these questions. When finally I broached the subject, Gran snapped, "That is not a subject for children. You're getting too big for your boots."

There was no use explaining it was in the *Common Prayer* book, though I offered to show her if she cared to see. Gran's oval face turned purple with rage.

"That is blasphemous. To your room. I'll deal with you later."

Another setback! How would I ever get into Gran's good books?

Sent to bed without supper, I took refuge under Gran's prized quagga-skin karros, a light bed coverlet. At least it was cozy. Marta, my Zulu nanny, took pity on me, sneaked in warm milk and a sandwich, and implored me to be a good girl and to beg Gran's forgiveness. I could not understand why something that was written in the *Common Prayer* book, given by Gran and inscribed with my name, could be so outrageous.

Marta replied, "Argh Joan, when you are older you will understand."

"I'm asking now. I'll forget when I'm older."

Instinctively, I knew that the conversation could go no further. As well, I did not want to alienate Marta and knew that it was necessary to appear to agree, for at least she was on my side.

The battle had only just begun. Gran ordered me to attend Bible study classes twice weekly and forgo play in the park as punishment. "That ought to keep you out of mischief," she said.

I was not so sure. It was not long before reports reached Gran that I distracted serious students and that perhaps when I was a little older, I could return. More disgrace!

"You're wilfully disobedient and out-spoken. What's to become of you?"

Relatives were consulted, and by chance, I overheard the general consensus: "She's just a child, it is best to let her be." Oh, how it paid to eavesdrop! Armed with this information, I renewed the campaign against Gran. I did not set out to be blatantly difficult or disobedient. I really wanted to be good, if only Gran understood. But she permitted no explanations. She regarded any response as impertinence. It was impossible to have a conversation with her because I knew how she felt about children being seen and not heard. Why couldn't I be seen and heard? That was exactly what I longed for.

One sultry afternoon, I was reading on the veranda and Gran was darning socks when two neighbours appeared. After a brief greeting, Gran invited them to have tea. I listened while pretending to read *Great Expectations*, where I made an interesting discovery of the relationship between the characters and myself. I saw myself as Pip, imploring to be forgiven, and Gran was the unyielding Miss Havisham.

Gran noticed that I was paying attention to the adult conversation. "How would you like *ME* to go out and play, so that you may talk to the ladies?" she mocked. The ladies snickered.

My face was aglow. My head felt on fire. Why did I always blush? Had I answered back, I may have had my ears boxed for being rude, except Gran never lifted a finger. She had no need to; her barbs prickled and did enough damage.

I went inside and through the open window I heard the ladies gossiping. I was delighted I had outsmarted Gran. But my triumph was short lived. From inside the doorway, Gran intoned, "You deceitful child. Up to bed at once."

A chorus of nattering old women chortled as I left. The world was conspiring to keep me in servitude and perpetual punishment. I was concerned. Why was I so different from my pretty younger sisters who never got into trouble? Perhaps it was because of the influence of Pisces, those twin fishes who swam in reverse tides in a restricted space. They lay, one above the other, head to tail—that is, upside down. Was that why I did not fit in?

Feeling all alone, it was little wonder then that I grew muddled. My entire world appeared upside down, with everything always seeming to go wrong. Grandmother's faith in horoscopes and fortune tellers only served to strengthen her prediction that I would come to a sticky end. I realised that was the reason she tried to exorcise the witch that possessed me. Thank goodness they no longer burned people for being odd. Being born under the sign of Pisces had correctly confirmed the topsy-turvy world I was destined to inhabit.

CHAPTER 2
Milestones

THE YEAR 1935 WAS INAUSPICIOUS. I WAS UNAWARE THAT AN UNFOREseen change was about to take place. My seventh birthday was days away, and my eleven-year-old brother christened Vincent but nicknamed Barney, and I were playing in the garden when Marta, our nanny, called out that it was time for my afternoon nap. I thought it most unfair that my brother was never called away from whatever he was doing. I had three younger sisters; five-year-old Beryl, three-year-old Jean, and my baby sister Leatrice, who was just under two and only answered to the name of Peggy, which she associated with her stuffed piggy. The three little girls were already taking their rest. As usual, I protested in vain that I was not tired or sleepy. I hated the enforced rule, and in spite of Nanny's constant scolding, my habit during naptime was to visit the bathroom at two-minute intervals. That afternoon, I heard the tradesman's bell. I ran to the bedroom window and saw a van draw up to the side entrance of our old, Dutch-gabled house. I watched Nanny dry her hands on the striped apron that covered her wide girth, and then she signed what must have been an invoice. She called out to our Zulu gardener and ordered him in their native tongue, "Ben, help driver put big box in garage and come to kitchen when you finish."

By this time, I was hopping around.

"Why you down here?" an irate Nanny asked.

"I can't help it if I need to make water," I said, hopping up and down. "I'm excited, and that makes me go. What's in the box, Nanny?"

"You must rest if you want go to park later. In box is something for gardener, you nosey child," she scolded.

"What's in the box?" I persisted, tugging on Nanny's apron. "But what's in it?" I stamped my foot and tugged even harder.

"Joan, don't be cheeky. You ask too much questions. Go have your nap," she scolded as she waddled away. "Your father, he will be angry that you don't listen when I say to go."

"I'll ask the gardener."

"He can't tell you. Go back to your room, and don't wake your sisters."

"I'm sorry, Nanny, but tell me what's in the box? Then I promise I'll go. Do you think it's a birthday present for me?"

Ben interjected in Zulu, "*Hau Sugah*—get away." He wanted to get back to work, but I was detaining Nanny, who gave his orders.

"Tell me. Please tell me. I'm not tired. I'll ask Father."

Nanny shook a plump finger and cautioned me once again but with little effect. It was strange that my disobedience had no adverse impact on my younger siblings' behaviour. Quite the contrary. They were obedient. Perhaps my constant answering back was a warning to them to behave themselves, speak only when spoken to, and answer politely.

Not waiting for an answer from Nanny, I ran off in search of my father. He was not in his office, but I noticed the calendar. On impulse, I picked it up and in the process, knocked over the pencil box. It clattered with a thud and scattered crayons, pencils, and erasers all over the floor. I had difficulty picking them up. The crayons kept rolling and slipping away from my grasp. Eventually, I managed to collect and return them to the box. I selected a red crayon, picked up the calendar from the desk, and circled my birthday. In my haste to replace the calendar, I nudged my parents' wedding photo. It fell to the floor with a thud, smashing the mirrored frame. I cried out and Father rushed into the office.

"What's all the commotion, Joan? Have you hurt yourself?"

"Oh no, Father. I'm sorry I broke the mirror. And now we'll have seven years of bad luck," I blabbered.

Nanny came to see what all the fuss was. "Look at all mess you make. You not listen," she said, shaking her head.

My father gestured to Nanny to say no more. "Joan, listen to me. You're not to believe those stupid superstitions. Where do you pick them up? Breaking the frame was an accident. However, if you were napping as you were supposed to be, then it wouldn't have broken. You must be obedient and more careful in future."

"Yes, Father. I only wanted to mark my birthday." I was still trembling.

My father's scolding had not dispelled my fears, but he patted my head and noticing the encircled date, very gently he said, "Joan, my dear, each birthday is a milestone, but this one's special."

"Why? I asked. "And what's a milestone, Father?"

"Every birthday is a milestone. And anytime something special happens to affect your life, for better or for worse, then that's another milestone."

"Just like the stones that mark the signs on the road?"

"Yes," my father laughed. "You'll be seven years old, the age to be admitted to junior school. You'll be starting in Grade Two and that will mark another milestone."

"Why not Grade One, Father?"

"Because you read above the Grade Two level, and that gives you a head start."

"Father, I'm so happy. I can't wait to start school." I started jumping up and down and hopping about, the van, the box, and the broken frame all forgotten. "I can't wait for my birthday so I can start school. Will I have a uniform? And a satchel? I want one. And also a pencil box with lots of coloured crayons, just like Barney's."

"Yes Joan, just like your brother's."

Nanny interrupted. "Joan, don't fuss and make noise. Mummy has a headache."

"Joan, please do as you're told," my father said. "Be careful now or you'll drive Nanny mad with all your questions, and Mummy is resting. Let's not disturb her."

I continued to tick the days off a little more carefully now. There were only three more days left before my birthday. Then, quite unexpectedly, Gran arrived from Cape Town, where she had been on holiday, visiting family. Usually, Gran sent a birthday card with lots of instructions on how to behave in a lady-like fashion. I decided that I did not want to be a lady. It was such a bother, and I certainly did not want to be like Gran.

"Nanny, do you think Gran has a present in her trunk for me? It must be special for her to visit with so much luggage."

"Don't go worry old missus. Grandmother is tired from long journey. Tomorrow Grandpa also is coming. Please, you must be a good girl," she pleaded.

"I promise, I promise, especially now that I know Grandpa too is coming."

The following day, my uncles and aunties also arrived. They brought boxes of long green mangoes, big bunches of lychees, and tiny lady-finger bananas. The family too would be in time for my birthday. I was happy to see them, but where were my cousins? It was strange they had come without their children. On previous visits, the uncles would play cricket in the back garden with my brother and all the cousins would join in the fun.

Today, the aunts and uncles stayed in their rooms 'til four o'clock tea-time, when they gathered in the sitting room and spoke in hushed voices. It was very different from all their other visits when everyone took part in boisterous conversation and played games. What fun it had been when we all played Snakes and Ladders, Ludo, Chinese Checkers, and cards. My father did not join them for tea. He spent his time in the bedroom with Mother, who had a headache. I thought the behaviour of my family odd. *Why?* I asked myself. Or was it another birthday surprise? But somehow things did not excite me. On the contrary, I was downcast.

Later that evening came the arrival of my Scots grandpa, Arthur, who poked his head in at my bedroom door and delighted me with his usual jovial greeting. "Hello, my darling child. Not asleep yet?" he asked, smiling as he approached my bed. I noticed his wrinkled face, and his curly dark hair accentuated his furrowed brow and twinkling eyes as he twirled his moustache between his thumb and forefinger. The pockets of his rumpled tweed jacket bulged—they held a constant supply of sweets; Callard and Bowser nougat or butterscotch drops and wine gums. On special occasions, there were tiny penny Nestle chocolates, which he dispersed liberally, especially if Gran was not around. Grandpa was a magician who could produce pennies from behind our ears, and he had a wonderful sense of fun and told us stories, which made us howl with laughter. He gave us piggy-back rides on his broad shoulders, but his favourite pastime was to take his beloved grandson, Barney, horse riding during the summer holidays.

Despite my being in bed and having brushed my teeth, he slipped me a peppermint drop and hugged and kissed me goodnight.

Part One

"Grampa, can you please stay with me and tell me the story about Mother and Father?"

Grandpa acquiesced, sensing that my need to be comforted was as great as his. He began: "Your mother, Lily, our eldest daughter, is tall like Gran and good looking like me."

"Oh Gramps," I giggled.

"She has a lovely voice, dark hair, and large, grey eyes. She was made to be on stage—she designed and made her own clothes and costumes. She is a stylish flapper, and she met Charles Salsoni, your blue-eyed, Italian father, who was a salesman who happened to be at our small furniture shop."

"Gramps, do you think I'll get married to someone handsome and good like my father?" I asked.

"Not if you talk so much, my darling. Do you want me to continue?"

"Oh Gramps. Yes, please, please. I'll be quiet."

Arthur smiled as he continued. "Your father was a business client. We knew it was love at first sight when your mother served him. Even Gran approved of him. He travelled all over the Union of South Africa, as well as Kenya, Rhodesia, and as far as Tanganyika for months at a time, inspecting forests and buying and selling timber to furniture manufacturers. Your mother invited him to see her in a play and brought him home to dinner afterwards. They got engaged soon after their first meeting, and they had a beautiful, quiet wedding. After the ceremony, Charles had to go abroad but could not take his bride on a honeymoon."

"Why?" I interrupted, forgetting my promise to be silent.

"Because he would be visiting densely forested regions not fit for women. So, Charles promised that when business slowed they would visit Italy. Several months elapsed before your father returned. By this time, Lily was about to have a baby and soon after, your brother was born. He was christened Vincent, in honour of Charles' father. The birth of my first grandson made me a proud and excited grandfather. Ah, *a bonnie wee bairn*, he was. I called him Barney, as you know, and I taught the wee one to ride. I was never happier than when tending to him until four years later when you came along. That reminds me, soon your big day is coming."

"Father says it's a milestone, Gramps."

"So it is," said Grandpa wearily. "I think that is enough for tonight. It's late. You must go to sleep now." He kissed me and turned on the night light. "Good night, darling."

In the morning, I ticked off another day on the calendar. "Only one more day to my birthday." Suddenly, I recalled the box in the garage. What was in it? Was it a present for me? It was so big! Somehow, the mystery compensated for the pall that blanketed my home. I started dancing around but was interrupted.

"Joan, Gran she wants talk," Nanny said.

"Yes, I'm coming." I hopped into the dining room, my Quaker-style shoes squeaking.

Gran was seated at the head of the table. She appeared distant, sitting erect and rigid like a sergeant-major ready to give an order. The unopened morning newspaper, the *Rand Daily Mail*, was clutched firmly in both her hands. I noticed Gran's spectacle chain dangling against her cheek. Her spectacles were perched on the edge of her aquiline nose. She reminded me of the wizened old owl who sat on the church steeple. I'd once heard Gran say that owls hooting and dogs baying at the full moon were signs that someone was about to die. I shivered at the thought, remembering the broken mirror and seven years of bad luck!

"Stand still when I'm speaking and don't fidget," Gran admonished. I had been making cat's cradles with string that hung from my neck. "Your mother's very ill. She'll be going into hospital later today. The doctor's with her now. So, please behave yourself and don't make a noise."

"Gran, will she be back in time for my birthday? There is only a day left."

"Can't you think of anything else rather than to ask silly questions? You should be praying for your mother to get well." She put down the paper and removed her spectacles, which she polished with a handkerchief that she took from her sleeve, and then she took a pinch of snuff in her bony fingers from an enamelled box.

Unlike Grandpa, Gran was tall and slender, always dressed in severe, tailored clothes. Her auburn hair was streaked with grey, tied in a chignon at the nape of her neck, and held up by two tortoise-shell combs. Like my mother, I had inherited Gran's hazel eyes, but not her long, beautiful hands and tapered fingers with rings, which glistened when she played the piano. Gran waved her hands, a sign that I was dismissed.

Part One

Nanny was calling: "Come, Joan. Mummy, she wants to see you. Wash your hands. Tidy your hair. Pull up socks and be quiet."

Entering my parents' bedroom, I noticed that it looked different. The bamboo blinds were drawn, suffusing the light. A strong, medicinal smell almost took my breath away. I missed the fragrance of my mother's special *Phul-Nana*, and her *Eau de Joy* perfumes, a present from her actor friends. I noticed that the bed was pushed against the wall and not in the centre of the room, where I was accustomed to seeing it. The foot-end of my mother's bed was raised, supported on a board resting on bricks. My mother's feet were elevated so that her head was lowered. It must be a treatment for headaches, I thought. I remembered that I had been cautioned not to chatter or to ask silly questions. I stood inside the doorway fiddling with my hair and biting my nails, not knowing quite what to do.

"Come Joan. Don't be afraid," my mother said in a weak voice, and she beckoned me to enter. I went to the bedside. I took my mother's cold, limp hand, and twined my pudgy fingers around her long, thin ones, toying with her gold wedding ring, which swivelled round and round. I stopped playing for fear it would slip off.

I stared into my mother's lustreless eyes. She bit her under lip and a solitary tear trickled down her cheek. Carefully, I brushed it away, but this started a torrent of flowing tears. I wished that there was something I could say to make my mother feel better and stop her tears, but I could not find words to comfort her. Instead, I listened to her laboured breathing and was surprised how it escaped in little spurts. As she exhaled, her chest heaved up and down. Mother's breath was acrid, and the breath mints did little to camouflage the sour smell. The cologne and lavender water that Gran had used to swab her forehead did not mask the dank odour. I turned away to hide my own tears and for the first time, I realised how truly ill my mother was.

The two long, black pigtails that formed a halo around my mother's pale face had come undone and had been replaced by a wet flannel. One of the plaits hung loosely over the edge of the bed. I lifted it and gently stroked and caressed the braid against my cheek before I put it down on her white silk nightgown, where it lay curled up like a dull, pied snake.

"Mummy, I prayed for you," I said. "Please, please get better."

"Joan, you're a good girl. Promise me you'll be brave and look after your little sisters."

Suddenly, Gran appeared in the doorway before I had time to answer and said, "The ambulance is here. Joan, go with Marta."

Father entered and took my hand. "Joan, kiss Mummy before she leaves for the hospital."

I kissed my mother, whose lips were parched and dry, her tears welling up again and flowing into the hollow pools of her sunken cheeks.

My father put his arm around me. "Be good, darling. Listen to Gran and Marta."

The attendants came and carried Mother away to the waiting ambulance, her outstretched arm dangled over the side of the stretcher.

Nanny wrung her hands in despair and wiped them on the apron that clung to her ample hips. Then slowly she shook her head and retied her *doek*, a head scarf, tightly around her head.

I did not understand why everyone was telling me to be good. Was my mother's recovery dependent on my good behaviour?

A little later, Nanny had finally stopped crying and said, "It's time to go to the park." As we were about to leave, I saw the adults assembled in the sitting room talking in lowered voices. More people arrived. Accompanied by his wife, our neighbour, an Afrikaans *dominie* (a pastor), was praying for my mother.

"Nanny, I don't want to go." It was the first time I had refused to go to the park. I wanted to stay in the hallway and eavesdrop, hoping that they would not notice me. Nanny relented and for once gave in to my request.

All the excitement that had built up over my impending birthday plummeted like the lambent sun before a thunder storm. It seemed as if a gigantic cloud had blanketed my world, smothering me in darkness. All the air was depleted and replaced by sadness and melancholia. I was disconsolate and lost, longing only for my mother's comforting embrace as I squatted in the hallway outside the sitting room. I wondered why all my prayers went unanswered. I resolved to say more prayers without being told, hoping that they would help my mother's recovery.

All the relatives and guests, including Father's brothers and their wives, were very sad, but my father's stylish younger sister, Katie, whom Gran disliked, did not appear as sad. She spent her time in my father's study playing gramophone records, and at intervals the melodic strains of "Smoke Gets in Your Eyes," a song from the musical *Roberta*, wafted through the house, vying with prayers that were being said for my mother.

"She's a self-centred hussy. She has no respect," I overheard Gran confide in Grandpa.

"What's a hussy?" I asked.

Gran responded, "*Never you mind!*" Her favourite saying. "Do you know what killed the cat? Go and play with your sisters and your dolls, Joan. Children should not listen to adult conversations, much less repeat them."

Grandpa merely smiled and patted me on the head. Reaching into his pocket, he handed me a peppermint Life Saver.

It was a rare occasion for all the relatives from both sides of the family to gather together. Although they were friendly, they did not seem too pleased when they were introduced to my mother's Anglo-Indian cousin, a priest from Mauritius, who brought me a prayer book.

"Thank you," I said, remembering my manners, but before I had a chance to speak to him, he moved on to join the grownups. I had wished to ask him about Mauritius because my mother was born there. Perhaps I would visit it someday.

The excitement that had built up over the past week had been dampened by the solemn atmosphere, usually reserved for the Holy Week before Easter. No one had mentioned or even referred to my birthday.

On the morning of my seventh birthday, a grumpy Barney came back a day early from Boy Scouts Camp. He did not wish me a happy birthday, but said brusquely, "Mummy's dead! Don't say I told you. Gran wants to tell you herself." He kicked the door stop and chased the cat, who skittered out of the way as he went out into the garden to stop Fritz, his dog, from howling. I shivered and remembered what Gran had said about dogs howling when someone died.

I was stunned into silence. For once I asked no questions. I'd known that Mother was sick, but Gran had not said she was dying. Why hadn't she? Gran knew that I knew about death. I had been present when the earth tremor rumbled on the dumps, and a little kid had been buried alive in the quick-sand, which was always dangerous, hence the reason we children were forbidden to play on it. That day I had pleaded with and begged Barney and Michael to allow me to play with them. They'd refused, and so I followed them to the mine dumps. I too was almost a casualty but for the quickness of Michael, who pulled me to safety on the wooden ramp.

Now it was clear why the relatives had come. The adults had been aware that Mother was dying, and their visit was not to celebrate my birthday, but to bid her goodbye. That was also the reason that Gran thought me selfish. But how was I to know? In spite of my agony, I could not cry. One is supposed to cry when someone dies. All my prayers had been in vain, and though I had been a good girl or tried to be, Mother had died. I shuddered, bit my nails, and gnashed my teeth. Why, why had she died?

"Joan," Gran called in a voice I had never heard before. Gran was slightly stooped and looked frail and troubled. Her eyes were red and glittering. I knew what she was about to tell me. I trembled, unable to control myself. Gran took both my hands in hers, trying to stop my shaking, but she could not. I felt I would wet myself, and now my teeth were chattering. It was difficult to tell where I hurt, or if I hurt.

"Joan, my dear..."

I jerked my hands away from Gran. For the first time, she was not herself. She did not scold, but appeared softer. However, I was neither able to respond nor pay attention to what she was trying to say. My mother's last words kept echoing through my mind: "Be brave and take care of your little sisters." My sister Beryl, five years old and two years my junior, would never listen to me because we always quarrelled, and often she managed to get timid Jean, who was only four, to side with her. Perhaps if I gave them all my toys, they would listen. But I decided I would keep my books and read to them. But what of my baby sister Peggy, who was barely two? She would cling even more. I promised to love her more than I loved my dolls. I was deeply troubled, but I would heed my mother's words and find the courage to fulfil my promise as best I could.

The following day, I observed that Gran, despite her grieving, had regained her composure and instructed Nanny to take care of me and my sisters during the funeral. Gran said a funeral was no place for children. Another maid was engaged to help until some order was restored.

Our neighbours offered the help of their maids, who came to help look after the little girls and in the preparation of tea for when the mourners returned from the cemetery. They rearranged the greenhouse and cleared space for chairs and tables. The maids swept away the remnants of the cedar branches the florist had cut from the front hedge. The branches had formed the base of the wreaths that held the beautiful flowers that adorned my mother's coffin. The florist made a wreath of white roses from me and my sisters. There were calla lilies from my father with a simple card that read: "For my Darling Lily."

Later, I confided in Nanny, "How odd the adults behaved. First, they were quiet and spoke in hushed voices. And when the funeral was over, they acted as if they were at a party." Everyone wanted to hug and kiss me and my sisters. I hated the old lady with the wattle neck and hairy moles poking out of her chin. But I had to be polite and accept the horrid kisses. The mourners talked and gossiped over tea. The neighbours introduced themselves to my father's relatives. Only Gran and the Mauritian priest talked quietly outside in the garden. "Nanny, I wish I could hear what they're talking about."

"Joan, you such naughty child, always wanting to hear what big folks say."

"But Nanny, I like to hear them."

"That's why Gran she's always scolding you."

"Nanny, I'm sorry, but how else will I ever know what's happening?"

Nanny shook her head in disapproval and clicked her tongue.

No one, not even Father, had remembered my birthday.

CHAPTER 3
Recollections of the Past

IN THE DAYS FOLLOWING MY MOTHER'S FUNERAL, ALL THE RELATIVES left and a semblance of normal life returned to our home. The sun shone brightly on the variegated purple and mauve wisteria that was in full bloom and covered the veranda where the family was having afternoon tea. Yet life had changed and it would never be the same. My grandparents were now resident. My father had gratefully accepted the offer of his mother- and father-in-law to make their home with us. Barney was sent to boarding school and Father took time off from work to spend with my sisters and me.

"Come Joan, come girls. I have a surprise for you. Joan, it's your birthday present," he said.

"Oh Father, you remembered!" I was elated. "What is it? I thought you had forgotten all about my birthday."

"It's in the garage. Shall we find out what it is?"

"Is it in the big box?" I asked. "I just knew it was my present."

I was joined by my sisters, who skipped into the back garden, and there it was, a *Punch and Judy* stage, complete with puppets. Ben had hoisted it onto a platform that he had erected between two oak trees. Nanny was busy untangling the puppet strings.

I beckoned to my siblings to try the puppets. "Oh Father! It's beautiful! I'm so happy." I called out to Nanny, "Please ask Gran and Grandpa to come and join in the fun."

"Yes, yes! Do call Gramps. He'll know how to work it," echoed my delighted sisters.

Part One

Our grandparents joined us at play, and for once Gran did not scold me for being loud and spirited. Grandpa was his usual self and entered into the fun. He realised that we needed the distraction.

Later, Nanny supervised our baths and prepared us for bed. Gran ordered Nanny to maintain our regular routine. She feared that our father would spoil us, but Grandpa cautioned her to be lenient. "Stop scolding, Emma."

Our father, often absent at bedtime, asked, "Shall I tell you a story?"

"Yes, please," we responded in unison.

"Of Jack an' a glory?"

"Yes, yes, please Father. Do tell us."

"Well, shall I begin it?" He paused as we waited. "There's nothing in it."

"Don't tease us. Please begin, Father," I said, leading the chorus that became louder and more urgent, anticipating a story.

The nonsense rhyme had become a ritual, a prelude to our bedtime stories. It was our father's way of amusing us.

"Please Father, do tell the story of how our grandfather sailed to Africa," I pleaded.

"All right then, but no more questions or interruptions and straight to bed afterwards."

Our father's five-foot-nine frame fit neatly in the easy chair at the foot-end between the twin beds with his slippered feet resting on a low stool. My sisters sat up in bed, and I stood beside my father combing his auburn hair.

Father began: "Once upon a time, a long time ago, a young fisherman lived in the seaside village of Viareggio in Tuscany, Italy. His name was Vincento. Unlike me, he was tall and strong with blue-grey eyes the colour of the sea in which he fished, and he had a beard streaked with grey. His fingers were gnarled and calloused, the mark of a good fisherman, your grandfather said. Each day with his three older sons, Peter, Paul, and Domingo, Vincento set sail with the other fishermen in their fishing boats. At the end of the day, they brought in the catch that included palamita, prawns, and the favourite bonito or blue fish that the local people enjoyed. Sometimes, they fished for days before returning to shore.

"Their village by the sea had attracted a group of English writers and artists who settled in the seaside hamlet where they mixed freely with the villagers.

The fishermen supplied them with fish and produce from their gardens. In appreciation, the writers established small informal English classes for the village children, and that's how my older brothers, your uncles, Paul, Peter, and Domingo, who were born in Viareggio, learnt to speak English.

"My grandfather said that as young fishermen, they were fishing in the vicinity of Livorno and Viareggio when the great romantic poet Shelley drowned. All the boats in the area helped in the search. After two full days and nights at sea, the fishermen finally recovered Shelley's body. All his English friends and the villagers, including the priest, attended the cremation. When the fire had completely died down, his friends gathered up the ashes and from the shore that Shelley loved, they scattered them in the ocean. All the fishing boats dipped their sails to honour the dead poet."

"As a small boy, I never tired of hearing how my father got to South Africa and why I wasn't born in Viareggio like my older brothers. They had sailed away from Italy because my Uncle Domingo was accused of smuggling. The disgrace was such that my father, your grandfather, a pious and proud man, could not bear all the village gossip. My uncle was not charged nor convicted, except by the public, but the stigma and disgrace of being a smuggler was too much for my father to live with. So, with his family and other loyal fishermen, they set sail for the land that was rumoured to be rich in gold and treasure. My father's boat and another fishing trawler left Viareggio for a new world.

"Your grandfather told how after many, many arduous weeks at sea and braving the fierce storms, they crossed the equator. And guided by the stars, they followed the Southern Cross as all fisherman did, for they knew that it would lead them on the rest of their voyage. Then one day a sailor atop the rigging shouted, "Ahoy! Land ahead!" There was much rejoicing, for at this time the hardy fishermen were beginning to run short of supplies. Your grandfather and all who sailed gave thanks to the Grace of the Lord, who had guided them safely to the shores of South Africa.

"They docked in the small seaside town of Port Elizabeth. The town was perched high above a cliff overlooking the Indian Ocean. Your grandfather said it reminded him of Genoa, and that is where the party decided to start a new life.

"I was born on November 29, six weeks after the family arrived in Port Elizabeth. The year was 1900 and thus, I was entitled to South African citizenship. Not long afterwards, my two sisters, Katherine and Maria, were born, and they too were entitled to that privilege."

When the story ended, my younger sisters, Jean and Peggy, were fast asleep. Beryl and I clamoured for more. "Please Father, tell us how you met and fell in love with Mummy."

"No girls, that's enough for tonight. Now pray for Mummy, who is watching over you." He tucked us in, kissed each child, and switched on the night light as he left the room. However, I was never ready to sleep until I heard the familiar music from my father's gramophone records. The strains of Franz Lehar's waltz from *The Merry Widow,* "Frasqita's Serenade," drifted into our bedroom and reminded me how our parents had danced to the music to the delight of all of us and Nanny. I tiptoed to my father in the sitting room. Getting out of bed was strictly against Gran's orders, but despite the warning, I knew father would not scold me.

"Father, what's cremated and stigma?"

"Joan, you promised to go to sleep. Tomorrow you can look up those words in the dictionary."

"Father, are you crying?" I said. "And how do you know that Mummy is watching over us?"

"Because you said your prayers, and when you're a little older you'll understand."

"But Father, everyone wants me to wait until I'm older. Nanny says I ask too many questions now. And when I'm older, what if I don't remember? Why can't I understand now?"

"Good night, Joan. Gran is not to be disobeyed, and she will be angry if she catches you out of bed," Father stated firmly.

I knew that was the end.

CHAPTER 4
A Victorian Grandmother

I PIECED TOGETHER MY GRAN'S STORY FROM TIDBITS I HAD PICKED UP from her and after her death from her diary. There were important points to incorporate into my own story.

Gran had inherited the unenviable responsibility of raising her late daughter Lily's children. The task was daunting, but with firm British resolve, she accepted the challenge, and she certainly dominated our lives. In the absence of our father, whose business in the lumber trade kept him away for long periods, Gran had sole charge of us—aided by our faithful nanny, Marta. Gran had an overwhelming influence on my character and behaviour. It is not surprising that we shared the same astrological sign and that I had inherited a penchant for horoscopes and some superstitious beliefs.

Emma Colville (Gran) was old school, a rigid Victorian lady who boasted of her proud British heritage. When she was a young child, her father, William Colville, moved his family from Mauritius to Durban in Natal, and finally they settled in Oudtshoorn in the Little Karroo, Cape Province. She was raised in a strict High-Anglican household on her father's modest horse farm. Gran told us stories of her youth and her love of horses and growing up as free as the wild *quagga* that roamed the *veldt* (bush). I was surprised how this high-spirited young woman had turned into the inflexible and often irascible Gran. I recalled the many winter evenings when four little girls snuggled under the warmth of her quagga skin karros and sipped hot cocoa listening to bedtime stories told by our doting grandfather. That karros was Gran's talisman, and she thought of the quagga as an icon that should have represented the land of her birth.

—24—

Part One

Gran had spent most of her childhood following in her father's footsteps. He treated her as the son he never had. He taught her to ride, shoot, fish, and swim, and his passion was horses and hunting the wild quagga. One day while hunting, they rescued an abandoned quagga foal that was being attacked by a jackal. Gran took charge and nursed it. After a few months, it was well enough and fully appreciating that it needed to roam free, she released it into the wild.

At age fifteen, Gran could be seen galloping bare-back on her mare across the veldt, leaving behind a cloud of red Karroo dust that matched her tawny mane flying in the wind.

Her father was hired to manage the governor's stables, and Emma accompanied her father to the interview. The governor, it was rumoured, was the reprobate scion of an English aristocrat, who had been banished to the colony in disgrace. His family was determined to avoid any more of his scandalous behaviour on their home turf. South Africa was the ideal hideout for the young man. Being so far removed from England, it would spare his conservative family any further embarrassment from his licentious activities. The governor's residence in the Cape Province, a predominantly Afrikaans-speaking region, served the governor's purpose. There he established his racing stables, where the cost of native labour and grazing was cheap. His stable of horses brought in much-needed cash, which supplemented his income, but was inadequate for his gambling needs. The annual stipend barely covered their expenses. The governor's prudent father, wary of his son's extravagance, had cut down his son's allowance. Her Ladyship's small private income helped to defray household costs.

"And do you ride?" the governor had asked Gran.

"I do, sir," Gran replied.

"As well as any groom. The horses champ at her bidding," said her proud father. "She understands horses. She talks to them, and they obey her."

"Then she should ride with my lady wife. Come and meet her tomorrow morning at ten," ordered the governor.

Her Ladyship hated the fact that they were tucked away in what she described as "this God-forsaken country." Her life was so different from the social whirl she had enjoyed as a debutante in London where she had met her handsome husband. The adventure she sought had not materialised and she was disillusioned. The parched, sandy, hot, dry climate did not suit her, and she complained that her lady-in-waiting was a gossipy old hag. There was little to do except for the boring official functions she presided over. Most of all she loathed the unsophisticated Boers, whom she was forced to entertain. She complained that their manners were appalling and that they either could not or would not speak English.

"My life is one big bore. What life and love I enjoyed evaporated a long time ago." Her marriage to the debonair bachelor had been arranged and had faded soon after their transfer to South Africa.

The governor's peccadilloes were legend, but appearances had to be upheld, which contributed to the frequent headaches Lily, Her Ladyship, suffered. The arid summer heat added to her woes and she sought comfort in alcohol. Her dog was her sole companion until she met the free-spirited Emma. She took Gran under her wing and instructed her in the social graces. Lily thought, *I know how to mould her and that will give me something to do.* Later, the consequences of Gran's education would impact the life she chose.

Gran was precocious and an apt pupil and managed to coax Her Ladyship into riding on a daily basis. In fact, Gran soon became indispensable and was asked to move into the house as Her Ladyship's companion. The governor was delighted. The lady-in-waiting could be sent packing, which would save a considerable sum of money in his perennially cash-strapped household.

Her Ladyship found Gran an intelligent and personable companion, which she so desperately needed in this foreign land. Gran was someone she could confide in without fear of repercussions from idle gossip.

Gran too benefited from the relationship. She found a mentor who grew into a reliable friend. Gran, the tomboy, turned into a swan. Soon after, her status changed to lady's maid. She developed a style any lady would have been proud of. Regrettably, Gran imbibed the lessons taught her by the governor's wife only too well.

One was her fondness for tippling. First, it was the gin and tonic sun-downer she enjoyed in Her Ladyship's company; later, the after-dinner sherry or port with a pinch of snuff, which Her Ladyship claimed cured headaches.

It was not until after Gran's death that I discovered her secret. Her frequent headaches were probably the result of being a closet alcoholic. Few family members knew of Gran's well-kept secret, or if they did, they remained silent.

Part One

Those were the salad days of Gran's youth. She was the envy of her sisters, who were mere provincial housewives.

At eighteen, tired of being a lady's maid in the governor's household, Gran craved adventure and excitement. Defying convention, she fell in love and eloped with Arthur, a stable hand. He was a handsome, fun-loving groom, who had been employed by her father. They rode away on two of her father's prized horses and reached Paarl, where they were married in a registry office. Her father followed and threatened to whip the Scotsman. However, his daughter persuaded him that it was true love, and he could not deny his favourite child. He gave his blessing, provided money, and sent them to stay with his wife's brother, Erez Jolliette, a priest, who lived in Mauritius. This satisfied Gran's mother and prevented any scandal.

Her Ladyship had not been privy to her protégée's plans and was heartbroken at the loss of her young confidante. She thought of Emma as the child she never had and encouraged Willian Colville to persuade his daughter and her husband Arthur to return to the farm.

Two years elapsed before they returned and by then my grandmother had a young child, a daughter she named Lily after Her Ladyship. After my grandmother's death, I poured eagerly over her diary, as any mention of my mother was a balm to my longing heart. Gran was happy to be back with Her Ladyship, as she was pregnant with her second child. Grandpa continued to work as a groom. Her Ladyship admired Gran's pluck and continued to befriend her until the governor was transferred to a Caribbean island. They left a few months before Gran gave birth to her second child. Her Ladyship was delighted to leave but was sad that once again she would be parted from her beloved protégée. Her parting gifts to Gran were a silver claret jug, an antique biscuit jar, and many household wares to set up a home. Promises to write frequently were exchanged. The correspondence lasted for years until the death of Her Ladyship. In her will, she left Gran a pearl and diamond-studded necklace.

After the governor's transfer, my great-grandfather, William Colville, settled his wife Tina; Emma, his daughter; her husband Arthur; and their two children in Johannesburg. The discovery of gold had attracted many immigrants and investments to the booming city. My great-grandfather, William, used his Clydesdale horses to start a hackney service and taught riding as a side-line. The two buggies were driven by William, and my Grandpa Arthur. The business prospered and soon William was able to invest in a small furniture shop.

On the outskirts of the city, the family acquired a house with an attached cottage on a large parcel of land on which to exercise and stable their horses. They were happy and wanted for little.

Then tragedy struck; both of Gran's parents, William and Tina Coleville, contracted Spanish flu. The epidemic of 1918-1919 was widespread and both parents died within weeks of each other. My grandparents, Arthur and Emma, were devastated by the loss of both her parents. In later years, a bereft Gran especially mourned the death of her beloved father William, who had been a companion as well as her father.

Emma and Arthur inherited the furniture business. My grandpa was a laissez-faire man, and he left most of the decisions, both domestic and business, to my conscientious grandmother, who immediately took charge of all their household affairs. Gran was the practical partner, and the upkeep of the horses drained their finances. Although she adored Grandpa, reluctantly she was forced to sell the hackneys, as motorized vehicles began replacing the horse and buggy. A disappointed Grandpa had little choice but to undertake the management of the small factory, which afforded them a good living.

Gran's brood had grown to five children: three girls, Lily, Leah, and Vivienne; and two sons, Collie and Jonathan. Gran, a strict disciplinarian, had her children educated at the Anglican School, where they sang in the church choir. From an early age, my mother and her siblings were obliged to work in various positions at the factory.

My mother Lily was Gran's eldest daughter, who was married to my father, Charles, a businessman. He travelled frequently on business trips abroad, while my mother occupied her time dressmaking and acting in amateur theatre productions. She had solo parts in plays and sang in concerts. But then, quite unexpectedly and without any warning, my mother died. All I remembered was that she had not been ill, but that I'd been told that she had a headache. My mother's death was a tremendous shock for the entire family. It is not possible to describe my own feelings then, I can recall only that my nanny tried to pacify me—I was inconsolable.

Aunt Leah, Collie, and Johnny all worked in the family business.

Part One

Gran's youngest daughter, my auntie Vivienne, became a school teacher and eloped with a jazz-band leader soon after her graduation. Gran was scandalised and sought to have the marriage annulled.

Grandpa for once spoke up. "Emma, have you forgotten our own marriage?"

"You were a gentleman, not some rag-tag musician," she replied.

"Be fair. You must give them a chance. Same as we had," said Grandpa.

Gran was not convinced. She refused to meet Vivienne and her husband. "I will not have him darken my doorstep."

Six months after Lily's death, Gran's middle daughter, my Auntie Leah, received an urgent cable from Vivienne, whose husband was on tour. "Please come immediately! Stop." The sisters had kept in touch after Gran banned Vivienne and her husband, who lived in a flat in the city. Leah sent for a cab and rushed to her sister.

Leah was shocked to find Vivienne lying in a pool of blood, pale and barely breathing. She called her uncle, Dr. Godwin, who sent an ambulance. Vivienne was taken to the hospital, haemorrhaging and unconscious.

Later her maid told Gran, "Miss Vivienne, my madam, she sent me to post office to send cable. When I come back, I find her like this." Vivienne had miscarried and died without ever regaining consciousness.

Gran was grief-stricken. She reproached herself. She was compunctious for not being available when her daughter needed her. That negligence would weigh heavily and it would haunt her more than she let on. She had lost two daughters in less than a year. Grandpa could not bear to see his wife's suffering and urged her to visit her sister Belle in Cape Town. "It will be good for you to get away. You'll need all your strength and energy to cope with the wee ones when you get back. Don't worry, we'll be fine," he said.

"I am very tired, my dear. Are you sure you'll manage? Seeing the ocean and my sister Belle will help to revive my spirits," Gran said wearily.

"Marta's niece will help out. And you'll come back rested and refreshed with renewed energy. You need time to grieve and heal."

Gran arrived in Cape Town happy to be with Belle. The ocean and Table Mountain had a soothing effect on her. On the fourth day, she received a telegram from my father, who had stayed home to help with us girls while she was away. "Come immediately. Stop. Grandpa gravely ill. Stop."

Belle accompanied Gran back to Johannesburg. They were met at the station by Dr. Godwin. He drove straight to his home. "Why to your house?" asked Gran.

"Arthur has pneumonia, and what with the children, I thought it best to nurse him at my place. In your absence, it was wiser for my nurse to care for him here. Both you and Belle are welcome to stay until he is fit enough to be moved."

Grandpa's condition terrified Gran. How had he taken ill in such a short time? There was little to be done. She sat at his bedside holding his hand and sponging his forehead with lavender water. She whispered gently to him, but he barely acknowledged her presence. Two days after her arrival, her beloved Arthur died. Gran was unprepared for his sudden death. There had been no warning and no goodbye. The anguish she felt was beyond anything she had been forced to endure. Gran ruminated—was this retribution? It was the single greatest tragedy of her life, coming less than twelve months after their daughters' deaths. Arthur had been her rock.

Gramps had been a Mason, a Fraternal Brother of the Scots Order of Free Gardeners. Cousin Godwin too was a member and took charge. He notified the brethren, who arranged for the funeral service at St. Mary's Cathedral.

Gran never quite recovered from her loss. However, she gathered what strength she could and put duty before all else. "Lily's girls must be brought up properly. Joan especially will need a firm hand," she told Belle. Gran mustered the courage and took control once again of her family. Under all circumstances, appearances had to be maintained. At night, undisturbed in the privacy of her bedroom with the quagga skin karros draped across her shoulders, Gran retired to commune with her beloved Arthur on her Ouija board.

Years later, I recalled how as a little girl, I dreaded sharing Gran's four-poster bed when my bed was needed for visiting relatives. I would pull the covers tightly over my head and put my fingers in my ears to avoid the one-sided conversation Gran conducted with Grandpa's ghost, who she claimed stood at the foot-end of the bed.

Gran raised us children and continued to live with Charles, who was grateful that our home life was not unduly disrupted. It set his mind at ease during his frequent trips abroad and freed him from worrying about his girls. The

Part One

children would miss their beloved grandfather, for he had been an indulgent, moderating, and loving influence.

A stoic Gran questioned, "Why am I being punished? I have no tears left and no heart to break. Oh Arthur, can you see my suffering?" If I was within earshot, I would blanch, for I had a morbid fear of ghosts, and Gran spoke to them all the time.

Nemesis had struck once again!

CHAPTER 5
Life at the Convent

I WAS ELEVEN YEARS OLD IN SEPTEMBER 1939 WHEN THE ALLIES declared war on Germany. Benito Mussolini, the Italian dictator, had attacked Abyssinia and that was a prelude to World War II. I remembered how in faraway Abyssinia, Hailie Selassie, the emperor made our daily news headlines, and my brother Barney and his friends had mock battles and sang, "Will you come to Abyssinia? Will you come? Mussolini will be there shooting peanuts in the air. Will you come?" I watched my brother and his friends having loads of fun, and I begged to join them. I was desperate to fit in and play with the boys. Grudgingly, I was permitted on condition that I became the Axis enemy. I was obliged to lie down on the ground and play dead while the chorus of boys chanted, "Will you come to Abyssinia?" and pelted me with peas or nuts from peashooters. I thought being a girl was unfair; my only choice if I wanted to participate in the game was to play by their rules. After all, what did I know or even understand about either Hailie Selassie or Mussolini?

Despite their frivolous games, there was a serious undercurrent and much apprehension caused by the war propaganda. The young men were determined to fight to defend the Commonwealth. Barney, who was of average height, turned sixteen and posed as an eighteen-year old—there were no checks on the ages of young men. He joined the Cadets and later was transferred to the Signallers Corp.

My father, the son of Italian immigrants, was a South African citizen. He enlisted and was drafted into the Air Force. Those Italians, like my uncles Paul and Peter, declared their allegiance to South Africa by enlisting in the army as well. All Italians and Germans who were not citizens and did not enlist in the army, including those who did not even speak their native language, were imprisoned in internment camps as a precaution against espionage.

Also interned were the revolutionary Afrikaners who formed the group *Ossewabrandwag*, or Ox-Wagon Guard as they came to be known. Their opposition and loyalty were to the Afrikaans "Tribe." All these years after the Boers' defeat by the British, they still harboured their anti-British grievances, and they were opposed to the war. They espoused the doctrine of the German enemy, whom they supported, adopting their policies of racial superiority. The Afrikaners regarded themselves the *Herren volk*, God's people, ordained by God.

As an enlisted soldier, my father was reluctant to leave his daughters in the sole care of our aging grandmother, fearing that if he were killed in the war, we children would be split among the relatives. None of our family members were prepared or could afford to care for all four girls. Boarding school solved the problem. Thus, my father decided that Beryl and I were to be enrolled in a convent. Jean and Peggy were under the age for boarding, but due to the war, regulations were lifted and special permission was granted for them to live at the convent too, under the supervision of a kindergarten nurse. Mother Superior became our legal guardian.

I became anxious and persistently tried to dissuade my father from enrolling us as boarders. "Father, Barney says we'll be bullied and locked up like prisoners! He also said, 'Don't be afraid to stand up to bullies, who will make your life a misery.'"

"Your brother, as usual, is exaggerating and teasing you."

I had no choice, and so at least for the next five years, together with my sisters, our primary home would be the convent, except for short holidays with Gran and relatives. I promised Father to be obedient. The time had come to honour my late mother's last words: "Be brave and look after your little sisters."

That first week at the convent was a huge adjustment; my sisters and I were split up according to age and were assigned different dormitories, which caused me more anxiety. I dared not think what it was doing to my younger siblings. Boarding school contrasted with the family life we were accustomed to. I resolved to find ways to maintain the bedtime-story rituals. At night, I left my dormitory, pretending to go to the lavatory, and would slip into Jean and Peggy's room to read or just talk to them. I agonised about the lack of a familiar face to tuck them in. In the washroom, out of sight, my tears streamed and I resolved to be strong. It was far more upsetting for my younger sisters, I rationalized. Apprehensive and ever-conscious of my duty, I promised to do my best as I settled into life at the convent, where the talk of war was disturbing. However, in a way it served to mitigate the war that raged within my heart and mind. I recalled Barney's complaint of his first term at boarding school, where he'd had to fend for himself. Fortunately, no one bullied me, despite the petty jealousy common among children, and Beryl was quite able to take care of herself. Jean and Peggy had the protection of the governess, but being separated was difficult, and the reality was that we were akin to orphans.

One day shortly after our arrival, Mother Superior summoned all the students and staff to assemble in the Great Hall to listen to the radio broadcast from London. Filled with curiosity, but sensing the urgency, I wondered if King George VI was about to speak to the Commonwealth.

The impatient and anxious audience fiddled and shifted about, increasing the tension. There was considerable static on the radio, and when finally the sound was restored, the sonorous voice of Prime Minister Winston Churchill boomed: "We are at war! And we expect every man, woman, and child to do their duty."

The rest of the speech was met with stunned silence until Mother Superior announced, "We must all heed Mr. Churchill's wise counsel and concentrate on helping the war effort. You are dismissed."

Each evening after completing our homework, we girls listened to the reports that were broadcast over the radio while knitting socks and scarves for the troops. The news was often quite frightening. Talk of war dominated most of our leisure time. For many girls like me, we were constantly concerned about our fathers' and relatives' safety. Mass was offered daily for the wounded and suffering soldiers. We prayed for an end to the terrible war that was reported to be causing havoc among the Allied troops. The German, General Rommel, named The Desert Fox, waged a relentless war in North Africa, causing thousands of victims and taking prisoners.

Part One

It was unlikely that the war would reach South Africa. However, as a precaution against air raid attacks, especially after the fall of Tobruk in 1942, blackout curtains covering all the windows were installed, and we practised fire drills. The students in middle and high school were enrolled in first-aid classes under St. John's Ambulance, which were conducted twice weekly to prepare us to aid in nursing, should the need arise. There was a shortage of trained nurses, as many had joined the army and were sent to staff military hospitals, both abroad and at home.

We followed the news of the war intently on the radio, and from odd scraps of carefully censored, infrequent letters that were generally post-marked "Egypt" or "Somewhere in North Africa." Souvenirs were sent back to a few lucky girls from relatives who were stationed "Up North," and for a time it helped to alleviate some of our fear. A tiny parcel from my father in Egypt contained a pretty necklace decorated with pictures of the pyramids and the sphinx. My sisters received beaded bracelets. It was a relief to receive these tokens; the trinkets provided some solace and confirmed that our father was safe. Or was he? His letters had become rare; it had taken many months before his presents reached us, and we had received no letters since. Once again, my usual habit of second-guessing myself left me with an uncanny feeling.

As the war progressed and the army's needs increased, rationing was introduced and many products became scarce. At breakfast one morning, I helped myself to what should have been buttered toast, but it had been replaced by doughy brown bread smeared with something called peanut butter. It looked quite unappetising and horrible, and it tasted worse. I disliked it instantly. I recalled that often I was made to finish my bread long after the meal had ended. But I was saved by the kindly cleaning staff, who relieved me because they were in a hurry to clear and reset the tables for lunch.

Matron, who supervised all the meals, scolded me, "You should be grateful to have anything to eat. People are starving and you're being fussy. You're setting a bad example to your sisters and other students!"

Never at a loss for an answer, I replied, "It sticks to my palate, Matron. But I will try to eat it. It'll be my sacrifice for the war effort."

"Enough, or do you want a detention?" Matron scolded.

I was a precocious child, and although I was a minor and only twelve years old at this time, my father considered me responsible. He had arranged that together with Mother Superior, I be named as the legal guardian of my siblings. This was essential and necessary so that his army pay could be collected each month to fund our upkeep. Chaperoned by Sister Jessica, I went to the post office to sign for the monthly stipend paid to soldiers' families. I signed the cheque, witnessed by Sister Jessica, who after deducting the school fees and other expenses, deposited the balance in an account set up by my father.

I felt proud and grown up having to sign, although I regretted that I never even handled a single farthing. If I'd had had my way, I would have instantly doubled my paltry allowance. However, the Puritan Convent upbringing influenced my attitude. At the monthly confessions, I felt obliged to add pride and avarice to the list of my sins. Once I had added stealing, and the priest questioned, "What did you steal?"

"A tin of canned peaches, Father."

"Were you hungry?"

"No Father. I was sent to the larder and I saw tins of canned peaches. It looked so good that I was tempted, and I took one and hid it under my apron. Later, I gave it to the gardener because I did not have a can-opener."

For my penance, I was instructed to own up to the sister in charge of stores. I did not, and at my next confession I felt that I was cheating by not confessing as I had been instructed and my disobedience was tantamount to lying, thus incurring another sin.

The numerous activities at the convent allotted time for taking part in theatricals and sports. A great pleasure was to participate in field hockey and tennis, at which Beryl and I both excelled. However, I lacked the patience to practise the piano, something I would come to regret in later years. On Sundays, the lengthy sermons were boring, and to endure them I would leave a book in amongst the hymnals and read it during these occasions. Fortunately, I never attracted the attention of the nuns. My preferred pleasure was to spend time in the library with my friend Ruth. We got lost in a world of make-believe. She was clever and we competed against each other on a regular basis. Ruth, on the other hand, never took a single chance and often worried on my behalf. Somehow, there never seemed to be enough time to read. From the age of five,

Part One

my sister Jean often sang solo parts in our school choir, for she had a lovely voice, and as she got older, she excelled at table tennis.

Life at the convent was fully occupied with all the rules and regulations, and I discovered that the regular routine and the sameness of every day became fairly mundane, and I often tested or broke the rules. I was rarely punished for my disobedience; for some unknown reason I was treated by the staff as an older girl during my pubescent years. I managed to get away with my wilful behaviour to the annoyance of my peers, who sometimes did and said spiteful things like hiding my books or spilling ink over my essays. "You think you're so smart and better than us," was a taunt I had to put up with. My sister Beryl was a good student and an athlete—she responded to any attack on her and she never understood why I, her senior, did not retaliate.

I simply told her, "I wish you wouldn't. I hate fighting and quarrelling. Isn't it enough that there's a war on?"

If one has not lived in a religious institution, then it is difficult to explain the nuances of behaviour that affect treatment meted out to students. Perhaps honesty, and my integrity, and the fact that I was always at the head of my class, may have played a part in what my peers deemed the special treatment I received.

I believe the staff realised that my siblings and I were like orphans and made allowances for us. I understood why the other girls envied my status with the staff, but in turn, I was jealous of them. I never quite fit in, and an unexplained notion of alienation remained. I had far less pocket money and things than they had. Sister Jessica was quite frugal and agreed on the allotted allowance my father had stipulated. I spent mine almost as soon as I received it, mostly on sweets. Quite often, I would cajole my thrifty sister Jean to lend me some of her savings, which she hoarded carefully. I envied most students their parents and especially their mothers. My life had a void that could not be filled in spite of my accomplishments. There was no mother or father to be proud of me on Prize-Giving Day.

CHAPTER 6
Curious and Curiouser!

The war had raged for more than four years and I was sixteen and in my final year of high school. I was called to Mother Superior's office. *Now what have I done?* I wondered. Had Matron finally reported me?

"Joan, you are to dress in street clothes. Pack an overnight satchel then return to the waiting room."

"Please Mother, may I ask why?"

"Sister Jessica will explain later. Now, go and do as you're told."

A car was waiting, and Sister Jessica beckoned me to follow. My curiosity grew; where were we going? Before I could ask, Sister said, "We are going on a visit, and all will be explained when we get there. In the meantime, you may want to pray for peace and for all people affected by the war."

Prayer was the furthest thing from my mind. The mystery deepened. I was anxious and I could not help wondering whether my indiscretions had finally caught up with me. My palpitations increased. Why the secrecy? We drove for what seemed hours until we reached an unfamiliar part of the countryside. "Where are we?" I asked.

"Almost there. We are going to visit a hospital. Now, no more questions."

Now I was truly frightened. I fidgeted and bit my nails, not knowing what to expect. I needed to go to the bathroom. It always happened when I became nervous or excited.

"Stop biting your nails," Sister Jessica ordered.

Part One

Driving along, I tried concentrating on the sun setting on the western horizon, which invariably was an artist's dream, but I was too anxious to appreciate the magnificent magenta sky. It was dusk when at last we reached the outskirts of the town and came upon fields that were fenced with barbed wire. The iron gates were guarded by two soldiers armed with rifles. Trembling and fearful, not knowing what to expect, I recalled hearing of a girl who was sent to a reformatory because she kept running away. Was this it? Sister Jessica was unperturbed and calm except for the annoying frowns and glances she cast in my direction. The car was allowed to enter and from the dimmed lights emanating from the low, one-storey buildings, it was impossible to tell where we were. By now I was tapping my feet and Sister was quite angry. "Can't you sit still?" A mile farther in from the gate, the car stopped in front of a low building, where a soldier escorted us from the car. "We're expected," Sister Jessica said.

"Please follow me." An orderly led us into a waiting room. "Someone will be with you shortly."

The mystery deepened. I was close to panic but forced myself to try to remain calm. My heart was pounding, and I feared I would faint and be admitted to this forbidding place.

A slender, middle-aged man in a white lab coat appeared. He toyed with the stethoscope that hung loosely from his neck and kept looking at his watch. "Good evening, I'm Dr. Rosen. Sister, please be seated. And your name, young lady?" he said, bowing his blond head toward me.

"I'm Joan," I whispered.

"Well Joan, don't be afraid," he said, taking my hand. "You must be wondering why all the secrecy. And why you're here. We did not want to alarm you."

But that is precisely what you did! I thought.

"This is a military hospital. Your father was wounded at the fall of Tobruk. He was severely injured and sustained a head wound. He is recovering. He has been here for almost two years."

I thought, *That accounts for the absence of his letters.*

"It's a very slow process and he has some loss of memory. We believe it to be temporary. He is showing signs of recovery and that is why I sent for you. Do not be afraid."

Now my heart began throbbing and my head was thudding and I needed more than ever to use the washroom.

"I'll take you to see him. There's nothing to be afraid of, but talk to your father as you normally would. I'll be watching his reaction through a one-way window."

I discerned Father's condition, but I was relieved that at least he was alive and right back here in Johannesburg. I wished that my sisters were with me, and I could not wait a minute longer to see Father. I took a deep breath as I entered a pleasant room. Another bedroom came to mind but I'd been younger then. Magazines were strewn on the floor. Father was seated in an armchair. He did not acknowledge my presence. He was wearing a dressing gown and slippers. His dull blue eyes were staring into space.

Thankful that I had been warned, I approached him rather cautiously and said softly, "Hello Father." I bent down and kissed him on his cheek. He flinched. It was disconcerting and I was at a loss. He did not recognise me. I was hurt and I knew it was hardly his fault, but all the same, it worried me. I sat on the arm of the chair and peeping out from beneath the bandage, I saw that my father's once-auburn hair had been shorn and the few strands that remained around the edge had turned grey. Tenderly, I tousled the straggly hairs as I had done when he had told us stories at bedtime. But that was before he'd joined the army. "Are you in pain, Father?"

There was no response. I knelt down and looked up at him stroking his hand. "Please Father, tell me a story about Jack an' a Glory. Do you remember how you teased us?"

My father fluttered his eyelids. *He is remembering.* I felt my heart would burst as it flared into action again. I had no handkerchief to dry my tears. I was grateful Father was recovering, albeit so slowly.

The doctor entered. "That's enough for now, my dear."

As we left, the man in the armchair sighed and susurrated, "Joan."

I was sorry to leave him just as I thought he was remembering. However, I was excited to get back to the convent to share the news with my sisters. I felt confident that Father would recover. Why else had they waited so long before I was told about his condition if he was not well on the road to recovering? It also explained the scarcity of his letters. We had been led to believe that letters were being stopped so as not to give the Nazis a clue of the army's whereabouts.

Part One

My father spent more than two and a half years in hospital before he was pronounced fit. The doctors did not want him to be exposed to any sudden loud noises or bangs, which could quite possibly trigger a setback in his recovery. After peace was declared and all the firework displays were over, Father was discharged from the army hospital and transferred to the Retired Servicemen's Home. Apart from the odd loss of memory, Father recovered with a protective "plate" in his head.

— ⚜ —

A peace treaty between and the Allies and the Germans was signed. The war in Europe ended on V.E. Day, Victory in Europe, May 8, 1945. It was a day I would forever remember. A public holiday was declared. There was rejoicing and church bells rang in every town and village. Motorists tooted their horns. People blew whistles and danced in the streets, and all over the United Kingdom and its colonies, they were celebrating the end of the war.

I had just turned seventeen and that evening, to our delight, Barney came home. It was his final day in the army. He had been demobilized and he wanted to stay home but Beryl and I, who were home for the celebration, begged him to accompany us to the park to hear the band and to be a part of all the festivities. Gran permitted us to stay out late, on condition Barney accompanied us. The entire town was celebrating and watching the fireworks display in the park. There were victory parades and amid the flags and hoopla, which was loud and jubilant, the band played, "There'll always be an England," and, "It's a long way to Tipperary," and other patriotic songs.

On our way to the park, we were stopped and several young soldiers in a sports coupe driven by a car salesman insisted Barney, who was still in uniform, join them and follow the parade. At first he hesitated, but Beryl and I urged him to go, assuring him that we could find our way home. We felt the young men had returned from the front and were entitled to some fun now that they were back home. Their army pay had accumulated while fighting, and they were inundated by car salesmen offering deals. Barney climbed into the back of the car and sat on the fabric hood, which was folded down. He waved to us and they were off. It occurred to me that he was perched rather precariously, but I thought no more about it. He had just survived the war.

Later that night when he did not return home, we thought that he was still celebrating. Naturally, we were somewhat anxious as the noise had slowed down considerably, and we were hoping to spend time with him and to hear all about his adventures in the war. There was a knock at the door, and to my surprise, it was a policeman wanting to speak to my father.

Gran appeared and asserted her authority as head of the house. She explained that father was resident in the retired soldiers' home, and she was in charge. "Was there a message for him?"

"There's been an accident," the policeman reported.

The family gathered to listen.

"Some young soldiers were celebrating and driving along in the sports coupe, and another automobile rammed into the sports car. The young soldier was thrown out, and he landed on a stationary trailer parked at the side of the road. His abdomen caught on the spikes. He was severely injured and taken to the Johannesburg General Hospital. Unfortunately, he died soon after admission, before his next of kin could be informed."

The adults were speechless. Beryl and I convulsed into tears.

"I have a car here and will take you to the hospital to identify the body," he said.

I begged Aunt Leah and Uncle Jim, a dour, stern individual, to accompany them to identify Barney's body. For once, they and Gran did not forbid my request.

At the hospital, we were ushered into a waiting room and told to wait. Barney's commanding officer was present and accompanied my aunt and uncle to identify the body. Although he had been demobbed, Barney still had to obtain the official army discharge before the undertaker could claim his body. I was relieved to be spared the ordeal of actually seeing my poor dead brother, as I possessed a morbid fear of the dead. Instead, I prayed for him. Remorseful, I contemplated the irony—Barney had survived the war and on the same day that he was demobilized, he was killed in a civilian accident. His young life had been snuffed out in less time than it took to blow out a candle. The suddenness of his passing was traumatic. Our family was grief-stricken, as were many of his friends. My father had a setback. He was never quite the same and he lived for the remainder of his life in the Retired Servicemen's Home.

Part One

At Barney's funeral, a large gathering of relatives and many people unknown to us attended. I recall how my father stood beside the open coffin and placed his hand on Barney's still good-looking young face, and said, "My poor, naughty little boy." Barney had been a rumbustious daredevil and had loved to speed on his cycle. Once he had borrowed an uncle's motorcycle without permission, for which he had been severely punished and was confined to our backyard minus his trousers. His friend Michael leaned over the fence and teased him as "the bare bum cyclist."

Gran commented, "We are not alone. So many young men have died. We will pray for all of them."

The war had ended, and with it my brother's young life.

CHAPTER 7
Art College and Interior Design

Peace was declared on May 8, 1945, but there was no peace in South Africa— instead turmoil and political chaos reigned. All the Afrikaners who had been interned by the pro-British Jan Smuts Government during the war were released, and the Voortrekker Movement was reborn. The Apartheid era had begun.

At sixteen I had graduated from the convent high school and went back to live with an aging grandmother and an equally old Nanny. I had won a scholarship to attend the Witwatersrand Art and Technical College in Johannesburg to study Interior Design. Simultaneously, the award included an apprenticeship, working for a prestigious interior design company, Wallace of Sloane Street, London, with a branch in Johannesburg.

Gran allowed me to accept the offer. "The experience will be invaluable," she said, pleased that I had done well. She had handed over the management of the shop to Aunt Leah and her husband. However, Gran continued to run the home with a firm hand. The apprenticeship with the English company spared me the ordeal of working with my family, but I was expected to join them in the business at the end of my apprenticeship, at which time I would be nineteen. I envied the freedom other young people enjoyed. They came and went as they pleased. I had practically to beg for permission any time I went out at night, and there was no guarantee that it would be granted. When I was allowed out, I had to be home by eight o'clock. It did not help that one of the neighbourhood girls was pregnant out of wedlock. Pointing a gnarled finger at me, Gran said, "See what happens to loose women."

Part One

I had no ready answer but I felt a response was necessary. "Gran, you continue to treat me like an irresponsible child and never give me any credit, no matter how hard I try. You're lucky it's not me."

"And what do you mean by that?"

Gran called Aunt Leah. "Listen to this child. We're too soft with her."

"Most young people my age control their lives. I've graduated from college and I've been working for two years, and I'm still treated as an irresponsible child."

"That's enough, Joan," Aunt Leah interrupted.

I was aware that this was not the end of the discussion. It was the first time I had dared to defend my actions. I was frustrated and wondered how I could escape from this bondage. Gran even collected my pay and doled out an allowance. My father was of little help as he resided in the ex-serviceman's home, and following Barney's death, he seemed to have lost all zest for life and left Gran to dictate terms. I decided to seek the advice of Mother Superior. If all else failed, then I might as well consider a convent, so I made an appointment to seek Mother Superior's advice.

"Good afternoon, Joan. What's the problem, dear?"

"Mother, you're still our legal guardian. I cannot live with my family. The restrictions have become impossible. It will be even worse when my two younger sisters return at the end of term. I've suggested joining the Order but Gran nixed that idea as utter nonsense."

"Joan, you're not a serious candidate for the novitiate. You are too headstrong. The vows that are required to be a nun are poverty and chastity, and possibly you will have no difficulty with those two, but the third and most important one, that of obedience, will give you much trouble. Let me think about your problem. Now go in peace, and may the Lord be with you."

"Thank you, Mother, for understanding my position." I was somewhat relieved; perhaps there was a solution. All I wanted was a normal life without all the restrictions my family imposed. Girls did not leave home to live on their own without causing a scandal. I placed all my hope in Mother Superior.

A week later, I was summoned to an interview.

"Joan, I've prayed and thought a long time about a solution to your problem. I've consulted with your former teachers, who have confirmed that indeed you are a responsible young lady. Have you any idea of what you would like to do? Now that the war has ended, have you considered nursing? I realise you've not considered it as a profession, but the advantage is that there you will be in residence, which I believe is your main concern."

"I have not given any thought to another career."

"Nursing is a noble profession and is something even your grandmother cannot contest. It will mean a change of lifestyle. No more varnished nails and makeup, or high heels. Do you wish to think about it?"

"No, Mother. I'm prepared to do whatever is needed that will permit me to live away from my domineering family, without bringing shame to them. And I promise to work hard and not let you down."

"Very well. I'll speak to the matron. She is a member of our church board."

"Thank you, Mother."

"You have my blessing and may the Grace of our Lord be with you."

I said nothing about my plans to anyone. The fact that I was about to embark on an entirely new project without any parental permission excited me. If it all worked out, then I would take charge of my life and make my own decisions.

I kept my appointment with the matron of Bridgman, who said, "You are younger than the age at which we admit girls. However, Mother Superior speaks highly of you. Since you have a diploma from the art college and have worked for two years, you will not be required to do the obligatory two-year probation before taking the preliminary exam. The work is onerous, but I'm told you are up to the task. There is a two-year intensive training for midwives. At present, there is a shortage in that field. So many of our nurses were recruited by the army."

"Thank you, Matron. When does the programme begin?"

"The course starts in a fortnight's time, and it is to prepare you to write the entrance exam. Here is the required list and an explanation of what is expected."

"Thank you, Matron."

"Please cut your nails and no make-up. Braid your hair, cut it, or tie it back. And wear sensible shoes."

With trepidation, I loitered before I went home to break the news to Gran and Aunt Leah. They were certain to scold me for not first obtaining their permission. However, they respected Mother Superior, who had had a great

Part One

influence on me. Gran and Aunt Leah conceded that it was to my credit that I was guided by Mother Superior and not by my father's sister, Aunt Katie, whom I admired and Gran despised.

I phoned Mother Superior to thank her once again for providing me with an opportunity to make my own decisions. I was thankful and excited that I had the opportunity to escape from a restrictive home life. Finally, I would be taking charge of my life.

CHAPTER 8
Only Fools Pay for Experience: Drama in the Labour Ward

D R. CLARE BRIDGMAN, AN AMERICAN MISSIONARY, ESTABLISHED Bridgman Memorial Hospital in 1928 to honour her late husband and to serve the Native women of Johannesburg.

On my birthdays, I generally consulted my horoscope, and it occurred to me that the stars were aligned—or was it a co-incidence that 1928 was also the year of my birth? I was ecstatic to be accepted into the midwifery programme at Bridgman Memorial Hospital. I would be exposed to a life beyond the narrow confines of my home, convent, college, and general social milieu, which was restricted to Europeans. It was an opportunity to live and work amongst people of a different racial, cultural, and political stance. Further, nursing had never occurred to me, but I was prepared to give it my best, and I was confident that I would succeed.

South African society was divided into Europeans and non-Europeans. Segregation was endemic and practised since the inception of the country in all spheres of life. It had always been that way; the signs "Europeans Only" were plastered everywhere: government offices, schools, colleges, universities, churches, park benches, and the list went on and on. But the aim of Apartheid was to introduce legislation that would enforce the existing practice of separation. It was an attempt to prevent the white gene pool from becoming "contaminated," and more importantly, it was to emphasise the superiority of whites over non-whites.

Part One

I moved into the spartan nurses' residence, so unlike my convent dormitory. It lacked the warmth and camaraderie of my alma mater. I was to share a room with another student, older than myself. Twenty-one was the age of acceptance into the midwifery programme. I was nineteen, but since Bridgman was a missionary hospital with its own regulations, an allowance was made as a favour to Mother Superior. I was grateful, and I resolved to do my best. At last, the freedom I craved was within sight.

Matron MacDuff was a tall, reed-thin, no-nonsense Scot. She wore a starched veil over her carefully centre-parted sandy hair, drawing attention to her eyes, which were strangely disconcerting: one blue eye, the other brown. Her hooked nose was reminiscent of certain aviary species. She was nicknamed "The Polly," and I soon found out the reason. Matron MacDuff would suddenly appear, her raspy voice heralding, "Nurse, what ARE you doing?" She would repeat the student's answer, sending chills down the offender's spine. Matron believed that every new nurse was an ignoramus who lacked basic intelligence. She was equally blunt in her assessment of the young medical students who had to complete a six-week training session at the hospital.

"Medical students are oversexed boys with brains that end in their pants. I forbid my nurses to fraternise with them, and woe betide anyone guilty of disobeying my orders," was her explicit warning to new recruits.

Matron's injunction to nurses did not faze me, for I had no romantic interest in boys. I found the work stimulating and the lectures interesting. One such lecture on the implantation of the embryo and foetal circulation fascinated me. I was absorbed in it, and when the lecturer asked if there were any questions, without hesitation my hand shot up and I blurted, "How did the seed get there?" Thunderous laughter ensued and suddenly I realised my *faux pas*. I blushed and hid my red-hot face behind my hands. I thought, *I really am naïve. I've led such a sheltered life.* My solace was that this was the last formal lecture before I would be transferred to the labour ward. I was fully occupied, but on my days off, rather than return home I attended political lectures and meetings and dances and parties, something my grandmother had forbidden. I soon learnt to sneak back into the hospital residence well after the night curfew. I was careful to avoid being caught, as the punishment was the cancellation of off-duty hours, and it could lead to expulsion.

Night duty proved a challenge in the labour ward, where the work was exacting and difficult and nurses could not afford to make mistakes. Often there was no time to take a tea break. One unusually quiet evening when I was on duty, there were only three patients in the labour ward. One was a young girl of uncertain age. I suspected her to be between fourteen or fifteen years old. She was in labour, but her contractions were weak. She was not confined to bed but was permitted to walk around. She seemed to spend an inordinate amount of time in the lavatory. I decided to check on her. "Is everything all right?" I asked. I was concerned about her reluctance to leave the washroom.

"Yes, I waiting for water to clean," she said, as she flushed the toilet again and held on to the handle. Still holding onto the handle: "I like to see water."

It dawned on me that the toilet was a novelty. The girl was from a remote farm and unfamiliar with a flush toilet. In all African areas, there was no sewage or running water. Night soil was collected weekly and the buckets were replaced with clean ones. Incongruously, the largest sewage disposal units were in Nancefield and Kliptown, two coloured and Indian townships, a scant five miles away from Soweto.

Gently, I led her back to the ward, but in a short while she was up and wandering around again. She said, "I go lavatory," and without waiting for an answer, she ambled off. She seemed in no distress, so I let her be. There was a lull, and an unusual stillness in the labour ward. The lights were dimmed and the other two patients rested comfortably. I continued making swabs.

Some time passed before I noticed that the girl had not returned to the ward. I went in search of her and was startled when I heard a voice from behind the toilet door.

"Argh, shame," the voice said again and again.

I rushed in and to my amazement, I found the young girl squatted on her haunches. In her blood-stained hands she held a tiny, lifeless baby so small it might have been a doll. Tears were streaming down her cheeks. The placenta with attached umbilical cord was lying on the blood-spattered floor. I scooped the bloody mess, and I tried to comfort her, but anything I said had little effect. Gingerly, I placed the lifeless, miniature dead baby in a dish. The unfortunate mother continued to wail, and I rang for assistance. I bathed the distressed young woman and put her to bed, awaiting the doctor's examination. The patient would be discharged to the care of the district nurses the following day. How to commiserate with grieving mothers was not a part of our midwifery curriculum. It was emphasized that we not become emotionally involved with patients. But how could one prevent becoming sympathetic to their plight?

The poor girl was bereft. In her culture, it was customary to prove fertility prior to marriage. A child would ensure a good marriage proposal and increase the *Lobola* or bride price. I wondered about the girl's fate after the still-birth. In a short space of time, I was slowly being exposed to the culture of black people. It dawned on me that I was being educated in the social structure of my country and how necessary and important it was for my understanding and growth. I resolved that as a young person, it was incumbent on me to play my part in trying to rectify the situation.

As was often the case in the labour ward, everything suddenly happened at once. The two other patients were now fully awake. A screen separated them. One of the patients was a social worker, and this was her first pregnancy. She was rather old for a primigravida. A nurse was checking the foetal heart and asked me to check it as well.

"You are right. We have to call the doctor," I concurred.

The patient looked worried and asked, "Is everything all right?"

"It is time for the doctor to examine you. Please try to relax," I said, coaxing her.

Two more nurses came on duty. The doctor arrived and gave the older mother an injection. She was in strong labour and he confirmed that her labour was advanced, as the head was crowning. However, there had been no foetal heartbeat for the past thirty minutes. The doctor had to perform an episiotomy to extract the baby, its head was impacted and the mother was in distress. The umbilical cord was wound tightly around the baby's neck and had strangled it. Anxiously, the mother watched as we struggled to resuscitate the stillborn child, but unfortunately, all our efforts were in vain. It was one of the most difficult tasks, how to inform the mother, who was shivering and stoically staring at us with pleading eyes, clenching her fists. The doctor prescribed a sedative and he crossed over to the second bed, where the other young mother-to-be was moaning and rolling about. Earlier that evening, she had been brought in by the district nurse, who said she was expecting twins and that she was from the farms and had had no prior pre-natal care that she was aware of.

The first baby was delivered quite normally amid screams from the distraught mother. But now she started screaming as the contractions became stronger. Doctor gave her an injection and after a while, the second baby was delivered. The babies were very small, two and a half pounds each, yet they yelled lustily and were wrapped up in warm blankets. "There's another one," the doctor said. For a moment, there was disbelief and the doctor asked both nurses to check.

"We were aware of twins, but the third baby went undetected, as she was already in labour when she was brought in." The poor mother had no strength to push the third baby out. The doctor had to apply forceps to deliver the under-weight baby. The mother was exhausted and could barely lift her head, indicating that she was thirsty. She took only a few sips then pushed the feeding cup away.

I was concerned for the triplets' safety, if they all survived, for it was brought to our notice that they would not be welcomed into the family. We were informed that a superstition existed among certain African tribes where multiple births were unwelcome. I never understood why, and thus the fate of the extra babies could be in jeopardy. On discharge from the hospital, they would be handed over to child welfare to ensure that all the babies were kept safe. The mother was uncomfortable and refused to communicate with anyone. Understandably, she was exhausted and lay with her eyes closed. Strangely, she did not request to see her babies.

I was concerned about the older mother, who in all likelihood would never conceive again, and the agonizing sadness for the young girl who'd had a still-birth. I thought, how unfair. I had been witness to the drama of that night's deliveries, which demonstrated the random nature of life in the maternity ward. Three live babies and two distraught mothers. If I could, I would have sneaked one of the triplets to each of the bereft mothers. However, it was not my place to interfere with destiny.

I continued to learn about the cultural lives of people I had taken for granted all my life. Having grown up in a privileged milieu, I had never considered our domestic servants' needs or backgrounds before. Most people accepted that servants were there to work and knew little about them, and they cared even less about the lives of those who toiled on their behalf. Growing up in a society where separation was the accepted norm, my ignorance is understandable, but

Part One

not forgivable. The majority of servants came in from the farms and lived on the premises hidden in the backyards of their employers' residences, and they were at their employers' beck and call all hours of the day. They had one day off a week, generally Thursday, which came to be known as "maids' day off," and one Sunday per month.

A year passed and training at this quasi-religious institution had given me another perspective on life. It had opened up a new vista and opportunities to associate with people other than those I had known and grown up with. My direct contact studying and working alongside black people made me realise the freedom I had enjoyed was at their expense. I had choices and many privileges denied the black midwives.

My growing social consciousness now included regular political meetings. I joined the Progressive Forum (P.F.), whose mandate was to raise the morale and the political consciousness beginning with students in their fight against Apartheid. The P.F. was affiliated with the non-European Unity Movement in Cape Town, where the people of mixed race, that is "coloured," were on the common voters' role, and they enjoyed the franchise the same as Europeans, but that too was about to end. The P.F. consisted of many fellow travellers, both European and non-Europeans, and members of different colours and religions.

Academically, I had exceeded all expectations and proceeded to the final year. There was a two-week holiday before the next term began, and I was determined not to return to the family home. I solved the problem by accepting an invitation to attend a political conference in Cape Town. My funds, however, were limited and I could not afford the fare on my meagre student's pay. Paul Smythe, a genius, political guru, and chief founding member of the P.F., hitchhiked everywhere. It was his preferred mode of transportation. Paul agreed to take me under his wing. He said, "Joan, don't let the lack of money prevent you from attending the conference—you can hitchhike with me."

Somewhat apprehensive, I agreed. I realised Gran would be scandalised if she knew of my intention to hitchhike, especially with a man. It was just not done!

In my mind, I could hear an outraged Gran admonishing me, *Who ever heard of nice girls chasing off with strange men, much less hitchhiking?*

Paul told me to organise a lift to the airport, where we would meet, and he would take charge from there. A trusted friend who drove me cautioned me about the dangers of hitchhiking. However, I was not to be dissuaded. It was preferable to going back home to Gran and purgatory, I thought.

On arrival at the airport, Paul was lolling up against a barrier at the entrance. His usual unfiltered Springbok cigarette dangled from the side of his mouth. "Wait here, and don't talk to anyone."

He returned a while later and said, "Joan, I've clinched a lift all the way to Port Elizabeth and the Tsitsikama Forest."

"And what car does he have?" I asked.

"Joan, you're a babe in the woods. No, I don't know the guy, and it's his private plane."

I was speechless but excited. "What a lucky, unexpected adventure," was all I could muster.

Paul was his casual self. He appeared to be only half awake and often gave the impression that he was barely conscious of his surroundings, but instinctively one became aware of his genius.

My excitement was overwhelming. The closest I had ever been to an aeroplane was at a small private airport at Baragwanath, close to the hospital where two young doctors had obtained their pilot's licence, which was essential if they were to practise in the Bush-veldt. They had invited a few of us to see the planes in the event we too would seek work in the bush. Unfortunately, flying lessons were beyond our means, but we were permitted a look inside and inspected the small aircraft. Thus, the opportunity to actually travel in a plane was beyond all my dreams. I was overjoyed and it came free of charge—a delightful bonus. I could barely wait to board. The sheer novelty of my first flight was a highlight of my young and inexperienced life. I would forever be grateful to Paul for guiding and allowing me to accompany him. Many years later, after Bis and I were married, we had the pleasure of helping Paul to hide out in Potch, before his escape from South Africa.

Since we would be travelling on a private plane and we were not leaving the country, there were few preliminaries except for putting on safety vests. Paul sat in the co-pilot's seat, and I sat in the back. I was impressed at how much Paul knew about aviation. He kept up a lively conversation, but the droning noise made it difficult for me to follow the conversation. I picked up odd snatches, but my lack of knowledge prevented me from understanding what was said.

Instead, I enjoyed the scenic beauty of the turbulent Indian Ocean, watching it roil back and forth for miles along the undulating golden beach, all the way to the horizon on one side. There was a large ocean liner in the distance and a few fishing boats were mere dots close to the shore, with the dense forest on the opposite side. The plane easily ploughed through billowing white cumulous clouds that enveloped it for minutes at a time, playing hide and seek before it emerged into bright sunshine. The pilot made what he said was a special detour to point out the Recife Lighthouse, a spectacular sight, the black and white striped structure reminiscent of a giant zebra on hind legs. The droning noise of the engine induced a twilight sleep. I dozed on and off during the approximately three-hour flight. Somewhere along the journey, Paul offered me a flask, which I declined.

"We'll be landing shortly," Mike the pilot said. "I have a jeep parked at the airport."

"Do you do this route often?" Paul asked.

"Yes, fairly frequently," he answered. "You're welcome to join me at the Tsitsikama Forest Inn for tea."

Paul had told him little about us, only that we had plans to meet up with friends in Cape Town. He was careful not to mention any political connection. On arrival at the Inn, we settled to a scrumptious English high-tea of cucumber and sardine sandwiches, cheese straws, buttered scones with strawberry jam and clotted cream, and delicious fruit cake. After some trivial conversation, Paul excused himself and left me alone with the pilot. Mike was a big-game hunter who conducted safaris in the bush. He knew and was familiar with all the game reserves south of the equator.

"Do you often hitchhike with Paul? And what do your folks say?"

"No, this is my first time. And what an adventure! My folks are unaware of my activities. They do not even know that I'm on leave from the hospital."

Paul returned. "Joan, pick up your bag, we have to leave. We've got a ride into Cape Town."

We thanked Mike for the ride and the tea. We left him sitting alone. Out of earshot, Paul said, "Now we have to scrounge another lift into Cape Town. It's only about two hundred miles at best."

"But didn't you just say we had a lift?"

"That was an excuse for your benefit. He kept ogling you."

"What?" I hadn't noticed. I'd assumed he was merely being polite.

"A cardinal rule, especially for young girls who hitchhike, is don't make friends with strange men on the road."

"Thanks for the belated warning. And what of those they know?"

Paul ignored my remark. It would soon be dusk and we must have walked for about two miles along a steep road. The forested gorge was lush with beautiful flora, purple and white agapanthus, coral pincushion protea, red-hot pokers and a variety of gerbera and white daisies. Paul's knowledge of botany, like everything else, was extensive, and he pointed out things of interest. Then suddenly, we heard the approach of a pantechnicon (transport truck) lumbering uphill behind us.

"I'm going to stop the driver and ask for a ride." The engine spluttered to a halt as Paul flagged him down. "Are you going to Cape Town? And can we get a lift, if you are?"

"Not all the way to the Cape. You'll have to sit in the back and no smoking. The load's flammable," he said, noting Paul's cigarette.

It was dusk and the twilight evening would soon give way to nightfall. Momentarily, Paul hesitated. "Thanks. Well, beggars can't be choosers."

We climbed into the back and the driver bolted the door securely. My heart was racing, but I was tired. It took a few minutes to become accustomed to the musty interior, but it was preferable to waiting on a lonely stretch of road.

No sooner had we settled in when I fell asleep, only to be woken later by Paul's snores. It was dark, hot, and stuffy in the cabin and my throat was parched. I realised that without waking Paul or thumping against the side wall to attract the driver's attention, there was no way of knowing what the time was. Or where we were, or how far we had travelled. *Please remain calm and don't fuss*, I told myself. Just then, Paul rolled over and knocked his head against a crate, which woke him. As he reached for his cigarettes, I swatted at his hand.

"Oh Christ! I forgot. What time is it?" His watch had stopped.

I had not brought mine. He thumped against the back of the truck. The driver knocked back and shouted, but we could not make out what he said.

We were like caged animals. After what seemed forever, the truck came to a sudden halt, throwing us against each other. We gasped. The driver opened the door to a rush of fresh sea air, revealing a starry night. "This is as far as I go, but it's only a mile or so into town."

"Thank you for the ride. We'll enjoy the walk. We need to stretch our limbs, and the fresh air will be good. Thanks again."

The walk was pleasant under the stars, and Paul identified the various constellations. "Unless you have other plans, we could go directly to the camp," he said. "There are bound to be lots of people there and something to eat, and a place to sleep."

I nodded in agreement. I certainly had no plans and would have to follow my instincts. We reached Froggy's Pond at Cape Point. It had a camping ground close to the ocean, where the conference was to be held. Many people were about and were delighted that Paul had made it. He was one of the main speakers and casually he introduced me, saying, "We're starving and thirsty."

Fresh fish that had been caught earlier and grilled over fire-pits had never tasted better. Cheap wine flowed. A teetotaller, I refused the wine. I did not fancy the taste and the convent had instilled the horrors of alcohol, thus I had never acquired a taste for it. Some young people sniggered and shrugged their shoulders. The night air was filled with cigarette smoke. A young man offered me a cigarette, which I accepted, simply not to be thought a wet blanket. In the dim light, I put the unfiltered end into my mouth, and I was forced to spit the tobacco out. I had never felt as stupid as in the presence of these knowledgeable young people. I realised I lacked the worldly background and the fervour this group displayed. While their banter and heated passionate discussions were taking place, I was tired and asked where I should put my satchel.

"Oh, anywhere. Find a place wherever you can. No one here is fussy."

Several girls had commandeered Paul, who appeared to be enjoying all the attention. People began pairing off. I was uncomfortable and felt out of place. It was my first foray into a gathering of Bohemians, for want of a better description. I realised that the conference invariably meant that it was party time as well. Everyone appeared more worldly and older than me. I was awkward and prudish; my convent training was still too deeply imbedded. I decided to sleep fully clothed in the first empty tent I came upon. I wished the night would end, and questioning myself, I wondered whether I had made a poor choice. Someone started playing a piano accordion and a chorus of revolutionary songs broke out. Eventually, the revellers drifted away, and Table Mountain was obscured by dense clouds. I gazed up at the stars but they too were hidden. Then, lulled by the cool ocean breeze, I finally fell asleep.

I awoke early the following morning to a wonderful view of the mountain covered by a white cloth of clouds, and surrounded by dense bush and colourful blooms with reds and yellows predominating. Most people were still asleep, not surprising after the night of carousing. Unwashed and grubby, I went to the poorly attended welcome session. Somehow, I was not inspired. It was more like a picnic for would-be "free-thinkers," referring to people who did not commit to any political group but were social fellow-travellers. I met up with Izzy, an old acquaintance and a drawing partner from design college. We had always teamed up on art excursions and visits to various art galleries. His father owned one of the biggest art galleries in Johannesburg.

Izzy was amused to see me. "Whatever are you doing here out of your natural habitat? I remember an earnest young girl who always handed homework in on time, while I fooled around trying to learn something about the finer points of art, knowing full well that I had a career in Pa's gallery."

"I'm learning the ways of the world. I came as Paul's guest. He's lost in the crowd."

Izzy raised his eyebrows but did not say anything. "I drove up from Joburg to watch the cricket test match between England and South Africa but decided to have a look in first. I'm not enamoured with the rustic life, so I won't stay. You're welcome to join me. I'm staying at my aunt's, the one you met in Joburg when we were both students at art school."

I was relieved. I had no qualms about leaving the so-called political conference, which in reality was an excuse for a social get-together. I could not imagine staying, especially feeling left out. Hitchhiking had been an adventure, but I would not attempt it again. Knowing Paul, he would not miss me. He had rendered me a favour. I was a novice and unschooled in the ways of these worldly young people. I was reminded of my father's favourite expression: "Only fools pay for experience."

I accompanied Izzy to his aunt's home at Cape Point, where I was stunned by the magnificent view of the ocean fronting the house and in the background,

Table Mountain. She greeted me warmly, but predictably, Izzy's aunty was shocked when she learned about me hitchhiking.

"Whatever will your family say?"

"They don't know that I had a short vacation and I do not intend to tell them." As usual, I felt the need to explain my actions, but I omitted the part about the truck and any further incriminating details. "I came by plane," I said casually. That instantly seemed to change my host's impression, and I went up in her esteem. Perhaps she thought I came from money and therefore I deserved to be allowed to discard the normal form of behaviour by acting out. Young women were expected to act with decorum in accordance with the set mores of the times.

The aunt was hospitable and during the day took me sight-seeing. In the evenings, I spent time with Izzy and his two brothers and friends at the beach, enjoying lobster and crayfish barbecues. The delectable Cape watermelons, prized by South Africans for making Konfyt, a preserved sweet delicacy, were in season, and mock battles were staged, forcing us into the surf to wash the stickiness off.

The brief sojourn to the cape had afforded me a pleasant interlude away from work.

Back in Johannesburg, I had to return to work at the hospital. My trip had been another eye opener. In retrospect, I had gained an insight into how people survived the pressures of Apartheid. I appreciated that a diversion from the depressing political conditions was essential in order to cope. On reflection, I promised myself to be less critical in future, and thus I continued to support the P.F. The meetings were important because the discussions on the political situation in our country were serious and helped to spread a political awareness among people who normally had no recourse in how to combat or to further their knowledge of the tyrannical system. I encouraged the midwives to join as well. Weekends when I was off duty, I distributed pamphlets at bus stops and locations, explaining the need for people to be informed about the political situation and to attend the P.F. The Unity Movement was an attempt to unite all factions of political groups opposed to Apartheid. In time, it was hoped that the united movement would be strong and help to change the status quo.

CHAPTER 9
Falling in Love

Living in residence finally allowed me the freedom I had always craved. Having joined the P.F., I was not in a position to make a monetary contribution, as they were constantly in need of funds to print leaflets and posters. Therefore, in my spare time I volunteered my service along with other members and undertook to assist in the distribution of the pamphlets that had been printed by an anonymous donor.

One evening, laden with a large sheaf of posters, I entered the undergraduate common room at "Wits," the abbreviated form for the Witwatersrand University of the Transvaal in Johannesburg. I encountered a solitary young man standing at the front. He was slender and of medium height. He wore a cricket sweater under his "Wits" university blazer and a tennis racquet lay on the chair beside him, a testament to his athleticism.

"Hello, where's everybody?" he greeted me, smoothing back his jet-black hair. "I assumed there was to be a meeting this evening, or am I wrong?" he said with a nonchalant air, straightening his ascot.

"Hello," I replied. "There's a meeting of sorts, but the members are seldom on time to informal gatherings. Stack these on the table, please," I said and shoved the pile towards him.

"Sure," he said smiling, and he took the load from me.

His brown eyes were shaded by the longest lashes I had ever seen. I stared, he held my gaze, and I felt the colour rising to the roots of my hair as I blushed. I was self-conscious, my cheeks were aflame, and my pulse quickened, but I could not avert my gaze. Confused, I continued to stare, wishing that I was anywhere

Part One

else but there. I was spared further embarrassment by the arrival of friends, and I turned away to greet them. I shook my arms, glad to be rid of the heavy load.

Gradually, students drifted into the common room. They picked up posters and found seats. Before long, the prattle of voices rose to a crescendo as their heated arguments debated the political situation, and in particular the university policy regarding admission of non-European students. Their arguments drowned out the chairman's plea for attention. The university permitted only a limited quota of non-European students, who studied alongside their European counterparts. Each year the medical school admitted a token number of Indians and even fewer blacks. A select number of non-European students who could afford it applied to study medicine at universities in Edinburgh or Dublin. The law faculty in South Africa at that time was the sole preserve of Europeans.

"Attention! Attention! Silence! Please. Please, may I have your attention?" The chairman called everyone to order. "We're not open for discussion this evening. Remember this is an informal gathering. We're here simply to confirm the date for the annual picnic and to find out the results of the dance and the annual street parade. The proceeds will go to the crèche in Alexander Township."

The crèche in the impoverished native location on the northern fringe of Johannesburg had been founded by liberal-minded students. They were appalled by the economic and social injustice of poor black women who worked as domestic servants, and who had to abandon their own young to fend for themselves while they cared for their employers' children. In addition, they cleaned, cooked, and kept house, leaving their white masters free to enjoy their leisure activities. The irony was not lost on the students.

"We should all be looking after our own children," they reasoned. It was unfair and time for change. However, change was still many years away!

"Proceeds from the dance and the street parade, with the addition of several large anonymous donations, totalled £6532," the treasurer said.

"Hear! Hear! Hurray for Wits! Wits!" was the jubilant cry from the students.

"That's an excellent effort, taking into account that we had so much fun. The annual picnic will take place this Sunday at Meier's Farm, and please do not forget to bring your contributions. We're adjourned," said the chairman.

Everyone bundled out in haste, and the young man and I missed the chance for further conversation as we hurried out.

The day of the picnic arrived and I had the day off. I waited for a bus that would transport people to the picnic spot on the Vaal River twenty miles north of Johannesburg. This was the students' last fling before the year-end final exams began.

No cloud marred the brilliant azure sky, which was in sharp contrast to the murky grey from which the Vaal River derived its name. Young couples strolled about. Some braved the river to swim. Others played ball games or lounged around playing cards, when without warning out of the clear-blue sky, a peal of thunder crashed like the cymbals in a Tchaikovsky symphony. The sound reverberated in crackling spurts and was followed by streaks of lightning. Moments later, a torrential rain sent people scurrying for cover—but not soon enough, as the sudden downpour drenched the picnickers.

I was blinded by the heavy summer rain. I floundered and lost a shoe in the sodden undergrowth as I fought my way in the storm. Stumbling and groping along, I clutched at the overhanging branches that impeded my path on my way to shelter in a bus.

"Come with me," a man's voice ordered, and I felt a hand grasp my elbow. The voice sounded vaguely familiar and I was grateful for the support. The relentless rain lashed, and marble-sized hailstones pelted down. Minus one shoe, my toes were caught in the slush, and I had difficulty keeping my footing. I had to concentrate, as I kept slipping and sliding on the spongy grass. My rescuer held me firmly, but the torrential storm blinded me so that I had no idea who he was. He steered me safely towards a car parked on the bank and pushed me into the front seat before making his way around and climbing into the driver's seat beside me. In the few minutes that it took to reach the car, we were soaked. The trek had winded me.

I was grateful for the respite and the safety of the car, which sheltered and protected us from the fierce storm and the dreaded streaky lightning.

"Thank you," I said breathlessly, wiping the wet hair from my eyes. I turned to look at my saviour. "Oh, it's you. I'm sorry. I don't know your name," I said, and I recalled our brief encounter at the Progressive Forum meeting when I had ordered him to take the pamphlets from me. That brief contact had ignited a spark. I remembered his smile and his personable attitude. He was Indian.

Part One

"Everyone calls me Bis."

"Now I recall; you're the tennis star whose picture was printed in the recent Wits news bulletin?"

"Yes, I'm a med student, and it's easy being a star when there's not much competition," Bis said, laughing.

"I'm Joan," I said, shielding my wet breasts with my hands. The flimsy blouse clung to my body and my discomfort was obvious, but I felt grateful to him for rescuing me from the storm. I had a morbid fear of lightning, ever since I had witnessed a young child who had been struck and killed.

"We'll have to wait it out, but we'll be safe in the car." Bis did not wait for my answer as he tried to start the car. Visibility was poor and it was tricky extricating the car from the muddy bank. After many stops and starts he managed, and drove off until he reached the road. "Thank goodness I managed to free the car, or we might have been stuck there indefinitely." He parked at the roadside while the storm raged. Recurring flashes of lightning accompanied by booming peels of thunder assaulted our senses as we waited for the rain to slow down. We were marooned and shivered in our wet clothes, trying to get comfortable. Finally, the storm abated, and only the sound of our audible breathing and the patter of gentle rain could be heard. Bis broke the silence and quoted: *"And what art thou? Said I to the soft falling shower..."*

"I am the Poem of Earth, said the voice of the rain," I interjected. "Walt Whitman?" I queried with a sideways glance at him.

"Yes," he answered and took my trembling hand and held it between his. I was embarrassed and shyly withdrew my hand.

"We could go to a friend's not far from here to dry off?" he offered.

"No, thanks. I feel too grubby and like Cinderella, I've lost a shoe."

"And will the prince find it? And go searching for the princess?"

"In this storm, who knows?" I said, laughing.

"We could try a drive-in cinema?" Bis said hopefully.

Before he finished, I said, "Look, the rain's beginning to let up," as the sun peeped out from behind a golden cloud bathing the sky in shimmering light and revealing a double rainbow—a sure sign that the storm was over. It ended almost as quickly as it had begun.

"That's a good omen. You're meant to make a wish," I said.

"Really, and what's your wish?" Bis started the car and turned on the radio, but there was too much static. "Sorry, that happens during a storm."

"Actually, making a wish is an old wives' tale and my wishes seldom come true, and I don't believe in everything my grandmother says."

"You're cynical. What do you believe?" Bis asked, as he continued to drive at a leisurely speed. The atmosphere inside the car felt charged. Bis opened the window to let the cool fresh air in as the steam rose from the road after the downpour.

"I'm not superstitious. The nuns at the convent get credit for that."

"No, I expect you're not. What do you do?" he enquired.

"At present I'm preparing to write my final midwifery exam. I was a designer and decorator. I worked for a London company with a branch in Joburg. I was supposed to work in the family firm, a small decorating outfit. But I wanted freedom, and to take charge of my life, so I took up midwifery. My P.F. friends said it was a good thing, as decorators were petite bourgeois, and when the revolution came, we would be redundant."

"Do you always explain everything you do? And take your friends' advice?"

"It's a habit. I hate to be misunderstood. But it was the perfect excuse for me to leave home and live in the nurses' residence. And also an opportunity to recruit nurses to the P.F."

"You're doing it again. But that's very noble of you," he jested.

"I've no idea why I'm telling you my life story. Leaving home to live in residence was a real chance for freedom, and to get away from a tyrannical grandmother who still treated me as a child."

"Quite laudable," he laughed. "Again, do you always explain your actions?"

"I do talk too much, especially when I'm uncomfortable." I flushed. It felt as if the roots of my hair were on fire. "Now you're making fun of me."

"I'm not. But why are you uncomfortable? You're too young to be so earnest," Bis said.

"I suppose that too is the result of my upbringing and having lived cloistered in a convent."

"Do you consider it a disadvantage?"

"Not really. Sometimes I am inhibited. I'm not accustomed to the freedom most young people enjoy and take for granted."

"Actually, I do understand. I left home to go to school in Natal. My community is as insulated as your convent, and Apartheid hasn't helped us break free."

"It seems that we have more in common than I thought," I said.

We were at ease, as if we had known each other a long time. And without waiting for a reply, Bis speeded up and drove up to Northcliffe. It was a lookout point high above the city and he found a parking spot on the wide plateau.

"This is a wonderful place to watch the sunset," he said.

"You've done this before?" I said archly.

"Now who's having fun?"

The sky was ablaze with colour: vermillion and amethyst clouds inlaid with golden streaks from the setting sun that floated on the west horizon, and it added an enchantment to the moment. Bis recited from Omar Khayyam: *"A Jug of Wine, a Loaf of Bread and Thou..."*

"You're quite a romantic," I interjected. To hide my sudden confusion, I laughed, brushing the wet hair from my eyes.

"You should laugh more. Your eyes sparkle, and they're beautiful."

I felt myself blushing again. I recalled Mother Superior's words, *you're so sensitive. You give yourself away. You turn the colour of beetroot.* Thank goodness the light was fading. I prayed he did not notice my rising colour, which was a constant bother and an embarrassment.

Without warning, Bis leaned over and kissed me. I was caught off guard, but to my surprise, I responded, and I did not reject his advance. Bis drew back and said, "We're almost dry. We ought to go."

The sun was disappearing slowly beyond the horizon like a giant, saffron-coloured eye. A peeping Tom or a witness to first love? We drove off in silence, comfortable, oblivious of our damp clothes.

"Where would you like me to drop you? Or we could go to the drive-in cinema?" he said again, giving the impression that he wished to prolong our time together.

"Thank you, another time. I need some dry clothes."

"I could lend you a shirt."

"But not a shoe." I laughed. "The nurses' residence, please, at Bridgman Memorial Hospital."

CHAPTER 10
Holy Unction

In my final year at nursing school, I was summoned to Matron's office, perturbed, wondering what wrong I had committed.

"Your grandmother is in hospital with a fractured hip. There is no need to concern yourself. She is receiving good care. Now back to your duty," was Matron's terse statement.

"Thank you, Matron."

Despite Matron's assurance, I was concerned, and in my lunch hour, I called Aunt Leah, who informed me of the gravity of Gran's condition.

It transpired that my indomitable Gran had slipped and fallen on the highly polished passage floor and broken her hip. Bessie, her maid, had discovered her groaning in agony. She was barely conscious, and Bessie, unsure what to do, covered Gran with her favourite quagga skin karros, which produced a shrill cry from the stricken old lady. All the trustworthy Bessie could do was sit beside her and wait for the family to return from Sunday-morning church service.

To her horror, Grandmother was admitted to Johannesburg General Hospital, an imposing building where both my mother and my brother Barney had died. She would be hospitalised for a minimum of six weeks. The prognosis was not encouraging. Gran was seventy years old, and her silent drinking was at issue, disclosing her secret, which was one explanation for her wraith-like figure. But, as usual, appearances had to be maintained.

Gran occupied a private room, but she was extremely difficult and an unco-operative patient. Aunt Leah said it was an ordeal to visit her as she refused to talk to her visitors or even to answer their simple questions. From the elevated bed with her leg suspended by a pulley, Gran glared down in stony silence. Her discomfort was evident, but she sustained her steely reserve.

On my day off from duty, I visited her. I was shocked by Gran's appearance. Age and sorrow had withered her parchment skin, which now was wan and wrinkled and it highlighted her sharp features. Only her eyes retained their lustre.

After a month in hospital, Gran's condition deteriorated. She had contracted pneumonia. Her main complaint was that she was deprived of her Ouija board, and she missed the séances she had conducted. In her delirious state, she kept calling for me. Gran believed that she had the preternatural gift of clairvoyance, and that it would be passed on to me. Aunt Leah appealed to Matron to give me extra time off to visit her.

"Joan, I'm so glad you've come," Aunt Leah said when I arrived. "She's called for you repeatedly, and the doctors do not believe that she will recover. At times, she calls out to your grandfather, but then she always talked to him, as if he were still alive. The priest has administered the last rite, the sacrament of Holy Unction."

I watched my delirious Gran lying helpless and was overcome with guilt. I thought of all the scoldings I had received for my wilfulness. Why had it taken me so long to admit that it was to teach me and to ensure that I grew into a responsible young woman? Gran was a stickler for good behaviour, etiquette, and integrity. As the eldest, it was my duty to set an example.

In silence, Aunt Leah and I held vigil at the bedside, helpless witnesses to Gran's suffering. My troubled thoughts were a hazy blur as I dozed on and off, but Gran's words rang fresh: "Joan, must you always have an answer for everything, and the last word? One day you'll come a *cropper*."

Now fully awake, I reached over and kissed the stricken lady.

"Forgive me, Gran. I'm sorry," I whispered, hopeful that Gran heard me. I was mortified and sick at heart. It had never occurred to me to be grateful or considerate for the care Gran had willingly bestowed. Why had it taken me so long to acknowledge that my adolescent behaviour had been a constant worry to Gran? I was ashamed. She had sacrificed her life for me and my siblings, and I had taken it all for granted!

The early morning light crept through the shutters and cast shadows on the wall when suddenly Gran started tugging at the pulley, her leg swaying. She groaned. "Oh, Arthur, at last you've come," she moaned.

"Gran, what is it?" I asked, holding Gran's fragile, bony hand.

Gran stared straight ahead and mumbled in a voice that was barely audible, "Arthur, free the quagga." For a few minutes, she continued to babble incoherently. Gran gurgled and for a moment, I thought she was choking, but I surmised that the end was near. There was a gentle rattle, almost like a gurgling sound, then quite unexpectedly, she exhaled her last breath.

I acknowledged that Gran's adult life had been one of sadness and continual upheaval. She was a mother who had buried two daughters and a beloved husband. She had devoted her life to care for her family and her late daughter's children without complaint. I pondered Gran's apparent dual personality—the practical and strict no-nonsense woman, and the superstitious lady who delved in and firmly believed in the supernatural. But I too was a Pisces, and although I claimed not to subscribe to the occult, I was curious and read my horoscope which appeared monthly in the *Outspan* magazine.

CHAPTER 11
A Surprise Gift

Gran was buried in the family plot next to her beloved Arthur and her two daughters. After the funeral, I returned to my duties at the hospital, where a busy workload left little time for socialising, and I needed to prepare for my final examination. I sighed, and for a moment, I wondered whether I would ever see Bis again. The memory of his kiss lingered. We barely knew each other, but I was impressed by his courtly manner. There was slim hope that we would meet. All the P.F. meetings were suspended until the end of summer, and I concluded that he had probably left town for the holidays. Anyhow, I had to write my final midwifery examination.

With confidence, I entered the examination hall, which was filled with matriculation students and college graduates, there to write their university entrance exams. Present also were the nurses and midwives, writing certification exams. Some would go on to post-graduate nursing studies at university, whilst others would enter hospitals. Here, Apartheid was strictly enforced and the few non-European applicants were sequestered in a side room.

While waiting for my results, I spent the summer working at the hospital for room and board, thus sparing me a return home while I awaited the outcome. At the end of summer, all results were posted in the medical journals. I had passed with honours. I had also won a scholarship I had applied for to the Almoner[1] Division at Witwatersrand University.

---

1 Almoner: a distributor of aid

I had a scant few days before moving from one spartan dormitory to a room on campus. It turned into quite a chore what with registering, choosing my curriculum, and purchasing supplies. To find my way about the campus required more time and energy, as the different faculties were scattered miles apart. In addition, as an honours graduate, and before classes started, I had been invited to the International Students' Union to attend a lecture by Rev. Junod on penal reform. The topic: *The Plight of Pregnant African Women Prisoners.*

The post-lecture discussion went on much longer than I had anticipated, and the temperature reached ninety degrees. The common room was hot and stuffy. I had gotten up and gone in search of fresh air and a drink when I saw him. Was it an illusion? But he was heading towards me.

Smiling, he took my arm. "Are you looking for anyone in particular?"

"Oh Bis, I'm glad to see you. I presumed that you were still at the caves on the archaeological dig or on holiday."

"No, and I'm glad to see you. Come, I've parked illegally," he said with a grin.

Racing to his car, and barely able to check my emotions, I stumbled but Bis held me firmly as he had done once before. "We must stop meeting like this!"

We both laughed.

Bis started the car and drove away. We reached Northcliffe, one of the few non-segregated areas where we could meet away from prying eyes.

"I tried contacting you, but I had no way of knowing where you were," he said.

I jabbered away, barely giving him time to answer all my questions. He found a parking spot and flicked the headlights for service for the take-out eatery. A waiter took our order. "We've done this before," Bis said, and he ordered chicken sandwiches and tea. Then he leaned over and kissed me. "I've dreamed of doing that all summer while I scraped sand away from Neanderthal bones in the Sterkfontein Caves, which now have become world famous thanks to Phillip Tobias's pioneering work."

"How did you know I'd be at the meeting?"

"I didn't. I saw it advertised, and since it concerned pregnant women, I took a chance. I had spent the summer scheming how to contact you. I didn't even know your surname. I could not phone the hospital, knowing Matron's attitude to med students. And I was unsure whether you were still there. Actually, I drove past there a couple of times, hoping to see you."

Part One

I reached for his hand. "We were destined to meet. I continued to work at the hospital, praying you would show up there."

Our order arrived, and we ate in silence. Suddenly talking did not seem important. Having found each other, merely being together was blissful.

It had started to rain, a slow drizzle, which dissipated the humidity. I broke the silence. "It's been so hot. The rain is a relief. Unfortunately, we will not see a rainbow this evening. We barely know each other—I said that once before, but I'm delighted to be here with you."

"So am I," he said, and gently put a finger to my lips. "Please, open the cubby, there's something for you."

I obeyed, and a leather-bound copy of Whitman's *Leaves of Grass* wrapped in a Wits scarf slipped out. For once, I was at a loss for words. It seemed so natural to be here with him, but to receive a gift was quite beyond my expectation.

"Thank you." I blushed, and for a moment pondered if my behaviour was unseemly. Had I appeared too eager? And would I never escape my Puritan upbringing?

"I knew you'd pass. I expected you to pass with distinction. Congratulations! It's your graduation present. I've been carrying it around in my car on the off chance we would bump into each other. Please, read the inscription."

I felt the colour rising to the rhythm of my rapidly beating heart, for inscribed on the inside cover, *"And what I assume you shall assume...*
For every atom belonging to me as good belongs to you."

I was overwhelmed, and I felt an emotion unlike anything I had ever experienced. Whitman's poetry epitomised what I felt to be true. I was bewildered by the suddenness of his confession, his gift of love, for that's what it was, and it had taken me by surprise. Was this truly love? The old cliché "love at first sight" was indeed true. Accustomed as I was to second-guessing myself, in the far recess of my mind, I imagined Gran admonishing me: *Get that twaddle out of your head. Do you even know this fellow?*

None of my male friends had had the impact that Bis had on me and I knew almost nothing about him, or he about me. All the boys and young men I knew were merely friends or competitors.

Questioning myself was second nature. It was part of my psyche. After all, I was born under the sign of Pisces, those yin yang fish, and flinging all caution aside, I had just annexed my yin to his yang.

CHAPTER 12
Against All Odds

ONCE WE STARTED DATING, WE SHARED OUR DREAMS AND EXPECTA-tions, and we confided in each other aware of what our respective cultural mores stipulated; mine European and his Muslim-Indian. However, unlike most couples, we could not always meet openly, and we chose to keep our relationship secret. Apartheid, with its strict racial laws, coupled with the fact that we were young political activists, posed a problem.

I accepted a staff position in the labour ward at Baragwanath hospital, which was fifteen miles outside of the city limit. We made lengthy phone calls to each other and indulged in the usual patter that young couples are familiar with. Both of us shared a passion for literature and poetry in particular. In our spare time, when Bis was not competing in tennis tournaments and we were not at P.F. meetings, we attended all the speakers' events put on by the university cultural club. As a non-white, Bis had no access to the theatre or to symphony concerts, except for the few that were convened at the university Great Hall. Fortunately, Bis could afford to purchase all the books and records and indulge his love of music, which we listened to in his flat. Bis said that dating among Muslim youth was forbidden, and even for engaged couples it was discouraged. Marriage among different ethnic groups was definitely out of the question. Inter-racial relationships between whites and non-whites were forbidden by law. I had a European birth certificate, and Bis, who was Indian, was classified an alien under the Apartheid law. Neither Bis nor I alluded to our different social and especially religious status, he a Muslim and me a High Anglican, but there were constant reminders from families and friends about the impropriety of our relationship.

Part One

"Where does that leave us?" I asked.

"Joan, I'm confident that we will find a solution. Don't be disheartened. We just have to keep our relationship a secret for now."

It was known only to a few intimate friends. We spent as much time as possible together. Bis often missed lectures in order to meet. He had not attended a single lecture on public health. The night before the final exam, Kris, a friend, went to Bis's flat with his meticulous notes. Fortunately, Bis had a phenomenal memory, and was able to memorise them and attend the exam the following morning.

Bis and I were deliriously happy and wrapped up in our own world, but grave problems lay ahead. We were acutely aware that we faced a battle. The political situation was becoming worse. The Communist Party had been banned. It had been a convenient hideaway where young couples of diverse racial groups met, and it continued to operate underground. Any criticism or open display of dissent against the government was a cause for a conspiracy investigation. Informers were everywhere, and distrust reigned. There was no actual ban on mixed gatherings, although we were aware suspects were under surveillance. Many people were banned out-right and confined to their homes. Some people could not attend gatherings of more than four people and required permission from a magistrate in order to leave their homes. Everyone tried to avoid the attention of BOSS, an acronym for the "Special Branch." When Bis and I did meet, we gave the impression that it was casual and quite by chance. A few known Special Branch operatives sometimes attended social gatherings and were conspicuous as they sat silently to one side, observing and making notes, while we pretended to ignore them. We wondered whether it was a clever ploy, devised in order to catch us if we let our guard down.

Many other couples faced similar obstacles. It became necessary to avoid the scrutiny of the Special Branch by switching partners and changing our routines.

The final-year medical school examinations had ended, and before the results were made public, an excited Bis phoned me to meet him. He was ecstatic. "We must meet. I'm coming over right away, and please take the afternoon off!"

It was my Wednesday half-day, and I waited outside the staff sister's residence until Bis pulled up in his car. He left the engine running and waited for me to get in before he drove away.

"I wanted to tell you personally before the results are officially published. Will you honour the new doctor by attending his graduation ceremony? I've taken for granted that you would. I'll give my car to my flat-mate Ahmed Kathrada, who will accompany and drive you to my graduation ceremony."

"Congratulations! I'm truly honoured. Nothing will please me more than to attend." I smiled at his presumption, a gesture foreshadowing my future, which he would orchestrate. Being in love, I acquiesced willingly to his request without any protest or argument.

A few weeks later, I attended the medical school convocation in The Great Hall at the University of the Witwatersrand. Relatives and friends dressed in their finest summer attire packed the hall. I had a lovely, linen, navy-blue two-piece outfit. The post-war "New Look," ankle-length skirts, were all the rage. No more short skirts! The war had ended, rationing was at an end. At last, life in general was returning to a pre-war time.

The audience waited impatiently for the ceremony to begin. A procession of dignitaries in their academic regalia marched in and took their places on the platform. The stage was awash with crests of the Witwatersrand University, the City Coat of Arms, that of the country, and finally that of the British Commonwealth. The smiling graduates, including the four Indians and two Africans, filed in and took their places in the front rows, and when all were seated. The audience rose as the organist played the opening bars of both national anthems, "God Save the King," and "Die Stem van Suid Afrika." It was a pleasant surprise to see the non-white students were not separated from their peers, but were seated alphabetically. Wits was known for its liberal policies. Seats rumbled and scraped as all sat down again. A hushed silence ensued but soon was interrupted by coughs and clearing of throats.

Commencement was in session.

"I now declare the ceremony open. A warm welcome to the parents, graduating students, and our honourable guest, a distinguished World War II veteran, and an alumnus of this university to give the opening address."

The renowned veteran drawled on in a monotonous tone about post-war duties and the task the graduates faced. A restless audience fidgeted and stirred in their seats, and a baby whined and had to be taken outside.

When the speeches were over, the graduates marched up to the stage to be capped. Bis was among the first of the hundred-odd students. I recall I watched with pride as he was confirmed a medical doctor. I was filled with joy, and I could only imagine what Bis and his family were feeling. He was one of four Indian students and two Africans graduating that year. The dean congratulated him, shook his hand, and handed Bis his diploma. He moved back to his seat. There would be a long wait until all the graduates were installed and before the ceremony ended with the closing prayer.

Later, when we were alone, Bis confided, "All I wanted was to hold your hand and share my feelings with you. I was euphoric, but my heart was pounding so loudly that I was deaf to most of what was said. Bis recalled a phrase from the lengthy speech that moved him. "'To strive for excellence.' A precept I will endeavour to live by," he stated.

I realised that my involvement with Bis was opening a new understanding of how Apartheid affected Indians. The ruling society had decreed all non-whites were second-class citizens. Bis was sensitive to the denigration, and he felt a certain degree of shame for something he had no control over. Bis, the other three Indian students, and the two Africans who had graduated with him had defied the odds.

Later he told me, "Joan, I got through the lengthy speeches by recalling past incidents that had occurred and brought me to this point," and he related an incident from his youth.

He had been accosted by white louts as he was carrying his books and wearing his school blazer. They followed and taunted him, "Koolie, koolie, curry poop no good." They did not stop until they too were set upon by thugs, allowing Bis a chance to escape.

Looking back, it seemed a miracle that his dream had become reality. He continued, "Joan, graduating from medical school was a surreal experience. It legitimised my own worth." He confessed that all the pain and angst he had been forced to live with had made him stronger. He explained his development; how he had grown a long way from his roots, and how amid great excitement and trepidation at age twelve, he had boarded the train for the overnight journey to Natal. He was to attend the legendary Indian school in Durban, Sastri College, opened by the Indian Poet Laureate and Nobel Prize winner of 1909, Rabindranath Tagore. At school, his classmates had shortened the patronymic Bismillah to Bis. It stuck and followed him to varsity, and forever after he was known to all simply as Bis.

He recalled his father's parting words as he hugged him: "Abdul Haq, study and be a dutiful son, and do not forget your obligatory prayers."

It was a sentiment that was echoed by the religious elder who had accompanied them to the station, there to bestow his blessing on the young boy with a warning. "You're making a big mistake by sending your son away," the Imam had admonished Bis's father. "All our boys lose their faith. Some even eat pork." The Imam shook his head and nodded disapprovingly toward Bis. Once again, he warned Bis's father, "Big, big mistake to send him away to college. *Insha Allah* he will return as he goes. But no good can come of sending him away. Better he stays here and becomes an Islamic scholar."

"And what did your father say?" I asked.

"My father merely shrugged and ignored the unasked-for advice. He refused to be drawn into that particular argument. But there was more than a kernel of truth in Imam's warning to my father. The issue was that as a student, I had shown great promise at the *Madressa,* the religious classes all Muslim children attend daily after regular school hours. I was a gifted student and the Imam was reluctant to lose his star pupil, fearing Western education would distract me and all that orthodox teaching would be lost. Some of his fears were justified and his prediction was about to be fulfilled. Just think, I could have been an Imam and would never have met you." Bis chuckled.

"And I could have become a nun teaching literature."

"Is that where your love of poetry stems from?"

"No," I said with a smile. "My father encouraged it. He had inherited a signed copy of Shelley's poetry and he often recited from it. 'If winter comes, can spring be far behind?' It was his favourite maxim. He explained no matter what troubles or problems beset you, they would end, and a brighter solution was something to look forward to."

Looking back to our adolescent years, Bis and I discovered that we had taken similar paths. Both of us had to leave home at an early age.

"You've no idea how bleak the boarding house was," Bis said. "I survived the minor tensions and tried to fit in by joining clubs and sporting activities. It was the panacea to overcome my initial homesickness. Separation by ethnic group and caste was alive and well even at Sastri, where we were all supposed to be equal. We were all Indian, but a subtle caste system prevailed."

Part One

"At least I was not alone at boarding school," I said. "I had my younger sisters to watch over, and the nuns were kind. I actually enjoyed the school and found many ways to be disobedient simply to relieve the monotony of routine, but more importantly, it gave me a sense of being in charge, especially if I got away with it. Naturally, there were holidays and special outings to look forward to."

Bis smiled warmly at me. "I'm so glad that your experience was happier. It's a different story when bullying is sanctioned by adults and the government. And though I wasn't hurt physically, it can be damaging to the psyche."

He got back to telling me what he'd been recalling during the speeches. "I thought about the long, uncomfortable train ride as it chugged along, jerking and churning its way through the Drakensburg Mountain passes. The second-class carriages reserved for Indians, Chinese, and coloureds [people of mixed race who were not black]. Then the third class with its un-upholstered and bare wooden seats for black people. Of course, you would not have experienced this, as first class was reserved for Europeans."

"No, you're right. I never experienced that kind of discrimination. However, I witnessed how coloured students who were permitted to sit upstairs on trams were punched and kicked as they came downstairs, as they tried to alight. That was painful to see, as I was powerless to help them against the white thugs. It is appalling how prejudice undermines our ability to act."

Bis continued, "I was perched precariously in an upper berth. Each time the train rumbled, I was afraid that I would fall down and hit the obese body that was spilling outside of the lower bunk. The old man's noisy snoring, his intermittent grunts, and his thrashing about shook the upper bunk. Thus, there was little chance of sleep. The incident that stuck with me was the conductor's irritated call, 'Tickets! Tickets!' as he stood in the open door-way, tinkering with his clipper. Woken up by the conductor's intrusion, the old man stopped snoring. He rolled over and fumbled for his ticket.

"Man, where's your ticket?" the conductor growled, as the old man continued trying to find it. From the bunk above, I handed mine over. The conductor glared up at me and said, 'Koolie, you behave, and don't leave your garlic smell behind.' A remark I had no choice but to ignore. It stung my pride. Such comments only strengthened my will to succeed. Joan, I was resolved that I would be more than this ticket collector, whose superiority was accorded him by the colour of his skin."

The graduation ceremony had finally ended. Graduates, family, and friends streamed out into the sunshine eager to congratulate the new doctors. All appeared equal. Everyone mingled in carefree camaraderie, and Apartheid seemed a mirage as they exchanged good wishes, hugging, and taking snapshots with friends and relatives. It was refreshing to be a part of the collegial atmosphere. Prejudice, rancour, and narrow-mindedness was banished for the time being, but the evil of Apartheid simmered beneath the surface.

Later, Bis told me that he had spotted his father, his younger sister, Ruby, and his niece, Fatima, in the crowd. He went to meet them and they congratulated him. His mother would never attend public functions. She had difficulty appearing socially in mixed gatherings outside of her own community. His mother was the daughter of an eminent Imam, who was the head of the Islamic Madressa in Dabhel, India. She had been brought up in "*Purdah*," which dictated the seclusion of women in public, a custom she had difficulty discarding. She arrived in South Africa seven years after their marriage, and at her husband's request, being a dutiful wife, she discarded the niqab, the full head and face covering, in favour of a head scarf and a large shawl, which she drew protectively around her head and shoulders.

Bis met his father, who was very proud and said, "Well done, my son, but we won't stay for the celebratory tea party. We want to avoid the traffic, so we should leave soon."

Bis accepted the excuse. Bawa, a proud man, was uncomfortable in mixed social gatherings, which appeared to accommodate their social status on this momentous occasion, but did not alter it.

"Thank you, Bawa, for everything. I understand."

"Your mother is anxious to see you. When will you be home?"

"As soon as I've packed up here, possibly during the next week," Bis said.

Ruby interjected using his family pet name, "Hakie, I need some snapshots of you in your graduation gown."

Bis found it amusing, as he knew the real reason was to show him off to her friends. He disliked posing but obliged her, and he posed for several with his father and niece and got a friend to take one that included the four of them.

Part One

"We met Ahmed Kathrada, and he introduced us to Joan, his girlfriend. He gave me your car keys and asked me to give them to you," Ruby said, as she handed him the keys.

Bis saw his family off and went in search of Ahmed and me. We were with a group of friends and I had my back to him.

"Aren't you going to congratulate the new doctor?" he whispered in my ear.

I turned around. "Not if you sneak up on me. I've been waiting for you to find me. Ahmed introduced me to your father and your sister and niece."

"And now that I've found you, I want you to meet someone. Come." He led me to the tea pavilion. "Wait here a sec." Bis came back with his friend Bunny, who had been his anatomy dissecting partner. They had developed a close friendship throughout their years together at medical school. "Bunny, this is Joan." Before he continued, both Bunny and I burst out laughing. "What's so funny?" Bis asked.

"I tried to date Joan when I did my stint at Bridgman. She assisted me with the post-mortems on premature infant deaths. Little wonder she refused me. Bismillah, you are devious," said a jovial Bunny.

CHAPTER 13
The Madding Crowd

To understand South African terminology regarding the various racial groups without offending anyone, it is helpful to know and to distinguish between the appellations of its diverse people at the time I'm writing of. The interchangeable terminology is confusing, because the population was a stratified society divided into four groups. "Europeans," or white persons, included Afrikaners and Boers and were at the very top. Second were non-Europeans, or coloureds, which consisted of the darker-skinned people of mixed origin who were not white or black. Third were the Asiatic, which included Indians, also referred to by the derogatory term of koolies; the minority Chinese group, who were denigrated as Chinks; and a handful of Japanese, who had the title of "honorary whites." Finally came the Bantu, a collective term for the entire black race, alternatively referred to as natives and the insulting term kaffir, or nigger. Bantu in turn became native, a term that was replaced by African among the more liberal element of society and was finally changed to black in the modern era.

Under Apartheid, each group was distinct and reinforced stereotypes and our behaviour toward one another. Curiously, it encouraged the notion of superiority, where Europeans were at the helm and all the rest of the population were layered one below the other.

My time working at Baragwanath Hospital ("Bara") was stimulating, and it turned into a study in race relations. My contact with natives prior to Bridgman Hospital was usually with servants in a domestic environment and Asians through trade. Bara was a minuscule, cosmopolitan world depicting a cross-section of South African society. The staff was multi-racial, numbered in the hundreds, and treated thousands of black patients annually.

The strict laws reinforced the differences between people. Therefore, it was imperative to remain connected to organisations such as the P.F. and clubs that espoused democracy, which was further eroded by petty Apartheid. Baragwanath Hospital and its environment differed vastly from the parochial hospital of Bridgman. I had to adjust to the hustle, which was bewildering. My experience now gave me an indelible impression of the dire poverty and suffering, something that would never be forgotten.

Baragwanath Hospital had been built by the British Government during World War II to cater to the hundreds of soldiers and casualties of the war, including my father, who were flown in from the North African Campaign. In 1948, it was sold to the South African government for £1,000,000 and converted into a native hospital.

The hospital was erected in a series of between forty and sixty wards, all at ground level and independent of each other. Every ward was built to house forty patients. The wards were linked by concrete passageways and covered by corrugated iron sunroofs that protected patients as they were wheeled to their respective wards from the triage centre. Although the hospital was barrack-like, the beautiful, well-tended gardens surrounding each ward lent it a light and airy quality.

The vast grounds housed the staff living a quarter-mile away from the wards. The European-doctors' section was separate from the European-Sisters' quarters, and equidistant was the non-European doctors' quarters. The hospital had to accommodate about eight hundred native nurses who were in training there, and their compound required a huge section of the grounds, which was isolated a long way from all the other buildings. Also living on the grounds at Bara were the hundreds of Zulu men, called "boys," who were cleaners and gardeners. Baragwanath was a self-contained modern village of approximately ten thousand people.

The hospital was situated fifteen miles beyond the city limit of Johannesburg. Its close proximity to the sprawling black township of Soweto made it ideal to service the demands of the fast-growing native population. Simultaneously, it kept the natives in a reserve and away from the town, especially at night, which made it easier for the police to control.

On weekends when off duty and with other members of the P.F., we distributed pamphlets and mixed with the people in the immediate precinct of the hospital as well as those in Soweto. There was no law forbidding our mingling, but often the white police presence would be a deterrent. The police suspected that white people and Indians in black areas were dissidents, fomenting and inciting revolution. Therefore, it was essential to keep a low profile, and often we distributed religious pamphlets in order to confuse the police.

Here we witnessed the appalling conditions people were forced to endure, which had worsened under Apartheid. The plight and suffering of blacks in these locations[2] was far worse than it was humanly possible to imagine.

Baragwanath became the largest teaching hospital in Africa, if not in the world. It was the hub of the black community, and it was a relatively safe haven for undercover dissidents who plotted to combat Apartheid. It was also a venue for the covert backdoor thieves who peddled their stolen loot. The saying went that one could purchase anything from a pin to a bedroom suite at Baragwanath, merely by knowing whom to ask. I recall the number of times I bought stockings when mine laddered while on duty.

The hospital provided many young black women the opportunity to become professional nurses, the majority of whom would otherwise most likely have ended up as domestic servants and nannies. The legions of black secretaries, orderlies, cleaners, gardeners, and support staff toiled day and night under the supervision of white management. Scores of white doctors, matrons, and sisters came from European institutions to train hundreds of non-white nurses, who were needed to work in the wards and to maintain the hospital at the highest standard.

Apartheid was strictly upheld and non-Europeans were subordinate to their white superiors. My introduction to Bara was working in the labour ward as a staff midwife while continuing my social studies, and later I obtained a coveted position as almoner and patient advocate. The average number of babies delivered in the hospital was between twenty-five and thirty daily. These were mainly primipara with first babies, diabetics, and difficult births that could not be

---

2 "Location" is a term used in South Africa exclusively to denote black residential townships situated well beyond the town or city limits.

delivered in their homes. Over a hundred black midwives serviced the normal deliveries in the township.

In 1950, I escorted a visiting journalist and an American doctor around the obstetric unit. They wished to see first-hand how Bara operated and dealt with the large number of patients it catered to. When I was showing them around the lying-in labour ward, the American doctor waved his hand towards the patients. "You have an abundance of the best material here," he opined, referring to the women in labour. Sadly, this was a common sentiment shared by some European doctors too. On his way out, the doctor continued in his American drawl, "They lie there silently like docile black cows chewing the cud."

The condescending remark was offensive, but he was a guest, and I had to be careful how I responded, especially with a journalist present. There was so much I could have said, but I simply stated, "They are poor black women, and mothers-to-be!"

Bara became a refuge for the poor with masses of homeless people congregated in and around the hospital grounds. It was reminiscent of a marketplace in an over-populated and underdeveloped country. Poverty-stricken patients who sought medical aid were grateful and hoped to be hospitalised in order to obtain a bed and a free meal, but superstitious and rural Africans believed that it was a place one went to die.

On one occasion, a middle-aged woman was found wandering around the hospital. No one understood a word of her dialect. She did not appear to have too much wrong with her and she was admitted to "Masakein," an isolation ward for people who had been in contact with infectious diseases. Weeks went by and in the interim, she made herself useful by helping out in the wards, carrying trays, fetching water, and stacking dishes. The woman seemed quite at home until one day an orderly taking a poll in the wards understood her language.

"What are you doing here, Sister Mama? You don't seem to be sick," he said.

"I'm not. I came to visit and I couldn't find my friend. So, I was put into the ward because nobody knew what I was saying. But I like it here. Nice bed and lots of food," she said. "Please, I stay here for good?"

Her case was brought to the almoners' attention. She had been living at the hospital for more than four months. We were obliged to hand her over to the Department of Social Welfare.

The bustling triage centre barely coped with the volume of the trauma casualties. Medical, surgical, and obstetrical cases were admitted and directed to the respective wards. The out-patient clinics overflowed, and patients and their relatives camped outside or on the hospital grounds.

The YMCA set up a store on the grounds to provide discharged patients with the barest necessities: sugar, milk, stiff mealie (corn porridge, a staple of the African diet), and a rough, cheap, blue soap.

The staggering birth rate and associated complications posed additional problems and kept the hospital operating at maximum capacity on a twenty-four-hour schedule.

Baragwanath was the focal point of an impoverished community, and often the sole place of refuge. Directly opposite the hospital a bare, open field was taken over by vendors, squatters, and drug pushers. It became an instant location. Daily we staff members witnessed the scenes and mayhem as we approached the hospital entrance, and we had to prevent colliding with the mobs who loitered in front of the gates. Strangely, the hospital staff and doctors who were coming on or off-duty were never accosted but were respected, and the crowds, including thugs, ushered our cars safely through the gates.

On our trips into the location to hand out pamphlets, we witnessed first-hand the sad conditions of poverty and overcrowding in the crime-infested place. Mud huts and rough, red-brick shanties with tin roofs were the norm in Soweto, which sprawled for many miles. At the end of the dusty, unpaved streets, water-pumps were installed where residents collected their water in whatever containers they had. Incidentally, an enterprising Cape Malay businessman from nearby Kliptown, an adjacent coloured suburb, sold water at a penny a gallon to the residents who lived close to his property.

Black gangs called Tsotsi Boys did their share of damage by sending hundreds of victims to the trauma unit. In the townships, these gangs caused havoc, and the violence went unchecked. They pillaged and terrorized hard-working people. Stab wounds, shootings, and murder occurred in incidents too numerous for anyone to record accurately or to care about. Each day throngs of people formed disorderly queues outside the hospital gates. They pushed and jostled trying to gain entrance.

To maintain some semblance of order, Zulu security guards, night watchmen, and black policemen worked non-stop to protect the people. The police were armed with truncheons, knobkerries, and shamboks—whips akin to cat o' nine tails. These were the only weapons black policeman were permitted to carry, and they caused severe multiple injuries. European police were supplied with firearms.

The fear of police was second only to that of the dreaded gangs of Tsotsi Boys who hung around the gates. They were brazen and in spite of the police presence, they concealed their illegal guns and other homemade lethal weapons, fashioned from sharpened bicycle spokes, which they used to poke out eyes and ears, or to jab up a victim's anal passage. In this milieu, the pickpockets and the Tsotsis robbed and maimed innocent victims. There was little difference between the Tsotsi thugs and the official police force, who were equally ruthless, except the police were legal and held the upper hand.

On one occasion, we witnessed an incident when a terrified woman screamed, "Stop! Thief, stop! He got my bag."

A burly policeman grabbed a young thug, who had started running from the scene. The assailant fired a gun. And in the ensuing scuffle, other security guards tackled him before he had time to fire his weapon again.

"Where's the bag you stole?" demanded a policeman.

"Please, it no me. Somebody else, no, no not me," yelled the unfortunate wretch cowering and flailing his arms as he tried to fend off the blows from the menacing knobkerries. There was no reprieve from the vicious beating. He required treatment and had to be admitted as another casualty to the bustling and overcrowded triage centre. The bag was not recovered. Undaunted, several Tsotsis approached the gates and attempted to enter, but were stopped.

"What d'yous want?" asked a policeman. "Give me them bicycle spokes."

"We want our brother," said one, not surrendering his offensive weapon.

In defiance of the police warning, they continued to harass the policeman.

He lashed out at them with his knobkerrie. "Ain't no visiting hours now, so go away."

The young thugs sauntered off but continued to loiter, mixing with the masses beyond the hospital gates. Across the street, teeming crowds milled around in the open square that represented a microcosm of the native community. Buses and taxi cabs ferried passengers between the hospital and the townships.

The garbage-strewn square had been taken over by squatters and unlicensed vendors, where makeshift stalls were erected on the hard ground. Hawkers sold stiff mealie meal, roasted offal, and corn on the husk, which they grilled on coal braziers or galleys that had been made from discarded petrol drums. The drums leeched acrid fumes that mixed with the stench of sewage waste, and the pungent smoke of "dagga" (marijuana) filled the fetid air.

Dust-devils swirled around adding to the pollution. Hucksters and fat Shebeen[3] Queens in colourful turbans sold illicit homemade Kaffir beer.

"Where you hide them things?" policemen screamed.

"What you take us for?" shouted the indignant Shebeen Queens.

The police were not fooled, but the sellers outsmarted them and continued their illicit business. The policemen, using crowbars, poked around in the arid ground trying to locate the caches of the brew, which the vendors buried beneath the sand amid the ant heaps. Any contraband the police found was swiftly emptied, except in certain cases where a blind eye overlooked the offense and the profits were later shared. The spilled casks of Kaffir beer created muddy puddles that rippled along the rutted road, and stray emaciated mongrel dogs lapped up the gooey mess.

"Dumb, dumb pauleece!" the outraged Queens screamed.

Swarms of green-headed bottle flies picnicked and multiplied in the waste dumps. Hordes of giant red ants scurried about, a microscopic version reminiscent of the hundreds of mine workers who were disgorged and stampeded helter-skelter from special trains as they were herded and prodded through streets like cattle, enroute to their compounds on the edge of town. Little pot-bellied, snot-nosed children with matted hair, bleary eyes, and scabrous skin foraged for scraps of food, or ran errands for drug traffickers, for *dagga* was a palliative for unemployed and destitute *rookers* (smokers), who were considered pariahs and scorned by society.

Tsotsi Boys kept a lookout for the police, alerting the villains by beating bicycle spokes against Coca Cola bottles or tin cans and shouting, *"Arrah, arra-rai, Arrah, Arrah,"* a warning that the police were on their way.

The babble and raucous noise of the crowd was drowned out by shrieking sirens and flashing lights that warned of approaching ambulances. The crowd scattered in all directions as the vehicles closed in. Without stopping, the

---

3   Shebeen: An illegal bar where alcoholic beverages were sold without a licence.

policemen waved them through the gates, directing them to the emergency entrance, admissions centre, and the obstetric ward.

The scale of suffering among ordinary black people was unimaginable, and yet, along with the hospital staff, they contended with it on a daily basis. The hospital, in effect, provided a sanctuary for those in dire need. But it represented only a fraction of those who needed help. There was little that could be done.

My colleagues and I believed that education would eliminate some of the poverty and hardship. The principles of the P.F. and other political organisations were based on helping to educate people, and to unite them in the struggle against Apartheid. The hospital precinct became a casual venue, and what the hospital provided was a Band-Aid solution to the insurmountable conditions of poverty and the under-privileged masses.

During the late fifties and sixties, I learnt that the famous hospital had become a scavenger's paradise where anything that was not under lock and key or nailed down was stolen. Only the poor and desperate sought admission there.

In my day though, teams of almoners and rehabilitation staff helped the poor and homeless patients to recover and find some form of refuge. However, the aid was inadequate to satisfy the demand that exceeded the facilities.

CHAPTER 14
Chinese Interns

Three Chinese doctors, two men and a woman, interning at Baragwanath Hospital were very unhappy. They were relegated to the non-European quarters and resented having to live there. Their discontent stemmed from the fact that they had attended private European primary and high schools. Now they considered it beneath their dignity to live amongst the non-white doctors.

After complaining of being the only female in the non-white quarters, and fearing for her safety, one doctor was granted permission to move into the European quarters. The two male Chinese doctors were disappointed that they were not granted the same privilege. The irony was that all their homes were in the Coloured Group Area of Kliptown, a designated non-European township, roughly three miles from Baragwanath and Soweto. Here their fathers operated grocery stores, and their living quarters were behind their shops. The shops were popular hangouts for the indolent *"dagga rookers,"* who congregated in front of the buildings. Often the sparsely stocked shops were fronts for the operation of their illegal *Fah-Fee and Pukka-pu* numbers game, which they plied six days a week. The "runners" or salesmen were recruited from amongst the local communities, who in turn solicited people to gamble on the numbers games. Twice daily, the winning numbers were drawn and announced before the next lot of numbers were sold. It was penny gambling on a very large scale. The odds were ten to one, and the numbers ran from one through thirty-six. Runners peddled the game amongst the under-privileged, who could ill afford to play but who were so desperate to make a few shillings that they chanced their luck. It allowed the

Part One

Chinese shopkeepers to derive lucrative profits, all tax free, although the police kept a wily eye and often arrested the "runners" for illegal gambling.

One of the Chinese doctors was a clever fellow, short with unusually narrow eyes and pock-marked skin. He tended to be surly, and he was teased mercilessly by Indian doctors.

"Doctor, what number will you pull today?" they asked. He did not find the jibes funny. He isolated himself from the Bridge players and their ragging, and he spent his leisure time in the library reading thrillers

The other Chinese doctor was a playboy: tall, fair-skinned, and good looking. Unlike most of the other Chinese, whose families had originally been recruited in the nineteenth century as indentured labourers and miners to build the railways, he prided himself that his family had paid their fare to make a fortune in the new country. He claimed that he was of Mandarin stock, which accounted for his height and looks. He regaled the other interns with tales of his amorous exploits. He was impatient to finish his internship, as he was preparing to leave for Ireland as soon as his contract expired. "Baragwanath," he complained, "is a backwater and too far out of town to travel into Johannesburg." This made him very unhappy. He was a film buff and had access to all the European cinemas in the city where he could watch the new releases. Above all, he resented that he was compelled to live in the segregated non-white quarters.

He was the lone graduate from the University of Cape Town. He drove an MG sports car, and he missed the joy of driving with the top down and a girl at his side along the scenic Cape route. He complained that the Transvaal was drab and dull. He missed surfing and sailing and having fun at the beach. "I had a great time in the Cape. Not to mention the pick of the beautiful Malay girls," he often boasted.

In the Cape Province, the coloured community—that is, people of mixed race but not black—enjoyed more political freedom than in the other three provinces and were on the voters' rolls. As a resident student, this doctor had voted in the general election. But now under the Nationalists Government, coloured people were being removed from the common voters' role and placed on a separate one. He hated the Apartheid rule, but he refused to join any group that opposed it. "I have no desire to attract the attention of the Special Branch that could condemn me to this infernal hole. I'm determined to get out."

He boasted of a wealthy uncle in Ireland who was completely Westernised, and this appealed to him. The added attraction was that there were two unmarried daughters. "I'll just give them the once-over," said the irrepressible young man.

The non-European doctors' reaction to their Chinese peers was good-natured scepticism. There were more important things to worry about than a few disgruntled interns. The consensus among most South Africans was that the Chinese were reactionary and that they could never be relied on for any political support. Unfortunately, they were trapped between two divided sides: neither white nor black.

Gambling apart, the Chinese were law abiding, but a problem presented in the form of a few Japanese businessmen who had obtained European status.

The Apartheid regime had sold tons of pig iron worth many millions of pounds to the Japanese, and their bonus (bonsella) was that the few Japanese in South Africa were given honorary white status. However, this privilege applied only during daylight hours. The reason was that at night the local police claimed they would not be able to differentiate between Japanese and Chinese, who did not enjoy European status. The police lumped all East Asians together. They stated, "All Chinks look the same. Slanty eyes and straight hair. And Asian men love to sleep with white women, even though they know cohabitation is illegal here."

CHAPTER 15
African Residents

ALONG WITH THE TWO CHINESE INTERNS WERE TWO AFRICAN interns who shared the non-European doctors' quarters, Archie Rangebola and Rex Tatalane.

Archie was a quiet, taciturn individual. He could never be induced to play Bridge, but on occasion, he attended the parties held in the common room. Rex maintained that Archie felt uncomfortable and was out of his depth due to the repartee of the witty Indians and their different social customs. Archie spent most of his free time at the African nurses' quarters.

"Lucky him! We're jealous," was the chorus from the other doctors.

Nurses' quarters were strictly off limits to all doctors. Archie's father owned a funeral parlour, and one wit remarked, "Not to worry Archie, Daddy will bury all your mistakes." It was intended to be funny, but Archie was not amused. He believed it to be a slight on his ability. Interns teased each other constantly.

Rex was not known to have any black friends and spent all his time with Indians. A garrulous man who invariably knew all the latest gossip, he was an avid Bridge player but constantly cash-strapped and borrowed money from anyone who would lend it to him—even strangers were not spared his Fagan-like habits.

Rex was clever. His father was a "Boss-Boy," captain of the Black Miners Association in the gold mines and that entitled Rex to a full government scholarship. He was an excellent cricketer who became the eleventh member of the hospital non-European Team. Their success against the rival European doctors was legend. In the present society, they needed to prove that they were equal in everything but colour. Orwell's dictum that *some animals are more equal than others* certainly applied. "Yes, we have to work twice as hard and be three times as good as our white compatriots to get the recognition we deserve," was a saying that was echoed throughout the non-European doctors' common room.

Bis told me about the time Rex had accompanied the Transvaal Indian Cricket Team to Natal. While stretching their legs at a station in the Orange Free State, the predominantly Afrikaner farming region, Rex was approached by a little Afrikaans girl. Before he had time to find out what she wanted, her father pulled her away.

"What's wrong Pappy? Look he's black!"

"Come away, he's a kaffir," said the father.

"But Pappy, he's a person. You said kaffirs were monkeys."

Her comment provoked laughter. It was the only way to treat ignorance. Racial remarks were rife, and for the most part, there was no defence against them. But racial slurs occurred among the different non-European groups with equal frequency. Bis remembered that when he had invited Rex to his family home for a tennis match and dinner, his mother was anything but pleased. "Think of your sisters," she said.

"Whatever is that supposed to mean?" Bis questioned scornfully.

Those careless, negative comments never ceased to amaze him, and the frequent question, "Would you allow your sister to marry a kaffir?" was a common sentiment expressed throughout the country by other non-whites and non-Africans alike, who were all contemptuous of blacks. The irony was that non-blacks were not averse to sleeping with "kaffir girls." These statements caused discomfort, but they did not require a response. After years of indoctrination and endemic racism, it was a difficult and slow process to wean people away from their entrenched prejudices, which grew more virulent under Apartheid.

One day, Rex burst into the common room. "Chaps, I'm off to London!"

"That's rather sudden. What will you be doing there? And does the Bank of England have sufficient money to lend you?" remarked an intern. "You still owe me a fiver."

The snide remark went unchallenged. Rex never repaid his loans. "I've had a windfall. I've won an American Scholarship through my church to study at the world-renowned Moorefield's Eye Hospital in London."

Part One

"Well, congratulations. We hope that Fort Knox is the sponsor and that they will repay any loans you borrow from blind patients," quipped another intern.

Rex ignored the remark but continued to fill in the details of his windfall. "I'm excited, as I will be staying at a post-graduate boarding house operated by a retired general in Regent's Park. I'm off as soon as my papers come through. So bye, bye."

There was speculation and envy and more disparaging remarks after Rex left. "Lucky him. I wasn't aware that he was a practising anything, other than one of Fagan's tribe, let alone a Christian!"

CHAPTER 16
A Forbidden Tryst

When he'd escorted me to Bis's graduation, Ahmed Kathrada introduced me to Ruby, Bis's youngest sister. She was under the impression I was Ahmed's girlfriend. Bis corrected her, and his confession pleased her. She admired my self-assurance, and it inspired her to further her own education. Bis and his sister confided in each other, and she pleaded with him to intercede with their parents on her behalf to allow her to further her education at a private college in Johannesburg.

"Hakie," she said, using his pet name, "I must continue my education, but I know Mother will object."

Bis pleaded with his father to allow Ruby to attend the private college. She could stay with Uncle Mamajee, and in her free time she could spend time as a volunteer at the hospital. Bis promised to keep an eye on her. Finally, their parents consented.

"Thank you, Hakie! I promise I won't cause any problems," she said. Ruby appreciated that Bis understood her need to have a life outside of the insular town. She was fortunate in that she was the youngest of his siblings and allowed to further her education. In their ethnic community, rigid social customs were imposed on Muslim girls and women. Decorum demanded that proper conduct be practised at all times, and that entailed being modest and observant of their social customs.

A year earlier, Ruby had approached Bis with an unusual request for an unmarried Muslim girl. "Hakie, I have a friend, a former classmate, who is applying to Bara for internship. He graduated with distinction and wondered if you would put in a word on his behalf?"

Part One

"Who is he? If he is as good as you say, then he should get in on merit."

"Actually, he's a pen pal and we've corresponded since high school. Ishmael's wish is to intern at Bara," Ruby said, ignoring Bis's query. "The only other place where Indians may intern is in Durban, and he's not keen to go there."

"How come you're acting on his behalf?"

"Ishmael was embarrassed to approach you himself. So, I offered."

"Ishmael, is it? I'll mention it to my chief, but you know I may not have any success." Bis raised his eyebrows. He realised that this was Ruby's way of informing him that she and Ishmael were more than friends. "What else are you not telling me, or am I supposed to guess?"

He did not upbraid her for not conforming to the strict social code. A tacit agreement existed between brother and sister, and neither would discuss their affairs with other family members. At Bis's request, I met Ruby and secured her a position with volunteer services and soon we became friends.

In their Muslim culture, dating was against the rules and strictly forbidden. Going all the way back to the inception of Islam, it was a means of safe-guarding a young girl's chastity. Bis did not subscribe to these entrenched parochial mores, and he offered to assist his little sister. Fortunately, Ishmael was Muslim and his marriage proposal would be accepted when the time came. Ruby's secret for now was safe with him.

Ishmael was a gold-medal recipient. He had gained an internship at Baragwanath Hospital on merit. Bis had nothing to do with his appointment, but he appreciated his sister's choice of the reticent young man, who when spoken to often answered in mono-syllables, which people interpreted as being rude and abrupt. He was tall and shy and self-effacing, and his pale face turned bright pink when meeting new acquaintances. He hoped to specialise in anaesthetics, a branch of medicine more suited to his personality, as all contact with patients would be limited to pre-operative routine questions. His family were bound to be disappointed with his choice. They had sacrificed much to send him to medical school, and they expected him to be a general practitioner in their home town, where he would enjoy the respect of all. Ishmael had wanted to be an engineer. However, his family had insisted on medicine because doctors held a privileged position in the Indian community. It raised a family's social status and it ensured that his younger sisters would obtain better marriage proposals.

Bis's success had proved this to be true. Ishmael's family pinned all their hopes on his success. Dutifully, he complied with parental wishes and became a doctor. At least the choice of a speciality was his.

One day at the Bridge table he announced, "I will never be the main attraction, I'm satisfied as a supporting actor in the operating theatre. I don't have the temperament, or the bedside manner, nor the ability to deal intimately with patients. I intend to get married as soon as my internship ends, and I will continue to work in a hospital." This was the longest monologue Ishmael had delivered. He was a man of few words and not given to idle chatter. It was known that he had a special pen pal with whom he corresponded. He loved working crossword puzzles and often had one tucked into the pocket of his lab coat. He was a keen Bridge player, and once at the Bridge table he was quizzed about his future.

"Who is the lucky girl?" an intern asked.

Ishmael stared past the nosey intern, and then an impatient player said, "It's your turn, Ishmael. If you're not interested, let someone else play."

Ishmael ignored the comment. Rumour swirled that the girl was Bis's younger sister, Ruby, who on occasion had visited her brother at his quarters. Neither Ishmael nor Bis would discuss, confirm, nor deny the rumour. In the Muslim community, unless a formal announcement of an engagement by the respective parents was made, any discussion of a young girl's name linked to that of a man jeopardised her reputation, especially if they did not end up married to each other. The community would deem the girl to be tarnished.

I had met Ishmael through my contact with illiterate patients. It was my duty to obtain signatures from patients for him before anaesthesia and we had become friends. Bis had informed me about the strict Muslim code on dating, and that Ruby and Ishmael were an item. Boys regularly dated surreptitiously, but this was completely ignored.

I was sympathetic and did not object to the couple meeting in my office. Considering our work, it was not unusual for Ishmael to be there. Often-times while he waited to meet Ruby, we would indulge in simple philosophical conversation, and I had come to know and respect this earnest young man.

"It is unfortunate that we live in a society that not only separates, but also forbids those we choose to love," Ishmael said, and I nodded in agreement.

Part One

Ishmael had voiced what I knew to be true. I thought that at least his path to happiness with the girl of his choice was assured, while the uncertainty of my own aspirations posed many problems, both social and legal. Ironically, I was to be proven wrong on that score.

Ishmael told me that on his days off, unlike all the other residents, who had cars, he boarded the hospital bus for Fordsburg, a suburb of Johannesburg. In 1948-1950, the Group Areas Act designated Fordsburg an Indian area, as there was an established mosque. Indians were herded out of the town and forced to live there in crowded suburbs or they would have to move out to Lenasia, an Indian enclave (more of a ghetto) fifteen miles beyond the city. There they were compelled to compete with each other in business, and it was becoming more difficult to eke out a decent living. Ishmael's uncle and aunt had recently moved into the area, where they operated a tiny corner grocery store. On his off duty from the hospital, he took charge of the bookkeeping and acted as their general factotum. His generous offer spared them paying an assistant.

Mosques were not banned under the "Suppression of the Communism Act," and the local mosque became a logical gathering place, where Ishmael attended Friday prayers. However, it was not too long before political meetings were convened and attracted the attention of the Special Branch, who were well endowed with unlimited funds. BOSS had undercover informers, for they were determined to stamp out rebels, whom they believed were communists whose intention was to overthrow the government.

It was common knowledge that the spy network and police surveillance was pervasive and reached into the private lives of unsuspecting victims. The police extorted bribes and had the power to arrest people on the slightest pretext. But the youth persisted with their political meetings, and many of them landed in Marshall Square, the dreaded interrogation centre on the edge of downtown. Raids during the wee hours became regular. No one was exempt, and few detainees emerged unscathed. Reports appeared in underground newspapers, and the *Guardian* newspaper printed the story of three prisoners who had managed to escape from Marshall Square and had made their way safely to London. There they reported the barbaric methods employed by their interrogators. Torture was used to extract information. Prisoners were subjected to absolute darkness or to blinding lights, and the alternate switching confused and disoriented them.

"Take off your clothes and stand up straight," was the first order barked by the detectives. The naked prisoners' hands were shackled behind their backs, and then they were frog-marched and thrown into cubicles barely larger than coffins. The most sadistic method was to place electrodes on their naked genitals. It was excruciating, and it left no visible marks.

The escapees recounted that prisoners' screams and howls were deafening. This had the desired effect of intimidating and frightening other victims even before they were summoned. It was rumoured that for a price certain non-white detectives in the employ of BOSS, were responsible for some of the leaks that reached the news. Rumours abounded, and sometimes the horrors perpetrated on victims were deliberately let out into the public sphere to encourage others to "squeal" as a protection for themselves, and to ward off atrocities in the event they or relatives were picked up as offenders.

One Friday, Ishmael was at prayers and he was swept up in a raid on the mosque. No questions were asked and he was thrown into the "Black Maria," the police van, along with all the other captives. He was known to be apolitical and he had never been heard to express a single political opinion. Unfortunately, he was in the wrong place and was scooped up with the assumed plotters.

When Ishmael did not report for duty, his colleagues were concerned. It was uncharacteristic of him to absent himself without notice. Three days later, Rex burst into the common room to bid his colleagues a final farewell before leaving for London. "Incidentally," he said, "while waiting for my passport I learnt from a cleaning boy that a doctor was among those detained at Marshall Square. I'm sorry to learn that it was Ishmael."

At the Bridge table, the doctors discussed their concern. "What can we do?" said Thakor. "Is there any solution?" The players reached a consensus to seek legal advice. As seniors, the onus fell on Bis and Abram. However, they would first have to report Ishmael's plight to the chief-of-staff and obtain his permission.

"Sir, with your permission, we need to engage a lawyer to act on Ishmael's behalf," Bis said.

"Well, it's your money. Damn fools to get involved with riff-raff," was the chief's response as he glared at Bis.

"Sir, we can't abandon him. Think of the trouble it will cause. Detectives will be swarming all over the hospital looking for accomplices," said Abram.

"Everyone will be under suspicion," Bis added.

"I suppose you're right, Abram."

Bis winced. He was aware the chief had recently received a new set of motor car tires from Abram's family, who owned a motor-car dealership.

Abram, as usual, was eager to oblige. Bluntly, he told his colleagues, "In these times, it doesn't hurt to grease the greedy palm."

The doctors engaged a lawyer, Allan Sherman, who went to Marshall Square and told the authorities that he was there on behalf of Ishmael Hassen's family to enquire as to the nature of the charge.

The detective in charge told him that Ishmael was a conspirator, and a trouble maker.

"What proof do you have?" the lawyer asked.

"We don't need any. He refused to co-operate. We have evidence that he was a leader of a seditious group opposed to the Group Areas Act. People listen to doctors."

"Well, I'd like to see him," Sherman said.

"No, you can't. He jumped out of an eight-storey window this morning," said the detective. "He's dead."

"What do you mean he's dead?" Allan Sherman trembled from shock. He was outraged by the callous attitude of the detective. "I demand to see your chief! This cannot go on without protest."

"I'm in charge, and I've told you what happened. You can request an enquiry. There will be an official one."

This behaviour was indicative of the cruel treatment the police practised and the fear that they instilled in the general population.

"Has his family been notified? May I see the body?"

The detective in charge at first refused to talk to the lawyer. Later, he said the body had been removed and taken to the coroner's for examination. "All in good time. The parents will be informed as soon as the autopsy is completed. We'll work this one by the book," he added.

"But he's Muslim and the body must be buried today before sunset. That is their custom," said Sherman.

"He's a conspirator and he's lost his rights. Tell me, if he wasn't guilty, why'd he jump?"

The lawyer knew the futility of arguing with the Special Branch. It was not the first time they had refused to co-operate, and he could stake his life that it would not be the last. The pretence that justice was done was a travesty. Under these circumstances, there would be no further inquiry into Ishmael's presumed suicide.

On behalf of the family, Sherman petitioned to collect the deceased. Two days later, permission was granted to retrieve the body for burial. Accompanied by a local Imam, Ishmael's distraught father, his uncles, and the two doctors claimed the body. A strict Muslim ritual regarding ablution for the dead was a religious obligation and was performed by the Imam and Ishmael's male relatives. The doctors noted that the injuries did not support the coroner's findings. The body was badly decomposed, and the soles of the feet showed signs of burns.

As Ishmael was a political prisoner, there would be no inquest nor redress for his death. He was merely another statistic in a long line of disappearances of youth who died while in police custody at Marshall Square. His distressed family would have to be content with the meagre details the lawyer was able to glean from the authorities.

Ishmael and his family were orthodox Muslims. They would pray for him and accept his fate. At the wake, his father said, "Ishmael was a good boy and a dutiful son. It is Allah's will. We will ask for forgiveness for all our sins, and for those of his jailors." However, all the dreams, aspirations, and sacrifices his family had made, were just that. They were buried with their son, another casualty of the morally corrupt regime.

The tragic news spread, and a sombre atmosphere prevailed in the normally noisy doctors' common room. At the Bridge table, Ishmael was honoured by a minute of silence.

The doctors were despondent and after a few attempts to play Bridge, the game was suspended. Ishmael's untimely death and the manner in which he had died cast a pall over their activities. All the air had been choked out of the common room. Discussion centred on the circumstances of Ishmael's cruel death and how a noble young colleague had met an untimely end.

Bis informed Ruby of the tragedy. Both were distraught, and Ruby spent most of the day crying in my office. I was unable to pacify her.

"Joan, I'm lost and I don't know what to do."

Part One

"You are welcome to stay here. I'll ask Bis what you should do."

There was no easy solution; their love affair had been secret. And I did the only thing I could under these difficult circumstances. I called Bis, ignoring all the precautions I usually took when needing to speak to him at the hospital. "Please, come to my office, Ruby needs you."

Bis collected Ishmael's personal belongings and his last letter to Ruby, and also a sheaf of letters tied with a green ribbon to which a small gold locket was attached. Bis, Ruby, and I met at the YMCA entrance and drove off.

"Ruby, we can drive around for a while, or I can drive you home, or to Mamagee," he said gently to his sister.

"Hakie, let's drive around for a bit, then drop me off at Mamagee's, and thank you and Joan for everything."

There were no words of consolation, and I was unable to reply for I was sick at heart.

Ishmael's death did not permit Ruby to grieve openly, nor to declare her love. Their love would remain a secret and be buried with him. In time, Ruby would accept the burden their culture imposed on her. She was young and resilient. She sobbed on her brother's shoulder, and he lovingly folded her in his arms. At the entrance to Mamagee's flat, they clung to each other for a few minutes before she left her brother's embrace.

"No, don't come inside. I'll be okay," she said. Then she dried her eyes before going inside. Bis got back into the car. Tears spilled down my cheeks and Bis squeezed my hand, grateful that at least we had each other.

The time had come to leave Bara, and Bis drove off to Northcliffe.

CHAPTER 17
Trauma in the Labour Ward

THE CHIEF OF OBSTETRICS AND GYNAECOLOGY HAD ENCOURAGED both Dr. Bismillah and Dr. Abram to apply to the registrar's programme, and he assured them a place under his tutelage. Only doctors who had completed their residency or who had general-practice experience were eligible to enrol in the programme that was reserved for Europeans. Bis had completed his residency in Durban at McCord's Hospital. The training period was a minimum of two years, or longer, depending on the speciality.

Their acceptance into the Obstetrics and Gynaecology Unit was a victory in the stand against Apartheid, as non-white doctors were prohibited from giving orders to the European sisters in charge of wards. The law was strictly enforced in all government institutions, but in this instance, it was relaxed to accommodate the two Indian registrars, demonstrating the contradiction and the absurdity of the divisive law.

The non-European doctors' accommodation was spartan, but a common room that served as a dining room became the centre for their social activity. The Indian doctors were avid Bridge players and during off-duty hours together with a few European doctors, we frequently joined in the game. We were party to much that occurred in their common room.

Non-European doctors comprised a small fraction of all doctors employed at Baragwanath Hospital, and like everyone in South Africa at the time, they were consigned to a segregated residence. Housemen were first-year interns and were on call six days a week. The long hours were worth the experience working in the busy teaching hospital.

Part One

The intercom system and telephones took up an entire wall above the dining tables with loudspeakers that summoned doctors to report for duty. The doctors held a more cynical view and speculated that a bugging device was concealed in the contraption in order to spy and report on their conversations.

Few serious subjects were openly debated and definitely not politics. It was an inauspicious time. People kept their opinions secret and suspicion was rampant. Who was friend or foe? The political climate sowed the seeds of distrust, and no one ever knew on whom to rely. Stories of arrests abounded. Friends and relatives disappeared and often they were not heard of again. Colleagues were interrogated and censorship of personal mail was routine. The country under the Apartheid government was likened to the Nazi regime—a police state. Liberals and their sympathisers were in constant fear of reprisals for their democratic ideals. Mixed gatherings were carefully scrutinised. The oppressors believed that the doctors were among the opposition that subscribed to the anti-Apartheid cause.

There was no end to police powers and the atrocities they inflicted on a fearful public. At Baragwanath Hospital, the overcrowded triage and emergency rooms bore witness to their handiwork. Caution became the watchword of the day. In the common room, case studies, sports, and Bridge were the only safe topics for debate. No one dared to speculate who reported to the Special Branch, although there was a strong suspicion that amongst them there were informers. On the surface, life carried on and people tried to forget the oppressive atmosphere by enjoying innocent pastimes such as Bridge and dance parties.

Four o'clock tea was the ritual hour when work came to an abrupt halt. As eight-hour shifts ended, a cup of tea and a game of Bridge provided restorative energy and relieved stress, if only temporarily. Tea time added to a convivial atmosphere in the non-European doctors' common room. They straggled in, each eager to find a seat at the Bridge table as they picked up sandwiches, cake, and tea, the elixir that calmed and soothed a weary body. The dash for a vacant seat often ended in playful scuffles.

Cards were shuffled and dealt out to the first four players. Dr. Bis and three interns—Mohamed, Thakor, and Rex—sat down and without further delay began to play. Bis was a proud, charismatic, and good all-round sportsman. He had a dry wit and was admired by his peers. Good looking Mohamed was brilliant but something of a dreamer. Thakor was a fun-loving prankster who had difficulty arranging his cards, as an extra digit on his right thumb stuck out like a twig and slowed him down. It was cause for amusement among his peers. Rex's, acceptance to medical school was an achievement of merit and a privilege as there was a strict quota for native applicants. All four were expert Bridge players. Bridge was more than a game; it was a means to demonstrate to your peers just how smart you were. Theirs was a profession that spawned egotists.

There was much fun in kibitzing by the other doctors, who commented on play while waiting for someone to vacate his seat. Much laughter and banter were an antidote to the gloomy political atmosphere that hung over the country. Bridge was the glue that cemented their friendships, and even drew some in on their days off. Although Dr. Abram was a tournament league player, he preferred to kibitz. It was an opportunity for him to display his superior skill of the game and almost everything else. He took pleasure in goading weaker players who erred. His ribald remarks did not endear him to his peers. He was rich, sarcastic, haughty, and on friendly terms with his obstetrical chief, who often demanded favours in kind from him. He and I got along and we understood each other. His mother was of Malay and Dutch descent and his upbringing was pervasively European, thus we had much in common.

One day the game had barely begun, and the intercom, which could be heard all over the vast grounds of Baragwanath hospital, crackled, "Calling Dr. Bismillah to the OB Unit." The baritone voice repeated the message again and continued until Bis answered his page. "I'm on my way." He shrugged his shoulders and handed his cards to Ibrahim, a self-confident young intern, who was grateful for the chance to take his place at the table.

Bis put on his lab coat and headed for the ward, which was about a mile away. His step was light as he hurried along, and the loudspeaker again repeated: "Calling Dr. Bismillah..." It did not stop.

Bis hurried to the labour ward. The familiar, pungent odour of disinfectant and ether, which camouflaged stale urine, assaulted his sense of smell. Bis and I were familiar with the procedures in the labour ward, and often we discussed significant cases, especially when he wanted me to transcribe notes for him.

Bis was met by the ward sister. All the beds were occupied with patients in various stages of labour. Some groaned as they moved their heavy bodies, others were silently lying in, waiting. The sister in charge handed him a mask and chart and led him to the far end of the ward, where a fifteen-year-old girl at term was in distress.

"Doctor, this is the young mother," Sister said. She drew the privacy curtain around the bed and beckoned a nurse to assist.

"Demella, Ohsie," Bis greeted the young mother, using the African term in an attempt to set her at ease.

She was too distressed to respond. She was sobbing and groaning in pain.

On examination, Bis noted the complication; it was a breech presentation. "Sister, she will not be able to deliver her baby normally. Please prepare her for a C-section," he said. "I'll notify the chief. Have her mother sign a consent form with the Almoner, as she's under age."

Bis reported his findings to his superior, the chief of obstetrics. "Sir, it is urgent and I suggest an immediate Caesarean section."

"I agree. Medicate her but await my arrival. I want the medical students to observe this case," the chief said.

Bis administered the medication and in a gentle voice, he tried to reassure his patient. He ordered extra blood and proceeded to await the arrival of the chief and the medical students. He monitored her pulse and listened to the foetal heart. It was stable. Bis swabbed her fevered brow and held her hand as he talked softly in an attempt to gain her confidence and settle her anxiety. The morphine had calmed her, and she appeared slightly less restless, but her contractions were getting stronger and irregular. Anxiously, Bis awaited the students' arrival but kept an eye on the clock. He did not leave her side and watched the nurses prepare her for the operation. He held her hand and reassured her as he waited and waited.

It was in these moments of waiting that he recalled his medical-student days. As an Indian student, he had been ordered out of an examination room and not allowed to observe an autopsy because the cadaver was the body of a white woman.

Later, Bis told me, "Joan, I still feel the anger and distress I experienced and that awkward feeling when one is shamed in front of one's peers for something one is not responsible for."

In the labour room, Bis had kept his fingers on the young woman's pulse. Suddenly, it became irregular as her rapid heartbeat increased, and with great force, the patient wrenched her hand from his grasp and started kicking and rolling about. Convulsing, she started to shake and shiver. Spasms wracked her body. With difficulty, two nurses attempted to hold her down and another nurse inserted a tongue depressor. Now more anxious, Bis waited for the chief and the medical students, while nurses sponged her clammy body. Her eyes bulged. Bis added a sedative to the intravenous drip. Her pulse became faint and irregular and her contractions lasted longer and were becoming stronger. The foetal heartbeat was erratic. Nurses struggled to control the young girl as she kicked and contorted her body. She wailed and let out a shrill cry. Bis applied the oxygen mask and gave her another injection. She ripped the mask off, gasping for air. Quickly, a nurse tried to reapply the oxygen mask but could not keep it in place. The patient's body heaved, and her throat rattled. She gurgled and sputum flowed. Bis swabbed it away. Suddenly, she shrieked as a violent spasm shook her, and her body slackened as she went limp. Her uterus had ruptured. A low mew-like rattle, then a final slow gasp escaped. With a shudder, she exhaled her last breath. All attempts at resuscitation were in vain. Bis's expression was one of absolute disbelief and horror. His bowed head and bent shoulders testified to his failure. The ward sister touched his sleeve, and he looked up and checked the time on the ward clock against the time on his watch. He ordered Sister to chart the exact time of death.

Bis discarded his rubber gloves and threw them rather roughly, missing the kidney dish as they fell to the floor. It had been over an hour and a half from the time he had phoned the chief. Bis's taut mouth registered his frustration and anger as he stalked out of the ward.

Sister stopped him as he was leaving. "Doctor, the patient's mother is in the corridor, and she speaks English," Sister said.

Bis sighed and took a deep breath. The difficult part of his work was dealing with the distraught next of kin. "I hope that she was given some tea and taken care of while she waited," he said. He straightened his shoulders and went in search of the young woman's mother.

The mother was seated in the corridor holding her hands to her face. She stood up as he approached her. Bis beckoned her to remain seated, *"Sabona Mama,"* but she ignored his greeting and she started ululating as if she were possessed. Bis was unable to calm her. The commotion attracted curious patients and staff. Orderlies came to the rescue and tried to calm the distraught woman. She could not be pacified and became hysterical, clinging to Bis. The hospital wardens appeared and she was taken away to the triage room for treatment.

A subdued Bis returned to the noisy doctors' common room. The Bridge game was still in progress. He had no inclination to play and watched in silence, trying to forget the turmoil of the past two hours. He was deeply affected by the young mother's death and he resented his chief's casual attitude to the gravity of the situation. He had a report to write, and protocol demanded that the patient's advocate be informed. Bis needed time to collect his thoughts and write the death certificate. He had to be calm and rational before he did anything in haste. The report would have to be accurate and succinct. It would form part of a case study in his thesis on ruptured uteri.

Bis poured a cup of tea but allowed it to grow cold. He needed time to reflect and to cool his anger. He watched the players in a distracted manner. He could not forget the distressing situation. He believed that the lengthy delay was a direct cause of the complication. The tragedy should have been prevented.

"Bis, would you like to play?" Cassim, an intern, asked.

"Thanks, no. I've a report to write and a death certificate to fill out."

"What? Surely not in the labour ward? What happened?" Abram enquired.

"You'll know soon enough. There's bound to be an enquiry, and as a registrar you'll be ordered to attend."

"Little wonder you're so glum." Abram frowned, knowing that whatever the cause of death in the labour ward, it would impact him too. There would be serious consequences for those wishing to follow in their footsteps. It was well to remember that their senior positions were a privilege granted on sufferance by an avaricious chief of staff.

The game continued. "It's your turn, Thakor," his partner said.

"Arranging my cards," Thakor said.

"Why don't you have the damn thing amputated?" Abram snapped, referring to the extra digit that caused the delay. "It should have been done at birth."

"I expect my parents were superstitious," Thakor replied. He was embarrassed by the unwanted attention. "I am seeing a surgeon…"

"Oh, leave him alone, Dr. Abram. You're only kibitzing anyway. Why don't you go and see if Bis needs your help?" an indignant Ibrahim said. He knew that Abram resented that Bis was highly regarded by his peers. Now Bis was responsible for some infraction, and Abram too would come under scrutiny.

Bis returned to the ward to pick up the patient's chart. There were a couple of notes in his mailbox. He recognised the handwriting on both but decided to open them later.

In his report, Bis stated that the young mother was admitted in advanced labour. He underlined the time of death. However, it was his belief that the lengthy delay was a direct cause of the "Bandles Ring," a complication caused by the continuous contractions that ruptured the uterus, resulting in the death of both mother and baby. Bis signed the report and made a second copy. He paused, hesitated, and then he posted one in the chief's mailbox and went to the almoner's office.

There was bound to be an enquiry. As almoner and patients' advocate, I too would be in attendance. In my office, Bis was visibly upset as he related verbatim the events of the past two hours. There was little I could do but listen to him, feeling his outrage at the death of the young mother and her baby.

The following day, Bis was summoned to the chief's office. "Dr. Bismillah, I want you to reconsider and rewrite your report on the deceased young woman," his chief said.

"Why is that, sir?"

"You implied that her death from a ruptured uterus may have been averted if you had intervened earlier."

"That's correct, sir. There was a ninety-minute delay waiting for the medical students. They arrived after the patient's uterus had ruptured."

"It's not a request, Doctor. It's an order. I wish you to state that death was due to a complication of pregnancy."

Bis pondered before he answered, "I'm sorry, sir. I agree the Bandles Ring was a complication of pregnancy. Had I operated immediately, however, the complication could have been avoided. The ninety-minute delay made all the difference."

"Doctor, it's not for you to question my orders."

"With all due respect, sir, you left me in charge, and I obeyed them."

"Do you question my authority?" the chief asked, and he stood up from behind his desk and pushed the report away. He removed his glasses and polished them for the second time.

"I respect it, sir, but I would be compromising my integrity if I did not raise the issue with you. I do not understand how teaching trumps a patient's welfare."

"Well, have it your way." The chief walked out.

Bis knew that this conflict would later pose problems for him, but it was important for him to use this case as an example of the effects of delayed intervention in such cases in his dissertation on ruptured uteri. Before writing the report, Bis had researched the complication. There was supporting evidence that a delay in operating usually ended in death. What Bis had hoped for was to have a discussion on the topic. However, what he knew to be true was that non-European patients did not always receive quite the same consideration as their white counterparts, and that non-European subordinates were definitely not supposed to confront or antagonize their European chiefs.

CHAPTER 18
The Hospital Board Inquiry

THE INQUIRY INTO THE DEATH OF THE YOUNG MOTHER WAS CONvened by the chairman of the hospital board. He was a formidable and a pious Afrikaner, well known for his political bias. "This is not an inquest," he declared in his opening remarks. "It is merely a routine inquiry to ascertain the facts pertaining to the death of a young mother and her unborn baby. There is no blame attached to anyone. Legal presence here is simply a formality to observe that hospital protocol is carried out."

Present were the chiefs of both obstetrical units; the registrars, Dr. Bismillah and Dr. Abram; the matron of obstetrics; a recording legal secretary, Michael Goldstein, acting for his brother Josh Goldstein, who was legal counsel for the hospital; and me, the almoner who represented patients' interests.

The chairman stated, "This inquiry is unwarranted. I don't see the reason why the matter wasn't settled amongst you." He took a sip of water, allowing his admonishment to hang in the air. "The case presented is that of a fifteen-year-old girl who died in childbirth, and we are here to ensure that the hospital is free from blame. I can't waste time on sentiment. The girl, a teenager, was unwed, and she had a positive Wasserman [a routine test for sexually transmitted disease]. God alone knows what her life would have been like, or even if the child she was carrying would have been normal. Perhaps it's kinder where they are now. Hundreds of these native women die each year in childbirth. Given the way they live, she was no exception."

Bis's chief concurred. "I agree that the girl would have died anyway. We can't be sure of anything. Dr. Bismillah, you acted in accordance within the precepts of this teaching hospital. You obeyed my orders and did your duty."

Although the chief had exonerated him, Bis felt insulted, and a response was essential. He was not convinced that teaching took precedence over a patient's needs.

"With all due respect, sir, have we forgotten the Hippocratic Oath: to do no harm?"

The chairman snorted and walked out, putting an end to the inquiry. He was followed by the chief, who opined as he left, "Given the circumstances, the girl's death was inevitable!"

Bis stormed out after them. He was angry and again felt the injustice on behalf of the deceased patient, but more important was the lack of empathy from his chief and no excuse for the tardy response to the emergency situation. Rather, Bis had expected a discussion regarding the complication, but he realised it was a cover-up by the chief to safeguard his honour. Bis felt humiliated and that continued to bother him.

As everyone left, the recording secretary and I were last. From behind, I heard, "Joan Salsoni climbed on a pony to buy her macaroni."

I looked back and for a moment, I stared at the young man. I felt a flicker of recognition and I smiled. "Michael Goldstein," I said, and he touched my forehead with his index finger. Suddenly, the intervening years were lost and memories came flooding back. "Oh Michael! It's been such a long time. It's so good to see you again. What are you doing here?" I asked.

"My brother is legal counsel for Bara, and he sent me here to observe."

Before I had time to reply, we were ushered out by an orderly. "Look, we can't talk here," I said. "There's a party at the Shapiros' on Sunday night. You do know their place at Northcliffe, don't you? Here's my card. Please, please do come."

"I'll certainly try. How well do you know the young doctor? He impressed me."

I blushed. "Is it that obvious? You do remember that you are responsible for the scar on my forehead?" I said by way of changing the topic.

"Yes, you always wanted to play with the boys and that scar, right in the middle of your forehead, is a reminder."

"My recollection is a little different. I'll see you on Sunday."

Bis took the notes from his pocket; one was from Bunny to meet him and the other was from me, inviting him to a party at the Shapiros'. Bis was extremely upset over Ishmael's demise and the enquiry and in no mood for a party, but he knew us being together would take his mind off the tragedy. With some misgivings, he decided to attend the soiree.

Bunny Tabb had been admitted to Wits on a scholarship. His rotund physique and his large, oval blue eyes matched his personality. He had a comic sense of humour that endeared him to people on their first meeting. As well, he was a gifted raconteur and was in demand to put on skits at concerts that raised funds for various charitable organisations.

Bis met Bunny at the appointed place and time, and Bunny handed him a book by their mutual friend and classmate, Phillip Tobias.

"Thanks for the book," Bis said.

"Bis, many of our classmates have left or are in the process of leaving to do post-graduate work in London. And you would do well to join us."

"I knew the book was an excuse for our meeting."

"Yes, I have it on good authority that you're under surveillance. There is evidence that you consort with 'banned persons.' There are spies everywhere."

"If you're referring to Ahmed Kathrada, who was convicted with Mandela for conspiracy and is now a prisoner with him on Robben Island, Ahmed was my roommate for six years while I was at varsity."

"Look, that's all I know. Please heed the warning. BOSS has a file of your activities."

"I've had a difference of opinion with my chief and I'm toying with leaving Bara anyway. My term is almost over, and working conditions are not ideal now."

"All the more reason to leave the country."

"You know about Joan and that problem, don't you?"

"Yes, and that alone should be reason enough to leave. There's a note in the back of the book. I'll pop in briefly to the Shapiros' party, but I won't stay." Bunny left the book on the table.

Bis was aware that it was possible that he was under surveillance—an unmarked car had followed him on several occasions. One night, he saw it parked near his flat and again at close range as he left the hospital. He knew he had to act normally and he stayed in the library for another hour before he too left and headed back to hospital. For once, the noisy common room was deserted. Bis was perturbed more than he would care to admit.

Bis picked up the daily newspaper and went to his room. There was a public phone in the hallway. On impulse, he called me. I answered immediately, saying "Hello."

Before I could say anything else, he said, "I'm back at the hospital. I'll see you at the Shapiros' on Sunday," and hung up. Bis used the public phone as a precaution. It was a prearranged signal in case a problem existed. Our conversations had to be brief and limited to urgent messages.

Bis went back to the ward, where Sister asked, "Is there something you needed, Doctor? It's very quiet. Now having said that, we'll probably get busy."

"No, thank you, Sister. I left a chart in the office." Bis sat at the desk and called me again from the ward phone. "We need to talk."

"Hello, is anything wrong?" I asked.

"I haven't seen you in a while and we need to plan for our future. I'll pick you up in an hour."

And what of me? I too would be under surveillance! We would have to avoid attending political meetings for the time being. I would have to stop helping out at the P.F. office, and we should not appear together in public, only meeting casually at functions. Even that was unlikely to protect us from the spy network. Police surveillance was pervasive, with tentacles that spread into every aspect of life. It was common knowledge that the police extorted and used bribes, and they had their power to arrest people on the slightest pretext. On the other hand, desperate people were coerced into becoming paid informers.

CHAPTER 19
Remembrance of Things Past

UNTIL THE NATIONALISTS CAME TO POWER, THE COMMUNIST PARTY was legal in South Africa. It dated back to 1921 when the party was formed, and it was banned by the Nationalist Party in 1950. As young students, we were attracted to them for the rich social life they offered, and the fun-filled mixed social gatherings on weekends. According to Apartheid doctrine, the communists contravened the basics of the law. They were forced to go underground, but continued their activities. It was an insane time. Everyone was suspect, and illegal movements sprung up like weeds.

Dr. David Shapiro, like many liberal-minded people, had been a supporter. He lived in a large home at Northcliffe with his wife May. David was Bis's mentor and he and his wife were friends sympathetic to our plight and offered Bis and me the hospitality of their home.

Dr. Shapiro conducted an emergency medical practice from his home, and it became the pretext to hold meetings there. The outpatient clinic was a foil; it was a relatively safe place, as there was a constant flow of people to the clinic. This hopefully obfuscated the police, who were suspicious of any gathering.

May Shapiro was a closet political activist. She kept a low profile in order to maintain their home as a relatively safe venue for meetings. A large hall adjacent to their property was for hire by sporting clubs on weekends for "Snowball" parties and dances, which raised funds for the clubs and various charities. In 1955, May joined the "Black Sash Movement," an organisation of white women who protested the erosion of human rights that the Nationalists were intent on destroying. Thus far, she had evaded the attention of the authorities, possibly because the organisation consisted exclusively of white women, who were regarded as social workers. They were pacifists who wore black sashes and paraded in front of government offices whenever laws were being rescinded or tampered with.

Life was becoming increasingly difficult now that Bis was convinced that he was being followed. A policeman stopped and asked him to produce his driver's licence, merely to check that it was up to date. Normally Bis would have fussed at such an intrusion, but now he was careful to keep calm and to observe the speed limit. Often, he was asked for directions to places he was unfamiliar with. People were wary of casual acquaintances who suddenly appeared and started asking questions or condemning the system. It was difficult to know who to trust.

The party was in full swing when Bis and I arrived, and we were warmly greeted by David and May. We mingled about talking to acquaintances, and then I spotted Michael Goldstein at the door and I rushed over to welcome him. "Michael, I'm so pleased you came. Tell me all about yourself. How come you were at the inquiry the other day?" I asked.

"Steady on, and I'll try to fill you in. I'm articling with my brother at present. He is on the legal counsel for Bara. He sent me to witness the enquiry and observe how the system operated. It certainly was very interesting."

"Yes, so much window dressing. It was all there, nice and tidy. Protocol had been maintained."

"I gathered as much. The chairman, a true Afrikaner?"

"Yes, but tell me about yourself."

"I read law at Cape Town U. I loved the ocean. Real surfing, unlike the mine dumps. Remember?" he said, touching the scar on my forehead.

"How could I forget? I replied to my brother's childhood bosom pal, and we continued to reminisce about our childhood which now seemed so long ago.

The Goldsteins had three sons, all older than me. They were our neighbours prior to my mother's death. They were Barney's friends. Michael and my brother were sworn blood brothers and I longed to play with them because they had all the fun. In their eyes, I was only a girl, and I recalled their teasing, which reduced me to tears. My brother made no attempt to defend me. Still, I persisted in following them at a distance, hoping they would allow me to tag after them or not notice me. One day I trailed them all the way to the mine dumps where the excavated sand formed *kopjes* or hills as tall as twelve-storey buildings. The quicksand contained traces of lethal cyanide that was used to purify the gold extracted from the ore, and the run-off water formed large pools called "pans," which were adjacent to the dumps and fenced in. These pools were extremely dangerous and poisonous. Trespassing was forbidden and signs warned: "POISON," "DANGER KEEP OUT" and "BEWARE SINKING SAND." But these were magnets that attracted the boys to explore and to challenge each other in attempting daredevil exploits, like sliding down the sandy slopes on improvised cardboard mats.

The boys dared and goaded each other to get from one side of the pans to the other side. The only way to traverse the huge pipes that emptied the contaminated water into the pans was to carefully balance like a tightrope walker, placing one foot in front of the other until reaching the opposite side—a feat I once tried. Panicking, I looked down and I would have fallen off, but for the quick action of a rope thrown by Barney, who shouted, "Hang on!" as I neared the end. That was a close shave. "I told you not to do it," he scolded. "I'll never bring you again."

Parents cautioned their children and could tell when we disobeyed because the lethal cyanide sand left a tell-tale residue of gold dust on the skin, which had to be scrubbed off with soap and warm water. A Dutch herbal salve, *Zambuck*, was applied to stop the itching and swelling.

"Michael, do you remember another memorable day? I had followed you and Barney right onto the dumps. I watched with envy as you frolicked on the sand, shooting clouds of golden dust that sparkled in the air. Suddenly, there were screams as the ground shook and I started to roll down the slope. Fortunately, you and your brother Josh spotted me and quickly pulled me to safety on the stone ramp that linked two kopjes."

Earth tremors were common in Johannesburg and normally could be ignored. However, on the mine dumps, the danger lay in the shifting sands. Later that day, we learned from a policeman that a young *piccanin* had been buried alive. The policeman had come to take statements from the boys and to implore their parents to warn their children of the danger the mine dumps

Part One

posed. He admonished the boys and threatened to lock them up if they disobeyed his orders.

"Thank God, it wasn't one of ours!" the policeman said, and he reprimanded the boys again in front of our parents. "And you, missy," he said, pointing a finger at me, "Don't follow the boys!"

The incident caused me to have recurring nightmares. It was about this time that I discovered that all lives were not equal. I related the incident to Alida, who was three years my senior and the daughter of our neighbours, the dominie and his wife. I admired Alida, whom I thought of as very smart.

"You were so lucky it was only a black kid," Alida said. And she recited a ditty: "God, He made the niggers. He made them in the night. He made them in a hurry and forgot to paint them white." Then she continued in a sing-song voice, "Ching Chong Chinaman born in a bar. Christened in a teapot ha, ha, ha. Harry black berry, King of the Jews, sold his wife for a pair of shoes."

I thought the rhymes were amusing and easy to memorise. Basking in my achievement, I could not wait to get back and recite them to my father. My grandmother was present and she scowled at me, and said, "I should wash your mouth with soap and water, young lady."

My father too scolded me and explained why reciting those ditties were wrong. "Joan," he said, "Don't ever sing those rhymes again. It's disrespectful. How do you like it when the boys make fun, or say nasty things about you?" My father reminded me, "How did you feel when your mummy died? Think of the poor boy's mother and family losing their child. I am disappointed, Joan."

I was mortified and said, "I'm sorry, Father. I didn't mean to be disrespectful, and I'll pray for the parents."

"That is the least you can do. Let this be a lesson," my father said.

As punishment, Gran ordered me to bed without tea to impress on me that it was not only insulting and rude, but that all people deserved to be treated with respect. Gran chastised, "Alida's too big for her boots, and too old for you to play with."

My father paid a visit to the dominie to complain about the ditties his daughter Alida had taught me. He objected to the racial slurs, as it endorsed and encouraged intolerance and prejudice.

"Argh man! It's child's play. Don't take it seriously. Are you a kaffir lover, or what?"

My father was perturbed by the dominie's attitude, and that finally put an end to my friendship with Alida.

Michael smiled at our recollections. I reflected how times that seemed so much simpler held warnings of things to come.

"Oh Michael, I had so few friends except for Alida. You remember her, the dominie's daughter, who was older than me? The kids in our neighbourhood were mostly boys and you always chased me away. All I wanted was to play and have fun with you and Barney."

Michael laughed. "And the one time I agreed to play with you, it got me into trouble."

"Yes, the scar on my forehead is a constant reminder of those days. Nanny had warned me repeatedly about playing with the boys, and you in particular. One afternoon at the park, I challenged you to see who could swing higher and touch the overhanging branches of an oak tree. The bet was on. If I won, you promised to take me to play on the mine dumps. If you won, I promised never to follow. I disobeyed Nanny's order and I won and beat you. I touched the highest branch, and then plunged headlong onto the concrete base of the swings. My trophy was a gash on my head and my clothes were spattered with blood. You ran off, afraid of a scolding from Nanny."

Nanny was beside herself. "Joan, why you listen to Michael? Him bad boy! What Madam gonna say when she see you, an' blood all over?"

To make matters worse, Parky, the groundskeeper, rushed over and scolded Nanny, "If you'd paid attention and weren't gossiping, this wouldn't happen. All you nannies think you're so important, but you neglect to take proper care of your charges."

I felt sorry for Nanny. Parky's comment was unfair, but the sight of blood had unnerved me, and I knew that Gran was sure to scold Nanny as well. I wanted to defend Nanny, but Gran's favourite words rang in my ears: "Children should be seen and not heard." Many years later, it still bothered me each time I thought about the incident. It had been entirely my fault, but who would have listened to a child then?

"It's still there, Joan," Michael said touching my scar, and we laughed.

Just then Bis walked over. "Hello," he said.

Part One

I turned to him. "Bis, this is Michael. We were kids together. He and my brother were bosom pals."

"Hello, I'm pleased to meet you," Michael said. "It was quite a performance at the enquiry the other day. You impressed me."

Bis shrugged. "The bureaucracy. What's to be done?"

"Nothing," said Michael. "We live in difficult times."

"I'm all too aware. It will only get worse," replied Bis, who excused himself.

I watched him leave and continued talking. I was aware that Bis was still thinking about Ishmael and poor Ruby. Talking to Michael about our childhood temporarily seemed to alleviate some of my distress.

"Michael," I said suddenly. "Barney was killed in a motor accident amid the VE day celebrations, incidentally on the day he was demobilised."

"Yes, how ironic. Josh informed me about the accident. I was sorry to have missed his funeral," Michael said.

"He was only twenty-one years old. We were devastated." Thinking of Barney's sudden death once again taught me a lesson, which was to make each day count, despite the obstacles in my path.

Just then, a maid brought a tray of canapés, an excuse for me to slip outside and see Bis, who was gazing up at the sky.

"A penny for your thoughts," I said.

Bis turned around. "You seemed to be enjoying yourself."

"Just catching up on old times," I said, tugging at his sleeve.

He put his arm protectively around my shoulders. "Are you cold?" he asked.

"Not when I'm with you. Let's sit down." We sat on the garden bench. I leant against his shoulder and through his tweed jacket I felt the comforting warmth of his body.

At night, the city as seen from Northcliffe stretched out like a shimmering jewel below us. E-Goli, the native name for the city that produced much of the world's gold, lay spread out before us, hiding its flaws. The streets were not paved with gold, but the city was rich and prosperous. However, the wealth was strictly controlled and in the hands of the few at the expense of thousands who toiled below ground and lived in extreme poverty.

Johannesburg, like much of the country, was in turmoil. The turbulence and violence spread far beyond the idyllic night scene that hid the despair. Come daylight the sun's rays would highlight what night had hidden and the problems confronting the young lovers would still be there.

We had stayed out too long. The party was ending and as a precaution and to allay any suspicion, Michael agreed to escort me home. I kissed Bis good night and left. Bis continued to linger alone on the hill top, pondering our future. He wiped the sweat off his brow and tried to slow his rapidly beating heart. He was the last to leave. Later, he confided that he'd felt a pang of jealousy. Would it always be that way? He wondered whether I'd be better off with someone else, perhaps Michael. And should he settle for a wife of his family's choosing, and finally put an end to their constant nagging about that suitable wife who they believed was precisely what he needed? His mood no better than when the night began, Bis thanked his host and left.

CHAPTER 20
Dangerous Moonlight at the Zoo Lake

WE PLANNED TO GO TO THE ZOO LAKE, I WAS EXCITED TO SEE BIS, but I detected the tension in his voice. Of course, his family were of little help with their constant nagging for him to marry that suitable bride and settle down to practise medicine in his home town. But the larger issue for us was the insidious and sinister threat of Apartheid that threatened our relationship. He was Indian, an educated, second-class citizen in love with me, a white girl, and that could scuttle any plans for the future.

Bis agreed to pick me up at Bara—there was a separate gate for European sisters, well away from the bustle of the front gates, and except for a night-watchman it was usually deserted. I was waiting when he arrived, and we drove to the Zoo Lake in silence, listening to a concert broadcast from London. Music invariably soothed our troubled minds. Romance in the moonlight, is how I preferred to think of our trysts.

The Zoo Lake was an oasis in the heart of the city. Couples parked their cars there on hot summer evenings. The relatively peaceful, romantic setting offered temporary relief and an escape from the problems of living under the repressive regime. It was a haven for lovers. Absent were the offensive signs that read "Europeans Only," that constant reminder that barred non-white people.

In that troubled society, the beauty of the lake, nestled in a temperate forest with its colourful *kaffirboom* (coral trees) and herbaceous shrubs, contrasted and compensated for the drabness of the overcrowded non-white suburbs where the coloured people were compelled to live.

The lake glistened in the luminous moonlight, inviting sweethearts to meet undisturbed under the watchful eyes of the starry night. Bis parked beside a giant willow tree. I recall the susurrus breeze that rustled through the branches and the sound of water lapping against the bank, the frogs' staccato ribbet... ribbet, and the chirping cicada's nocturnal song to the accompaniment of Debussy's hauntingly beautiful and melodic "Clair de Lune" over on the radio. But that night, we had to forego star-gazing and concentrate on our future.

I was agitated. "Bis, what are we to do?"

"Shush. Let's enjoy the music first." Gently, Bis put his finger to my lips, my head nestling against his shoulder.

"No!" I turned to look at him. "We can't carry on meeting in this clandestine manner. I'm becoming a nervous wreck. Sneaking around and lying all the time. I can't do this."

"What's the alternative?" Bis said. "I've yet to finish my contract at Bara. More to the point, have you considered the consequences of contravening the Mixed Marriage Act, which forbids marriage between whites and non-whites? And the Immorality Act goes a step further for it forbids 'co-habitation' as the law quaintly insists on referring to sex between whites and non-whites. Marriage will land me in jail—or worse—and God knows what your fate would be. It could be the excuse needed to charge us with who knows what else."

"No. Yes... Oh, I don't know what I mean. It's all so ridiculous and unfair."

"Leaving the country is our only option," Bis said.

"I suppose you're right. I only have to give the hospital a month's notice."

"In the meantime, we'll still have to be very careful."

"What will your family say? I'm neither Muslim nor Indian."

"Yes, that's true. And I'm not a Christian nor white," Bis said playfully. Pulling me closer and putting his arm around me, he whispered softly, "My annoyingly pedantic older sisters, both of whom married doctors I introduced them to, will be more critical and outraged and they'll berate me more than my parents. They'll fuss and fume and call me ungrateful. Mother will cry and say she won't be able to show her face in the community. I'm their golden boy."

"But you're not the eldest son."

"No, but I'm the doctor. 'You've dishonoured our family,' they'll say to make me feel guilty for not allowing them to choose a suitable wife. And gleefully,

Part One

Imam will remind my father, 'I told you so. I said he'd be lost if you sent him away to college. Better he'd stayed here and become an Islamic scholar.'"

I interrupted, "Is your family orthodox? You are not at all like the few Muslims I know."

"No. Not really. They observe tradition and their wish for me is to find that suitable wife. Preferably one of their choosing."

"Are you implying that I'm not suitable?" I laughed and snuggled closer, inhaling the scent of his aftershave lotion.

"You're certainly not suitable. And what would your Victorian Gran have said, and what will your father say now?"

"Gran wouldn't have been pleased only because of the second-class status of Indians, thanks to the British Raj. I told you my grandmother was Anglo Indian, something she never admitted to in these colour-conscious times."

"Ah, colour-consciousness! The legacy of the British Empire," Bis said.

"Yes, we Anglos celebrate our British heritage and are silent and even deny our Indian or any other ties."

"That's certainly true. And we Indians are obsessed with fair skin."

"Is that why you chose me?" I chortled.

"Of course! Why else?" Bis teased. "Seriously, will your father object?"

"My father is a sceptic. He'll recite his famous homily, 'The Jews and Indians stayed home and made money while we fought the war.'"

"There is a kernel of truth in what he says. My family's business increased from a tiny convenience store to a general dealership during and after the war."

"The reason my father enlisted and that all the other South Africans of Italian heritage did, was to avoid being interned. Something else my father says: 'Today you're fighting Apartheid, and mark my words, tomorrow it will be tribalism.'"

"Is that really what he believes? I thought he was a liberal and that he believed in the future of the country," Bis said.

"Oh, he does, with the proviso that we're not governed by a lot of greedy monkeys, white or black. He maintains a touch of the 'tar-brush' won't do any harm. Integrity is what counts, something sadly lacking in the present crop of politicians."

"Things seldom change. Look at the mess the country's in."

"The stigma of colour has always existed," I said. "That was the reason Gran's family left India for Mauritius. You know my mother was born there. Once there, they became Mauritians and High Anglicans. One uncle even joined the priesthood."

"Did you know that Indian men who advertise for brides specify that they be light-skin..." and before Bis uttered another word, we were interrupted by shrieking sirens and flashing lights as two police cars descended and blocked his car. A policeman jumped out brandishing a firearm, while two others forcibly pulled Bis from the car and pinned his arms behind him.

Most policemen spoke in Afrikaans; it was the accepted language of the Herren Volk and was employed mainly to establish their superiority. One shouted, "Koolie, what're you doin' with a white woman?"

Bis trembled with fear. "Please leave her alone."

"Do you think we'll touch her after she's been with a koolie?"

I screamed, "Leave him alone. My Gran's Anglo-Indian."

"The law says if you're more than seventy-four percent white, then you're white," said the burly policeman.

A crowd began to gather but were rudely dismissed by the police, and their only option was to leave.

Pinned against the car, Bis trembled in the grip of one policeman while another flashed a torch up and down his body and examined his crotch.

"Koolie, you're lucky your fly's closed."

The gun-toting policeman jabbed Bis in the groin. It must have been excruciating, for Bis let out a howl. We were helpless. Later Bis said the pain did not compare with the humiliation and degradation he experienced. Yet his concern for my safety was more important. I recall how he summoned all his strength and willpower to keep from passing out in front of the bullies. It was well established that the police used their power to intimidate and reduce their victims to snivelling prey. Any sign of submission bolstered their superiority.

The policeman trained his torch on me, and I cowered and covered my face with tremulous hands. I was sobbing, mewling like a caged animal caught in a trap. He searched the vehicle, and not finding what he was looking for, he knocked his baton several times against Bis's ordinary Baby Austin motor car.

"Koolie, you're playing with fire. I'm gonna teach you a lesson," he said, and he kicked Bis in the groin. This time Bis screamed. A few bystanders came to see what the commotion was, but they too were shooed away. "What do yous want? Get the f... away." He threw Bis to the ground and kicked him again. "Koolie, it's your lucky day."

The policemen got into their cars and drove away laughing. They had accomplished their mission. This had been a warning, and speaking Afrikaans, which both of us spoke fluently, only emphasised their authority.

Painfully, Bis got up, and without dusting himself off, clawed his way back into the car. He tried to comfort me, for I was speechless and shivering. Then he held me close and whispered my name. I was limp. Comforted by his warmth and the softness of his tweed blazer, which was covered in moss and blades of grass which I ignored, I snuggled closer to him.

We sat in silence for what seemed ages, lost in thought and oblivious to the ballad of the croaking frogs and the chirping crickets, who continued their mating calls on that moonlit night unaware of the human insanity. The music on the radio played on.

"We were fortunate," finally Bis said. "They could have shot me and dumped me into the lake, or worse. We were at their mercy. Fortunately, there were other people around who might have witnessed their foul deed."

Bis was convinced that this was not a random attack. There were dozens of cars parked at the lake, yet the police had swooped down on his ordinary, two-seater motor car and ignored all the others. Their obvious mirth confirmed his suspicion. Informers were everywhere. He reflected on his workplace. Was it because he lent his car sometimes to Ahmed Kathrada, his flat mate, a known communist party activist? The police had been tipped off, but who had informed them? And why?

The following day, Bis was on his way to the common room, still pondering the previous night's drama and his fortunate escape, when he ran into Rex, who was there to pick up some references before leaving for London.

"Late night, Bis? You look as if you've been through the mill," Rex said.

Bis was about to answer and then checked himself. Very casually he answered, "No, not really. I thought you'd already left for London."

"I'll be leaving shortly. I've been held up. I'm still waiting for some documents."

They entered the common room, where many doctors had already gathered to play Bridge. It was a few minutes past four o'clock, the ritual hour when all who could stopped work to take tea. Tea, the elixir that restores and relieves stress and quenches thirst. "Tea time is the most civilised custom introduced by my countrymen," an English doctor opined.

A new game was about to begin. Cards were shuffled and dealt.

"Hey Thakor, when did you say you were going to have that thing amputated?" Abram asked testily.

"Actually, the surgical unit has scheduled me for next week," Thakor said.

"A jolly good thing too. You'll probably miss it," Abram said, massaging his own well-manicured hands. "I've noticed you blowing on it. Is it a lucky charm? You're always dealt a good hand."

Everyone laughed.

"Sorry, no pun intended," smirked Abram. "Bis, would you like to play?"

"No. Sorry, I'm off to the ward."

"Why so glum, Bis?"

Bis ignored the remark and left the common room.

CHAPTER 21
Sighting the New Moon

Bis was off duty for the weekend, and his mother had begged him to celebrate Eid with the family, which is the feast that ends the month-long fast of Ramadan. Dutifully, he obeyed and he accompanied his father to the mosque, where the community elders were gathered to witness the birth of the new moon, which would officially end Ramadan. But where was the moon? The orthodox Muslims did not accept the date of the new moon as listed on the Gregorian calendar.

"The moon must be seen with the naked eye by a true believer," claimed the sages. Eid festivities could not begin until the moon was spotted. Men with beards and clean-shaven boys scanned the sky, but the overcast night was dark and moonless, and the elusive crescent remained hidden from sight.

One man reported, "I've seen the moon with a pair of binoculars." Another said, "I've seen the moon from my balcony." Yet another added, "An aeroplane went into the sky to locate it."

"We can't accept the word of men without beards," said an orthodox believer.

This remark enraged Bis's father, who rebuked the speaker. "Man, when will you shed your ignorance?" Beards signified piety and were worn by devout Muslim men, but it was not a tenet of the Holy Koran.

The young men present were delighted that Bis's father had chastised the bearded speaker.

Finally, an Imam confirmed that indeed the moon had been observed in an adjacent village and Eid celebrations could begin. It was time for families to gather, to feast, to give thanks, and to make charitable donations, and dole out presents; all traditions that the Bismillah family upheld.

Bis honoured his filial duty and attended Eid luncheon with his family on Saturday, but he planned to return to the city that same evening. He was determined to make an escape from the claustrophobic home atmosphere that stifled and brought out the worst in him. He became restless and moody, and he loathed the way his family fussed over him with their constant niggling. Their not-so-subtle talk of girls who would make him a suitable bride never failed to irk him. "I know you mean well," Bis said repeatedly to his family, who were wont to see him settled.

Bis had confided to me time and again: "Joan, they fail to understand that I've grown up and discarded their out-dated social customs. What they do not realise is that Apartheid reinforces their moribund way of life." Bis vowed to rise above the limitations forced upon non-whites by their European overlords. He intended to excel and prove them in error.

"I have confidence that you will succeed in the end," I had replied, unsure of when or how that would come about but with absolute faith that he would succeed.

Falling in love but being unable to be open about our relationship demonstrated the ridiculous and unnatural situation that was a crime under the law, and a betrayal in the eyes of our families. Neither family would condone marriage outside of their community. This was a triumph of Apartheid, because it made it easier to implement their laws of separation. Bis was about to defy both the law and tradition.

"Ma, I hate to disappoint you, but I must return to the city tonight."

Amina, his mother, was a proud and elegant lady with silver-grey hair, and Bis noted the disappointment in her lustrous brown eyes. He was sorry but it was unavoidable. She had taught her children to be obedient and to respect their elders, but she was unable to persuade her son to spend more time at home. He had inherited his father's stubborn streak.

"Abdul Haq-Bhai," said his mother, using the name that she preferred to address her son by. "We expected and were prepared for you to spend the weekend. We see so little of you." Mother and son were seated in their comfortable sitting room, and it was not often that they were alone together. The rest of the family were out in the garden distributing Eid gifts to their neighbours' children, and to the servants.

"It can't be helped, Ma. I came specially to wish you Eid Mubarak."

"We've invited the Karim's to celebrate Eid dinner," she pleaded. "They were looking forward to meeting you. Their elder daughter's been accepted to medical school, and they hoped you could give her some helpful hints before she started."

"I truly am sorry, Ma. I really can't stop. I'm leaving shortly," Bis said emphatically. "I'm certain I'll be of little or no help to their daughter." And he got up to leave.

The long drive back to the city was pause for reflection, and for the first time, Bis understood what his older brother Ahmin had been forced to contend with. Their father, without Ahmin's knowledge, had ignored the tradition of sending emissaries to propose marriage on Ahmin's behalf. He had dealt with the proposal himself. Against his desire, the dutiful Ahmin obeyed his father, who believed that his niece had limited prospects and would make a good wife for his oldest son. Thus, Ahmin was married to a suitable wife, according to his father's wishes.

As a married man, Ahmin was obliged to take a position in the family's haberdashery and general store. The opportunity to attend university was obliterated, depriving him of the intellectual stimulation he craved. Ahmin proved his aptitude and was indispensable to the family business, which he expanded during the war years and managed with profitable success. However, he was resentful toward his father, which resulted in constant quarrelling with his old man. This went unnoticed by the family or was simply ignored, as an individual's needs were secondary to those of the clan. Bis was not about to fall into the same trap.

Driving back to the city that night, Bis pondered his future. It occurred to him that now that he had graduated, there was little to prevent his father from exercising his parental authority by offering a proposal of marriage on his behalf. Was he correct to assume that the Eid dinner invitation to the Karim family and his mother's pleading with him to stay and meet their medical-student daughter was to lure him into an engagement to marry the daughter? She was Indian, Muslim, good looking, and educated—she possessed all the attributes for a most suitable bride!

Bis abhorred the notion. He began to perspire and his anxiety increased. His brow was moist, and he clutched the steering wheel tighter as sweat dripped from his palms. His agitation increasing, he realised his plans for his future were in jeopardy unless he acted immediately. He was less than an hour's drive away from town when he stopped at a petrol station with a public telephone and made a quick call.

"Hello, Bis," I answered. "Where are you? I assumed you were home in Potchefstroom."

"Listen Joan, I can't talk now. I'm on my way. I should be there within the hour. Please meet me at the Shapiros'."

Bis made two more phone calls. A sigh of relief escaped as he got back into his car and he drove away whistling.

On the drive to Northcliffe, Bis surveyed his life to this point. He had realised his boyhood ambition to become a doctor, and he could be independent and free of the cultural constraints that had bound his brother. This was his chance at independence and freedom. He had to escape from the humdrum existence of the small town and the constricting life that would be imposed on him in a country where he was a second-class citizen. It was something he intended to rectify.

Bis believed that he had much more to accomplish. At medical school, he had been exposed to a wider world. It was there he had started to question a traditional way of life, where time appeared to have stood still. The small Muslim-Indian community had prospered economically, but socially they had not moved forward. They had stagnated—or so Bis thought. "I was born in South Africa, and unlike my parents I'm not an immigrant but a native son. Still, I have none of the legal rights—rather, I'm reduced to second-class status, and I'm made to feel ashamed because I'm not white." It was an argument Bis raised regularly with fellow Muslim students, who were apathetic and accepted the status quo without complaint.

"Our faith has to come before all else, or we are lost," was their refrain.

"No one is suggesting you give up your faith, or your culture, but there is no attempt to assimilate or to meet on some level with other communities. After one hundred years in this country, are you still immigrants?" Bis asked.

"No, but we are true believers. Our teachings command us to be faithful to our creed."

Part One

Bis thought their arguments were illogical and they made little sense to him, but he was aware that any further discourse was hopeless. His peers were chained to secular practices that masqueraded as religious rites.

Bis contended and had explained to me, that the Muslim religious stance fuelled the Nationalists' Apartheid agenda to repatriate Indians to India. The government stated, "Indians are an unassimilable people," and it was rumoured that they offered to pay £250 per head to any Indian who chose to co-operate. Bis knew of no one who had actually accepted the offer to repatriate.

The sequence of arguments that led Bis to the decision he was about to embark on was fraught with problems—religious, social, and legal. Bis's father was a Hadjee, who is one who has made the pilgrimage to Mecca and can recite the Holy Koran by rote. Bawa, as the children used to address their father, discarded certain social traditions that were based on ancient superstitious custom only when it suited his purpose. People consulted him constantly to act as arbitrator in their family disputes, especially regarding inheritance and marriage settlements. Bawa was a stubborn man. Ghandi-like in appearance, small and lithe with short, stubby grey hair, the old man was myopic and wore wire-rimmed spectacles. He glared at one, which made him appear stern. With pursed lips, he spoke with authority, but he was a man of few words and he did not tolerate fools. Bis remembered his father's aversion to outdated orthodox practices. His father was a prudent and practical man who prized education both religious and secular. However, his father's attitude was that marriage was sacred and he deplored the fact that many Muslim men had more than one wife or kept mistresses. Bawa found it dishonourable that they used the excuse that Islam permitted a man four wives. This only displayed their ignorance and petty, base natures. In fact, in South Africa, the second wife more often was not Indian, but coloured or Malay, and these women had full rights to own property. Therefore, it was a marriage of convenience. These dual marriages accounted for the numbers of step-siblings in many Muslim families.

Bis reasoned that marriage to me without his father's permission would not find favour, but the memory of Ahmin's arranged marriage resonated and stiffened his resolve to follow his heart. Bis figured that the question of religion would resolve itself, but the legality of our marriage presented a problem. To marry me under the present law was impossible, and not to marry me left him open to an arranged marriage.

Bis resolved the dilemma. He would marry me by *Sharia*. That is Islamic law, which had been legal under the former government and was still recognised in South Africa. The Apartheid government had not yet rescinded the law. However, it was on their agenda and given time, it would be annulled. Bis took for granted that Islamic law would be acceptable to me. His father would have to concede that our marriage was indeed legal and binding, and Bis was certain that I would agree. I was not religious, but I adhered to many religious scruples; living in sin without the sanction of marriage was one. We would have to deal with the legalities of a mixed marriage later.

CHAPTER 22
A Marriage Proposal

It was past eight o'clock when Bis returned to the city with a renewed sense of purpose, and he vowed to chart his own course. He drove directly toward Northcliffe, the home of his mentor and friend, Dr. David Shapiro. Bis sighed with relief and opened the car window to inhale the cool night air. It had rained earlier and fresh puddles of water were scattered along the curb reflecting the stars.

Looking up, Bis noticed the day-old "Eid moon" had retired. The black night sky was a panorama of scintillating beauty; the Milky Way a swathe of brilliance in the heavens. Bis took his cue from Orion, the warrior girded with glittering belt and sword, ready to do battle. His favourite constellation, the Southern Cross, that navigational beacon of light south of the equator that for eons had guided sailors to the land of his birth, this night would witness his proposal of marriage—a surprise Eid gift.

Bis parked his car and went inside to greet his hosts. "Hello," he said.

"Hello, David's at a meeting," May said. "And Joan's in the garden."

Bis hurried out into the garden. I ran to him. He took me in his arms and held me close. "Let's sit down," he said, and he brushed the leaves from a bench with his handkerchief as a bunny rabbit scuttled away. We sat in silence, our arms entwined and my head resting lightly against his shoulder as we inhaled the sweet, scented air. It had rained earlier and the air was redolent with a potpourri of honeysuckle, verbena, mimosa, and eucalyptus. In the distance, an owl hooted, while a pair of *kieviets* twittered their mating call as they circled around fluttering their wings in a courting duet. For a long time neither of us spoke;

we were content to be together and savour the moment. The African night sky was enchanting and far below the flickering lights of the golden city stretched out before us. Words would annul the serenity, and from the dance hall below, strains of music drifted up and serenaded us adding to the aura of the night.

The setting was romantic, but I interrupted the silence just as a shooting star streaked by. "Bis, we ought to make a wish," I whispered. "This is heaven. I'll always treasure this place."

"No darling, heaven's an illusion. Yes, this place is special, and unlike you, I'm cynical when it comes to making wishes."

"Don't spoil the mood. You're always so practical."

"Since you've broken the spell, I'll tell you what brought me back to town tonight. After my call to you, I spoke to an Imam, a trusted friend, and he's prepared to marry us according to Muslim rites."

I was taken completely by surprise, for it was quite unexpected. We had often talked about marriage, but I knew we would have to wait until the ban on mixed marriages was changed, or we left the country.

"Bis, are you actually proposing? This is so sudden." I broke away and turned to look at him.

"Yes. We can't afford to wait any longer, or I could find myself in the arms of a suitable wife with no chance of escape."

"So, I'm the lesser evil. You're admitting that I'm the damsel that is to spare you from having an arranged marriage to some chosen beauty?"

"Yes! You snagged me in time before my father married me off as he did my elder brother. They spoke of little else at home and that it was time for me to settle down. They'd invited a family with two pretty daughters to celebrate Eid dinner tonight."

"You missed a bargain. You could have had both from what you've told me about Muslim men and their multiple wives! So, that's your reason for the proposal. And I believed you to be the true romantic hero."

"That's your fault for harbouring romantic notions. Joan, don't be difficult, even in jest. Yes, I confess that I'm a victim of a clever ploy, and it's all because I'm in love and you know exactly what I mean." Very gently, Bis put his arm around me.

"Oh, you're insufferable and conceited. Am I supposed to be flattered or grateful? And what will your family say? You haven't told them, have you?"

"No, it's our secret. We'll make it public when we leave the country."

"Now you'll make me cry. When is the big day?"

"Tuesday evening. If you weren't so coy and such a prude, marriage wouldn't be necessary."

"You're so smug. It serves you right for choosing a good convent girl." I broke from his embrace, poking him in the ribs. "Incidentally, have you forgotten that Tuesday's my twenty-third birthday?"

Bis pulled me close again, and for a while, neither of us spoke. Then he said, "How often have you reminded me that you wouldn't live in sin? So, I've honoured your wish. I've made all the arrangements by setting the date, for I know only too well how you like to be in charge and muddle through. So, I'm your birthday present."

"How masterful. You're so practical. Any trace of romance is lost. You are devious, Bismillah. When did you make the arrangements?" I asked, snuggling closer to him.

Bis ignored my remarks. He was resolute once he had made up his mind. "Unlike you, my darling, I'm a realist. I spoke to our friend Samir Inja just before I phoned you, and to Moulvi Sheik. Samir offered us his flat, and he'll arrange for the *Nikah* ceremony to take place at his gallery. It will be a simple affair. Tuesday evening is the only time Moulvi's available because he leaves on Wednesday for the start of his pilgrimage to Mecca."

The strains of "God Save the King" drifted from the dancehall, a signal that the dance was ending and a new day was beginning. We were reluctant to leave the splendour of the garden, yet it was late and both of us had to work the following day. We went indoors to impart our news to May and found David had arrived. He was delighted for us and could be trusted to keep our secret.

"Congratulations! May and I want you to use the summer house for as long as you need. You realise that you may have to leave the country."

"Thank you, we're so lucky to have you for friends," Bis said.

"Thank you, I'm truly happy," I said, unable to stem my tears. My impending marriage reminded me of the loss of my mother as I embraced May, whom I regarded a trusted friend—almost a surrogate mother. At last, all the envy and petty jealousy I had harboured over the years over not having a mother to love and guide me evaporated. I counted among my blessings the unconditional love bestowed on me.

On the drive back to the hospital residence, the ever practical Bis said, "I need to explain *Sharia*, that is, Islamic law. The *Nikah* is the actual marriage contract, and it is not attended by the bride. Her father and male relatives appear on her behalf to give her in marriage and accept the dowry. Divorce is even simpler. The groom merely has to repeat three times, 'I divorce you,' in the presence of two witnesses."

"What of the woman? Does she have any say?"

"Certainly not. She's chattel. Are you still game?" Bis said, with all the authority he could muster, unaware of how that statement, in the not too distant offing, would prove to be true.

"Now you admit that I'm a suitable wife, and you'll make all the rules! If I weren't in love with you and gullible, as you keep telling me, I ought to reject your proposal." I smiled as I stared out of the window. I was about to pass another milestone. My life was about to begin anew, and I could not decide whether it was in the stars, destiny, or plain serendipitous luck!

CHAPTER 23
Secret Nuptial

It was my birthday, and a boom of thunder had aroused me from a sound sleep, putting an end to my muddled dream, not that I remembered any of it. It was pouring rain. I got up to shut the windows, but it was far too early and too dark to be up. I climbed back into bed, but sleep evaded me. Excited and happy, I lay in bed and smiled. My gift would be a husband. The rain continued—it was a good omen. My thoughts were on the day ahead, and I reflected on Bis and our first meeting. We had discovered each other in a storm, and that was the beginning of our relationship. Often cloistered in his two-seater car, we enjoyed driving in the rain for hours, discussing whatever came to mind, and it afforded us a sort of privacy away from the world at large. Our marriage was to be a secretive affair, nothing like what young women dream of, and unlike the wedding of my two younger sisters with all the trappings and fuss. There would be no exuberant planning of the venue, dresses, flowers, or invitations, no relatives to celebrate my marriage, or photographer to record the event. Mine would be a solemn affair, but I was ecstatic and found I quite enjoyed the mystery. Bis and I were to be married that evening, and together we would face the future.

I was fortunate to have the day off, it allowed me time to prepare for the event that was about to change my life. In keeping with the man who acted on principle, Bis had left little to chance. He'd made all the arrangements, and all I had to do was to follow whatever he had planned.

I remember reading my horoscope, and I liked the favourable prediction: "Fair weather but be mindful of a few bumps along the road ahead." I could live with that, and naturally I did not tell Bis, for I was aware from our sparring; our arguments and discussions political, literary, domestic, and religious, but he eschewed horoscopes and fortune-telling of any kind, which he regarded as superstitious drivel.

After all these years I recall vividly being off work that day: I was excited and I did not want to attract attention for fear I would give myself away. I needed to compose my emotions while waiting for the appointed time. Usually my birthday triggered sad memories but that day they were banished, and made way for what I hoped with all my heart would be a happy future.

Later in the morning, to while away the hours and to calm my nerves, I used my day off to visit the hairdresser. Passing a French dress shop on my way to the salon, I paused on the sidewalk, hesitated, and on a sudden impulse went in. A pale-blue Barathea suit trimmed with black velvet lapels and cuffs appealed to me. It had a fitted peplum jacket that showed off my tiny waist. It fit perfectly, although the skirt needed to be hemmed. The outfit was expensive, but how often did a girl get married? Mine was not the traditional wedding, but the old adage "something new and something blue" seemed appropriate.

After the salon, I visited the university gift store and purchased gold cuff links embossed with the Wits crest. In the book department, I found a leather-bound copy of Khalil Gibran's *The Prophet*. These were to be my wedding gifts for Bis. It was the first time that I had spent so much money on a single day, and to cover the cost I ransacked my savings account.

I returned to the dress shop to pick up the suit, and realised I needed a place to change. I could not go to the residence or to any of my friends or family for fear of arousing suspicion. Instead, I settled on a small, discreet hotel where I knew my father had often stayed on business trips into the city.

After a leisurely bath, I took out my mother's art deco earrings that I had inherited, and held them against my heart. They were to set off my wedding ensemble. Although the pearls appeared too large to be real, the small diamonds were authentic. I considered the earrings a talisman, a charm I hoped would bring me and my betrothed good fortune. Something old and borrowed, they symbolised my mixed heritage and were a tribute to my cosmopolitan family. I smiled as I recalled my father telling me how he'd had the earrings made to complement the heirloom necklace my grandmother had inherited from Her

Ladyship, the governor's wife. My mother Lily had worn the matching set at her wedding to Charles, my father.

A trinity of momentous milestones marked the day: My twenty-third birthday, the anniversary of my mother's death, and now, my wedding. The memory of losing my mother had haunted me on birthdays past, but for today, I tucked it away. I fastened on the pearl earrings but did not wear the necklace.

I stared at my reflection in the mirror and I vowed not to let memories of bygone things mar my happiness. However, certain scenes and acts are indelible, and unable to control my thoughts my seventh birthday came to mind along with the image of my dying mother with one arm dangling over the edge of the bed. I saw the sideways tilt of her head and her forehead swathed in a camphor bandage. My mother gazed at me with mournful eyes as she was borne away to the waiting ambulance. That gaze remained etched in my brain and it often recurred to me in troubled dreams. The drama of that final day had had a profound effect and had influenced the trajectory of my life. It had taught me to take nothing for granted, to be aware of my responsibilities to my siblings, and to be grateful for everything I had been given. "Be grateful for small mercies and be respectful of your elders," Gran had often emphasized.

I undid the tissue wrapping of my wedding costume, admiring anew the straight skirt with a single kick pleat in the back. I buffed my black suede pumps and removed the shoe trees. I straightened the seams of my first pair of nylon stockings, a new material developed during the war that had recently replaced silk. I sprayed toilet water on my wrists, behind my ears, and on my chestnut hair, which was styled in a page-boy, a current craze that showed off the earrings. In one last glance in the mirror, my hazel eyes glowed, seeming to say, *I hope you're aware of what you're getting into.* Second guessing myself, I knew the problems with the law concerning my marriage loomed ahead, but that was for another day! I hoped that somewhere, in another realm, my mother was watching and giving her blessing.

The hotel was a short walk from Samir's gallery, but I did not wish to ruffle my appearance, so I hailed a cab. On arrival, I knew I could not have wished for a more luxurious venue. Samir came out to greet me wearing a dark Saville Row suit and sporting a white rosebud in his lapel. "Hello my dear," he greeted me with a smile, giving me a warm hug.

Samir was a part-time lecturer on oriental art at the university, and Bis had bonded with him through their shared passion for Persian carpets and poetry. Bis's love of beautiful things had drawn him to the gallery, which was filled with ancient screens, furniture, silk tapestries, and art work.

I had met Samir through my family's furniture and decorating business. He was the consultant they called upon for advice regarding antique furniture. Later, as a budding interior decorator, I called on Samir for his expertise and advice.

Samir's agate-coloured eyes reminded me of the cat's-eye marbles of my childhood. His waxed handlebar moustache matched his pomaded grey hair, and his impeccable tailored suits gave the illusion that he was tall. Samir chain-smoked gold-tipped Black Sobrany cigarettes from an ivory cigarette holder that lent him an old-world glamour. His refined and courtly manners added to his charisma.

Together, Bis and I had often attended readings at his gallery. Samir favoured the great Persian poets Rumi and Omar Khayyam. I could tell that Bis and I intrigued him. I was convent-educated and Bis was Muslim. How would it all end? Samir was familiar with the difficulties we faced under the present law. Added to these problems were the opposition, the restrictions, and expectations we would encounter from our respective families. We appealed to Samir's chivalric sense of honour.

"It will be my pleasure to be Joan's champion and arrange an Islamic ceremony," Samir said when Bis had telephoned him.

Samir ushered me into the little sitting room hidden behind a two-way mirror. "You're on time, and Moulvi's saying his prayers. I should tell you that a Muslim wedding is quite informal. The bride does not participate in the *Nikah*. Rather this is the contract between the father and male relatives, who answer on behalf of the bride. Today, I'm your sponsor and guardian and I pledge to be responsible for your welfare."

My father had not been consulted on nor informed of our marriage.

"Yes," I whispered. "Bis explained Muslim marriage to me. Oh, Samir, how can we ever thank you?"

"No—no thank you. Be happy. I've watched you grow to the lovely young woman before me. Be a good wife and mother and be respectful to elders."

"Yes, thank you, Samir. Your friendship, kindness, and generosity to both Bis and me are a blessing. We're so very grateful to you and Moulvi for enabling us to overcome a major obstacle."

As though summoned, Moulvi entered the room. He was a tall gentleman with a shock of grey hair covered by a macramé *kufi*. His long, dark beard was streaked with grey and covered most of his face accentuating his glowing, dark eyes. A long, white robe added to his stature. Moulvi walked slowly over to me and took both my hands in his. "Welcome, daughter." He brushed away a tear from my cheek and patted me on the shoulder, causing more tears to fall. "Our groom should be here soon."

I was puzzled—the front door to the shop had been locked for the night and they would have to open it again to let Bis in. Just then, I heard a grating sound as part of the wall behind the screen slid away. Bis walked in, smiling. He was wearing a navy-blue suit, a cream silk shirt, and his convocation tie.

"Asalaam Al-heikum," he greeted our host.

"Waleikum Salaam," the two men responded in unison.

Bis took my hand. "You look beautiful," he whispered.

"Shall we begin?" Moulvi asked. Without waiting for a reply, he began to perform the *Nikah* in Arabic. I did not understand a word, but the guttural sounds recalled pagan music. The contract between a husband and the wife's male representative was sanctioned. Moulvi briefly outlined the duties of a husband to his wife. Samir answered on my behalf and the ceremony was over. Moulvi explained to me the prayers and the significance of a Muslim marriage. It was valid, legal, and binding as any other.

Both men and Bis signed the documents and Moulvi pronounced, "Now you are husband and wife. Go in peace, my children." He helped himself to a Turkish delight from the tray of sweets Samir had provided. "It's our custom to offer sweets. A token of good health, long life, and happiness."

Moulvi then took his leave and Bis handed Moulvi an envelope with a donation of a gold sovereign as he left. I later discovered that gifts from my new family were generally gold coins.

"I wish you happiness and a long, trouble-free life together," said Samir. "Here is your marriage document. I'll put it away for safe keeping."

"Thank you, Samir, for everything," Bis said, handing him a small package that contained a gold signet ring Bis had received as a graduation present. Later when I quizzed him about it, he said, "I never wear the darn things."

"I too must be off, and I will not be back until ten tomorrow morning to open the shop. Bis, you know how to exit and lock-up behind you. Here is Joan's dowry," Samir said as he handed Bis a small leather pouch containing three gold coins. Then he left us alone.

Bis kissed me. "You're worth exactly three pieces of gold," he joked.

"Oh! I'm too happy to argue with you."

"We should go upstairs. I don't think you've ever been," Bis said, pulling me along.

For some strange reason, the three gold coins resonated, reminding me of thirty pieces of silver. It felt ominous. Why was I now recalling Judas' betrayal? Was it merely a coincidence? I chalked it up to my habit of questioning everything and to second-guessing myself. After all, I was a granddaughter of a Piscean, a superstitious woman who had influenced my subconscious thoughts, so I left it at that. I was too happy to spoil the mood. I had been brought up with strict Puritan values in a High Anglican household, and I had two uncles who were ordained priests. Then religion had been reinforced by my years at the convent. Having renounced all Christian ritual, perhaps hidden in the recess of my brain a tinge of guilt persisted as a reminder of how I had been reared. On the other hand, it could simply be a reminder that marital vows were sacred irrespective of religion.

Hand-in-hand we mounted the stairway to the second floor. The timbre of Bis's voice aroused me from my reverie. "Happy birthday! Welcome to the bridal chamber, Mrs. Bismillah." With that, he lifted me across the threshold of the luxurious flat.

Am I truly married? How can such happiness last? A pity I can't share my joy with everyone, I mused. I did not want to linger on such thoughts, and turned my attention to the exquisite flat. On the hall table, a bouquet of cream and white roses with a card read, "Welcome to a refuge away from the world." A huge expanse of lead-lighted windows lined one wall. The drapes were heavy indigo silk, tied with gold tassels. The delicate furniture was antique, pieces of different periods—some French and others Chinese. Two large, round, carved mahogany screens replaced interior doors. A grandfather clock ticked away. There was much to admire, from the delicate Chinese porcelain and Koranic scrolls framed in gold, to the rich tapestries and carpets. I likened the flat to Aladdin's cave. Although I had known Samir as a decorator, I had only seen the gallery, and never his flat.

"I came straight from the obstetric ward and I need a shower," Bis said, excusing himself.

I sat on the plush settee and took stock of the lavish surroundings. I was in a contemplative mood and mused on our good fortune while the anxiety I had felt earlier ebbed away. I got up and inspected the series of seventeenth-century Persian miniatures hanging above a Chinese cabinet.

"That's better," said Bis as he entered the room, resplendent in a gray silk dressing gown; a present from Samir. It struck me how handsome my husband was, his jet-black hair was sleeked back. For the first time I noticed his large ears. "What big ears you have, Grandma, and such a large nose," I joked.

"The better to hear and smell you," he said, and he gathered me in his arms and sniffed my hair. "Samir's left a present in the bedroom for you," he whispered, letting me slip from his grasp.

Minutes later, I entered wearing a heavily embroidered Chinese cream silk dressing gown and matching gold-tipped doe-skin slippers. In my hand, I held a copy of the *Rubaiyat of Omar Khayyam* with a note. Tears were streaming down my cheeks.

Bis came to meet me and took me in his arms. "Darling, what's wrong?"

"Even as a little girl, I never experienced the unconditional love I feel at this moment," I sobbed, handing Bis the note.

Dearest Joan,

The *Rubaiyat* will give you great pleasure and comfort. Enjoy it with my blessing. Wear the Chinese bridal dressing gown in good health and may the slippers remind and guide you on the Golden Path. In honour of this day, God speed on the journey. I wish you and Abdul Haq all the happiness that your own parents would have wished for you if only they could have been present. It was my privilege to act as your surrogate father. Never hesitate to come to me should the need ever arise.

Yours affectionately,
Samir.

Bis put his arm around me and we sat down on the plush sofa for a while. Finally he said, "A ring will attract attention and ours is not a traditional wedding. I got this instead." It was a gold watch, which he fastened onto my wrist. "Note, it has a second hand to remind you of me each time you look at it. Remember that each second we're apart, I'll be thinking of you."

For a second time that evening, tears streamed down my cheeks. I realised that all the tears I shed so freely now were from the reservoir where I had stored them these twenty years. I opened my attaché case and handed Bis his presents. Khalil Gibran's book was simply inscribed, "Ever-thine, Joan."

There was a bottle of champagne in the fridge, but as neither of us drank, Bis poured a glass of milk for him and orange juice for me. We toasted each other: "To our life together."

When the sun rose, we reported to work as two people united but separated by circumstances beyond our control. *How strange,* I thought, *both bound for the same work place but prevented from arriving together.* Bis would drive and I would take the bus for hospital staff. The bus left St. Mary's Cathedral at seven a.m., two blocks away from the flat. I boarded the bus and saw the faces of the privileged whites who travelled daily, merrily chatting away. Unable to divulge my secret, I was steeped in my own thoughts. I fondled my wristwatch and for a fleeting instant felt a pang of regret. I thought of my siblings, saddened that they were not there to share in my happiness. I felt certain my mother, whom we'd been taught to believe watched from another realm, rejoiced and blessed us.

CHAPTER 24
Hide and Seek

Now that we were married, Bis and I were careful about being seen together in public. We had to preserve our secret to avoid trouble with the law. Our furtive rendezvous had to appear as casual encounters, and whenever possible we met at the Shapiro cottage, or at the homes of a few trusted friends. To be found guilty of any crime meant confinement and being doomed to an unknown fate. It was stressful having to keep looking over one's shoulder.

Ishmael's death, the Zoo Lake incident, and finally Bunny's warning had alerted Bis to his precarious position, which was exacerbated by his questioning of the chief's handling of the internal inquiry. The time had come to leave Baragwanath Hospital, and the country. Our relationship made me vulnerable and it was only a matter of time before I too would be under suspicion by BOSS. In fact, it was possible I could already be suspect. Aunt Leah had informed me that a man had been spotted watching the house, and he'd turned out to be a plain-clothes policeman. He had made enquiries about me in the neighbourhood and he'd knocked at the door and asked after me. She had reported that I had left home and practised midwifery, and that I had not kept in touch with the family.

The trauma of the attack at the Zoo Lake haunted me and every time I saw a white policeman, I was reminded of the sordid incident. I wondered how the policeman knew of my racial classification status. It had never occurred to me that such detailed profiles even existed. But times had changed under Apartheid, and race and identity had become paramount issues, particularly in the case of anyone of mixed heritage. In the attempt to preserve the "purity" of the white race, the law was designed to group people into categories like species of animals or insects. Laws now forbade any dark races from contaminating the sanctified white gene pool. I wondered how that magical number of seventy-four percent white that entitled people to European status had been arrived at. The government policy under the white Nationalist Party introduced segregation as a means of ensuring racial purity in the land of beauty and unrest. They maintained that the proof that whites were superior to their darker-skinned brethren had its origins in scripture. This premise was endorsed by the Evangelists, and conservative dominies of the Dutch Reformed Churches, who believed they were merely implementing the status quo as ordained by God.

Thus, it was impossible to ignore the implications of being guilty on any count, and the possibility of being exposed became a threat to our safety.

I confided in my childhood friend, Michael, and asked him to escort me to meetings and parties to deflect any suspicion of my relationship to Bis. Michael agreed and warned me, "Keep your plans secret. There are spies everywhere. I promise to chaperone you. After all, you are the pesky sister I inherited through my sworn blood brother."

Michael had worked in the passport office one summer and he advised me how to apply without attracting the attention of the authorities. He cautioned me to leave the country on immediate receipt of my passport. That way there would be no time for an investigation, which could prevent me from leaving. However, in the interim, I should stay on at the hospital and meet Bis at the Shapiros.

Bis's contract at Bara was ending, and he would not renew it. He would return to the safety of his home town of Potchefstroom, where there was little or no political involvement. He would work there until he was ready to leave the country.

Bis was under tremendous pressure from his family to marry and settle down. He was caught in a dilemma. The pressure would only increase when he returned home, and he loathed the thought of me spending more time with Michael. Already there were whispers that we made an ideal couple. He was envious, but he had no choice but to accept the situation and act indifferent. In less than a month, he would leave the city and return to Potchefstroom.

Part One

Bis called to inform me of the latest development in Potchefstroom. "My father had an office built and it is equipped and all ready for me to go into general practice."

"Did you agree, and how do you know?" I asked in a plaintive voice.

"Ahmin was in town to replenish stock for the store. He stopped off at Bara to see me and to enquire when I would be opening my practice now that the office was completed. Bawa had the office built as a surprise graduation present. He consigned a medical supply company to outfit it in readiness for the 'Doctor Sahib.' Please Joan, try to be patient. I have to return to Potch to talk to Father."

Bis left that evening and returned early the following morning. He came directly to my office. "Joan, my father reminded me how fortunate I was to be debt free and able to start practising immediately once I retired from the hospital. He assured me that patients are lining up waiting for me, and he believes that he acted in my best interest. I thanked him, but I extracted a promise not to involve me in any other plans. I implored him to hold off on marriage until I had time to settle into practice."

"Were you able to convince him?"

"I played for time, and I felt guilty for my duplicity. I was tempted to tell Bawa of our marriage, but I resisted knowing that at this time it could cause more problems for us. We would probably be obliged to settle in Potch, and that would scuttle any of our plans to leave the country. Moreover, it would give the authorities time to investigate our marriage."

I had no choice but to agree with Bis. "Naturally you must do what is best."

"My only hope is to entice one of the doctors to take over the practice from me. The expense alone is something I could not afford to repay."

"I suppose it can't be helped."

"I promise to resolve the problem soon. I'll get the word out to the doctors that the practice is there for the asking. Joan, please try to be patient."

"Bis, it's not your fault. Something's bound to crop up. You know my philosophy that things happen for a good reason."

"One good thing: I'll be free weekends. I promise I'll spend them with you, but we'll have to play it by ear."

A year had elapsed and Bis had settled into general practice. Potch was a safe haven as all political activity was discouraged, thus making it easier for him to concentrate solely on his medical practice. It afforded him time to save and invest his earnings, which were essential for our survival once when we left the country. Now that the practice was fully established, Bis made enquiries but had difficulty finding a doctor to take over. His father had kept his promise and beseeched the rest of the family to wait until Bis was ready before finding that suitable bride.

I continued working at Bara. We had settled into a routine, spending most of our weekends together tucked away in Northcliffe or at Samir's flat, seldom daring to be seen as a couple in public. The Shapiro servants had the weekends off, and David's emergency office at the main house ensured there was a constant flow of people. Our situation was becoming tenuous, and we both realised that we could not continue to live that way much longer. The political conditions were deteriorating, and life was becoming more difficult. There was suspicion at every turn. More colleagues were being investigated and then disappearing. Bis was under the impression that he was being shadowed on his forays into the city. Among his patients were several black policemen who appeared to be friendly, but Bis refrained from having any discussion other than professional ones with them.

I was anxious and unwell. I phoned Bis to come in urgently that evening. "Please, pick me up at the Sisters' entrance gate at eight p.m."

"What's so urgent?" Bis asked, laughing at me as I got into the car.

"I think I'm pregnant," I blurted out by way of greeting. I was clearly agitated. "Bis, what are we going to do?"

"What all married couples do. Celebrate! And the rest be damned. Actually, I've been waiting for you to tell me. I wondered why it's taken you so long to find out. I noticed the changes a while ago. You forget it's my trade. Did you say you were a midwife?" He chortled.

"Oh, you're so clever. After all the babies I've delivered, I should've known."

"Have you seen a doctor?"

"No. I wanted to tell you first."

"Sorry Joan, I beat you to it. You *did* say you were a midwife?"

"You're insufferable. You always have the last word, don't you?"

Bis turned serious. "You do know the rule about doctors treating their own? You realise having a child here will cause untold problems and the baby's registration will be a nightmare. Well, this is the catalyst we've been waiting for, and it will force our decision to act right away."

"Are you suggesting that we leave the country now?"

"Yes. We've become complacent. You must leave immediately, before you start showing and the baby's born."

"Oh Bis, not now and not without you. Bis, we're hardly a normal couple. How often have you told me rules don't apply to us? You make it up as we muddle through the morass of Apartheid restrictions. Surely, there's another way?"

"The timing's not great, I agree. Unfortunately, you can't wait for me. You'll have to leave first, and I'll follow as soon as I sell the practice and receive my passport. Dr. Yusuf has been working with me these last two months. He'll be grateful to take over. He has few options. He's worked all over the place and the terms will suit him, although my father will not be pleased. His bias towards him is that their tribe are regarded as the Jews of India and are not to be trusted. Things do not change! Failing that, I'll leave and hope that my old man finds someone to replace me."

"I hope you're right."

"Joan, it's urgent. You have to apply for your passport right away and do as your boyfriend Michael instructed," Bis teased.

"Yes, my tax clearance and the forms were filled out months ago. I've been waiting for the right time to apply. Now you'll have to get yours."

"You forget I'm Indian. Deliberately, I've not applied yet, for it would be an excuse by the powers-that-be for an investigation. That's another reason why you have to go ahead of me. It will be more complicated for me to get a passport and will take a while longer. I'll apply through the travel agents. They play ball with the Afrikaner clerks. I'll buy one if necessary. Everything has its price. Desperate times... You must book your passage to London as soon as you get the passport. The Union Castle Line had extra ships for the Queen's coronation. The demand for passage wasn't up to their expectation."

"I dread the thought of going without you."

"It can't be helped. I'll follow as soon as I'm able. I want you safely out of the country first."

"What if you're prevented from leaving?"

"Don't even think about it. If for any reason I can't get away, I'll leave on an exit visa, or sneak out of the country via the African Protectorates like many of our friends have done. If need be, I'll accept the Nationalists' offer of £250 to leave. That may be my only option."

"Can I trust them, or you for that matter? Remember the old adage: the mice will play when the cats away," I joked.

"That could equally apply to you. You've no choice. Now, am I going to examine you?"

CHAPTER 25
A Marriage Licence and a Passport

Bis sought the counsel of his friend and mentor, Dr. David Shapiro, who had trained as a lawyer before switching to medicine. He advised Bis that it was essential to obtain a South African marriage certificate before leaving for London. The Islamic licence may or may not be valid in England.

"A day before the Mixed Marriage Act became law, the courts were deluged with people all attempting to beat the ban before their marriages became illegal. Judge Malherbe was outraged by the act. He is the magistrate at the Special Licensing Office. I could have a word with him, and no questions asked. He will give you a legal document. I'll vouch for you," David said.

"Better safe than sorry. We live in strange and dangerous times," May added.

"You can worry about the mixed marriage later, should you return," David advised.

May was very fond of both of us, and she regarded us her special protégés in our unjust, segregated country. Her support for us was her stand against the erosion of human rights by a crazy government.

Bis and I presented ourselves at Judge Malherbe's office at the appointed hour. No secretary or clerk was present. The judge was an amiable older gentleman who welcomed us in a cordial manner. He stroked his goatee and his clear blue eyes peered at us as we stood before him. He did not ask us to be seated.

"You wish to be married today by special licence?"

"Yes please, sir."

"You will require two witnesses, and I notice you do not have any. I will arrange for a clerk, as my secretary is off for the day. There is an additional charge of £25 in cash for his service."

"Sir, I am aware of the cost," Bis said.

"So then, fill out these forms while I fetch the witness."

The judge returned with a coloured orderly. "He will have to do," he said.

I signed the form, followed by Bis, and witnessed by the orderly, who signed in the space for the first witness.

"I'll just have to be the other witness," the judge said. "There now, you have a legal marriage certificate, and you may pay the young man the £25. Naturally, there is no receipt for his service." Bis handed the orderly the £25 and then paid the judge the £5 Special Licence fee, for which he received a receipt.

Bis thanked the magistrate but was waved away. In Afrikaans, the magistrate said, *"Dit is my plesier."* It is my pleasure.

Leaving the office, I remarked, "That was the weirdest and quickest marriage ceremony."

"No, we bought a licence. That was sophistry at the highest level. A demonstration of how the legal system is subverted."

CHAPTER 26
Aboard the Blue Train

THE TIME HAD ARRIVED TO APPLY FOR A PASSPORT AND I SOUGHT Michael's advice. Michael had worked in the passport office one summer. He was familiar with the habits of the Afrikaner clerks who were permanent staff and employed in all government offices. Invariably, they were always in a hurry to leave work. He recommended I go minutes before closing time on a Friday to hand in my application forms, which I had applied for in my maiden name of Salsoni, as that would ensure no awkward enquiries or questions asked by impatient employees. For the next week I was on edge—what if I didn't get my passport? But a week later, on a Friday afternoon just before the licencing office closed, I returned and I received and signed for my passport without a single query. I proceeded directly to Thomas Cook Travel Office to book my passage.

The ship sailed in four days from Cape Town, and the train journey to the boat would take a day and a half. Our secret was still intact, but I confided in my youngest sister Peggy, who offered to accompany me. It would be an excuse for her to meet her fiancé's siblings, who resided in Cape Town. I asked my sister not to divulge my secret until I was safely out of the country. Pegs would be at liberty to use her discretion once I had safely left South Africa.

On the eve of my departure, Bis and I spent our last night together at Northcliffe. The Shapiros wished us luck and presented me with a beautiful travel rug. It was a solemn parting. We bid the Shapiros farewell, and thanked them for all they had done for us. We sat outside in the garden, as we had done so many times before. That night the panoramic view from the eyrie on the hill top was obscured by a dull, overcast sky, matching our sombre mood. Neither moon nor stars were visible, and it was foreboding. I wondered if it was an omen for what lay ahead.

I could not staunch my tears and Bis held me close. He whispered words of love to console me, as he kissed them away. He promised that he would leave the country as soon as he obtained his passport.

"Please try to be happy and take care of yourself and the baby," Bis said. "I've written to Bunny and Kris to look out for you. And do not worry about money. The Dahbel House agent in London has instructions to open an account for you at Barclays Bank. All you have to do is produce your passport."

He took my hands in his. "Joan, I told my father of our marriage and the need for secrecy. It is the only way to put a stop to the endless nagging of finding me a wife. He had to know. Had I not told him, you might have heard that I'd become engaged. My older sisters were plotting to take the matter in hand."

"Was he angry? What did he say?"

"Surprisingly, it was difficult to gauge his feelings, as he had met you at graduation and then at your home with Ahmin when they picked up the reading lamp for my flat. He probably surmised as much and guessed that we were more than friends. All he said was, 'I suppose you know what you're doing. *Insha Allah,* thank God, she's of *The Book* and not a Hindu.'"

Jews, Christians, and Muslims, history relates, are all the children of Abraham.

"I suppose he's disappointed, but he accepts our marriage and wanted to know when you would join the family. He will wait until you are safely out of the country on Friday before breaking the news to the rest of the family. It was quite touching. He gave me the name of the London agent before I asked for it. However, I will not be spared the wrath of my two sisters, who'll berate me for dishonouring the family for marrying a Christian and not one of our own, and for breaking my mother's heart. Not to mention their disappointment of not being allowed to show me off and arrange my marriage. They will never appreciate that I will make my own decisions. I'll phone your father before I leave, whenever that may be."

On several occasions, Bis had met my father, who maintained that I was old enough to manage my own affairs, especially since he had left me in charge of my siblings during his term in the army.

Part One

"I've left a letter for him," I said. "He has not been himself after the war injury, and Barney's death added to his sorrow. He grew even worse since, although he still does his daily five-mile walk. He is retired and will understand the need for secrecy and my hasty departure. I didn't think it necessary to explain about the Muslim marriage. It would not matter to him anyway. He's quite irreligious and he'll tell the rest of the family."

Peggy's fiancé, Monty, was working on an assignment in Potchefstroom, and asked his brother Josie to drive Peggy and me to the train station. Monty would drive Bis, who had gone back to Potch early that morning.

That evening, the station was packed with revellers. I craned my neck looking for Bis. Amid the excitement, I had perked up, but I was concerned that I could not find him. The porter stowed the luggage and I boarded the train, fervently hoping that Bis was somewhere in the jubilant crowd.

The Blue Train was wheezing and belching smoke as the stoker heaped coal into the engine firebox, ready for departure. Bis had insisted Peggy and I travel in the luxurious Blue Train. It was his present to compensate in a small way for his absence. The train ride to Cape Town was the first leg of my journey to meet the Castle Liner bound for England. Monarchists waving Union Jacks sang, "There'll always be an England," and "Dear Old Blighty." It added to the festive atmosphere. Many were going home to celebrate the coronation of Queen Elizabeth II.

Nervously, I waited. Where was Bis? Peggy remained on the platform to watch out for him and Monty, and then she spotted them hurrying along and waved her scarf to attract their attention.

"I'm sorry we were delayed. The storm washed the road away," Monty said.

"Bis, Joan's in the fifth compartment," Peg said. Bis found me looking through the opposite window. My eyes were moist, but I smiled when I saw him. Neither of us spoke, but we held on to each other.

"Phone me as soon as you get to Cape Town."

I nodded my head, afraid I would start to cry. My resolve was to leave him with the sense that I was fine. I broke away, laughed, and said, "You be good." Later I thought, *That was an odd comment*. But we had always teased each other, for both of us were popular with the opposite sex. Bis charmed women, while I was a "tomboy." My quick repartee was a habit that was hard to break, and I often spoke without thinking!

The whistle blew signalling that the train was about to depart and Bis left me. With a shriek and a crunching sound, the train lurched forward and it was off. Peggy and I stood in the doorway and waved until our well-wishers were mere specks in the semi-darkness.

"Pegs, would you like to go to the dining car or the bar before we turn in?" I asked.

"Yes, I'd love too. Now that we're actually on the Blue Train, I intend to enjoy the luxury and comfort it offers," said Peggy.

Entering the dining car, we noticed the windows were etched in gold leaf. It was elegant beyond anything we had expected, and the soft lighting enhanced the atmosphere. A liveried maître d' welcomed us and showed us to a booth. The dining car was half full, and the soft music was incidental to the low chatter of the diners.

"I'm happy that we're here to share this night together," I said.

Peggy reminisced, "Do you remember the year we travelled to a hockey tournament in Port Elizabeth? I wanted my hair in curls. You set it with Amami setting lotion and rolled it tight, and tied a scarf to keep it in place?"

"Of course, how could I forget?"

"In the morning, some of my hair was as straight as a horse's mane and the rest of the curls looked nothing like the advertisements."

"Yes, you were furious with me, especially when our friends laughed. I didn't know what to do. I took a nail scissors and cut the straight ends off. It looked a lot better."

"It was raining when we reached Port Elizabeth. All the curl washed out, and the straggly ends jutted out in uneven lengths. I started crying. The captain of the P.E. team who met us took me to a hairdresser and I returned neatly shorn. I've thought about the incident often. Beryl thought you did it deliberately."

"I think Beryl was slightly jealous that I paid so much attention to you. You were so very young when our mother died. Do you remember why you're called Peggy?"

Peggy shook her head.

"You had a rubber piglet, and each time you couldn't find it you called out for Piggy, and as you did not answer to any other name, our nanny assumed you were saying Peggy."

"Joan, I have a confession," said Peggy. "Don't be annoyed, but Beryl and Jean used to refer to you as St. Joan, the Puritan. Beryl felt she could take care of herself, but you often told her off when she did things you thought were wrong."

"Really, whatever gave them the idea that I was a goody-two-shoes?"

"You were always so right—you broke so many rules at the convent, and you always managed to talk your way out of it. It seems odd, but despite that you always set a good example for us and Beryl hated to obey you, she said it's a wonder you weren't burnt at the stake."

"I knew my duty, and what with Gran's constant moralising, I had no choice. Besides, the last day I saw our mother, she was dying. I was too young to know that then, but she made me promise to take care of you."

"We understood. Gran always scolded you. I think mainly because you weren't afraid to answer her back."

"It's still a problem. Father says I've an answer for everything, and do not know when to hold my tongue."

"You always got your own way. I think that is what irked us. Had we done some of the things you did we'd have been punished, yet you got away with it."

"Gran was strong and she had to deal with so much sorrow. Maybe her sternness was her way of protecting us."

"Do you remember our mother? I wish I did. Everybody says you look like her."

"I wish... she was lovely. I do remember her, especially that last time I saw her on the day she was taken to the hospital. It was awful. She was only in her early thirties when she died. Barely older than I am now. We're old maids by their standards. She was married at eighteen, and both Beryl and Jean have followed in her footsteps. It's strange how the women in our family are strong—we appear to have inherited Gran's genes. I was in my teens when Barney was killed. Father seemed to fall apart after his death, and he said it was his punishment. I can't think why. I'm sure his war injury had a lot to do with that. Peg, thanks for coming. Let's finish this delightful meal. Do you want coffee?"

"No thanks. It's bedtime. Joan, I'll miss you. You will write?"

"Of course. I'll send a cable as soon as I arrive."

We returned to our compartment and found the night porter turning down the bed covers, and he had brought fresh water and orange juice. He waited to see if there was anything else we needed.

We undressed and climbed into bed. Peg said, "I love the bed. Of all the times we've travelled by train, this is the first time I'm not in a bunk. I'm sure I'll sleep like a baby. Good night, dear St. Joan."

"Good night, Pegs."

I switched off the light but did not sleep. I listened to the train clickety-clack as it rumbled along the tracks. I was comforted that Peggy had accompanied me. It took my mind off Bis and I wondered how long it would be before we were reunited. I should concentrate on having a healthy baby, I thought. I had not told anyone other than the Shapiros about my pregnancy. No need to worry Peggy at this time.

The cabin was comfortable. Magazines and the daily newspapers in both languages were provided. Each compartment was fitted with proper toilet facilities and some even had bathtubs. I was aware of the noise from the other compartments where the revellers were celebrating and singing patriotic songs. The porter had tried to silence them, but they carried on until either too exhausted or too drunk to continue. I slept fitfully, Peggy soundly.

On arrival in Cape Town, the train led directly to the boat dock. Passengers had only a short walk to the gangway and the reception area where immigration officers were stationed. The luggage was carried by porters to the ship. Peggy was met by Monty's siblings, and she introduced them to me. They whisked Peg off and promised to be back in time to have tea aboard the ship in the visitors' area before it sailed later that afternoon.

Thankfully, I passed through immigration without any problem. I settled into my cabin and found to my surprise that I would be sharing with an acquaintance from the Progressive Forum, Hanna Gill, an eccentric post-graduate philosophy student from Wits.

I went to make a phone call. There was a landline in the purser's booth and he dialled Bis's home number for me.

"What took you so long? I've been going out of my mind with worry."

"Don't scold. I'm safely aboard and already I miss you."

"My father told Mother of our marriage and that he had met you at my graduation, and also that he had visited your home with Ahmin. Mother shed a few tears and did not understand why you left for England. Ruby sends best wishes and is positive we'll be happy. She can't wait to see you again. I've not told them about the baby. But darling, how are you?"

"I'm well, only hoping I won't be sea sick. Hurry and get your passport. I'm impatient. I can't wait for you to join me."

"I've called the travel agent. They often get results quicker. Bribery, I suppose."

"I'll phone you from London..."

The phone went dead. For a brief moment, I hung onto it, then I laid it to rest in its cradle.

I returned to the deck to wait for Pegs and Monty's siblings.

"We went looking for you," said Peggy.

"Sorry, I called Bis. We were cut off before we could say good bye."

"That's a positive omen. Gran always said goodbyes are final. It's hello that's important. You'll have a chance to pick up the conversation where you left off when you do meet," Pegs added.

"This time I want to believe in her old wives' tale. Let's go to tea." My guests stayed until the bell rang announcing visitors to leave the ship.

I went up on deck and waved to my sister and friends below. The gang plank was moved and the ship's horn blasted the final farewell. Amid the bunting and flag waving, we were off. Many passengers stayed on deck waving. I stayed as well and was joined by Hanna. It was pure coincidence that we were bunking together.

"I must go down and see Mephistopheles," she said.

"Who is he?"

"You know, Faust's Black Devil. I've named my Cairn terrier after him. He's in a pen in quarantine, and he does not share my glee.

I was happy to see Hanna go. I did not share her enthusiasm for the voyage, but I was pleased that I was aboard. Overcome by wistful sadness and my memories of happier times with Bis, I derived little comfort from them. I was filled with heartache and loneliness. I wondered how long it would be before Bis and I would be reunited. My life had changed so quickly and it was still evolving. Alone, I wanted to remember and watch Table Mountain recede as the sun set. Who knew if I would see it again?

CHAPTER 27
A Sea Voyage

JUNE 1953

SEVENTEEN DAYS AT SEA, AND THE PASSENGERS ABOARD THE UNION Castle Liner, an intermediate ship, were excited to be at the end of their long sea voyage. One more day and we were to dock in Southampton, but we were informed that the ship would sail directly into the Pool of London. No explanation for the change was given. The passengers' excitement turned to anxiety as they worried how to inform relatives of the change—there was no telephone service. In the aftermath of the war, speculation was rife and stories both real and fictional circulated. The rumour spread that the port of Southampton was unsafe. It was littered with the wreckage of sunken ships washing ashore and unexploded bombs. I was among the disgruntled voyagers. My concern was how to notify Dr. Krishna, a friend whom Bis had asked to meet me. Bis had known Kris, as he preferred to be called, ever since their high school days and later at medical school. He had left for London immediately after graduation. He would be expecting me to arrive at Southampton.

The loudspeaker blared: "The Union Castle Company is providing free tickets from the Pool of London to St. Pancras Station to compensate for any inconvenience to passengers by the short notice of change."

"Joan, don't worry. Do you know where you'll be staying?" Hanna asked.

"No, I was depending on Kris."

"I'm booked to stay at Sacks-Pick Residential Hotel in Swiss Cottage, but dogs are not allowed. You're welcome to take my reservation. I'll make other arrangements. Here's the address. I'll give you a note telling them of the change."

Part One

"What will you do?" I asked.

"I'm a seasoned Londoner. Collect your luggage and we'll take the train."

"Thank you. I must call Kris and tell him about the change."

Laden with luggage, I staggered along to the telephone booth to make my call and I left my luggage beside the booth. I placed my handbag on the inside shelf and dialled Kris's number. There was no reply. I dialled the hospital where he was a senior registrar and waited for an answer, but Hanna was waving frantically for me to hurry as the last of the passengers from the ship were boarding the train. The conductor blew his whistle to signal that the train was about to leave. Hanna pointed to me and asked the porter to assist me. He rushed to my aid and collected my trunk. I only just made it in time.

"Tickets!" called the conductor. In my haste to get to the train, and to my horror, I had left my handbag on the shelf in the phone booth.

Panic stricken, I cried, "Sorry sir, I've left my bag in the telephone booth. I'll have to go back for it."

The conductor pulled the emergency cord and hurried away. Near panic, I was at a loss, but minutes later the conductor returned, "There's an emergency siding and we'll let you off there and notify the next train to take you back."

"Thank you." I was beside myself with worry. My passport, money, and other important documents were in the handbag.

Hanna scolded me, "How could you be so careless?"

"Now miss," said the conductor. "Often people coming off the boat forget things. It happens. Fortunately, today this station is reserved for the exclusive use of the ship's passengers."

I stepped down with all my luggage. I was agitated and waiting seemed like hours, although the train arrived minutes later and I was soon back at the starting point.

The kindly porter took care of my luggage while I ran to the booth, and by the grace of St. Christopher and all the patron saints that protect travellers, my bag was still where I had left it. "Thank you," I whispered, and involuntarily I made the sign of the cross as I retrieved it. I was not religious, but old habits and customs die hard, particularly when one has had a narrow escape from what might have been a disaster. This was my first foray into an unknown world, and I would learn to navigate my way. What an introduction to London! I pondered whether the incident was a portentous warning or merely a reminder to be more responsible for my actions. Unlike my husband, I was not a pragmatist, but I willed myself to remain positive and to be more careful now that I was on my own. I thanked the porter and handed him a generous tip.

"Thank you, miss. Lucky you found it."

"Yes, I dread to think if I hadn't."

On the taxi ride to Swiss Cottage, I saw the ravages of the war. In 1953, much of the city was still a mess and reconstruction was very slow. Many streets were littered with debris, potholes, and burnt-out buildings, the result of the German Blitzkrieg over London. The damage and shabby buildings were partially disguised by flags and streamers, which lent a festive air. The city make-over had begun with the preparation of tidying the inner-city route for the coronation parade of Queen Elizabeth II, which would usher in a new era.

The colourful flower stalls on street corners and at the entrances to the underground tube stations helped to camouflage the drabness. Curious, I noticed that the daily newspaper stands were left unattended with only a dish that held the coins. It was a pleasant sight, something that I could not imagine in crime-ridden Johannesburg, where the masses had little to look forward to as they scrounged by their wits to eke out a living. The British people could envisage the future to improve their lives. They deserved to celebrate after the ordeal of war. Although rationing was still strictly enforced and goods were in short supply, the hardy British made do with what was available.

Welcome to post-war London!

I was puzzled. It was midsummer, and the sun had not yet set, though according to my watch, it was past eight o'clock. I was accustomed to six hours of daylight and assumed my watch must be wrong. I checked into *Sack-Picks* residential hotel without any further problems. After the events of the day, the large attic room at the top of a three-storey house was a refuge. It was homey and inviting. Two green-leather upholstered arm chairs complemented the white-painted furniture. The linen bedspread with matching curtains patterned with pink apple blossoms and pale-green leaves completed the decor, and a colourful potted plant filled the fireplace reminding me of Gran's *aspidistra*. A clock on the mantelpiece struck the hour—nine o'clock. I noted the time.

Part One

Surely, the clock must be wrong. The bedside phone rang. I allowed it to ring, thinking it was possibly the wrong room.

A maid came in to turn down the bedcovers. "Miss, should I answer?" she said, and before I could reply she picked up the phone, answered it, and handed it to me. "It's for you, miss."

Hanna was on the phone. "Good. You're in. Did you find your bag?"

"Yes. By some miracle, it was still on the shelf where I'd left it."

"This is London. It's safe as houses. I'm glad all's well," Hanna said.

"Hanna, please what is the correct time? It's still so light out."

Hanna laughed. "There's a clock in the room. Yes, it's still light. It's daylight saving and the summer solstice in the northern hemisphere. The long twilight summer evenings are some compensation for the drabness of the shortened grey winter days to come."

"Thank you for the lesson. This is my first encounter in a northern environment. I'd forgotten all about the time change. I must adjust my watch."

"Do you like the room? I stayed there last summer."

"Yes, it's lovely. And the stairs will give me all the exercise I need."

"I'll be around tomorrow. You must come with me to visit Mephistopheles. Poor baby's in quarantine," Hanna said.

I did not have the heart to refuse her. "Good night, Hanna, and thank you for everything."

It was too late to phone Bis. I was fatigued and I climbed into the double bed with its soft eiderdown coverlet and slept soundly. I was woken by a knock at the door. It was morning.

A maid brought in a tea tray. "Miss, breakfast's served until ten o'clock in the dining room."

"What time is it?" I asked.

"Just gone nine, miss."

"Thank you, I'll be down for breakfast."

Hanna was seated when I arrived. A few elderly gentlemen were absorbed in their newspapers but looked up long enough to acknowledge my presence.

"I wouldn't miss breakfast," Hanna said. "The food's really good here. They manage in spite of the rationing. You can expect me to dine here often. And now we must go and visit Mephistopheles, poor baby. He hates quarantine."

"I'm not sure that I can this morning. I must unpack and phone Bis."

"It's too early to call SA. There's a five-hour time difference. And you've months to unpack. By the way, what will happen when you get back—the Mixed Marriages Act and all that nonsense?"

"We'll cross that Bridge if and when we get there. It's anyone's guess."

"We all thought that Michael Goldstein was your boyfriend. Either way, you'll have to adjust; if not to Jewish, then to Muslim tradition?"

"Hanna, Michael was my brother's bosom pal, and we grew up together. He was concerned for me. Anyhow, what difference does it make? None of our group is religious. We renounced it a long time ago—perhaps not formally, but in theory."

"I suppose you're right. Our crowd are all agnostic. However, the lot of you are still pretty traditional and quite parochial," said the worldly Hanna. "Naturally, you're not to blame, having been brought up in a convent where you were protected from the outside world."

"Which reminds me, Hanna, do you recall one Good Friday attending a reading by Mort? He lectured on Gogol's *Dead Souls*. That was the first time I met you. I thought, what am I doing here? A Christian girl listening to a Jew blaspheme? Remember, he used the expression 'F....ing Jesus Christ,' several times? I was shocked. That was the very first and last time that I had not fasted or gone to the ritual Good Friday three-hour service."

"Of course, I remember. He was quite crude, and he swore all the time. It was part of his usual vocabulary, that's why I broke our engagement."

"I wasn't aware that you were engaged to him."

"I was afraid of being married to him; he reminded me of my father."

Hanna became a regular visitor and engaged in conversation with the other guests, the majority of whom were wealthy German Jews who had sought refuge in England prior to the Nazi pogroms. Most of them thought that Hanna was *meshugenah*. She insisted on telling everyone that her father was a psychological killer who had murdered her mother. It transpired that her mother was in an asylum. However, I was happy for her company, for she introduced me to a London I may not have explored on my own.

A few days later, Hanna brought two dignified American ladies to lunch. "I believe you need a substitute for religion, so I brought my religious American friends," she said. "Joan, meet Bahia and Doris."

Part One

I was nonplussed.

"We're pleased to meet you. We were not aware of a luncheon invitation," said Bahia. "But Hanna insisted we come and meet you and said that you might be interested in our religion."

"Oh, that's all right, I'm pleased to meet you, and you're welcome to stay to lunch. I'll notify the desk. Hanna had told me about her meeting with you. The management are accustomed to Hanna dropping in at meal times," I explained. "Hanna has a mind of her own."

During lunch, I learned that the ladies were members of the Baha'i Faith, and they were leaving for South Africa in six weeks. They had met Hanna at a South African rally in Trafalgar Square.

"And here we are," said Doris. "Hanna told us that you would be interested in our faith, as your husband is Muslim and you're Christian. The Baha'i Faith could solve any religious problems you might encounter in the future."

"That's true, but I did not discuss religion with Hanna. She took it upon herself to predict what I ought to do. I have yet to meet my in-laws and I know little about Islam."

"Perhaps you'd care to attend one of our meetings?"

"Thank you, I'd love to, but I'll wait for my husband's arrival. I must warn you that neither of us is religious."

"I'll leave a booklet for you," said Doris.

"We have a meeting to attend this afternoon. Once again thank you for lunch," Bahia said.

I went into the garden at the back of the house and read the booklet. It was a pamphlet on progressive revelation, a basic history of religions and how they all sprang from the same source. The Baha'i's originated in Iran—Persia as it was known then. I thought *Persia* sounded so much prettier than *Iran*.

I estimated that it was a good time to call Bis in South Africa, for I had been cut off abruptly, and I asked the switchboard operator if I could make the long-distance call from my room.

"You will be billed separately for it," the operator said, and handed me a card with the instructions for all long-distance calls.

It took several tries before I got through to the overseas operator, who put me through to Bis's home number. "I thought you'd never call. Are you okay?"

"I tried several times but could not get through. I'm sick at heart, but I'm settling in. Do you remember Hanna Gill? Pure coincidence, we bunked together on the ship. Lucky for me, she introduced me to a charming Swiss Residential Hotel, though it could be expensive for a long stay. I'll write you about it."

"Don't worry about that now. If you're comfortable at the hotel, then stay there until I come. Just look after yourself and write. Contact Bunny and Kris and go to the bank. It's at 1 Cockspur Street."

"I phoned Kris and explained about the cancelation from Southampton, but I need not have worried—he had expected me to phone him on arrival and Bunny's in hospital. He's had knee surgery but is doing fine."

"Joan, I miss you. God knows when I'll get my passport. It's in the works."

"Bis, I didn't realise how hard it would be. How is your family treating you?"

"My parents and Ruby have adjusted well. The Cinderella sisters [as he often referred to them], won't forget in a hurry." We both laughed and it lightened the mood. "Send me your phone number; it will be cheaper for me to call you."

"Many things are rationed, and London's still a mess after all the Nazi bombing. I miss you and love you."

"You know I love you and miss you more than words." The second three-minute signal interrupted. "Bye." I heard the click before I could reply. It seemed so final. I held onto the phone for a moment, shutting my eyes, and trying to conjure his image. Then I sighed and put the phone down.

I spent my time in London sight-seeing and doing the tourist rounds, generally accompanied by Hanna, who claimed to eschew that pastime, but I went along with her to walk Mephistopheles when he was finally discharged from his quarantine kennel at 10 Rillington Place. It was the semi-detached house of the notorious serial murderer, John Christie. Daily, the news headlines told of the atrocities he had committed as more bodies were being identified.

Sunday afternoons at Speakers' Corner in Hyde Park were a wonderful distraction. People of diverse political persuasions vented their anger, criticizing the establishment and everything they disagreed with. It was a clever institution to deflect criticism from the government, and it was an outlet for disgruntled constituents.

Life in the bustling city accented my loneliness and I missed Bis. I was fortunate to have Bunny, who referred me to an obstetrician at Hammersmith

Post-Graduate Hospital. He also invited me to all their parties where I met many of Bis's medical school classmates. Kris, who immediately after graduation chose to do a house job in London, had stayed on to specialise in cardiology, and he declined their social invitations. He was reserved and did not appear to fit in. I found him awkward; he never seemed to be at ease, but I continued to accompany him on outings. I believed that he had a complex of sorts. I introduced him to Hanna, who referred to him as an *ersatz pukka-wallah* (English gentleman snob). In a letter, I complained to Bis, who begged me to be patient with him.

It was autumn in London, August 1953, and I sent Bis a report extolling the joy of my enchantment with the city. "It is an open and free society, where world-famous speakers and philosophers make speeches in Trafalgar Square and mix freely with the crowds who join them there. It is exciting and above all, it is enlightening.

"The music scene and the variety of concerts offered is beyond description. I love Albert Hall, but to mention all the venues would be an essay in itself. Of all the entertainment London offers, the theatre gives me the most pleasure. The variety of plays is staggering. The cultural activities will surely please you, as most were denied you in our native land. To date I've seen two plays, *Guys and Dolls* with Sinatra and Marlon Brando, and a delightful comedy, *Excuse Me, We're British*. They lifted my morale, but it will not be wise to see any more plays until you join me. However, you will be pleased that Bunny and a few of your fellow class mates have secured tickets to join them to see Agatha Christie's *The Mouse Trap* on November 25. I have not even mentioned the opera and the symphony concerts, but that will have to wait for your arrival. I imagine you attending in person, and how different it will be from listening to your records.

"The galleries are too numerous to mention. The museums fill my time and it will be my pleasure to be escorted by you. I cannot wait for you to join me, and to share the luxurious art scene. In addition, the public parks and attractions in London are simply awe-inspiring. You must hurry and come."

CHAPTER 28
A Lonely Heart through Error Forlorn

In September of 1953, Bis informed me that he had finally received a passport and had booked his passage aboard the Edinburgh Castle liner bound for Southampton. In a few weeks, we would be reunited. I was elated. He invited me to fly out to Madeira, where the ship would be calling enroute to Southampton. If I boarded the ship there, then we would enjoy four days of sailing together to Southampton. It was to be a celebration of our long overdue honeymoon. Bis hoped it would compensate for his lengthy absence and also be a well-earned rest for me before the baby arrived.

Ecstatically, I contacted Thomas Cook Travel Agency to arrange the flight to Madeira, with a request to share my husband's suite.

"As soon as I hear from the Union Castle Line, I'll issue your ticket," the clerk informed me.

Later that day, the agent called. "Madam, I'm sorry, but there's no one named Bismillah aboard. Perhaps he is booked on another ship, or under another name? However, there isn't another ship until next week."

Naturally, the news deflated me, and I phoned Kris.

"Face it, Joan, his family have prevailed. That's the reason he's not on board."

"Oh Kris, I don't believe that for a moment. There has to be a reasonable explanation. Tomorrow the agent will send another cable to their head office."

"Don't say I didn't warn you. You've no idea the trouble Muslim families will go to protect their interests. I do know that crowd."

"Kris, you're biased, and you're not being fair or helpful."

"I don't mean to be heartless, Joan. I only want you to be realistic."

Part One

"Well you've not convinced me. We'll see; you'll eat humble pie before long."

Yet despite my pseudo-confidence, my insides were churning, and being pregnant did not help. I was unfamiliar with the customs of Muslim or Indian society, and countless times Bis had warned me his family was determined to find him that suitable Indian girl to marry. He had resisted, but what if Kris was right? I dismissed the thought instantly. I had faith in Bis, and I had to try to keep calm. I toyed with the idea of phoning his home but did not wish to alarm his family in the event something indeed had happened. On the other hand, if some mishap had occurred, I was certain that Ruby, would have contacted me. There was little to do but be patient and wait until morning.

I spent a restless and disturbed night. My intermittent dreams did not reassure me and only added to my distress. I was the romantic dreamer and Bis was the practical schemer—but where was he, and what was the reason for his absence? At the first signs of daylight, I dragged my aching heart to the bathroom. I was determined to be at the travel agency as soon as they opened.

The baby began kicking vigorously. The simple task of dressing, doing up buttons, and brushing my hair fatigued me, and I stopped several times to catch my breath. Finally, I was ready. On my way out, I collected the mail and shoved it into my handbag without looking at it, and I hurried to the waiting taxi.

It was Saturday, Thomas Cook Travel Agency operated from nine in the morning until one in the afternoon; these were the normal business store hours for London.

I arrived just as the doors opened and found the clerk had sent another cablegram to the ship enquiring after Dr. Bismillah, but still there was no reply.

"I'm sorry madam, if we do not hear before we close at one p.m. then we'll not have any word until Monday."

There was little else to do but return to my flat and await the promised call. My impatience and anxiety increased, and I found it difficult to concentrate. To stop from worrying, I read and reread Bis's letters, hoping to find something that would explain the mystery. I scanned his last letter looking for a clue to his whereabouts.

Potchefstroom 8th September, 1953

My love, I can't wait for us to start our life together. I am so thankful that we found each other in spite of all the differences and obstacles that may still lie ahead. You are my light, and I'm lost without you. This separation is tearing me apart.

The good news is, Yusuf will be happy to take over the practice when I leave. Naturally, Father is not too pleased about my leaving, or for Yusuf to replace me. Father surprises me. For all his progressive ways, he still holds some ridiculous and biased illogic ideas. Our families hailed from different villages in India. After a hundred years in this country, one would have hoped that petty grievances would have been forgotten. Now see what kind of family you've married into. Please remind me if I become greedy and intolerant and forget that there's so much more to life.

Incidentally, several large grocers and confectioners are sending food parcels to London. Our newspapers report the shortages over there, so Ruby is sending some parcels to you. I told the family that provisions are still rationed in England. She hopes to remain on your good side so that you will invite her! However, Mother will not hear of her going abroad, and she refuses to understand why you had to leave the country. She hopes you will join the family soon.

Enjoy the theatre and concerts while you have a chance. There will still be much for us to see and do together once I arrive.

Incidentally, I have received my passport, and I am in the process of winding up my affairs and should be able to join you shortly.

The political situation appears to be worsening, and I cannot wait to leave.

Until then, yours as always, Bis.

The letter provided some consolation, but no clue of where he could be.

I did not hear from the agent, and my concern increased. I could barely control my rapid breathing; I was all alone and expecting my first child, and

Hanna was away on holiday on the continent. At that moment, the baby kicked as if to remind me I was not alone. I smiled wryly and decided to phone Bunny.

"Joan, try not to worry. There has to be a logical explanation for Bis's absence. I finish work at six. I'll call you then, and we can have supper. I hope you're taking care of yourself and the baby. That's very important."

"Thanks, Bunny. I'll see you later." He was reassuring, unlike Kris, who meant well but only succeeded in upsetting me. I dreaded being confined to the flat, so to while away the hours until supper, I went for a walk in Regent's Park.

The beautiful gardens, with their colourful plantings and well-kept hedges, distracted me from my troubles. I sat down on a bench watching the children racing their boats and quarrelling among themselves, as their guardians read their newspapers, occasionally looking up to check on the children. Lost in thought, I did not realise the pallid sun had disappeared and a tepid grey mist now blanketed the sky. It was soon followed by a drizzle that sent everyone scurrying in all directions. I got up and hastened to take shelter in the nearby tea room.

Waiting for my tea, I remembered the mail in my bag and found a letter with a crude scrawl I did not recognize. A wavering hand had scribbled my name and address on the envelope, but there was no return address. I thought it strange, the postage stamps were South African, and were post-marked three weeks earlier. Why had the writer not used an airmail letter? I used a butter knife to open the letter and I read it slowly, trying to make sense of the contents, but I could not. I recoiled in disgust from the repulsive thing now scrunched in my fist. I sat, staring straight ahead, incapable of any action. The writer's name was familiar, and I wondered if she were simply making mischief. However, the author mentioned a certain birthmark known to me, which appeared to confirm the veracity of her sordid tale. Could it be true? *No, it must be a lie*, I thought. Yet the evidence appeared irrefutable.

The crumpled letter fluttered as the tea tray arrived. Quickly I stuffed it away back into my bag fearful someone would learn of my husband's perfidy. I could not bear for anyone to know and pity me. Was this the reason for his absence? To be fair, I should wait to hear from him directly. I was disheartened and painfully sad, and at a loss of what to do. The baby kicked, only adding to the problem. I was stranded. How would I manage without my husband?

Where was Bis? Had he betrayed me? It was beyond all reason that he would abandon me now that I needed him. I knew it was not the end of love but of trust. I rationalised these were two different entities, and apparently Bis had violated that trust. My pulse quickened, the staccato rhythm of my breathing increased, and a searing pain like the backwash of waves roiling back to sea leaving the detritus of heartache and despair behind caused me to gasp for air.

The rain had stopped. It was a passing shower. I did not drink my tea, the panacea in times of stress, and I left some money on the table and hurried away. It was the end of summer! My thoughts were a jumble. Was the letter an omen of things to come or a metaphor for my life? At the beginning of our relationship, I knew Bis had had other girlfriends, but it had not troubled me as he said they were mere flirtations before my time.

"They were not like you, my Puritan prude. You are the ultimate romantic, and I love you for it." At the time, I had thought it rather funny. I had been so naïve. Of course, I had expected Bis to be and think like me. Little wonder he had said, "Joan, men and women are different, with different needs." I did not doubt his love for me, but I knew now I had to be more realistic. I was confused, and rationalising did not conciliate my aching heart.

It was too far to walk back to my flat, but I needed to clear my head, and so I kept on walking unaware the rain had started to fall again. Few people were on the streets, and the cars that sped by over the sodden roads hooted as they splashed, spraying water over my already wet clothes. Random thoughts flashed through my mind like the advertisements on a television screen. There were fleeting images of Bis and our times together, but they did not last quite long enough to make sense or to tell a coherent story. I continued walking. The fog in and around me thickened, and I recalled the happy times at dances, holding each other close as we swayed cheek to cheek to the romantic "Stardust," by Hoagy Carmichael, and other melodic tunes of the day.

"You really are the last of the romantic heroines, Joan of Arc," Bis had teased.

"And will I be burned at the stake? And you, Prince Charming, are far too practical for your own good," I quipped. All these thoughts only served to remind me of my problem.

Somehow, I managed to find my way home. Perhaps a guardian angel, if there were such beings, had guided me, although long ago I had become an unbeliever.

Part One

My faith in organised religion had slowly slipped away soon after my convent upbringing, which had shielded me from the harsh realities of the outside was this retribution for heresy? I was confused, and old habits die hard. I wavered; my thoughts were muddled. I dropped my wet clothes on the bathroom floor and bathed. If only the hot water could have washed away my torment.

Towelling myself off, I hesitated between anguish and hope, wanting desperately to believe that it was all a huge mistake. Bis loved me! And he was honourable. But where was he? It was unlike him not to have called, or was he guilty? Again, was I jumping to conclusions? My apprehension grew, waiting for Bunny to phone. I could not bear for him to know. Suddenly, I felt something wet trickle down my leg. *Goodness, I'm wetting myself*, I thought and went back to the bathroom. I was shocked by the blood that oozed down my thighs.

"Don't panic," I said aloud, trying to control my emotions, but I became more anxious and shivered. A trained midwife, I knew the implications of premature bleeding at twenty-eight weeks of pregnancy. I had to try to compose myself. I called the Hammersmith Post Graduate Hospital Emergency number that was posted next to the telephone at my bedside. "Obstetrical ward, please."

"Obstets here. How can I help?" said a voice on the other end.

"My name is Joan and my reference number is 07961. I'm haemorrhaging and I'm all alone."

"One moment, please, and I'll put you through."

"How much would you say? A cup full?" another voice queried.

"I can't estimate. But it's a lot and the flow is faster now."

"Joan, listen carefully. Have your bag handy, leave your door unlocked. Then lie down, elevate your feet, and wait. A midwife and a hospital car will be with you shortly."

The flow of blood alarmed me. If only the midwife would hurry. What if I started a real haemorrhage before they got to me? Was I in fact miscarrying at this stage, at the second trimester of my pregnancy? Anything was possible. I knew I had to keep calm, but I was determined not to spend the night alone in the flat.

I recalled the tragic story Gran told about Aunt Vivienne, who was found dead in a pool of blood from a miscarriage. What if the midwife was held up in London traffic? And Bis, what would he do if and when he found out? I remembered my mother and how sad I had been the last time I saw her. I was too young know then that she was pregnant. Was history repeating itself, and would I too fall victim and lose my baby?

I was thankful for the efficient British system and obeyed the no-nonsense instructions, using the bag to elevate my legs. My toiletries had been packed for an emergency ever since I got to London. Years of experience as a midwife had taught me to prepare for the unexpected. However, what it did not teach was how to control thoughts and mend a tortured heart.

Mercifully, the midwife and driver arrived and helped me into the station wagon. They made me comfortable and elevated my legs by lowering the seat. There was no time to examine me. The nurse said, "We need to get you to hospital quickly. So, no need to waste time. According to your chart, you're twenty-eight weeks pregnant."

The midwife began filling in the particulars to avoid any delay, so that I could be admitted directly to the labour ward. She was efficient and smelled of carbolic soap. I was relieved and concentrated on her to stop myself from thinking. The epaulettes on her shoulder denoted her rank. She was a staff sister. A white, stiffly-starched veil was worn high on her forehead and exposed a few grey hairs. She wore a royal-blue belt with a silver graduation buckle on her pristine white pinafore, which covered a royal-blue dress. Her sleeves were rolled up but held back by pleated white cuffs. The driver, in a lab coat, was a paramedic who smelled strongly of cigarettes, which made me nauseated.

On admission to the ward, I recognised the smell of disinfectant that camouflaged the stale smell of urine. All hospital labour wards were alike. I was put to bed and an intravenous drip was set up. The bleeding continued. On the phone, I had deliberately exaggerated the amount of bleeding. They could discharge me in the morning if the bleeding stopped. I had at least another twelve weeks before my due date. But for now, I was safe.

A doctor arrived. "How are you? I'm going to examine you." The nurse stood by while the doctor scrubbed and donned rubber gloves.

"You're in labour. However, the contractions are mild. The baby is very premature according to the dates and also its size. Please don't be concerned. Dr. Ian Donald, the paediatrician, will be in attendance. Do you feel any pain?"

"No, doctor. I'm aware of the contractions, but they're painless. Doctor Wrigley diagnosed that I have an irritable uterus that can cause premature labour. I've had the contractions for weeks."

"That accounts for it. Sister, the patient is to have complete bed rest. She needs to sleep. I'll be back to give her an injection, which ought to help."

The morphine injection caused delirium and my entire body seemed on fire. My tongue was dry and my throat was parched. The itching increased. I writhed about, gasping for breath. Two nurses held me down and I was given another injection. A nurse sponged me and applied ice packs. It helped to cool my itching body. *If only it could soothe my wounded heart,* were my last thoughts as sleep began to dull my senses. When I woke up, daylight was streaming through the blinds. I was confused and wondered where I was. And why was I wearing mittens? All I wanted was a drink of ice water.

Then I heard Bunny's voice, and in that moment, reality dawned.

"Hello sleepyhead. Joan, everything's going to be all right."

I was too dazed to respond.

"You're morphine sensitive, and the mittens are to prevent you from scratching," said a nurse. "I'll prepare you for the doctor's rounds."

The doctor's findings were a strong foetal heartbeat and moderate contractions. "Nurse, the patient is to have fluids only. Measure all intake and output and keep an eye on the drip. Monitor the foetal heartrate every half hour. Any change, however slight, call me." He turned to me. "You, my dear, must rest and try to sleep. Nurse, I want her to have another sedative."

The pethidine injection was taking effect, sending me into a somnolent daze. I drifted off as if on a cloud. Then far below, through the window, I saw giant striped bugs lazily crawling about, but why were they smoking? I fell asleep watching them. Between waking and dozing, my dreams were more muddled. My contractions were stronger, but I barely felt any pain. In my somnambulist state I mused, was I a nurse or a patient? It was all familiar, yet unfamiliar, but I could not recall much of anything or how long I had slept, or if I had slept. Unsure of my bearings, I started dozing off again but a violent spasm followed by another strong contraction jolted me. Now I was fully awake. I attempted to shift...

"Please don't worry." The nurse intervened and rang for the sister and the doctor. I felt the bed wheeling around or was I imagining it? I was whirling around and around, and then I heard Sister's voice.

"We're taking you to the delivery ward. The baby's in a hurry." All I remembered was someone putting a mask on my face covering my mouth and nose, then oblivion.

"Wake up, Joan." It was Bunny. He tousled my hair.

"Where am I?" I tried to sit up but was too dizzy and fell back into the pillows. "Bunny, what's happened about my baby?"

"Hush, it's all right. You have a son. He is healthy with a good set of lusty lungs. He is very tiny though, under two pounds. He's being cared for by Dr. Ian Donald, who is a wizard. Preemies are his specialty."

I was filled with emotion. "Will he survive? Please, may I see him?"

"No, not yet. Wait until you're well enough. They won't move him for fear of infection. And he's in isolation."

"Is there any word of Bis?" I asked.

"No, we're hoping that today, being Monday, there's sure to be some news. You must rest now. I've sent an urgent cable to the ship's purser, and I've phoned Kris."

I was beginning to feel groggy. "Bunny, what are those bugs down below? I can see them through the window."

Bunny laughed. "You're hallucinating. They're not bugs, but prisoners. Wormwood Scrubs, the famous prison, is next door to this hospital, and that is the exercise yard you see from here."

For two days I was pampered and in a dizzy state. Everyone was exceedingly kind. The effects of the sedative had not yet worn off. Bunny had told his colleagues about the missing husband, and Kris continued to be the sceptic. It had been amusing when Dr. Donald had asked, "Which of the two of you is the father? I'd like a blood sample." Both Bunny and Kris were listed as next of kin.

"Neither. Joan's our friend's wife," they blurted out in unison.

A cable arrived for Bunny on Wednesday. It was from Bis, who was aboard the Edinburgh Castle. There had been a ghastly mistake. Bis had missed the ship from Durban, and his name had been crossed off the passenger list. He then had to drive to Cape Town to catch the ocean liner there. A journey between the two ports took seven days, as the ship had to make stops along the coast at Port Elizabeth and East London. Bis's name had not been listed again. Another problem had confused the issue. Apartheid segregation laws prevented Indians from travelling in first or second class, which was reserved for "Europeans." Bis had to wait until the ship was three miles out to sea beyond South African waters where the law did not apply before he could take his place in first class.

The switchboard operator was confused by cables for Dr. Bismillah, and finally referred the cables to the purser, who confirmed that indeed there was such a person on board, and then Bis replied to Bunny's cable.

Bunny hastened to the hospital to relay the good news to me. Bis was alive and well and celebrating his son's birth with the Royal Air Force lads who were returning to England after the war. He was blissfully unaware of the drama and panic I had endured. When I did not meet him in Madeira and he had not heard from me, Bis got the impression that I had changed my mind about flying out to meet him. Not for a moment did he suspect that I had gone into premature labour.

The captain had approached Bis to apologise for the error and ordered champagne for him to share with the R.A.F. boys with whom he played table tennis and snooker.

I burst into tears.

"It's time to rejoice. Don't cry," said Bunny. "Bis will be here tomorrow."

I touched his hand. "Bunny, you're such a good friend. Thank you."

"Come, come. Dry your tears. We'll celebrate as soon as you're discharged. Do you remember when we worked together at Bridgman Memorial? I tried to date you. I didn't know then that you were Bis's girlfriend."

"Yes," I laughed, glad for the distraction.

"That's better. Actually, Bis is so private he never let on that he knew you until that day at our graduation."

"Thank you for everything, Bunny."

I was alone with my troubled thoughts, grateful that Bis was safe, but how would I react to our reunion? I was distressed. Even the birth of our baby had not eased my tormented soul. I longed to see and hold my child, but that was not permissible—for his own sake, the poor baby was deprived of his mother and would have to wait.

Later Kris popped in to see me. "Congratulations on two counts."

"Thank you, Kris. No need to remind me. I believe you only tried to prepare me in case things turned out differently."

"I should've had more faith, but I do know how those people think. We go back a long way. But Bis is a gentleman. He is different."

"Is he? He arrives tomorrow."

"I can't stay, but good luck and get well soon. Oh, what will you call the baby?"

"I'll wait to hear what Bis has to say."

Kris was already out the door.

A nurse brought in a breakfast tray. "You must eat. We need to establish your milk. You cannot breastfeed baby directly, but the baby will be bottle fed on your expressed milk. And we do have a fair supply of milk from wet-nurses," she said.

I had no appetite. I requested a bath.

"Good. I'll help you after you've had at least a glass of milk," Nurse ordered. I felt grubby. I needed to cleanse myself. If only it could wash away the turmoil that raged within. I thought of all the confessions I had gone to as a girl, and I wished that there was someone to confide in. The bath was refreshing, and I changed into my negligee and dressing gown. My hair was a mess, but that could not be helped. Nurse offered to brush it, and I accepted thankfully. I was tired, and I knew it was emotional not physical. I could not concentrate on the magazines and climbed back into bed. I needed to sleep. It was the first time since I'd been admitted that I fell into a quiet, drug-free sleep.

I was woken by a tap on my shoulder. I opened my eyes and squinted.

"Yes, darling it's me," Bis said. He bent down and folded me in his arms.

I was speechless, and as the tears welled up Bis held me close and kissed me for the longest time. "I'm taking you home today."

Bunny entered with Sister and said, "You will be discharged into my care."

"But what about the baby?" I asked.

"The baby will stay here until he is and bigger and stronger," said Bunny.

"Please, may I see him before I go?"

"No. The hospital practice is to keep preemies completely isolated. You know how concerned we are about cross-infection," Bunny said.

Part One

I nodded.

Soon, an orderly wheeled me to a waiting cab. I had moved into Hanna's flat while she had gone on holiday for the duration of the summer. Bunny helped Bis move my things from the flat back to *Sacks-Pick*. He had decided that it was the best option until we made other plans.

My return to Sacks-Pick was welcomed. I had made friends with the older residents, who were disappointed that there was no baby to fondle, but they presented the baby clothes they had stitched from their own silk clothing. My old room was ready with fresh flowers and Hanna had sent a card wishing me *Mazel Tov*.

We were alone, and Bis took me in his arms. "I thought this day would never come." With my head on his shoulder, he nuzzled my ear as of old.

I was passive and I could not respond.

"Joan, what's wrong?" Tears were streaming down my cheeks, and he hugged me close. "Darling, please tell me what's wrong. I'm here now."

We had always been honest with each other. It was impossible for me to lie now. All attempts to speak were futile. No sound came. Shivering, I sighed and left his embrace. I fetched my handbag, gave him the crumpled letter, and then buried my face in my hands and flopped into the arm chair. The clock ticked away incidental to my muffled sobs, which were punctuated by the odd stifled hiccup.

Bis leaned against the mantelpiece and read the note. I heard him tear it. He threw it into the fireplace and in a stride was beside me, his arms around me. "Oh Joan, what have I done? Speak to me."

I was unable to find words. I was an emotional wreck, in pieces like that letter he had just torn. I felt lifeless and empty. The dinner bell interrupted us and simultaneously, there was a knock at the door. Bis got up to answer.

"Mrs. Pick thought you would prefer a tray," said the maid.

"Thank you," Bis said and took the tray.

I continued to hide my face in my hands, but I had stopped crying.

Bis spoke, "Please, Joan. Can we talk? There is so much I need to tell you. Yes, I made a horrible mistake, which I will regret forever. I believe our love can withstand the dreadful pain I've caused you. I am sorry for the manner in which you found out."

I found my voice. "There is nothing to say. We have to live with the consequences." I went to the bathroom and washed my face. After a while, I came out and said, "Please, eat your supper."

Bis was about to speak, but I silenced him. "No Bis, I love you and I always will. The timing and the shock was destructive. There is no need to explain. Anything you say will not repair the damage. In time, I will heal. The scars will remain, a testament to your betrayal. I could have dealt with your having a second wife, one chosen for you by your family because you would have been honouring their wishes, and we had deceived them. But this was all your doing. You betrayed my trust. I was taught that a confession brings absolution and wipes away the sin. I cannot absolve you, but I have to forgive you in order to get on without bitterness. Together we have a delicate child to rear."

Etched in my mind was the experience of losing a parent, and it was a lesson I did not want my child to bear. I remembered my younger sisters who were even more vulnerable than I was. I knew my duty, and the choice was mine. I had had my say, and there would be no further discussion nor confrontation. I was not prepared to hear his excuses or any explanation that would expiate his behaviour. His betrayal was something he would have to live with and resolve without my absolution. I had been wounded, and I needed time to recover. Time, I knew, was a healer, and I would try to forget. Our love had been tarnished, but it was deep and abiding. Despite my anguish, it had to be cherished and nourished with all its flaws. I recalled my father's dictum about things happening for good reason—what was the lesson here?

CHAPTER 29
A Stateless Baby

FEBRUARY 1954

First thing each morning, I called the premature unit regarding my baby. Daily he gained an ounce or two. I had been allowed to see him only once, when he was a month old, and then from behind a double-glass screen, where he slept undisturbed. How I longed to hold and cuddle him. Every precaution was taken to protect him from infection. We named him Enver. At four months old and weighing five pounds, it was time for his discharge from the hospital, but his doctors were not prepared to let him out into the black smog that enveloped the city. The predicted forecast for London was a lengthy unpleasant winter, and the worst pollution since the war years.

"For Enver to thrive, he will need a warm climate and lots of fresh air," Dr. Ian Donald ordered. Bis and I knew the logical solution was to return to South Africa, where our infant son would have a chance for a healthy life. We were excited to have him, and although we had received a daily progress report, we had not been allowed to visit our baby while he remained in hospital. The doctors were afraid he would contract an infection. I had only seen him for the second time when he was three months old, and it was still not possible to hold or cuddle him. That was not to be, as any exposure to infection would set him back.

Weighing five pounds, Enver was finally discharged into our care, with instructions from Dr. Ian Donald: "He is part of our research on premature infants, and you need to chart his progress for the next seven years, and I would appreciate a written annual report."

We had no choice but to return to South Africa, land of sunshine and abundance, but devoid of our political freedom, we'd have to confront the political implications and the consequences that awaited us. Our son's health was of paramount importance.

The South African Embassy had refused to register the baby or even to grant him a visa to enter the country. He was considered an Indian and therefore an alien. Baby Enver had to apply for immigration like any other Indian. I appealed to my friend, the young Afrikaans dominie, Dr. Chris Gray, who at the time was a visiting pastor to the embassy staff at South Africa House in Trafalgar Square. Prior to Bis's arrival, I had met Dr. Gray and his charming wife Anna at the weekly coffee sessions I attended on Wednesday mornings. There I read the newspapers and magazines, and enjoyed the luxury of hot drinks, South African pastries, and fresh fruit, as rationing in England was still strictly enforced and almost everything was in short supply.

Soon we developed a friendship, and I discovered that Dr. Gray was an alumnus of Potchefstroom University. He knew the Bismillah general store, Dabhel House. I explained that I was unfamiliar with the Bismillah family, but that I was married to one of their sons, a medical doctor. Since my husband was Indian, the South African Embassy was not prepared to register my baby's birth. The official explained, "The law states that any child born of Indian parents outside the Union of South Africa is not entitled to citizenship. They are aliens and must apply for landed immigrant status."

Dr. Gray was sympathetic and offered his help. He was one of a few liberal Afrikaners whose attitudes towards Indians was beginning to change. "It is imperative for the child to be in a warm climate with his parents, who are South African citizens," Reverend, Dr. Gray, pleaded with the authorities. His intervention secured a temporary visa for our baby to travel to South Africa, and we would approach the authorities on reaching Cape Town.

The climate in South Africa varies, but Johannesburg, six thousand feet above sea level, is more temperate—it is warm and sunny, precisely what Dr. Donald had ordered for his charge. Bis and I deemed the law concerning our illegal marriage secondary to the well-being of our child. Our only option was to fly back.

The African states including Niger, Mali, Sierra Leone, Ivory Coast, and Ghana were opposed to South African Apartheid, and they barred all aircraft from flying across their territories, thus forcing planes to fly around the bulge of the Sub-Saharan African continent. It was a Yellow Fever Zone, and anyone who travelled there was required to be inoculated against the disease.

Bis, baby Enver, and I were inoculated, but Enver unfortunately had an adverse reaction to the inoculation and developed encephalitis. He was readmitted to hospital just four days after his discharge—his condition was critical. We were very anxious and even more concerned, and it did not help that Bis, a doctor, was familiar with the complications that were possible. But Dr. Ian Donald once again came to the rescue. He drained all the fluid from the soft fontanelle on the baby's head and saved his life. Enver remained in isolation under careful supervision for the next two weeks before the stitches on his head were removed and he was deemed fit to be discharged. Considering his medical history, the doctors claimed his recovery was miraculous. Dr. Ian Donald prescribed a daily dose of phenobarbital to keep him sedated for the following six weeks. Enver was prohibited from travelling by air to avoid another inoculation. Thus, I was obliged to embark on the long sea voyage with my baby. Bis travelled back by air, and he recalled his earlier experience travelling with the Union Castle line.

"It is wiser for you and Enver to travel without me. You will be spared the indignity of being separated once we reach South African waters."

Bis flew to Johannesburg to prepare for our arrival in Potchefstroom.

The fresh sea air, a six-month's supply of baby formula, and the supply of phenobarbital, courtesy of the British National Health system, helped the fragile infant. He was a model baby, who had been well trained after his long stay in hospital. It was just as well, for he resented being picked up. A paediatrician on board assured me that being a preemie, the medication was precisely what the baby needed. The voyage was uneventful.

The three-week voyage at sea had put distance between Bis and myself, and it was relaxing. With little to do, it was a time for introspection and reconciliation. I had arrived in England, barely eight months ago, a naïve, expectant young woman promising myself never to return to South Africa. How ironic, I was *enroute b*ack to my starting point, but I was filled with apprehension and worry. How would immigration officials deal with our child? And how would we be received by Bis's family?

As the ship neared the Cape of Good Hope, noted for its rough seas, all was quiet. I stood on deck and was awed by the sight of the majestic Table Mountain as it came into view. Silken white cloud covered the mountain, giving it the appearance of a table top with its pristine white cloth. Now, in the early morning light, the ocean shimmered and it was unusually calm as the ship approached the harbour in Cape Town. All was still, but my heart throbbed. I recalled that less than a year ago, a forlorn young woman had departed these shores, not knowing when or if she would ever return. Now an anxious young mother stood and viewed the scenic wonder in all its grandeur, her pain receding into the background. On board ship, I had had the time to contemplate my situation. I wondered if my life was to be one of constant upheaval and separation. I knew I would cope regardless of any problems that impeded my path.

On our arrival, the immigration officials boarded the ship. I had no difficulty entering the country. The baby's document, a temporary visa issued by the South African Embassy, allowed him to travel, but the officials rejected it at the port of entry, and he was refused admission into South Africa. My marriage to an Indian prohibited my child from obtaining a passport. He would have to apply for immigration. I thought, *How ridiculous! He's my baby.* I was frustrated and suddenly exhausted by all the red tape, but I knew the cause was emotional. I had to be practical and keep my wits about me. "What am I to do?" I asked.

The officers conferred with each other. *"Ons sal die papier teken, behalwe sy twintig pont vir elk gee."* (For £20 each, then we'll stamp the child's papers.)

That is blackmail and bribery, I thought. It was outrageous and corrupt, something that I railed against. Conceding to their demand would be an admission of guilt, and I feared that it would come back to haunt me. "I won't give you a farthing!" I protested.

"So, you do understand Afrikaans?"

I ignored the comment.

"Well, in that case, you will have to travel on to Durban and deal with immigration there."

Travelling to Durban entailed another week at sea. More time to speculate.

I went ashore to phone Bis. "We have a problem. Enver is not allowed off the ship, and a nurse has been provided to watch over him in the event I try to smuggle him into the country. We have to sail to Durban and apply there for Enver to have permission to immigrate into the country."

"Oh darling, I'm sorry. Don't worry, I'll have a lawyer meet you there."

"They offered to take a bribe, but I refused. I suppose had I accepted, the complication might have been avoided, but I couldn't trust them because that would have played into a fraudulent scheme. Then who knows where we'd end up?"

I returned to the ship and was amazed by the hundreds of Cape Malay Muslims chanting and blocking the gangway. The ship was about to sail. The crowd swelled and the noise was deafening. Sailors used fire hoses to spray the people in order to clear a path to the gangway so that we passengers could embark.

Later, at dinner, we learnt that an eminent Cape Malay Imam and his entourage were on their way to Pilgrimage in Mecca. The crowd had been there to wish them Godspeed.

"Why are they not at dinner?" queried a passenger.

"Because they are coloured Cape Malays and have a separate dining room downstairs."

Welcome home, I mused. A dictum of Apartheid was that every racial group was carefully designated and placed with their own kind. The coloured community in the Cape Province had been entitled to vote, but that was now rescinded under Apartheid.

The journey to Durban entailed another week of worry and uncertainty. I was reminded of my father and the stories he told of his family who emigrated to South Africa, and the lesson regarding milestones. "Adversity makes one stronger," he told me. "Always look for the positive aspect in any set-back." This was my final chance for introspection and to come to terms with my husband's infidelity. The added week on board had been more time for reflection, and whatever Bis was guilty of could not be allowed to interfere with how we brought up our child. I resolved to put his entire affair behind me. Our love for each other would help to cement our future without bitterness. I was wiser for the painful experience, and I had grown in strength. My decisions now were not those of the starry-eyed girl, but of a mature parent. Together we would confront the urgent problems that were waiting to be addressed.

After stops in East London and Port Elizabeth, the ship reached Durban. The weather was hot and steamy, which did not improve my morale. My battle with the authorities was about to begin all over again. The ship pulled into port and all the passengers disembarked.

"Madam, you are free to go ashore, but the baby is a foreigner and must remain on board until we receive clearance from Pretoria. The nurse will take care of him until his papers are sorted out," said the officials. I had to remain calm and allow the lawyer, who was waiting at the dock as Bis had promised, to act on my behalf. I went ashore to phone my husband.

"Bis, I'm so tired of the whole affair. I'm sorry we came back," I said.

"What a bloody mess. Are you all right, Joan? Try not to worry. How is the baby?"

"He is so good. The motion of the ship lulls him to sleep."

"Make sure that he is not too hot and dehydrated, Durban is very humid."

"The daily dose of phenobarbital prescribed by Dr. Donald keeps him drowsy. He has to be woken for his feeds. I wish you were here."

"Much as I'd like to be with you, you know it will only antagonise the authorities. You realise their enmity towards us *verdomde koolies*. Damned koolies. That's their opinion, especially if we're educated."

"I'm outraged by their stupid prejudicial laws. It is difficult not to become bitter," I said.

"I can't wait to be with you. Listen to the immigration lawyer, and I promise everything will work out. The family is eager for you to join us. My two sisters, who live in Durban, will meet you. Sadik, my younger brother, will drive you back to Potchefstroom."

"I'm not sure which I dread more, the authorities, or meeting your sisters."

"I know you're anxious, but do not worry. The family will like you. Father has reassured them that he liked you. You have the best legal counsel. Take care of our precious son. My older sister Maryam's son, Rashid, drove down with Sadik. He will be attending high-school in Durban."

"Good, I'll look out for him."

The lawyer met me and we discussed the baby's case with the immigration officials on board. It was more complicated than I had anticipated. The lawyer posted a bond, and urgent phone calls were made to Pretoria asking for temporary asylum for the alien child.

Several hours passed before permission was finally granted to allow Enver to enter the country. He had slept peacefully, unaware of the trouble his birth had caused. I was to experience first-hand how the freedom of Indians was curtailed now that I had a child with an Indian father. Another permit was required to allow the infant to travel from Natal to the Transvaal, because a law prevented Indians from travelling freely between the four provinces without permits.

These permits had to be signed by a magistrate at the local police station each time an Indian left the province, and on his return, it had to be returned to the local police station. The permits were limited to a six-week stay and had to be renewed if the visit lasted longer.

The inconvenience and the cost of travelling between provinces was a constant worry, so Indians found a way to subvert the law. A simpler method was to pay a bribe to a clerk, but as many found, it was an unreliable chance. The Apartheid system, with all its petty rules and regulations, fostered corruption. Clerks and officials expected to be paid off.

Despite the order to leave immediately for the Transvaal, I was too exhausted. I spent the night in Durban getting to know my brother- and sisters-in-law and the young nephew. I felt foolish for being the cause of all the trouble. Little wonder Bis's sisters were opposed to their brother's choice of a bride. However, I was welcomed to a special dinner prepared by my sister-in-law. They were hospitable, but I sensed a certain antipathy. I was, after all, a foreigner. I deemed it a minor problem; I was not inimical and resolved to make every effort to fit in.

I found Rashid quietly sitting alone in an outer room of his aunt's house. He appeared lost and sad. I sympathised and spent time reassuring him that his Uncle Bis had experienced precisely what he was feeling, and that in the end it would all work out.

"You will benefit from your experience in Durban. The best way to offset your homesickness is to apply yourself to your studies, join the various sports clubs, and make friends," I advised.

"I'm worried about renewing my permit," Rashid said.

I assured him that it would be all right and said, "Don't worry, the aunties will take care of it."

I told my sister-in-law that Rashid was concerned about his permit. She said, "It was fairly simple. He has a travel permit from the Transvaal. He will mail it back to his parents, who will return it to the local police station, giving the impression that he had returned home within the allotted time. Then at the end of the school year, his parents will again apply for a travel permit for him to travel to Natal and back again. Thus giving the impression that he made two trips to Natal."

I was astonished, and the reality dawned that under the law, Enver was classified Indian, and thus, even though he was a baby, he was already subject to the law. I had just experienced it first-hand.

The following morning, Sadik drove me and the sleeping baby to Potchefstroom. After the long voyage and bureaucratic problems, I was finally able to relax in the car. The eight-hour drive gave me an opportunity to make the acquaintance of my brother-in-law—a quiet, reserved, charming young man. We stopped once at a petrol station and I observed how years of conditioned racism altered the behaviour and attitude of people of colour towards Europeans. Just moments before, I had been engaged in a lively conversation with my intelligent travelling companion, who suddenly became obsequious in the presence of a white man. It was *Ja Meneer* and *Nee Meneer*, as he bowed his head, politely answering the garage attendant. I had observed this servile tendency as soon as I stepped off the boat, where the baggage carriers and dock workers were mainly Indian, and I saw the deference with which they treated Europeans. The native Africans were allotted the more menial tasks, and they were treated with disdain.

After my sojourn in London, my perspective of the country had not altered—if anything, it was more acute. The political climate had worsened. Apartheid was sinister and added to the hostile and divisive structure of the country. I was about to embark on a new life without recrimination or bitterness, and together with Enver and Bis, whom I loved, we would find our way.

I had matured, and many years later in hindsight, I concluded that I had fostered an unrealistic notion of "romantic" love, which I attributed to my Puritan upbringing. However, ingrained as it was, I was incapable of differentiating

Part One

between sex and love; to me they were one and the same. People, mostly men, strayed given the opportunity, and they differed from women. I had placed Bis on a pedestal. That was my doing. My absence, due to the lengthy separation, the pressures of the practice, and the constant surveillance in the police state had deprived us of a normal married life, and in my absence, Bis had strayed. My revenge was refusing to listen to any excuse he might offer, and that was his punishment. Had I been unfair?

CHAPTER 30

Down the Rabbit Hole

The sun was sinking over the western horizon, and my courage with it. My baby slumbered peacefully as Sadik drove along the last stretch of the highway. It would be nightfall before we reached the town of Potchefstroom. My feelings of uncertainty and apprehension increased, while my silent companion concentrated on the road ahead. I was lost in a myriad of anxious thoughts wondering how I would be received as a daughter-in-law. What would life be like in an Afrikaner town with a relatively small Muslim community? Would I fit in? Would this be an end or a new beginning in my search for identity? I could only wonder as the car suddenly came to a halt.

Sadik parked in front of a garden gate, where Bis was pacing to and fro. On sighting the car, Bis rushed over. Barely giving me time to alight, he folded me in his arms. "Darling, I've missed you. Where's our baby?" he said, holding me firmly.

"Asleep in the hammock you sent." Despite all Bis's assurances, it was with trepidation and angst that I arrived at my new abode tired, not looking my best after the long car ride, and wondering what kind of impression I would make.

The historic town of Potchefstroom was very different from the splendour of London, and I felt as though I had fallen down the rabbit hole. Like Alice, I found myself immersed in a world of diverse realities with an interesting cast of supporting characters. There were the minority Muslim Indians with their social and cultural mores, to whom I would owe my allegiance, then the condescending governing Afrikaners and the smaller Jewish community of professionals, doctors, dentists, lawyers, and businessmen. The location opposite the

Part One

Indian area was where the coloured community resided; they were people of mixed origin, neither black nor white, but more black than brown. Finally, there was the subservient black majority.

I was back in South Africa, fully aware of all the adjustments I would have to make. Bis's parents and Ruby were waiting to welcome the baby and me. I had envisaged our first encounter during the lengthy sea voyage, but I had not expected the warm welcome that awaited me. Bis handed the sleeping baby to his mother, who hugged Enver to her breast and whispered a prayer into his ear. He woke up startled and emitted a soft cry. I handed Ruby the bottle with his special formula. She was eager to hold and to change him, but my-mother-in-law insisted on attending to the baby herself.

To my surprise, I felt at ease, and my apprehension was replaced by curiosity. Bis and Ruby had paved the way for me, and my in-laws had received me into the family. The thought crossed my mind, *so, this is my new beginning*. Living in the parochial Muslim Indian community and in a segregated non-European enclave would be a new experience. I recalled the same discomfort when as a girl I went into the convent. This was the world to which I was committed. I was no stranger to divisive race relations, and Bis had warned me that in the small town it was all-pervasive and unduly harsh; the non-white population was politically subdued.

Amina, my mother-in-law, spoke little English, but she was fluent in Afrikaans. I did not speak Gujerati, her native tongue, so we conversed in *Die Taal* Afrikaans, the second official language of South Africa. It was spoken in most rural towns in the Transvaal, and in the Orange Free State. It was the usual language of communication between masters and servants.

We were welcomed by the other family members. My father-in-law, Mohamed, remembered meeting me at Bis's graduation. He was a wiry man, who grasped and held my hand firmly in his bony one. Gandhi-like in appearance, he seemed to inspect me through his wire-framed spectacles. I soon learnt that he was a man of few words. He did not tolerate fools easily, but through pursed lips he uttered the few often scathing words that had the intended effect, and he always managed to have his way. On my first meeting with my mother-in-law, Amina, she smiled and welcomed me and her luminous brown eyes met mine as she acknowledged me. In her clenched palm, she clasped a string of beads, a *tasbi*, akin to a rosary, and she wore a head-scarf, signalling a pious, devout woman. I formed the impression that her large shawl appeared to be her refuge, a protection and her compromise in the foreign world she had been compelled to adapt to. I realised that I too would have to adjust to a culture foreign to me, but I was confident that with Bis's support I would manage. My meeting with Maryam, Bis's eldest sister, showered me with loving kindness and welcomed me into their midst. Sadik's wife Nafisa was very pretty, charming, and shy, but she welcomed me. Ahmin, the eldest son, was out of town. His wife, Ayesha, was reserved and quiet and she hugged me. Bis's two older sisters, whom I had met in Durban upon my arrival, had been cordial but restrained in their acceptance of me. Thus, my warm welcome into the family was all the more surprising.

The weather in Potch was sunny and warm, precisely what Dr. Donald had ordered, and Enver thrived under the supervision of his doting grandmother. His morning bath became a daily ritual. She massaged his tiny limbs with fragrant medicinal oils, stretching them and praying as she nursed him with loving hands. Enver's long stay in hospital had resulted in a well-trained baby who seldom cried. My mother-in-law fed him morsels of chicken, rice, and vegetables ground in her bony fingers, along with freshly squeezed orange juice and mashed papaya. She burped and cuddled him before laying him down on a silk eiderdown on top of a kilim rug, where he slept until woken for his next feed. I remained a spectator at these proceedings, but I was thankful for the tender love she bestowed on my infant son.

My first impression of Potchefstroom presented a facade of a clean, orderly, law-abiding Afrikaner colonial town. The picturesque country town had an Afrikaans university and a huge military base. Potchefsrtoom was simply referred to as Potch by the residents, the name derived from Potgieter, one of the leaders of the "Great Trek" of the group of dissatisfied Boers who fled in ox wagons from British domination and founded their own *dorp* or small town. Potch was the cornerstone of endemic racism, the cradle of Afrikaans orthodoxy and the heart and soul of Afrikaner Dom; a place like no other in the Union of South Africa, which consisted of four provinces: The Cape, Natal, Orange Free State, and the Transvaal.

I steeped myself in the history of Potchefstroom. It was necessary to understand now that I was to be a part of this netherworld. I recalled my history lessons at the convent. Afrikaners were the descendants of French Huguenots and Dutch settlers of the Dutch East India Company, who went in search of a sea route to India. They landed in Natal on Christmas Day, hence the name, and started a halfway station that would serve to replenish their supplies of fruit, especially lemons, which they had discovered helped to combat scurvy, a common plague of sailors in those far-off days. Later, in 1652, they established a colony at the Cape of Good Hope. It was fortunate, I thought, that they had settled and formed a colony there. Little more than two hundred years later, my father's family and scores of Europeans arrived there as well. The Dutch farmers, or Boers, as they came to be known, were dissatisfied living under British Colonial rule. They detested the English and wanted to be rid of the yolk of British dominance. Their only option was to flee the Cape and they were known as *Voortrekke*rs, or the front runners. In 1834-36, they migrated north in search of land and a new home.

The Boers' march northward, known as *The Great Trek,* was marked by violent clashes with the vast marauding Bantu Impis (indigenous blacks), who were moving south and this resulted in the two *Kaffir Wars*. The spear-wielding Bantu Impis were no match when pitted against the superior firearms of the *Voortrekkers,* who defended themselves from within a ring of ox wagons, makeshift fortresses called *laagers.*

The victorious *Voortrekkers* were greatly outnumbered. They gave thanks and praised Jehovah, who they believed had delivered them from the black hordes. Imbedded in the Afrikaner psyche was the idea of righteousness and entitlement. In gratitude, the *Voortrekkers* established the settlement of Potchefstroom along the banks of the Mooi River, a tributary of the Vaal River. It is incongruous that the grey, greasy river was named *Mooi,* an Afrikaans word for pretty.

However, the Boers still had to contend with British Imperialism in the province of Transvaal, which led to further conflict over ideology. In 1895, under the leadership of General Paul Kruger, Afrikaners fought for their independence in the First Anglo-Boer War. Their victory was short-lived when later they faced the entire British Commonwealth, including Canada, in the Second Boer War, which ended in 1902. The result was a stinging defeat from the British and her colonies. Many were captured and horror stories abound of their treatment under the British. It was reported that they were kept in work camps with barely sufficient food to subsist on, and their feelings of loss and hatred festered. Simultaneously, the gold and diamonds that were discovered were controlled by the British and added to their grievances. Over the course of a century, Afrikaner hatred toward the British escalated and their antipathy turned to bitterness.

As a sop to the Boers, the genial, esteemed Afrikaans leader *Oom Paul*, as he was affectionately known, was consulted on whether Potchefstroom should become the capital of the Transvaal, a proposal he rejected. Like many Afrikaner leaders, he had a limited formal education but was schooled on the Bible. He reasoned that the Afrikaners who traced their origin to the Voortrekkers were as bull-headed as the oxen that pulled their wagons. He said, "*Soo gemaak, en soo gelaat staan*." Roughly, the sardonic remark meant that they were stubborn creatures of habit and incapable of change.

Many decades later, after World War II, the Afrikaners had their ultimate revenge; they won a general election in South Africa in 1948, which witnessed the rise of the Afrikaner Nationalist Party that spawned Apartheid, and ultimately, the cessation of the Union of South Africa from the British Commonwealth in May 1961.

The pious Afrikaners traced their religious beliefs back to the Dutch Huguenots, who had been expelled from France. Holland accepted the Protestants, but finally they were sent to form the halfway station in Natal on the sea route to India.

All three branches of the Dutch Reformed Churches exercised a powerful influence over their congregations. They believed that Jehovah created blacks as creatures, not fully human and lacking brains, and that they were to be subservient to the will of the *Herren Volk*, who were God's People. They agreed on the literal interpretation of the Bible. Blacks were created to be the "hewers of wood and drawers of water."

Potchefstroom was the template for Apartheid. Social intercourse between whites and non-whites was limited to a master-servant relationship. The economy was dependant on cheap black labour, and consequently, blacks all over the country were forced to live in locations that were situated well beyond the town limits, without the conveniences taken for granted in privileged white communities.

Part One

The bloated Potch mayor boasted, "We have always lived separately from the blacks and Asiatic. We have kept them in their place. Residentially, they are confined to their own areas, except for one or two Indian and Chinese families who still live behind their shops in town. Soon, they too will be ordered to move."

One of the first things that drew my attention was how this small Indian community, ghetto-like yet divided from within, had migrated from different regions in India and were bound by their common religion, Islam. They spoke almost the same dialects and shared most of the same customs but were split into two groups: Memon and Surtee. Each group adhered to its own distinct social code. The schism may be attributed to the caste system of the sub-continent. To an outsider, it was impossible to tell any difference, for they were tolerant of each other, but an undercurrent of tension existed. Inter-marriage was discouraged. It was puzzling that so many decades later, petty distrust of the other still persisted. Apartheid bolstered prejudice, and unwittingly, the Indians complied with the enforcers of Apartheid.

History taught that the Indians were entrenched in their ancient lore and the caste system, which subscribed to a form of hierarchy that was exacerbated under British rule.

The Muslim community was fascinated by the "Christian foreigner" of mixed heritage who had married their most eligible bachelor. I piqued their curiosity by adopting the sari, the traditional Hindu dress, in place of the usual salwar kameez that Muslim women wore. The sari was trend-setting and preferable to my Western outfits, as it eased my entry into my new environment.

The women regarded me a welcome addition, especially the nosey Memons, who inundated me with invitations to their homes. Bis, a Surtee, was highly amused, for the Memons were more orthodox and confined than the slightly more Westernised Surtees. It was a source of amusement to me that wealth, good looks, and degrees of skin colour were endless topics of discussion among the Indian women.

There were strange characters and an unusual number of physically and mentally handicapped people in the small Indian community. Bis speculated that decades of family inter-marriages were the reason for the high incidence of abnormalities. There was the young unkempt woman who wandered around unescorted at night whenever she could steal away. During the day, she followed me whenever she saw me and demanded to hold the baby, who she claimed was hers. *Mal* (Mad) Sara appeared harmless, but children made fun of her, and she pelted them with stones.

I had to accustom myself to the odd nicknames of many of the people. One was a cousin. His name—*Tjoek-nie-kop*—implied he had a nail in the head, meaning that he was not quite all there. A neighbour's son was a deaf mute named Flying Cockatoo: a strange young man who wrung his hands constantly and vaulted over fences. He would make himself comfortable on people's *stoeps* (verandas) at four o'clock when they were having tea.

My introduction to the Afrikaners in Potch was an eye-opener. They were unlike their city counterparts I had known in Johannesburg. In the main, they were polite, but their white status allowed them to ask me intimate and sometimes insulting questions without batting an eyelid. One afternoon, I visited the store and was accosted by an inquisitive farmer's wife, who asked, *"Hoe kan jy met koelies woon?"* (How can you live with koolies?). The disdainful Afrikaners referred to me as *daarie wit koelie* (that white koolie) and did not hesitate to ask, "How could you, a *Christian*, marry a koolie?" These privileged whites felt entitled, took the liberty of questioning me, and had no idea that they were being rude.

Often, when Indians referred to Afrikaners as *Boers*, the term invariably had a pejorative undertone. Afrikaners were generally civil towards Indians, especially when they bargained for a discount at Indian stores, and their love of Indian food did not prevent them from asking for it. The Indians always obliged with ingratiating and obsequious smiles. From across the hedge of my in-law's house, I witnessed an odd exchange between an Afrikaner who stood on the neighbour's front doorstep. The owner emerged carrying an Indian stew pot and handed it over. In his other hand, he held a pastry. The man grabbed the pastry, took a bite, and said, *"Got,* koolie, did you wash your hands?" Not waiting for an answer, he gobbled the *samosa,* a savoury pastry filled with minced chicken, and left without a word of thanks.

The neighbour spotted me, and he waved and said, "He's a very good customer."

CHAPTER 31
Bis sets up a Medical Clinic

Bis's medical practice grew, due in part to his being the only non-European doctor in Potch. He started at nine each morning, coming home for lunch. After lunch, before returning to the office, he made house calls in the location. I often accompanied him to acquaint myself with his work. Here I witnessed the lives of black people. I was intrigued by the pride they took in their lowly mud and tin shanties, and those who could afford it had brick homes. They mixed cow dung with the red clay soil into patties, which were placed on the tin roofs to dry in the sun. The paste was smeared over the floors, where it acquired a smooth sheen like linoleum. People claimed that the mixture had the added effect of a disinfectant.

I knew Bis had a phenomenal memory, but I was surprised that he did not make notes, and after making dozens of house calls he would return to the office to record every detail of every patient, including the date, each patient's name, the diagnosis, and the prescriptions. These were later dispensed under his directions by Georgie Boy, a young coloured lad who worked in the surgery.

The Department of Health were responsible for all aspects of medicine, and they employed dozens of native midwives to service the location. Often they consulted Bis, but any serious cases were sent to the local hospital, a place to which Bis had no access—it was the preserve of the European doctors.

I had renewed my midwifery licence and Bis engaged my help working part-time, taking blood and delivering babies to the Indian mothers. He treated the Indian patients after the regular office hours, for no Indian would sit in a waiting room with blacks. Integration was unthinkable. There was no law against non-Europeans mixing among themselves, but in the Indian community, there was a social taboo of socially mixing with natives, who were considered not only black, but smelly and inferior. Nevertheless, everyone employed native servants and nannies—a somewhat hypocritical practice considering their disdain for blacks—and Indian men had no qualms engaging in sex with black girls.

"Miscegenation is a sin!" the Afrikaner lawmakers decreed. But that did not stop many white men from having sex with their black servants, as they considered it a sporting pastime. Bis was inundated by white farmers' wives, begging him to give them a potion that would deter their wayward husbands from copulating with black servant girls, who they believed were witches casting spells to attract their deviant spouses.

Some Afrikaners, men and women, who made appointments to see Bis were certain that he possessed magical powers that could cure their ailments. They were disappointed to discover that he was not the shaman of their imagination. "Your people know lots of magic tricks," was a common sentiment. They could not understand how an *Indier* could possibly be a doctor of white medicine. Surely, he must be a witch doctor.

All over the country under cover of darkness, it was common for men to indulge in sexual activity with black women. Often, I saw the Indian lads loitering in their cars outside the native ghetto, waiting to pick up girls. Married men acted more discreetly. Bis treated an Indian father repeatedly for sexual infections. The knave kept several native "girls." The incidence of sexual disease was high in the location, and Bis sent off blood samples to the medical research lab in Johannesburg. Most resulted with positive Wasserman. However, this salacious activity was not only the preserve of the Indian lads, and to my dismay, a Boer farmer charged with the rape of a very young black girl was acquitted. He maintained that sleeping with black girls was an old *Boer sport*, and he could not understand what all the fuss was about.

One day, a newlywed young Indian woman three months pregnant visited me. "Sister, I must ask you a favour, and you must help me."

"I will if it's possible. What is troubling you?"

The woman hesitated nervously, twisting her long plait, braiding and unbraiding the hair. "Promise you won't tell the others," she pleaded, trying to suppress her tears.

"All right, I promise."

"My mother-in-law hates me. My husband, we fight all the time. At night, he and his pals go with kaffir girls. He tells me it's nothing. 'We pull their skirts over their faces when we do it,' he says and laughs. Please Sister, please, you must ask the doctor to write a letter to say I must go home now and not when I'm ready to have the baby."

In the Indian community, it was the custom for first babies to be born at the maternal parents' home. I took pity and told Bis, who gave her the necessary letter.

Despite the busy work load, Bis made time to spend alone with me. On quiet Sunday evenings, he would take me for drives, pointing out his love of the meticulous gardens that surrounded the grand city hall, the world-famous agricultural and veterinary colleges, and *The Afrikaans Kollege van Akademie*, which catered exclusively to Europeans.

On one particular drive, Bis was pensive as he drove around pointing out these places of interest. "Now do you see why I could never be happy here? I can never be part of the academic life I dream of having. Here, I'm demeaned and denied the dignity I crave," he complained bitterly.

I had no answer but gently caressed his cheek, not having experienced the form of prejudice he was compelled to endure. We drove around in silence and I took note of the beautiful homes of the area reserved for whites. An impressive feature of the residential area was the concrete *sluits*, or deep gutters, that were filled with running water to facilitate the watering of gardens. These also formed a buffer that separated the properties from the pavement and the roadway. My initial thought was what a contrast to the native locations, where there was no running water, only the communal taps at the end of streets, from which the native people fetched their water in whatever containers they possessed.

Potch boasted a fair number of beautiful historic buildings. I was fascinated as Bis pointed out the white-plastered churches dedicated to Jehovah and surrounded by impeccable gardens. The number of parked cars indicated the church services were in session and attendance was high. Afrikaners took fierce pride in their belief in Jehovah. It was more than a religion; it was their system of justice and fairness. What irony. The bigots insisted that the lack of crime in Potch was because they kept the kaffirs in their place. Black policemen, specifically trained to enforce the law, were renowned for treating their own people harshly and with disrespect. One speculated whether they believed this would enhance their status in the eyes of their white masters.

Continuing on our way, we passed Bis's surgery two miles from the city centre. Huddled against the door, a man lay writhing in obvious pain. Bis pulled over.

"Doctor, them Boere *okies* [boys], they pull me off bicycle. They say me, '*Julle kaffirs behoef nie op die straat nie.*" [Kaffirs do not belong on the street.]

The poor fellow was groaning. "*Hulle* [they] say me bang the car in front of church. I tell *okies* not me. *Okies* hit me and break bicycle. They tell to owner when he come from church. 'Sir, this kaffir he dent your car.' Owner take off his belt and *donder* me good. '*Verdomde* kaffir,' [Damn kaffir] he say."

Bis treated the man for a fractured arm and several cuts, bruises, and injuries, including a severely damaged ear drum. The brutality meted out to natives was not new to me, and I recalled my days at Bara, but here I was seeing it on a much closer level. I became a witness to personal suffering, and my husband had to deal with the effects of the acts of violence perpetrated by prejudiced individuals on black residents who were cowed into submission by white louts. Sadistic racism merely for the fun of it!

CHAPTER 32
Potchefstroom – A Muslim Family

To fully appreciate and understand my new environment, I delved into the history of the Bismillah family. They were among the first to immigrate from Dabhel, Gujarat State in India, and settled in Potchefstroom in 1844. Like all immigrants, they came in search of a better life and started by working menial jobs or as indentured labourers working in the sugar cane fields in the province of Natal, or in the mines along the Reef in Johannesburg.

Over the decades, the enterprising rural Indian communities grew. In Transvaal province, many Indians became keepers of small shops, traded with the large black population, and made an adequate living. This was the norm in almost every isolated small town, and often the name on the shop front read *Algemene Handelaar,* meaning General Dealer. It was confusing to people who did not speak Afrikaans. Itinerant Indian salesmen were welcomed by these shop-owners, receiving a meal and a bed for a night. There were no hotels or inns that catered to non-Europeans.

Bawa, my father-in-law, had told me that when he first arrived in the country as a very young boy, he worked carting water uphill at a penny a bucket. As a teenager, he had worked as a clerk. He went back to his village in India and married, returning without his wife. Later, the enterprising young man had saved enough to open his own shop before he sent for his wife and daughter. Like most other general stores, Dabhel House, named for the Bismillah hometown in India, prospered during the war years under the astute guidance of Ahmin, my husband's elder brother. Ahmin was a gifted businessman—he expanded into other lines, selling not only groceries but haberdashery, clothing, and housewares. Situated on Main Street, two miles from the city centre, Dabhel House catered mainly to the wealthy Afrikaner clientele; farmers from the surrounding areas who came in monthly to replenish supplies.

Prior to the two world wars, the majority of families who owned these shops lived in the back quarters, or in the odd double-storey building. One day, a jubilant Bawa announced, "The town council has agreed to lease me land on which to build a house."

"Where about? And how did you manage it?" the excited family queried.

"It's the vacant land across from our shops, that parcel of land that divides us from the Boers. It's not freehold, but it's worth it, because the council has officially designated the land an Indian area as of 1945."

Bawa's newly earned wealth built the first yellow-brick house in the Indian area. He ensured the new five-bedroom home would have all the modern features with bathrooms and separate indoor toilets, although they were still the squat ones preferred by Indians. A proper sewage system was installed to replace the so-called "night buckets" used for outdoor toilets. Black municipality workers collected the buckets of night-soil weekly from the backyards, replacing them with clean ones, which had been dipped in boiling tar as a cleaning disinfectant.

A *rondavel*, or round cottage, was built in the garden to accommodate travelling salesmen, and was a place where Bawa and his friends played cards undisturbed on Sunday afternoons. A grapevine-covered *pergola* led from the garage to the vegetable and fruit gardens. My mother-in-law was a keen gardener and with the help of Moses, a young black epileptic, she supervised and cultivated these gardens, as well as a variety of roses in the front.

Bawa had started a trend. Shortly after, other Indians emulated his example and vied with each other by building even larger homes with double garages. Indians comprised hardly one percent of the town's population and they were predominately Muslim, with three exceptions: *Sombai*, the Hindu tailor and family; Kantie, his assistant, and his family; and the barber, Sniffy, who spoke with a snuffling tone. Muslims considered haircutting unclean and beneath them, but were content to patronise his service.

The balmy climate was conducive to sports and South Africans, irrespective of colour or creed, were sports enthusiasts. Teams in all sports had their segregated leagues. Bawa built a tennis court for the use of the Indian community, who invited other teams to play. The Bismillah ladies were keen tennis players, and they were extremely competitive.

During the summer months, cricket matches were eagerly contested, and the Potch community was well known for its hospitality. Each weekend, families catered to visiting teams. In the morning, the women would prepare lavish meals for the visitors, and my sisters-in-law taught me to cook and bake. After lunch was served and with little else to do, we women and children attended the games and cheered on our teams from the comfort of our cars, while the children scampered to the side-lines.

Football was a winter sport, supported with the same enthusiasm and hospitality as cricket. However, the families' courtesy of serving meals was never extended when they played against the local native teams.

I soon learnt that in this closed society, Indian women kept a low profile and were relegated to being housewives or helping out in family stores. It was economical, as it spared paying clerks wages. The Bismillah's were no exception, and they were excellent businesswomen. In fact, the Afrikaners referred to Dabhel House as *Mina's se winkel* (Mina's shop). Mina was the diminutive for Amina, who spent many hours working beside her husband and children, except for Bis, who was away at school.

At the time, there was no chance of higher education for women, except through correspondence courses. Indian women in small towns had to be content with junior school that ended in grade eight. It was unthinkable for girls to aspire to a secondary education because it would have entailed leaving home. Boys had all the luck.

Most Indian housewives in the rural towns were limited to a life of housekeeping, entertaining, shopping, attending engagement parties and weddings, and visiting relatives for short holidays. I found it surprising that the ladies in the community were unaware they lived in a cocooned island, in fact a ghetto. They were, however, content with such luxuries and conveniences they could afford. I was now part of that lifestyle and I had much to learn.

The Europeans had access to their own cinemas, which prohibited non-Europeans access. An enterprising Indian business man built a cinema in the Indian area, the *Koh-I-Noor* cinema or Bioscope, as all cinemas in South Africa were dubbed, and it opened in 1955-1956. Watching films became a popular source of entertainment, except for the older orthodox Muslims, who boycotted the movie house. The outside world had intruded, and Hollywood movies were screened, making an impact on the youth. Elders feared their way of life was being subverted, and the youth would be influenced and led astray. Here too, division was indirectly forced, with Indians occupying the upstairs balcony seats, while the natives sat downstairs. It was an economic segregation, as the balcony seats were more than double the price.

Saturday matinees provided a great escape for the young. It was quite an experience. The crowd was loud and raucous. It was a communal free-for-all, and I, who sometimes took my young nephews, was amused by the hi-jinks of the audience. Dialogue was drowned out by the African audience, who did not understand or speak English, though they loved interacting with the films. The native audience on the main floor jumped up from their seats and screamed, "*Litey, Litey pas op*" [young man, look out] to warn the hero of impending danger. The young Africans emulated the heroes. They cheered and mimicked their actions. *The Mark of Zorro*, with Tyrone Power, was a particular favourite, and Zorro graffiti covered the outer walls of stores, much to the annoyance of the Indian shop owners. Movies like the *Lone Ranger* and John Wayne Westerns were also popular because of the shoot-outs between the white settlers and the "red" Indians dressed in their colourful regalia. I observed a strange fact; the non-European audience always championed and identified with the white heroes—there was no expression of sympathy for the vanquished red Indians! The spontaneous antics of the audience reminded me of improv theatre in London. Although different, the experience of fun and laughter was a welcome relief in our present mundane world, cloistered as we were in the world of Apartheid. For Bis and me, Potch was a temporary escape and a relatively safe haven from the tentacles of Apartheid waiting for the chance to snap us up.

Bis and I, with our two children—Enver, who was now a healthy four-year-old, and his baby sister, two-year-old Nadya—continued secluded in staid Potch. On the surface, everyone appeared happy, living their restricted lives, a few eking out a livelihood in their small grocery shops. The community was thrifty, almost parsimonious, and it appeared to me that no one could be classified poor, yet a distinct hierarchy based on wealth existed. The Potch Indians were conditioned to blindly accept the separatist doctrine of Apartheid as long as it did not intrude on their business operations.

Bis continued to practise medicine, marking time until we could leave the country.

CHAPTER 33
Owning a Home in Potchefstroom

My life in Potchefstroom was an enormous adjustment. There was so much to learn on a cultural and social level, and the racial issue that plagued our country added to our discomfort. I was fortunate that a contrite husband was supportive and eased my way. However, he was unhappy.

"I knew that you would fit in, but don't get too comfortable. We will leave here as soon as the time is right and our son is healthy," Bis assured me.

I had discovered a completely new culture, and I adapted as best I could. Gran's teaching was tested: "Always maintain your dignity in the face of changing circumstances." It was a lesson learnt, and pride would not permit anything less.

Bis, on the other hand, was disenchanted with life in Potch. He loathed his second-class status and his discontent was exacerbated by the fact that Potch Indians did little to support any political or progressive cause. They believed that it was to their advantage to isolate themselves from the political struggle—it insulated them against Apartheid, and they went about the business of making money. Their businesses prospered and their standard of living was superior to that in many other parts of the country. Bis observed that the community was short-sighted, and their complaisance bothered him. The elders, including Bawa, said, "Don't rock the boat," and any political discussion or activity was discouraged.

It was ironic, but Bis and I benefitted from this attitude. Potch became a temporary hide-away, and due to the volume of work, time limited our participation in any political activity beyond Potch.

Part One

In the late1940s to 1960, people young and old in Johannesburg, Cape Town, and Durban joined together in the struggle against Apartheid. They were actively engaged in the campaign of "Passive Resistance," which had been started by Mahatma Ghandi in Durban in the 1940s. It was the movement to combat the evils of prejudice, the class system, and white supremacy. Their efforts to unite went almost unnoticed by Potch Indians, who remained passive, insulated, and aloof. As long as it occurred elsewhere and not in Potchefstroom, an attitude of *I'm all right, Jack* prevailed. The esteemed revolutionary Indian leaders—Dr. Yusuf Dadoo of the Communist Party and Dr. Naiker of the Indian Congress—could not get a toehold in Potch.

Repeatedly we were informed by the community elders, "They're communists, and we don't want them here causing trouble."

The Potch Indian community were perverse in their blinkered acceptance of political events. The entire world condemned the Sharpeville Massacre of 1963, a peaceful protest by blacks against the "Pass Laws," which required all black men to carry identity cards at all times, during which the white policemen mowed down dozens of innocent people in the street. But the Potchefstroom Indian elders used this as an example to warn against any form of protest. "See what happens to protestors?" they exclaimed, aware that any resistance to Apartheid would be ruthlessly crushed. Thus, they satisfied themselves by avoiding any mention of the struggle and continued to profit.

Fear of the authorities gripped the entire non-white population, and it forced them into subservience. Yet, all over the country, resistance groups sprang up, except in Potch, where the natives too were inactive. They were intimidated by the local authority and the black police force. The African National Congress could not hold a single meeting in Potch at the time.

Bis was dissatisfied with general practice. It had become routine. Writing prescriptions and the limited care that he was able to provide was inadequate. He was thwarted for he had no access to the local hospital, which was staffed by European doctors. He missed the stimulation and the camaraderie that Baragwanath had offered. Bis was aware that his training was being wasted. He became moody, as it had never been his intention to run a general country practice. He believed that he had paid his dues by establishing the practice, but now it was time for change.

Bis's aggression played out in sports. To my amazement, the gentleman husband I knew had a different reputation among his family. The first inkling of his fiery temper was at a cricket match, where his belligerent behaviour against the opposing side left me embarrassed. Gleefully, it was pointed out by the family: "What did we tell you? Your husband is not the saint you believe him to be."

I attributed Bis's combative behaviour to frustration; something few of the family understood. I had a better insight and understanding of my husband. I sympathised. He believed he was marking time in a dead-end world; a comfortable, domestic world that I had come to accept and was beginning to comprehend.

The lack of privacy in the family home contributed to Bis's discontent, and each night after supper, we retreated to his one-bedroom flat next to his surgery.

"Joan, we have to have a home of our own."

I laughed.

Bis was irritated. "What's funny?"

"Yes, perhaps privacy may alleviate some of your restlessness," I said, and I continued laughing.

Bis raised his eyebrows. "Well?"

"I was just thinking about my first night here in the main house. I got up and went to the bathroom. I was dazed and uncertain of my bearings. I had to check myself from screaming with fright. There in the semi-darkness, under the night-light, lined up on the window ledge were at least half a dozen water glasses, each one filled with teeth, including yours. My fright turned to amusement, and I wondered how often you accidentally grabbed the wrong set only to discover it didn't fit. Is that what you're objecting to?"

Bis merely snorted. "Joan, I'm being serious. I don't know how much longer I can live here. I can't give up the practice just yet. I need to secure our finances. But in the meantime, there are no suitable homes for us."

"I agree, but what are we to do?"

"We'll build a house. Your friend the architect, Chummy Graff, is back from London. He's practising in Joburg. I'll phone him."

"I'm sure he'll be delighted to hear from us. Why build if you're thinking of leaving?"

Part One

"A house will add to the attraction of the practice when we sell."

I knew the futility of disagreeing with Bis. He only told me his plans once he had them all worked out and was sure he could execute them.

"There's a plot of land opposite the parents'. That ought to please them. I'll ask Bawa. Building a house would be an excuse until my plans are in order," he said.

Aware of his son's restlessness, Bawa was eager to help. He believed that a home of our own would be an inducement for Bis and me to remain in Potch.

Bis, like his father, was stubborn, and they both set out to accomplish precisely what they had set their minds to. Within two weeks, Bawa had obtained the necessary permits for us to build a house. It helped that he knew all the right people and could get things done. I surmised that it was a gentleman's agreement, or more likely an agreement between a client and shop owner; the permit in exchange for discounts at bargain prices at Dabhel House.

Bis had insisted on central heating being installed, a new feature in country housing. Potch winters, although only six-weeks in duration, reached frigid temperatures. Bis also insisted on bidets and upright toilets in place of the squat toilets favoured in Indian households.

Most Wednesdays, Ahmin would go on a buying spree to the wholesalers in Johannesburg. I had become friends with this highly intelligent elder brother, who had been denied the opportunity to attend university. He invited me regularly to join him on the long drive into town. It spared him the tedium of making inane chatter with the neighbour who usually accompanied him and who repeated himself ad nauseam by asking the same questions over and over again.

Ahmin was widely read and well-informed. Bis ordered records, books, and magazines, which were delivered to the store, and Ahmin would open and listen or read them first before handing them over. Once, he took off an entire day to play and replay a Beethoven recording, at the end of which even his young sons were heard humming the famous refrain from the Fifth Symphony da...da...da... dum. No one dared ask him to change the record. Later in the evening, he told Bis and me that he also appreciated classical music, never having been exposed to it before. He found it stimulating yet also soothing. Music and literature were added to our discussions on the drive into Johannesburg. He would drop me off to do my shopping and after conducting his business, later picked me up at a friend's or at my sister Beryl's home.

A final stop would be to the Indian market where a very religious Uncle Mamagee was the lone Muslim stall-holder. He was devout and prayed five times a day, and the two large grey callouses that had formed on his forehead above his eyes as he bowed low touching the ground were a testament to his piety. Mamagee was aided by his three sons. Ahmin would collect the order of fruit and vegetables that would be ready, and then it would be on to Mamagee's home, where his younger second wife and daughters had prepared a delectable meal.

Within a few months, our house was ready to move into. I eschewed my family's traditional furniture and settled on modern Scandinavian sapele mahogany pieces. The dining chairs were upholstered in colourful fabrics. Deep sofas were upholstered in an off-white blend of linen and wool imported fabric. Everything else was ordered through Dahbel House. Two hand-blown, stained-glass light fixtures that I had bought as souvenirs in Stratford, England, came in useful to light the front *porte cochere* that led to an enclosed courtyard.

The garden was as important as the interior. It proved a temporary diversion for Bis. He chose the ornamental camellia and magnolia trees for the courtyard and a wisteria creeper for the back *stoep* (veranda). The back-yard split-pole fence was covered by passionfruit vines. My mother-in-law helped select apricot, peach, and nectarine trees that she planted against a six-foot tall white wooden fence. Years later, on a trip to Potchefstroom to introduce our youngest child Nisha to both our families, the four-year-old was handed a freshly picked peach by her grandmother, who never quite understood why we had left a comfortable living for the bleakness of London, as she perceived it. Nisha said, "I thought peaches came from the shop on Finchly Road."

My mother-in-law was horrified. "Look what you are depriving the children of."

At the garage entrance, we planted an enormous mulberry tree and when in season, young black children could often be seen gathering the fruit. Bawa, who also enjoyed shopping sprees, contributed a large spruce tree, which we planted near the rock garden. At Christmas time, it was decorated and lit up, a novelty in this community, and presents were doled out to the children and the servants.

Bis and I had barely settled in when the first of Chummy's (our architect) clients arrived to see the house. Scrape, a prosperous black entrepreneur who operated several dance halls in and around Johannesburg, had made his fortune as a promoter of jazz bands. One bitterly cold winter's evening, he arrived in a chauffeur-driven limousine. Bis and I were lounging before a blazing fire in the study.

Kristina, our maid, knocked. "Doctor, black fing in front door."

Bis hurried to find the acquaintance he had known in first year medical school, but who had since dropped out. "Scrape, it's been a long time. Please come in and meet my wife."

"It's good to see you after all this time. Nice place you have here." Scrape's English was impeccable, unlike that of most natives, who spoke with a distinct accent.

"Would you like to take your coat off? It's quite warm," Bis said, leading the visitors inside to greet me.

The introductions over, Scrape took the armchair, and as his young driver was about to sit down, in a loud voice Scrape boomed, "Not you, *piccanin*. You know your place. On the floor or stay outside."

Servants were a common feature in the majority of all South African homes, regardless of colour. Nannies and maids, who may have been employed for years and reared the children, were never entertained within the family home, but stayed outside in the servants' quarters.

I rang for Kristina to serve tea. After what seemed a long time, I went to the kitchen, where I found the maid sulking.

"Kristina, we're waiting for the tea."

"Psha, black fings sitting like people. I not they servant."

Yes, I thought, racism existed at all levels of South African society, and I had to placate Kristina to get the tea. I recalled a similar incident, except it had occurred in Johannesburg. Bis and I were invited to a Jewish friend's home for supper after a meeting. The kitchen boy refused to serve a *koolie*, even if he was a doctor.

A few weeks later, Maria, the house maid, announced. "Madam, some Dutch'erie's want to see the house." Before I had time to answer, three white women (I could hardly refer to them as ladies—perhaps this demonstrates my own prejudice) had already taken the liberty, crossed the threshold, and pushed past me.

"I'm the Master Builder's wife. I'm going to show my friends the house."

I was baffled. There was no greeting, request for permission, or apology. I was merely the koolie doctor's wife. Hence, it was taken for granted that she was well within her rights to show off her husband's work. They passed the built-in linen closet at the end of the passage. The door was ajar. "God, I didn't know *koolies* slept on sheets," one of the women remarked. I ignored them but told Maria to show the women out when they'd had their fill.

Endemic and organised, systematic racism was entrenched in the majority of white persons in South Africa. I'm sure that any person who has not lived in a society that segregates its citizens by race and colour cannot understand just how degrading it is to those people who have and enjoy all the material comforts, wealth, and education, yet are denied dignity. It is ludicrous and dehumanising—all the privileges of wealth do not compensate for the denigration and humiliation that is endured.

CHAPTER 34
The Importance of Colour

In the aftermath of World War II in 1945, South Africa witnessed the rise of Afrikaner nationalism. During the war years, hundreds of Afrikaners were detained in internment camps and released at the end of the war. The Nationalist Party was rejuvenated, and they swept into power on the platform of Apartheid in 1949. Like the Nazis, their mandate was racial purity and to maintain white supremacy. They had not learnt from the Nazi experiment that their philosophy was flawed, and that the disrupted race relations caused dissent and fostered underground movements.

The terms white and European were synonymous and interchangeable. The colour bar had been systemic and widely practised in South Africa. But now, under Apartheid, it was entrenched in the law.

The Mixed Marriage Act was cause for consternation throughout the land. The emphasis on being white or European had people researching their backgrounds to prove their ethnicity and identities before a tyrannical and xenophobic board. If there was any doubt, then the board had the power to decide purely on appearance to which group a person was assigned.

Stories abound of prejudiced officials who denied people of mixed race who had lived their entire lives as white and were classified as such. These people now found themselves at the mercy of a board who declared them coloured or insufficiently white. Children were removed from schools and forced to attend non-white schools. Tragic stories of suicides, broken bodies, hearts, and homes affected many families. The daily newspaper reported a sad story of a blond dress-shop manager from one of the most expensive stores in Johannesburg, who had jumped from the twenty-first floor of the prestigious building. Her fiancé had discovered that her nanny was in fact her grandmother and he'd broken off their engagement.

The consequences of these racial policies affected people irrespective of whether they were white, brown, or black. Skin colour was a vital indicator, and as with a chameleon that changed colour when threatened, colour was an important factor that determined survival. The lighter the hue, the better the chance for upward social and economic mobility. Therefore, the practice of "passing" became widespread, with dire consequences for families where some members were not fair enough to pass. The darker-skinned family members who could not pass as white suffered the indignity of being ignored in public, or worse, and even being disowned. The derogative term *fenstertjie* meaning "little window" was coined to describe those people who passed as white. When they encountered darker family members on the street, they simply stopped and looked into the nearest shop window to avoid contact or acknowledgment. Naturally, this had disastrous effects on relationships.

However, those people who were considered white but were not "pure" lived in constant fear of being discovered, especially if they held European identity cards. The strain was great, and it was not surprising then that many migrated to other parts of the British Commonwealth. I was familiar with and knew first-hand their concerns, as my cousins had fled to England and Australia, and others to Mauritius, to avoid having to appear before a board of prejudiced officials.

Colour became an obsession, and cultural customs surrounding colour affected all segments of the non-white population. The origin could be traced to European colonisation of Africa and the sub-continent of India. I recalled that when I practised midwifery, the first thing Indian grandmothers did was to inspect the nail-beds of the new-born to assess the baby's true colour. Among Indians, as among most South Africans of mixed heritage, fair skin was a blessing, and dark-skinned beautiful girls were not nearly as popular for marriage as their lighter-hued sisters.

The board adopted ridiculous measures to guarantee that no loopholes were overlooked, and it affected all aspects of everyday life. It is well documented that various methods were employed to test who belonged where. One of the more ridiculous practices was to stick pencils into the woolly hair of coloureds—if the pencil stayed put and did not slide out, then they had their coloured identity cards revoked and they were registered black.

Skin-colour obsession was not confined to whites, but permeated the black community as well. Colour was all-important, for blacks too saw colour in degrees of brown and blackness. A lighter-skinned black nurse employed by Bis refused to go outside during the day without a hat, as she was afraid of burning darker in the sun. This was a common trait among many people of all communities.

In London, I had met a black South African doctor, and on learning that I was leaving for Potchefstroom, he said, "You will be passing Bara, as it's on the way to Potch. Will you take a package to a nurse at the hospital for me?"

I agreed, but on reaching the hospital, I did not find her. "May I leave this parcel for Staff Nurse please?" I asked a secretary.

"You mean the one she's black in she's face?" he said.

I thought how pervasive colour consciousness was, and how it related to all aspects of life and society.

While the rest of the world was involved in post-war rehabilitation, South Africa's main interest was the preservation of white domination. The Censorship Board consisted of members of the Dutch Reform Synod and prominent Afrikaner members of parliament, who oversaw the film industry. They implemented strict rules to enforce segregation especially in the area of films. All films had to be screened for anything that mentioned or transgressed the colour bar, and if found wanting, the film was prohibited from screening in non-European cinemas. A ludicrous example was their unanimous consensus that *Gone with the Wind* be banned in non-white cinemas. The mixed cast of whites and blacks was considered unseemly and deemed unfit for non-white eyes. The objection to the film was that it was against Christian principles. In particular, a scene depicted freed slaves, who were portrayed cavorting around in bowler hats and carrying brief cases. The very idea of slaves prancing around as free men would send the wrong message and set a bad example to local blacks.

The mixed cast aroused curiosity and the film played to packed European houses for extended periods. I invited Bis to see it. I bought tickets in advance and tried to convince him to join me by simply walking into the theatre, as no identification at cinemas was required. All it took was the confidence to do it.

I reasoned that in such a diverse society, Bis could be mistaken for and "pass" as Syrian, Lebanese, Portuguese, or any one of the Mediterranean people who enjoyed European status.

Bis asserted, "I cannot see the film under false pretences. It adds to the indignity and inferiority I am compelled to endure. The experience will heighten my feeling of repression and discontent." He refused to go.

On another occasion, I had invited Ruby and Fatima, a niece, who were keen to see the film *Around the World in Eighty Days*. There is a scene of an Indian princess being rescued from a burning funeral pyre by the European hero. An excited Fatima called out in her native Gujerati, "Oh my God! There are our people." Other than some laughter, there were no troubling consequences, except for the embarrassed young woman who could not wait to leave the theatre undetected.

Bahia and Doris, the American friends I had met in London, were white Texans and were attending the opening of the ultra-modern 20th Century Fox Cinema amidst great fanfare in Johannesburg. Before the film began, the screen flashed, "We guarantee the patronage at this cinema is 100% European." The ladies were scandalised. Indignantly, they left their seats and demanded their admission be refunded. They complained that they were being discriminated against, as they were not European but Americans! It took some convincing before they understood that any white person in South Africa was automatically "European," and that it was their right to sit on the benches marked "Europeans only" rather than stand while waiting for public transport, which they had done while they waited at tram and bus stops.

Signs of Apartheid were everywhere and were impossible to ignore. The ubiquitous "Europeans only" signs were plastered on separate entrances at all public buildings. They appeared at bus stops, train stations, parks, washrooms, restaurants, and shops, and it highlighted the offensive colour bar. Blacks were even forced to give way to whites when walking on pavements in some towns, and they were beaten up by thugs when they refused to comply.

It was not surprising that in a country where the authorities were obsessed with racial purity they banned anything that they deemed detrimental, such as television. It was considered an evil black box from which no good could come, and it was prohibited. The board was not only fearful that television would introduce non-whites to radical views that would undermine the ideology of the governing party, they also feared that the English-language programs would undermine and subvert Afrikaans, as there were no Afrikaans programmes. Television was not introduced into South Africa until 1976.

The era of Apartheid from 1948 to 1960 was obsessed with racial purity and colour, while the majority of its people, particularly non-whites, suffered hardship and poverty. Meanwhile, the rest of the world was rebuilding and recovering from the after-effects of World War ll.

South Africa was a rich country where the poor white segment of the population was looked after by the benevolent Afrikaner Government. The rest of the white citizens indulged in their wealthy existence, leaving them plenty of time to pursue pleasurable pursuits. It is a country with a long sporting tradition, encouraged by funding. It is proud of its athletic prowess and its achievements on the international scene. But at this time, there was no racial mixing of teams. International competition was the preserve of white or European South Africans who excelled at sports. When they competed in cricket or rugby against England, Australia, or New Zealand, the non-whites were permitted entry to watch the games from a segregated seating area, and they vociferously supported the visiting teams, cheering them on to win. A poetic compensation of revenge?

CHAPTER 35
The Inquisition

ON OUR RETURN TO SOUTH AFRICA IN 1954, BIS AND I WERE CAUGHT in the web of the Mixed Marriages Act of 1949, which prohibited the marriage between whites and non-whites. The Registration Act of 1950 was introduced to ensure that the white gene pool not be "contaminated" by non-white people. The Classification Board decided the race of an individual and they were empowered to assign a person to a specific group. All people were issued Identification Race Cards, which had to be carried and shown on demand. I was not issued a card. In the interim, my South African citizenship passport sufficed. From 1954, we lived in a state of apprehension, not knowing when the axe would fall and the law be enforced.

The dreaded time to clarify my identity had arrived.

The marriage certificate signed by Judge Malherbe in 1953 was checked for its validity. We were guilty of having contravened the law, and accordingly our son was an alien. We were vulnerable, and our anxiety and uncertainty increased as I was summoned to appear before the Classification Board for contravening the Mixed Marriages Act. I was trapped in a racial quagmire. My birth certificate stated European, my husband was Indian, and it was clear that we had broken the law. Our British-born son was considered an alien and ordered to leave the country. We were guilty on all counts.

Once again, I appealed to my friend, the Reverend Gray, the Afrikaner dominie who had returned to Johannesburg. When I explained my predicament, he offered to intercede on my behalf. While we were in London, he had helped to pave the way for my return to South Africa with our premature baby

Part One

son. I was confident that once again he would help to resolve my dilemma. "I will personally seek an appointment with the minister in charge of Classification Affairs before your appointment," he offered.

After consultation with his colleagues, Rev. Gray wisely advised us, "Bis, it is preferable for me to go to Pretoria to assist Joan in her battle with the authorities. Your presence there will only antagonise them if you are to avoid prosecution for contravening the Mixed Marriages Act."

"I hope they are as compassionate and understanding as you, Reverend," Bis said.

South Africa was in turmoil and a referendum to withdraw from the Commonwealth to declare a republic was in process.

We left for Pretoria early in the morning of 29 June 1960. The meeting was scheduled for 11 am. The country would withdraw from the Commonwealth on 5 October later that year.

Driving along the scenic route was an artist's dream, and on entering the town of Pretoria, Rev. Gray, a cautious driver, obeyed the speed limit, which allowed me to revel in the scenic beauty. It was in sharp contrast to the ugly reality of our mission. Gigantic blue gum trees and sweet-smelling eucalyptus branches wafted in the breeze. Dozens of swallows nested in them and took turns flying upward, tweeting and circling round and round, feasting on unsuspecting insects before returning to nest. Black crows caw-cawed and swooped onto the street, sniping and pecking at road-kill, requiring Rev. Gray to stop to avoid a dead deer on the road. Pretoria was most colourful at this time of the year and attracted many tourists before they proceeded to the game reserve. The inner-city streets were planted with jacaranda trees that formed a purple haze of canopies overhead, then faded to mauve petals that fell in confetti showers and carpeted the pavements.

On arrival at the elegant Union Buildings, Rev. Gray and I were confronted with a parking horror. There were hundreds of cars and buses and thousands of people milling about. We did not know what to expect. The entrance hall to the building was clogged with people massed on the steps. The chatter of so many sounded like the twitter of hundreds of birds in flight that reminded me of a safari we'd taken to the game reserve. Rev. Gray steered me through the crowd to the area reserved for Europeans and parked in a reserved space.

"What's all the commotion?" he enquired of a clerk.

"It's a political rally."

Demonstrating against government policies that they believed were eroding civil liberties was the Black Sash Women's Movement, which had formed in 1955. My friend May Shapiro, the wife of Bis's mentor and benefactor, was one of the organizers of that movement. I was certain that May was somewhere in the crowd, but it was no time for me to be seen fraternising with any political activists.

I was surprised as we entered the interrogation office. It was a comfortable lounge designed to set people at ease. Rev. Gray pointed out the mahogany-wood panelled walls and the contrasting oak parquet floor. The stinkwood furniture and the chairs and sofas upholstered in costly damask complemented the silken drapes and pelmets that covered the leaded glass windows. Pictures of past prime ministers adorned one wall and landscape paintings of indigenous scenes by Afrikaner artists occupied another. On a sideboard, silver trays with coffee-pots and bone china cups and mugs bearing the Union Coat of Arms were displayed. There was a tea wagon laden with the national Dutch pastries, *melktert and koeksusters*. A realistic carving of the ox wagon, a sacred icon of the Voortrekker movement, adorned the mantelpiece.

All traces of British royalty was absent. I wondered if the Nationalists believed that the removal of portraits would wipe out British influence. Afrikaners had not forgotten nor forgiven their internment during World War ll, and their ill-treatment and defeat by the British during and after the Boer Wars of 1895-1903. Almost a century later, their revenge was Apartheid. They had won partly by the gerrymandering of seats, which had propelled them with a minority of the electorate into power, ousting the Afrikaner General Smuts of the Liberal Party, who had sided and fought with the Allies during World War II.

"The chairman will be in any minute. Please be seated. Perhaps you should sit here," suggested the attendant, pointing out a chair for me at the end of the long table. My apprehension increased. I felt like the felon in the witness box, especially when the Rev. Gray was asked to wait in the library, after meeting privately with the chairman. Later he would be called if needed, the attendant said. It added to my anxiety.

Part One

Despite the luxurious setting, my nervousness increased. I was hot and imagined the giant picnic ants of my childhood crawling all over me. I could barely remain composed when suddenly I was distracted as a procession of people entered: four men and three women.

"*Goeie More*" [Good Morning]. They sounded like an ominous Greek chorus. The pale-faced women were dressed as if to attend a Sunday church service with their sensible hats, flat shoes, and black gloves. I might have been one of them, except for my high heels, for I too wore a black suit and matching gloves. Like the chameleon, I adapted to my environment and donned whatever garb was suitable to the occasion. The men were equally sombre in nondescript dark suits and ties, looking like pastors ready to conduct a wake. They separated accordingly, men and women on either side of the table. The bald-headed, ruddy-complexioned chairman took his seat at the opposite end, facing me. He did not inspire confidence.

"Good morning," I answered as I pondered about these people, wishing that Rev. Gray could have stayed.

The chairman interrupted my thoughts. "Do you speak Afrikaans?"

"Yes sir. I'm bilingual, but English is my first language."

"Het julle vrae voor ons begin?" [Any questions before we begin?] he asked the assembled members, and on cue they shook their heads. "So then, let us begin," he said.

A waiter entered to serve the coffee and pastries. The pungent aroma of coffee was welcome. I felt queasy and did not want any pastry, even though I liked *melktert*: a cinnamon-flavoured creme brulee in puff pastry. But to refuse would be considered rude and send the wrong message. I helped myself to a *koeksister*, a cinnamon-spiced doughnut, and toyed with it, spilling crumbs.

The South African authorities had access to all information pertaining to individuals. Each member of the board had a dossier before him or her with copies of birth, educational certificates, passports, and who knew what else. The conversation centred on the school I had attended, but they did not address me directly. They conveyed the impression that they were not at all interested in anything I had to say, or any questions I may have had. They talked to each other and at one another. I was a spectator at an inquisition.

"Miss Salsoni," the chairman finally intoned, "a good *Eye-talian* name. You have three hundred years of white European civilization and tradition behind you, yet you tell me you are willing to throw it all away. For what? We are offering you a chance to maintain that right. Few people get that choice or privilege."

Before I could answer, he continued speaking. "I see your father was in the air force and your brother was also in the army. What does your father have to say about this so-called marriage to an Indian? Are you sure you know what you are doing? Do you know how it is to live among *koolies*?" I bit my lip. The questions were rhetorical, for he continued and addressed the members. *"Dames, hoe lyk sy? En wat van haar Taal?"* [Ladies, tell me what does she look like, and what about her language?]

"She looks like a white person and speaks English and she has a diploma in Afrikaans," one of the men answered.

The chairman continued, *"Sy is geleered soos 'n egte wit mens. Sy het die Taalbon eksamen afgele."* [She's educated like a proper white person and wrote the special Afrikaans examination.]

I was humiliated. They were talking about me as if I was not present. I clasped my hands in my lap to stop them shaking and to hide my embarrassment. I felt the colour rising, my red face proof of my discomfort. I was expected to listen while they lectured and humiliated me for my transgression. They were bullies and I had no defence. I was the mouse the cat toyed with. There was a lack of empathy from them. My heart beat rapidly and I felt that it would burst. I took a deep breath.

A woman chimed in, "And what about your children? They will be *koolies*?"

The insult stung. I felt anger percolating from deep inside, but I knew I had to maintain my composure. I remained silent as they glared at me, expecting me to answer. Then, in a quivering voice, I pleaded, "I have a child who is still waiting to be registered in our country. Both my husband and I were born here. Is it wrong for me to expect that our son may claim his birthright?"

"What birthright? He's Indian! And they're aliens. So, if you wish to stay in South Africa and avoid prosecution, you will be classified Indian. And you are lucky, you will not be prosecuted according to the law," the chairman said. "Do you have anything to say?"

I was speechless. What could I say? Even if I wanted to answer, I could not, and again, like the creature who had no control over its colour when faced with

Part One

imminent danger, I blushed red to the roots of my hair, aware of my changing status from white to Indian.

I had been thoroughly chastised for my indiscretion of marrying an Indian. Tears glistened on my eyelids, but I dared not blink nor shed a tear before these bigots who would derive joy from my discomfort. Slowly I inhaled, hoping to staunch the wayward flow and save my dignity.

"Do you understand?" the chairman asked.

I was expected to beg and yield to these bullies. I could not acquiesce to their demands and admit my guilt. I remained silent.

My refusal to comply was tantamount to treason. They considered me a traitor to the white tribe and my European heritage. I was not contrite, but they had triumphed.

A woman who had been silent up until then chimed in. "He isn't even Christian. Do you know in God's eyes *koolies* are heathens? And you a convent girl."

I had no answer. I thought the woman's outburst petty and spiteful, piling on insult to injury.

There was no point in appealing to reason. It was beyond them to understand. The hearing had been a courtesy to Rev. Gray. It was a formality. Bloated egos were satisfied, and it confirmed their superiority. The chairman rang a bell.

A Cape Malay servant wearing a *kufieh*, a conical Arab hat, entered. The chairman said, "*Vat die frou na die Indiers gebou. Staan op, en gaan met die bediende.*" [Take this woman to the Indian Affairs building. Stand up and go with the servant.] All pretence of courtesy was dropped. I was guilty, just like that other Joan for whom I was named.

"*Ja Meneer,*" [Yes sir], said the unctuous coloured escort.

I held my head high. It was my only gesture of defiance. Deliberately, I brushed the crumbs from my skirt, straightened it, and followed the orderly. Without glancing at the condescending henchmen, I left the comfort of the luxurious lounge.

Through a labyrinth of corridors, I was escorted to another section of the building. On the way, I heard shouting and scuffling, and policemen barking orders to the unruly mob.

"What's happening?" I stammered, trying to regain my composure.

"It's the Women's Black Sash Movement and the Voortrekker Women's Group and their supporters who are fighting," said the orderly. "The police have used tear gas to disperse the rabble-rousers."

Finally, we reached the Department of Indian Affairs, a drab and unfriendly place directly adjacent to the non-European men's washrooms. It was a drastic contrast to the salon I had just left. A pimply-faced young Afrikaner clerk sat behind the steel wicket. He demanded my passport. Without a word, I handed it over.

"Wag hier," [wait here], he said curtly, gingerly taking the passport, as though it was contaminated.

I waited for what seemed hours. Each time a door from one of the washrooms opened, a fetid odour leached out. The Rev. Gray found me waiting. Neither of us spoke.

The clerk returned and handed me a new passport, seemingly identical to the one I had handed in.

"Teken hier, voor my. As u blief." [Please, you must sign it in front of me], he said. In deference to Rev. Gray's presence, now the clerk was courteous, and when he asked me to sign on receipt of my passport said please and *"u,"* a sign of respect. I scanned it and noticed my surname had been omitted, I was about to ask, but then looking at it, I read, "Joan/w.o. Adbul Hak Bismillah." For a moment, I was confused *w.o?* Then it clicked—wife of. With a stroke of a pen, I had lost my identity and become my husband's chattel.

CHAPTER 36
Trouble in the Rabbit Hutch

Bis noted the irony and joked, "You really are my property now." My altered status had little effect on our apparently tranquil domestic situation. However, our life was interrupted by letters from the Department of Interior, demanding we apply formally for our son's immigrant status. Thus far, we had ignored the matter. Now we were compelled to deal with the problem. Failing that, Enver, our little boy, would be deported as an illegal alien.

Once again, I turned to Rev. Chris Gray for advice and help. He was anxious for me to tell my story to the Afrikaans synod that were meeting in Johannesburg. There appeared to be some shifting of domestic policy by the more liberal element of the government. Both Bis and I were invited to a meeting with the Dutch Reformed hierarchy. On the way, I quipped, "Can you imagine collaborating with the enemy, the *Broederbond* and cabinet ministers? What would our friends in the Progressive Forum say if they knew? Call us reactionaries, or worse, sell-outs and traitors."

"It's Hobson's Choice, but it could be the catalyst that gives us a legitimate excuse to leave the country."

"Strange the things we do, like compromise on certain principles and conspire with the enemy on others," I said.

Reverend Beyers Naude, an eminent Dutch Reformed dominie, chaired the meeting, where Prime Minister Verwoerd's son-in-law was present. They listened attentively as I recounted my degrading experience. They sympathised and there were red faces when I had finished. They apologized for the treatment I had received.

"I sense a revolt brewing," Bis said after we left the meeting.

"Who knows? It's anyone's guess how things will turn out."

After two anxious weeks, we were pleasantly surprised to receive Enver's immigration papers with a valid South African passport. "At least it's in his own name," I quipped.

"Yes," Bis said. "It all depends on who you know."

Enver had grown into a healthy five-year-old, and now he had a little sister, Nadya, who had been born in a private nursing home in Johannesburg. She too had been premature, and we were required to stay in the clinic for a couple of weeks. Her weight at birth, though, was double that of Enver's, and she did not need the specialised care that he had required.

When Nadya was three months old, she did not seem to need the normal amount of sleep, and Kristina, her Zulu nanny, took charge. The baby tired everyone by wanting to be carried, and Nanny solved the problem. She carried Nadya piggy-back in the native fashion. The baby nestled against her back supported by a cotton blanket tied firmly around her waist and knotted in the front under her ample bosom.

"We're not natives. The child will have bandy legs and stink like a native. Tell her to put Nadya down," my mother-in-law ordered. I perceived that my mother-in-law's concern stemmed from her racially biased sentiments, but to avoid a disagreement, I did her bidding. I had learnt to keep my views to myself, as I did not wish to be chastised, and I had no intention of being disrespectful. Native mothers were compelled to carry their children while going about their daily chores. It was an economic necessity for poor people, for as soon as the children were able to crawl, they were left on the floor to fend for themselves with the help of other toddlers and older siblings. Bis noted the result was that most black children walked by the age of seven months.

I had written a letter to thank Rev. Naude, who had made it possible for Enver to receive his citizenship. Rev. Naude was touched and on a visit to Potchefstroom, he visited us. Much to my surprise, our meeting prompted him to write a lengthy article to the *Johannesburg Star*, stating that he had visited an Indian home, and how impressed he was and that he was looking forward to visiting a native one in the near future. He also said that the government should review its policy regarding segregation, especially when it involved non-white professionals. The reverend was having doubts about the way Apartheid was affecting people's lives and he opposed the injustice people suffered under the system, due to ignorance of the other. He was concerned with the injustice non-whites suffered, and he attempted to intercede on their behalf whenever possible, stating that, "The time has come for change!"

Shortly after his visit to Potch and at the height of the Nationalists' power, the Rev. Beyers Naude railed against the divisive race relations in the country. He supported the trade unions and other organisations opposed to Apartheid. Years after we had left South Africa, he was defrocked by the Dutch Reformed Churches and imprisoned by the Nationalist Government, but he was honoured and recognised abroad for his humanitarian stance.

There was turmoil in the country, and sensing a rebellion, the Nationalist authorities enlarged the military base in Potchefstroom. Life in Potch appeared stable, probably due to the large military presence, but in the rest of the country, there was a growing concern of police brutality and underground political activity increased.

The Reverend Naude's article on his visit to Potchefstroom attracted many Afrikaans students, who began visiting the Indian area. I wondered what they were up to. They did not enter the homes but stood outside talking to the young Indian lads.

"What do they want?" I enquired.

"The pale-faces wish to discuss religion. They want to convert us Indians to Christianity."

"Why don't you bring them here? I don't mind talking to them."

Soon, some young Evangelists stood in my doorway. "Please come in. Would you like some tea?"

"*Nee Dankie*," they replied shyly. "*Ons will net gesels*." [We just want to chat.]

I set them at ease. "What exactly would you like to talk about?"

"How could you, a white *Christen*, marry a heathen koolie?" they asked.

I was amused by these young Evangelists, so direct, earnest, and naïve. "It's simple if you understand Progressive Revelation."

"We don't know what Progressive Revelation means. Can you explain it to our pastor, so that we can know if is against our belief?"

"Certainly, if he would agree to meet with me."

That was the beginning of many debates at our home with their Afrikaans pastor. A few weeks later, he erected a tent on a field adjacent to our house, and he invited the community to a discussion. His visit happened to coincide with a visit from the Baha'i ladies, Doris and Bahia, whom I had met in London and who now were resident in Johannesburg. Rev. Naude's article drew their attention and reminded them of Potchefstroom. The Potch elders were furious; they certainly did not want all the attention their little enclave was getting. They complained to Bis and admonished him for encouraging the foreigners.

"It was bad enough having the Afrikaans students sniffing about—at least we're used to them—but to have these anti-Islamic heretics is quite a different story. It's *Haram*" (not Kosher).

Meanwhile, the directive from the Baha'i hierarchy was to teach the native South African people, in the hope that they would be attracted to the Baha'i Faith. They were instructed not to bother the Muslim Indians, whom they knew would be resistant and averse to their teachings. Muslims would consider the Baha'i's anti-Islamic. Their assumption was correct. The tension among the Potch elders was increased by the presence of the Baha'i ladies and created unwanted dialogue. There was no open complaint but a whispered campaign to prevent us from entertaining people who would pervert the true doctrine of Islam. I surmised that Bis's sister Maryam's husband was probably responsible for spreading some of the inflammatory rhetoric. He objected to his wife's participation. She blithely ignored him as being outdated and continued to participate in Baha'i gatherings.

Bis was amused by the reaction of the Indian community to the Baha'i and found the rumours and gossip a welcome distraction. "At the very least, it'll give them something besides business to talk about."

It was assumed the authorities had eyes and ears everywhere and were content that religious discussions would replace any political dissent.

The Baha'is managed to recruit one black follower, Gabe Moralale, who owned several taxis. After a few meetings at our home, he resigned. His belief in ancestor worship, he said, forbade him from consorting with *koolies,* who cheated his people by short-changing them at the grocery stores. He maintained that *koolie* shop-keepers added fine stones to make up the weight of staples like lentils and rice, which were sold by the pound.

Part One

The Baha'is formed a study circle, and it attracted an assortment of misfits from that insular community, including Ahmin, Bis's older brother, their sister Maryam, and Bis and me, as well as the lanky, lugubrious neighbour Karim, who had a speech impediment. He stuttered and stammered and was opposed to local Muslim social customs. By way of protest, he had named his younger son Benjamin, after the Biblical son of Jacob. Then there was Sombai, the Hindu tailor. He had an engaging smile, agreed to everything that was said, and never offered an opinion. His family were the only Hindus among the Muslims, and for the first time he felt part of the community. I deduced that it was his first invitation to a Muslim home. Then there was Gus, who desperately wanted to be somewhere and someone else. He had inveigled Bis into approaching Bawa with a proposal to marry Ruby. This outraged Bawa, who disliked that family, whom he regarded as fools, and he turned him down. Lastly, there was Karim's younger brother Farley, who was in love with Eva, their Chinese neighbour's daughter. Marriage between Chinese and Indian was unthinkable in this small town. The couple escaped to London after Bis and I had returned and they were married. I thought, *We're all so different. Every single one of us is odd in this particular society, striving to find a place, but more importantly to find ourselves. Will we find what we are searching for? And if we find it, will we finally fit in?*

In the stultifying atmosphere of small town Potch, Bis and I found the discussions stimulating. We enjoyed entertaining Bahia and Doris, who in turn invited some of the Baha'i hierarchy from Johannesburg to attend our meetings.

"Progressive Revelation" was an all-encompassing religious history beginning from before Judaism, to Christianity and Islam, and finally to the Baha'i in the modern age. Embracing religious history was a substitute that compensated for our inability to be politically involved, and Bis and I felt it was important to teach the history of religion to our children. Bis was opposed to partisan religious indoctrination. He believed this to be the cardinal cause of strife between people of different faiths, and that it fostered fanaticism and promoted and maintained Apartheid, resulting in religious isolation. He insisted that only through education and understanding could we ever hope to eliminate prejudice, and injustice.

CHAPTER 37
The Group Areas Act

An article in the local newspaper claimed that the town council was about to announce the removal of all Indians from the town of Potchefstroom.

The conservative Boer Council of Potch invited the Indian community to a meeting to air their views and to discuss their removal and resettlement to a newly designated Indian area. The Indians complained and pointed out that the move would result in financial losses to their business and to the devaluation of their homes. They were offered freehold land as compensation, but no remuneration for any property. The council rejected all views presented by the Indians, and in all seriousness, an Afrikaans professor argued that poor whites existed because of their proximity to the Indian community who gouged and cheated them. He contended that, "The smell of koolie cooking, and garlic in particular, affects and dulls the senses of whites, and that prevents them from advancing." It was laughable. The contradiction and irony was lost on him, as many whites could not get enough Indian curry.

The new edict provided Bis with a legitimate excuse to leave, which suited him since he had been planning for some time to move.

To comply with government policy, the Indians were to move to the isolated designated area on the other side of town, eight miles beyond the town limit. There would be no compensation for their existing properties, which had been built on leasehold land, but in exchange, Indians were given freehold rights in the new location. A poor bargain! The Indian denizens of Potch were coerced into accepting this arrangement, and there was no further protest. In any other town, there would have been demonstrations. Here they were cowed into submission by the fear of imprisonment and confiscation of their existing property.

The stores in town bore the heaviest losses. Businesses had to start over again. Many shop owners feared that the Boers would not travel the long distance to shop in their newly designated area, and many families were compelled to move in with relatives in Lenasia, a new Indian ghetto that was created fifteen miles outside the city limits of Johannesburg. Indian Potch home owners were given extra time to vacate. A few home owners were fortunate to cut their losses and sell their homes at greatly reduced prices to white building contractors.

Many months prior to the Indian meeting, the military had transported thousands of native people to their new location in the segregated area many miles beyond the town. Their enforced evacuation was completed in record time. It complicated people's lives, making it difficult for them to get to work and abide by curfew laws. In the absence of native municipal transport, profiteering by black taxi drivers gouged an already impoverished people. One day, Georgie-Boy arrived late for work. He explained, "I didn't have enough fare because I got robbed by Tsotsi Boys, so I had to walk eight miles." A hardship many were forced to endure.

The relocation of the non-white population of Potch affected the Baha'i meetings. The group, or what remained of it, was forced to disband. Gaby was the first to leave. He went back to his ancestor worship. Maryam, Bis's sister, who was married to her first cousin, an acerbic man who despised his wife's family, followed their son, Rashid, now a medical student, to Dublin. Farley and his Chinese neighbour's daughter Eva fled to London. Gus gave up working as a clerk and escaped to medical school in Ireland. Only Sombai, the tailor, and Karim, who would never fit in, remained to soldier on. They found what they needed within themselves but remained at odds in Potchefstroom.

Ahmin and his wife Ayesha had embarked on a visit to India, but tragically, Ahmin suffered a stroke while aboard the ship. He was airlifted by helicopter and flown to a hospital in Bombay, where the doctors diagnosed a brain aneurism. During the operation, Ahmin succumbed. He was the first person to be buried in a newly opened cemetery in Pakistan.

For Bis and me, it was time to leave South Africa and to return to England. Bis had refused to relocate to the new segregated Indian area and had only stayed on in order to lend support to the other Indian home owners, who had been granted a grace period until their houses in the new area had been rebuilt.

Fate intervened and Bis and our family's departure for London was hastened by trouble that was brewing within the British Commonwealth. In 1960, the South African prime minister, Hendrik Verwoerd, had walked out of a Commonwealth meeting and taken the country with him. Britain offered asylum to those South Africans who wished to remain within the Commonwealth, but the time span was limited. To meet the deadline, the children and I had to leave almost immediately for London. Once again, I was leaving without Bis, who encountered difficulty renewing his passport. He would follow as soon as he could obtain a new one, finalise the sale of his practice, and secure our finances. As a registered member of the British Medical Association, he had an extended period, and would have no trouble re-entering England.

I was happy to be returning to London. I had matured and was wiser after the experience of living in Potchefstroom. There was much to be grateful for. I had been accepted into Bis's family and my children had benefited from the love and support of their grandparents and relatives. We were a part of a larger family, but another way of life awaited us.

The time in Potch had also allowed me to regain my faith in my husband. We had grown closer over the years, and I had a better understanding of him and his needs. Bis needed to be free from the oppressive system that defined, dictated, and denied him his dignity. He wanted to spare his children the ugly effects of Apartheid.

Potch had been a haven of domesticity, minimizing any political involvement. Bis surmised that our association with members of the *Broederbond,* the xenophobic and fanatic hierarchy of Afrikaners council who controlled the Nationalist party, had been influenced by Rev. Gray, and protected us from police interrogation, although he was aware that we could still be under surveillance. No one ever knew for certain. As long as one was not known to be actively involved in political intrigue, it was relatively safe, though one was always aware and on guard.

However, Bis was determined to take one last vacation. I was thankful for the opportunity of my sojourn down the rabbit hole, and like Alice, it was time to surface and explore the outside world.

CHAPTER 38
Lion Country, a Farewell

"Papa, the radio says South Africa is lion country, but we've never seen any, only those bored ones at the Johannesburg zoo, who stalk around and flick their tails to swat bothersome flies," Enver complained.

Nadya countered, "I feel sorry for them. They are so proud. They pace back and forth in their small, unfenced lairs glaring at us. Imagine if the moat wasn't there—they would jump over and maul us. We're lucky they aren't leopards or tigers."

Subsequent to that conversation, Bis and I planned a safari to the Kruger National Park before leaving for England. Who knew if we would ever return? It would be instructive to our young children and give them a sense of the beautiful country we were about to leave behind.

Bis borrowed the new Volkswagen Kombi from Dabhel House; it slept six. We invited two young cousins, Nasim and Patrick, to accompany us on the trip. Picnic baskets and blankets were piled into the vehicle.

Driving north through Pretoria, we passed the Ndebele village with its colourful rondavels[4] and kraals.[5] The women wore beaded clothes and stunning headdresses of copper wire woven through their hair, and wire bracelets that wound around their ankles. I recalled a patient in difficult labour who was brought to Bridgman Hospital and how the copper verdigris had rubbed off onto the white pillow cases and sheets, much to the annoyance of the sister in charge.

---

4   Rondavel: a traditional circular African dwelling with a conical thatched roof.
5   Kraal: a traditional African village of huts, typically enclosed by a fence.

We loved the South African scenery, and it was an opportunity for Bis and me to revisit places that were memorable to us and acquaint our children with some of the grandeur of the African landscape. The long drive to Kruger National Park passed through some of the most stunning scenic views in the Transvaal low *veldt*. The *kopjes* (high ground) studded with thorn trees added an undulating pattern to the landscape lavish with kaffirbooms, purple jacarandas, blue gums, eucalyptus, and the baobab trees that were sacred to the San, or Bushmen. The forest formed a colourful tapestry that nestled in the golden light of the setting sun, creating a magical picture. The children stared in awe. All that beauty compensated for the long drive they had endured to reach the park, but their excitement heightened as we neared the entrance. The culmination of their quest to see lions in their natural habitat could not come too soon.

The lodges in the park were restricted, and the signs read, "Europeans Only." Those signs were something one never escaped in South Africa. It was important that the children understood what it meant, and why we were leaving. Children are never too young to learn about racial differences, and that discrimination is not acceptable. A wealthy, influential Indian merchant had wangled a permit to erect two rondavels in the game reserve for Indian visitors. But as a distant relative, he had invited us to spend our first night in the comfort of his mansion in Nelspruit, which was close to the reserve. After the long, tiring journey, we welcomed his hospitality and the use of the medicinal and herbal hot-spring bath on his property. This was followed by an extravagant meal with baskets of fruit and bowls of exotic nuts and sultana raisins, but we needed a good night's rest to be up when the gates opened in the morning.

Dawn and dusk were the ideal times to observe predators. Most big game conserved energy by resting during the hot noonday sun.

Jackals were the only animals that scavenged regularly during daylight hours. Afrikaans literature abounds with legends of the wily, diabolical jackal who prowls in search of an easy meal and out-foxes other animals.

Bis woke us long before dawn. We were too excited to eat the breakfast prepared by our host but were happy to take *padkos*, sandwiches, *samosas*, fruit juice, flasks of tea and milk for our short stay in the game reserve.

Daybreak was still a few hours away. The gates were closed when we arrived and dozens of vehicles were already lined up waiting to enter the park. The

Part One

drowsy children settled down but were roused by elephants bellowing and uprooting trees a few yards away. They were unable to actually see them as they appeared as shadows in the semi-darkness. With bated breath, the children waited anxiously, fearing and fantasising in the grey mist that the ghostly behemoths would break down the barriers and trample them to death.

Streaks of lustrous silver light crept out across the early grey dawn, gradually exposing the indigo sky and heralding in the new day. The children's curiosity mounted, and they fell silent, for a few feet beyond the barrier was an unforgettable sight. A pride of lions was approaching while vultures and black birds squawked overhead, and even the tall grasses seemed to quiver. Anxiously and with renewed excitement, they watched, but the lions wandered off into the bush. What a let-down.

Wardens armed with chain saws and rifles appeared in Jeeps and they cleared away the uprooted trees that were strewn across the road. One of the guards used a horn that mimicked a lion's roar and frightened the pachyderms away before the barriers could be removed, allowing the Kombi and the fleet of vehicles to enter.

Driving at a slow pace, we saw the peaceful giraffes seemingly undisturbed by the convoy of cars, nibbling away at the choice leaves from the top-most tree branches. Beside the long-necked beasts what a contrast the okapi presented, with their short necks and striped bodies, as they feasted greedily on *veld* grasses, ignoring all the traffic. I explained that okapi were thought to be first cousins to the long-necked giraffes, and they may have been distantly related to the quagga, who in turn were related to the zebra. You see, they are all cousins, just like humans!

"Mummy, what are quagga?" Nadya asked. "What a strange name."

"The San, or Bushmen, the original inhabitants of Southern Africa, gave them that name. It was derived from the sound the quagga made. They are extinct now, but were closely related to the zebra, although unlike the zebra, their striped heads and shoulders faded to a pale tawny colour with white legs. They resembled foals. My grandmother told us how they were hunted to extinction because they competed with livestock for grazing land. Quagga skins, or karros, were treated and were prized as rugs and bed covers. My grandmother kept one on her four-poster brass bed where she talked to my grandfather each night as if he were still alive. The karros had been a gift to her from her beloved husband, Arthur."

As I explained about the quagga, quick as a bolt of lightning, a congregation of kudu appeared. In a trice, they were gone, except for one straggler who limped awkwardly behind. The poor deer. Its time had come. It was surely a marked meal. Many species of the long-striding antelope hurried by, while herds of impala sniffed the air as they grazed at nearby watering holes, and then they too took off.

Chattering monkeys scampered from tree to tree, and boastful baboons upright on two legs made guttural noises stuffing their jaws and pounding their chests. "They remind me of King Kong in the comic books, but not nearly as big," said Nasim, while Patrick drew their attention to a large snake curled around a tree trunk, which frightened birds, lizards, and chameleons away. Suddenly, what from afar Bis had taken to be a rock started moving, and a gigantic tortoise ambled to the side of the dusty road. The children wondered whether it had heard the whirr of the approaching Kombi and had taken it for a danger signal.

In the early morning light, Bis drove on. He signalled for silence. He had spotted a lion, probably going after the injured deer, but the Kombi impeded its path. Bis stopped and a lioness and her cubs casually squatted right beside our vehicle. The lioness stared straight up at the children, who were agape leaning against the windows. They made eye contact. Perhaps she was inviting them to alight?

In amazement, the children were speechless until Nadya spoke. "Mummy, you have the same coloured eyes." The other children stared into the eyes of the lioness to affirm that it was so. Unperturbed and without blinking, the lioness out-stared them.

"It's fantastic! Only the Kombi is between us and their breakfast," Nasim remarked.

Bis had switched the engine off. "What a shame we're so close, but it's not quite light enough to take pictures. Anyhow, the flash may frighten her away."

I commented, "What patience she has. I wonder where the male is." We did not have long to wait. A loud roar announced his presence. It seemed that the lioness meekly obeyed her mate and gracefully got up. Her cubs trotted behind as she sauntered off into the bush. Had he trapped breakfast for the pride?

"The show's ended. She certainly knows her place," Bis chuckled, nudging me, though I did not take the bait. Bis started the car and slowly, we drove on.

"Well, now that we've seen lions, we can go home," he teased, to the chorus of protesting children.

For the moment, the excitement was over. The many springbok that crossed our path did not illicit the same thrill—they were so numerous that the children were becoming complacent. Then out of the bush, at first cautiously, a huge ostrich wobbled, followed by a rush of fluttering wings as the tribe of gangly birds took off in the opposite direction, most likely escaping from imminent danger. We drove on for miles, seeing herds of kudu and more deer. We spotted several rhinoceros that chomped on the long grass and bathed in the muddy water. Many flights of birds flew by almost unnoticed, except for the vultures and the crows that circled above making their raucous noise, and who obviously had found some leftover carcass. This was of little interest to the children. It was big game they had come to see.

Sensing their ennui, I said, "There are always interesting things afoot in this great reserve. The animals are more astute than we give them credit for. They're trying to preserve their lives and their privacy."

"Mum, is that true about their privacy?"

"Yes, ask a naturalist. He will tell you even stranger tales. My grandmother, who grew up in the Little Karroo, told us the weirdest stories about animals and their habits. Even house dogs sense danger and howl when someone is dying. Or that was what my grandmother believed."

Bis and I were no strangers to the game reserve, having visited it together on our own many times. One of the special attractions that I was keen to show the children was the San rock paintings of deer between 1,500 and 3,000 years old. Most of these were in caves, but I suffered from claustrophobia. I assigned Bis to take the children in the company of the armed guards while I waited in the Kombi. I did know of a couple of Bushmen paintings of deer high upon a cliff and I was prepared to explore those with the armed guide, who was stationed beneath the shallow rock-face.

We had covered many acres of the park and had sighted a lot of big game, including hippopotami wrestling and bathing, obviously trying to cool off in the noonday heat. The wildebeest and their young were feeding at watering holes and usually close by were the utterly ugly warthogs. A lonely tapir, with its snout glued to the ground foraging for ants caught the children's' fancy. Unfortunately, they had hoped to see tigers, but Bis explained that they would have to visit India to see those. They did not see any more lions; however, they spotted a leopard reclining on a huge branch enjoying a noon siesta. In the late afternoon, they watched a hyena chasing after impala. Cute meerkats, with their mascara-like goo-goo eye make-up, frolicked and squealed and delighted the children, but they too took off at the sound of the Kombi as it negotiated a steep incline.

It was time to leave, but not before we spent a night camping in the safety of the rondavel to witness the glorious sunset, and to experience a typical night under the stars. I wanted to remember the howling jackals and the panorama of the black African sky filled with scintillating stars—a watchful canopy over the animals' natural habitat.

The evening began at twilight with the unmistakable chirping of cicadas and croaking frogs, sounds that I associated with my childhood. Later, in the stillness of the night, I lay in my sleeping bag listening for the sounds of Africa.

The safari was a memorable farewell, our tribute to the land of our birth, and a reminder of what we were leaving behind. As I watched the stars above, I would forever remember the magnificent African night sky, and I recalled the first nursery rhyme my mother had taught me: "Twinkle, twinkle little star." Overcome with nostalgia, I felt blessed and hoped that in some far away galaxy, my mother was watching.

CHAPTER 39
Reminiscence: The London Years

'Sunny south africa' was how all the travel brochures described my native land, but that was a facade that hid the ugly truth of extreme racial discrimination, shame, subjugation, humiliation, and the constant fear of police surveillance, which had induced us to leave behind those we had come to love and respect. We were happy to be leaving, but there was the sorrow of parting and also a modicum of fear. Would our children thank us for depriving them of the loss of their dearly loved grandparents, who had moved in with us when our home was completed?

Once again, I would be leaving for London without my husband, but this time, I had two children to care for. I was in no hurry to reach our final destination, for it was wise to avail oneself of the perks that the airline companies offered on long distance flights. They paid for hotel stays on stop-overs until another flight was available the following week. I took the opportunity to stop in Kenya to visit friends and explore the sites—it was a welcome relief for the children after the long, tedious journey. Then onto Geneva, visiting old friends. Seeing Switzerland would lessen the waiting time until we were reunited later with Bis in London.

Reflecting on how I would manage to care for my family without all the help I had become accustomed to occupied my thoughts. I realised I would miss the things I had taken for granted. I would miss my in-laws, who had embraced me, and the love they showered on my children. I acknowledged the many generous contributions from my father and mother-in-law. The children would be leaving their loving grandparents. Enver would be deprived of the game he played with

Bawa each evening as he totalled the store's daily takings and prepared the bank deposit sheets. Enver said that he was sorry to leave as he watched Bawa darning socks, something he had promised he would teach Enver to do. Nadya would surely miss her nanny, Kristina, who for the past five years had lovingly tended her. Then there was Maria, the maid, and Queenie, the coloured laundress, who took much pride in the stiffly starched shirts that she laundered for her beloved doctor. There was James, the gardener, a *dagga rooker* (a marijuana smoker), who did his best work when he was high. How often had I bailed him out of jail for smoking up and sleeping wherever he happened to fall and not carrying his pass as all native adult males were forced to? I knew that the comforts I was giving up paled in comparison to the freedom and respect Bis craved—he needed to feel whole. In spite of everything, another milestone was behind, and I felt blessed. Strangely, and it may sound contradictory, but in essence we had lived a privileged life. But in reality, it was not material benefits that were lacking, but dignity.

Bis could not accompany us on this flight. He was awaiting the renewal of his passport and securing our finances from the sale of the house and the practice. Our return was imperative. South Africa had withdrawn its membership from the British Commonwealth and those South African citizens who wished to remain members were required to return before the deadline expired. Bis, as a member of the British medical association, would be allowed entry after the deadline.

Nadya and Enver were excited to be going to London, Enver's birthplace, and they had often heard me speak fondly of it—they could hardly wait for morning. Saying goodbye to their grandparents brought tears, and it was equally hard to be leaving their cousins and the aunties and uncles, and other family members who had come to the airport to bid us farewell.

This was the children's first experience of air travel, and their unhappiness was short-lived in the excitement of boarding the plane. Once the plane took off and ascended into the sky of cirrocumulus clouds, the lustre began to wear off, for they had to remain buckled in their seats. The tedium was relieved by a baby wailing, despite the young mother's effort to pacify it as she walked up and down the aisle—to the annoyance of the other passengers. Sheer exhaustion and the purring drone of the plane finally lulled the baby to sleep. Nadya and

Part One

Enver dozed but were roused when the stewardess brought lunch and bags with treats, orange juice, and colouring books. Six-year-old Enver thought maybe if the plane crash-landed somewhere in the sands of the Sahara Desert, which seemed to stretch on forever, they could be rescued by camel drovers. Now that would be an adventure!

Cautiously, Nadya asked, "What if we get hurt?"

"Don't be such a baby," Enver said, pinching her and helping himself to her orange juice.

"Please fasten your seatbelts. We will be flying around Mount Kilimanjaro, Kenya. It is a practice that is being resumed," said the voice over the intercom. What the voice omitted to say was that all flights over the mountain had ceased due to a plane crash the previous year.

Any boredom was relieved and the noise from the excited passengers was a blessing as the baby had started squalling again. The plane neared the mountain, banked, skirted the mountain top, and flew at an angle. Momentarily, it appeared to stall and wobble. The passengers held their breath and a hushed silence ensued. Then with what sounded like a hiccup, the engine purred into action and circled Mount Kilimanjaro twice around so that the snow-covered crater was visible to all, from all angles. The cheers and hoorays of the delighted travellers drowned out the cries of the irritating baby. The experience was thrilling and unforgettable—a treat that compensated for the long and monotonous flight.

We arrived in Nairobi in time for dinner. The next two days were spent visiting friends and sight-seeing. The highlight of our Kenyan stay was the guided tour to the Serengeti Game Reserve, but in the jaded and biased opinion of the children, it came too soon: only four days after their exciting visit to the Kruger National Park. Enver found it interesting, while Nadya asked, "Where are the lions?" The children made comparisons and were disappointed not to have seen any big game, but they were captivated by the thousands of pink flamingos that lined the shores of Lake Nakaru.

"That's one thing the Kruger doesn't have," Nadya said, by way of mitigating her earlier criticism. Unfortunately, the stay in Kenya was brief. They hoped that there would be another visit at some other time with their father and more time to explore the Serengeti.

Enroute to London, I surprised the children with another stop-over in Geneva to visit friends: Anika and Harish Kapoor, who worked at the Indian Embassy. It turned out to be a pleasurable adventure. My friends were not at the airport to meet us, and there was no response to my repeated phone calls. Enver was delighted. "We're lost," he teased Nadya, who was very sleepy. We waited for what seemed hours before I decided to go to a hotel, as both children were tired and peckish. It had been a long time since supper.

After a couple of phone calls, the desk clerk informed me that Geneva was deluged with tourists and delegates attending conferences and there were no hotel rooms available that night. Next to me, a kind gentleman waiting to be served overheard our plight and offered us his room. He explained that he would bunk with friends. I graciously accepted. He ordered a taxi and gave the cabby the address of the hotel and handed me his card. He had observed the two sleepy children and had made his generous offer.

The room turned out to be a lovely suite. Suddenly, the children perked up and complained that they were starving. I ordered biscuits and hot cocoa, which was served with chocolates and marzipan. The children begged me to cancel London and stay at the hotel. Just then, the phone rang—probably it was not for me, but I answered. It was the Kapoors.

"How did you know to call here?"

"We're sorry, Joan. There was a horrible mistake. The flight time had been incorrectly listed. And since you're settled for the night, we will pick you up in the morning. Have a good rest and good night, we'll talk tomorrow."

The following morning, the Kapoors met us and Harrish explained, "The old gentleman was an acquaintance of ours, and as a good Muslim he had recognised your surname. 'Bismillah' means 'in the name of God' and is revered by Muslims. He overheard the clerk address you, and you named us. He felt obliged to help a stranded mother and her two sleepy children and he telephoned me."

Switzerland was an exciting interlude. I felt it necessary to have as much fun as we could. It helped to pass the time until we would be reunited with my husband and compensate for his absence. More importantly, it would keep the children from getting bored. Who knew how long it would take before Bis joined us? Harrish adored children, and he took them to see all the sights, including the Castle of Chillon on an island in Lake Geneva. Best of all was their visit to the fairground, where I'm told Nadya got sick on the round-about. Later that evening, Nadya and Enver dined with the adults, who ordered Schlur for them, a non-alcoholic apple cider drink, which they served in champagne glasses, while the adults drank the real stuff. This prompted a Herr Professor to stop at the table and admonish the adults for encouraging such *kleine kinder* to imbibe and for keeping them up at that late hour. The children's most memorable time was the hike halfway up a mountain to a hamlet, where a yodeller blasted away on his instrument, welcoming hikers to buy a special cheese for a picnic. Time passed too quickly and we had to move on.

Upon our arrival in London, it was raining and that dampened the children's enthusiasm. Airplanes sprawled across runways that seemed to go on forever in the enormous airport. It was unlike anything they could have imagined and quite unlike the tidy, pleasant, and welcoming airport of Geneva, where they'd been given marzipan chocolates. "We should have stayed in Switzerland," Enver complained. They had never seen so many people bustling around, and so many planes bound for places unknown. "What a pity we can't inspect them," Enver said. He suggested that it was a good place to get lost.

Nadya begged him to be good; not naughty like he was in Kenya where he did not have his way and threw himself down the staircase at the New Stanley Hotel in Nairobi. He was lucky a gentleman had caught him, or he could have been hurt. I was furious and made him promise to behave himself, or else he would feel the back of my shoe.

We arrived at Sacks-Pick Residential Hotel, Swiss Cottage, on a misty grey evening. The long summer day that stretched out before nightfall intrigued Enver and Nadya, who were curious about the lengthy twilight hours just as I had been. I explained the summer solstice to them. They would have stayed up all night had they been allowed to. Six years had elapsed since my last stay, but some of the older residents were still there, and they were delighted to reacquaint themselves with the little boy they had known as a baby. Five-year-old Nadya charmed the old Herr Professor, who said she reminded him of the grand-daughter who was lost to him at Auschwitz.

Our stay in Swiss Cottage was brief. I found a lovely flat in St. John's Wood with access to a garden, and a good preparatory school within walking distance. It would be our base until Bis joined us. With any luck, he would not have to wait too long before getting his passport renewed. Often Indians were deliberately made to wait, a spiteful quirk of the racially-biased Afrikaner clerks.

I placed a long-distance call to South Africa to inform the family that we had arrived safely. It was 1960, and telephoning long distance was eons behind. It was not nearly as advanced as the service we take for granted now. I waited for the operator to call me back. Finally, my sister-in-law answered.

"We've arrived safely," I said. At some point, I jokingly mentioned the blisters on my fingers after washing the kid's undies and smalls in the wash basin. I thought of all the comforts we had sacrificed for freedom. The three minutes were up all too soon and the call ended.

To my surprise, a few weeks later a Bendix washing machine was delivered to the flat. My father-in-law had called his London agent and ordered it. My landlady was not amused but reluctantly gave permission to have it installed. When the wash cycle ended, I would take the laundry out and hang it on the radiators to dry. Fortunately, all the rooms were equipped with them. Quite often on a Sunday, fellow expatriates visited me with their soiled laundry. I was happy for their company and they joked that it was preferable to sitting like zombies watching the laundry spinning at the laundromat.

Two months had elapsed before Bis arrived. He could not wait to tell me about his latest ordeal. After waiting for his passport and the sale of the practice, he had been booked on a regular South African Airways flight direct to London. The plane was cancelled and replaced by the British Airways plane, the lauded Whispering Giant, which developed engine trouble, forcing the plane to land in the sweltering heat of Khartoum, with its grubby fly and insect-infested airport. A replacement part from London was being sent out to fix the stricken plane, and it would be two days before they would be ready to depart. In the interim, passengers would be transported and accommodated at a hotel.

As they began leaving, an announcement over the intercom called, "Dr. Bismillah, please report to the desk."

What now? Bis wondered as the fellow passengers boarded the bus.

"Dr. Bismillah, we've had a complaint from a passenger. You're not white, and therefore, you will not be able to stay at the same hotel."

Bis was aghast. He had been forced into buying a first-class ticket, because supposedly there was no seat available in economy class. He had no choice but to accept what he was told. In all departments staffed by European clerks, they exercised their authority and demonstrated their superiority. This was petty Apartheid, which occurred frequently, and government employees from the lowest levels used their positions to dictate to non-Europeans. Bis was outraged at how far the tentacles of Apartheid had reached into this seedy corner of the world.

Before he had time to answer, the clerk emphasized, "We are providing you, sir, with a chauffeur and a guide at your disposal. You will be accommodated at a first class hotel." Bis acknowledged that this was a sop in retaliation against the powerful South African economic giant, which demanded concessions from the less-rich African countries it traded with. Thus, he was not surprised by the timid acquiescence of the Khartoum Air Officials.

"Thank you," was all Bis could muster. It was a kind gesture, but it did not offset the personal humiliation and anger he felt. Bis spent the rest of the time reading at the hotel. At least it was clean and air conditioned, and he did not need to meet his fellow passengers, who had objected to an Indian.

The children were delighted by their father's return and the summer holidays were in progress for another eight weeks. Bis spent the time entertaining them. He took them to Lords Cricket Ground to watch a match, to the theatre, on a visit to Madam Tussauds Wax Museum, and to the British Museum before accepting a senior registrar's post at West Herts Hospital in Hemel Hempstead, Hertfordshire. The two-year contract was in preparation for the specialist examination in obstetrics and gynaecology.

A week before the schools reopened, we gave up the flat in St. John's Wood and moved to a flat in Hemel Hempstead, where Bis was to be the senior registrar.

Hemel Hempstead was one of three new towns in Hertfordshire re-built after the war to accommodate the thousands of people whose homes had been bombed during the Nazi air raids. It had been newly reconstructed on the remains of an old rural village, and the ancient red-brick church had been converted into the obstetrical unit, where Bis would do much of his work.

The hospital board had acquired a newly-erected block of flats in the Marlow Mall property conveniently situated opposite the hospital. The flats were spacious and built on two levels with bedrooms downstairs. The large, attractive bathroom with a skylight was upstairs off the entrance hall. I found this curious—most English homes that we were acquainted with skimped on bathrooms, and the bedrooms contained a washbasin. Some expats and Americans joked that the British were averse to bathing, hence the basins. Word got round that if you were contemplating buying a house, it was preferable to buy from South Africans or Americans, for they generally contained all "mod-cons," including central heating! The hospital board had acquired the flats and rented them out to the doctors. They were subsidized, for the doctors could not have afforded them on their low salaries. Once again, I had to adjust to life in a parochial town.

The flat was cozy, and we were lucky to have under-floor electric heating, but when the bill arrived at the end of the month, Bis declared, "This is the end of twenty-four-hour heating."

"Why? What do you mean?"

"Because the cost is almost as much as I earn. You will have to wear jumpers to keep warm and turn on the heating as it is needed."

Bis carefully monitored the time and limited the use of heating, which is what most people in England did if they were fortunate enough to have heating.

On a back street across from the doctors' flats was an old Tudor mansion that housed a few single doctors, and it was used for the doctors' communal dining room and a recreation room where a blazing log fire burned in the grate. It was a gathering place and all our leisure time was spent in the warm, comfortable lounge.

The Rudolph Steiner primary school in Kings Langly was six miles away, and Enver and Nadya were enrolled there. Each day I drove them to and fro. Their fees were paid directly from our bank account in South Africa, where the money from the sale of our Potchefstroom home and Bis's practice were invested under his father's shrewd direction. There was a restriction on how much we could take out of the country. However, the car had been bought and paid for in South Africa but delivered to me in London.

The children had settled into the school, where the curriculum differed from the usual government school, and emphasised the arts and music, which pleased them. But Nadya pleaded, "Mum please tell them I hate 'gertrood salad', it's all red and horrible.

Part One

Enver, reported that Nadya gobbled pink meat, which he suspected was pork, a fact he reported in a letter to his grandfather. Having lived with their grandparents in a Muslim environment, he knew pork was taboo and considered it not Kosher. Thus, I refrained from cooking porcine products, in deference to the family who observed the rule of Islamic law.

— ⚜ —

My family settled down to a more ordered life. Bis was home every night and answered calls from the flat, and the hospital was a few minutes' walk away. We spent more time together without the distraction of nannies and maids, who had ministered to all the children's needs. They were old enough to no longer require those kindly people. It was a bonus that we spent more time with our children, but I admitted that I missed the service of maids and house staff. I soon learned to do without them, and I found housekeeping in the flat quite easy. The hospital supplied an Irish maid twice a week. Nuala was a middle-aged widow who regaled the children with tales of Ireland and leprechauns. More importantly, Bis and I were free and did not worry about police or surveillance and the contemptuous political society we had left behind.

We adapted to our new life, looking after our children and being responsible for their welfare. Bis and I were happy. His status at Hemel differed from that at Baragwanath, where he was treated as an underling. Here he was on equal footing with his peers. Our biggest problem, if you can call it that, was to adjust to the weather! However, it was conducive to study; Bis's final specialist exam was two years away.

Without warning, winter arrived and the white snow blanketed everything, turning the drab greyness of a British winter into a short-lived fairyland. The first snowfall closed the weekend market in the square. Young people bundled up and indulged in snowball fights, and children screamed happily. Enver and Nadya joined the fun but soon gave up. Nadya was marooned knee-deep in a drift trying to cross to the Tudor Mansion for hot chocolate. She was rescued by one of the doctors. Bis, her cowardly father, was not about to brave the cold. Snow seldom lasted in and around London, and within days the melting snow caused unsightly puddles, which was a hindrance and messy. The sunless days resumed their grey habit, and Nadya stated that the pale sun looked more like a faded paper moon.

After I dropped them off from school and parked the car, the children spent time reading or playing parlour games in front of the log-stoked hearth where a fire burned brightly. Later they braved the cold and dashed home across the way for supper, a bath, and bed.

Bis spent our time with the children reading stories and monitoring their reading. Enver was impatient and added his own words, while Nadya painstakingly pondered over them. Her school report stated that she worked like a Trojan and was good at eurhythmics. On the other hand, Enver was easily distracted. One day, I was summoned to see the headmaster. During an English lesson by an eccentric English author, Enver had calmly stated that the cows were in the wheat field. All the children rushed out, only to find the cows in the pasture lazily chewing their cud and the wheat field gates securely fastened. Enver confessed that the lesson was boring and he thought a diversion was called for.

The Rudolph Steiner School had served the purpose in acclimatising both children in their new environment. However, the time had arrived to consider a regular prep school if the children were to attend a secondary school that would prepare them for matriculation and university entrance.

Bis's two-year contract at Hemel was ending. He enlisted my help in researching data for his thesis, a task I enjoyed. It was constructive and my midwifery training was an asset, as I could help research and make notes for him at the Royal College of Obstetrics and Gynaecology situated in Regent's Park. The weekly trip provided an opportunity to resume my weekly lunches with friends in London. My time was taken up typing Bis's thesis, and in my spare time, I occupied myself with a marketing-research programme, fairly new at the time.

Periodically, the hospital medical staff received free theatre and concert tickets, which was a welcome bonus; it augmented the doctors' low salaries and provided relief in a busy work schedule.

One day I returned to find Dr. Rex waiting for me. We had not seen him since our Baragwanath days. I was surprised to find him in this out of the way place after an absence of so many years.

Part One

"Hello, what are you doing here? How did you know where to find us? We're unlisted."

"It's easy to find people here. I called the Medical Board, and they gave me the hospital address. From then on it was plain sailing."

"Of course. Are you visiting?"

"We're neighbours. I have a job in St. Albans."

Rex became a regular visitor who enjoyed a home-cooked meal and made many long-distance phone calls, for which he never offered to pay. That was not surprising, as he was always broke and continued to borrow money from friends to whom I introduced him. He took advantage of our hospitality, and it was left to me to entertain him. As Bis continued to prepare for the specialist's exam, he ignored Rex.

"I'm left to compensate for your boorish behaviour," I complained.

"It's entirely your fault for being hospitable. And further, I don't trust him."

"What do you mean by that?"

"There's something fishy about him that I can't quite put my finger on, and his tales do not add up."

I accepted Bis's opinion, but let it pass and took no further notice, as I was feeling unwell. Bis referred me to see his boss, who confirmed that I was pregnant. Now that my life was working out satisfactorily, I wondered how I would manage another child. I decided to have the pregnancy terminated. Nadya, our youngest, had just turned seven, and I could not entertain the idea of another baby, especially as we were so far away from family and friends. Moreover, could we afford another child?

"Bis, I don't think that I can cope with a baby. We do not have the resources, or family support, or a nanny, as I had with the other two."

"Joan, I'm sure we'll manage. I'm against an abortion."

"Bis, we always manage, but I don't relish the thought of a third child in this apartment. We've lived here for two years, and it is rather cramped. I put up with it because I knew it was temporary. I understand the life of a registrar and his family is of necessity peripatetic and we had no trouble adjusting, and moving around was part of the process of you becoming a specialist..."

"Look, darling, you know how I feel. I'll leave it entirely to your discretion. You will not be able to have it done at this hospital."

The more I thought about it, the more my morning sickness increased, and I was perpetually tired. "All right, I'll go to London and get a referral from Dr. Abram. He'll arrange it for me at his hospital."

Although Bis did not agree, he was too preoccupied with the written part of the exam, and his contract would end in six months. He had been offered a senior position at a London hospital, a situation that pleased me, as it meant moving back to the city. With the children at school, I could resume work full-time with a marketing research company, where I had worked part time from home before moving to Hemel. A baby would scuttle any plans I had. In spite of Bis's objection, I was determined to go ahead with the termination, but in all honesty, a twinge of guilt must have resided in a crevice of my brain. Initially I had been opposed to abortion because somehow it was immoral, and moreover, I had allowed Bis to dictate our lives according to his plans. Now I had changed my stance, and I was acting contrary to his will.

All arrangements for the termination of my pregnancy had been made. I would stay with our friends, Abram and Yasmina, before and after the procedure. I went out to dinner with them that evening before I was admitted to the ward at eleven o'clock that night. The midwife was not pleased with my timing, but she had her orders directly from the chief of obstets and gynae, Dr. Abram's boss, who would be performing the operation the next morning. She left me to undress.

I began undoing my buttons and to my consternation, I spotted a cockroach crawling along the bedside locker. I was horrified. It was followed by a few others. I loathed them. I grabbed my bag and, not waiting for the nurse to return, fled down two flights of stairs into the street. There I found a phone booth and made an urgent phone call. "Yasmina, please fetch me. Hurry, I'm in the phone booth outside the hospital."

I ran to the car even before it stopped. "I can't go through with it," I said through tears. "I must phone Bis right away." Yasmina comforted me and we drove off to her home.

The phone rang several times before Bis answered. "Bis, it's me." Before I could say anything, Bis interrupted, "Darling, what's wrong? Are you okay?"

"No," I sobbed. "I can't go through with it. Please don't worry. Yasmina will drive me home tomorrow morning and I'll explain then."

Part One

I heard Bis sigh. "What changed your mind? I'm relieved. I'm on call, otherwise I would fetch you now. Are you sure you're all right?"

"Yes, obviously my subconscious took over and I knew you would approve of my decision. It seems I spend my life pleasing you."

I did not regret my decision to keep the baby, but I suffered severe morning sickness. My doctor prescribed thalidomide, but Bis forbade me from taking it. Later, the tragedy and sad repercussions for those mothers who had taken the pills proved Bis's decision correct. In hindsight, the nausea gravidarum was a small discomfort compared to the tragedy and repercussions caused by thalidomide. It spared us the agony many mothers and their babies suffered. We were fortunate to be so blessed.

Like our other children, Nisha too was a premature baby, but she weighed six ounces more than Nadya at birth. Years later, I told my daughter, "You owe your life to a cockroach, and to the legend that claimed children born in the old converted parish church were blessed and were under the protection of an auspicious star." I wished that mothers too were protected, for I had to wear a warm bed-jacket throughout my stay. The heating was inadequate and I was discharged from the draughty ward with a severe cold and sore shoulders. Fortunately, Nisha was bottle-fed. I believed the legend confirmed; that Nisha too was fortunate to have escaped the consequences that so many other unfortunate children had suffered as a result of the thalidomide prescribed for their mothers.

Bis had completed his two years and an extra six months as a senior registrar and obtained his specialist degree from the Royal College of Obstetricians and Gynaecologists in London. He was offered a position at St. Mary Abbot's in Kensington, London. I could not have been happier, for we had to move back to central London. With a third child, we simply needed more space. Taking everything into account, we bought a house in Surbiton, a mile from Kingston. We were fortunate the money came from the Potchefstroom account, and that Bis's investment in a rental property in the heart of Potch was gathering interest. Through the London agent of Dabhel House, we were able to get sufficient funds from South Africa to purchase the house.

The front of the beautiful old Tudor house had wrap-a-round, leaded bay windows. The stairwell was lit by an oriel stained-glass window. The house required a fair amount of work and a contractor was hired to do the alterations. The coal cellar off the kitchen was converted into a space to house the Bendix washing machine. Bis had accumulated a four-week holiday, and he managed to help with the painting. It was the first time that he had actually done some manual labour and he found it therapeutic working in the garden. He maintained that it was a welcome break from studies. Here was an opportunity for me to use my decorating skills.

Bis loved the idea of gardening and tended the many apple and pear trees. There were a hundred rose bushes in the garden, which needed pruning. Bis spent his month holiday before starting his post at Kensington helping to get the place in order. We hired an old Scotsman to help with the gardening. He claimed that he had been employed there and was responsible for planting the rose garden.

Our home was comfortable, but I could not imagine living without heating in the cold, grey winter months, especially now that we had a young baby, and I insisted on central heating. Our neighbour, a retired doctor who had the identical Tudor house, was dubious about the effects of central heating and told Nadya, who often accompanied him on his daily walk around the block, how dangerous it was.

"Central heating is most unhealthy, especially for your baby sister."

"But it's nice and warm. We don't freeze like I do when I visit my friend's home," Nadya confirmed.

The holidays were over and the children, who had spent two years at Rudolph Steiner, were to attend a regular school. Enver was enrolled at Shrewsbury House Prep School as a weekly boarder, two streets away from our new home, and he would spend weekends at home. Nadya attended a day school St. Mary's Girls Convent. Fortunately, school fees were paid directly from our South African funds. We could not have afforded it on a doctor's salary.

A second car was out of the question. I dropped Nadya off at school, and then I drove Bis to work at St. Mary Abbot's after a weekend off-duty, with Nisha snuggled in a carry-cot on the back seat, stopping every now and then to check that she was comfortable. Driving with a baby passenger was entirely a novel experience.

Part One

Life in Surbiton was busy. I held open house for the many expatriates who sought a temporary place to stay. It became a home away for the relatives studying or those passing through London on business. Reg Turvey, a South African artist, was an old friend who was attending a Baha'i conference in London, and he spent a week with our family. He surprised me with a series of three water colours of South African scenes to remind me of home. He painted them on butcher's wrapping paper that he had found on the kitchen table. They are among my cherished possessions and still adorn a place on my present living room wall.

Summer ended and there was an abundance of apples and pears. People stopped by and asked if they could have those that had fallen. Bis and I were happy to share them, for we had stacked two crates of neatly wrapped apples, which we stored in the cool garage. They came in handy during the winter months for pies and desserts. I offered them to the children's schools. The boys' school requested two hundred, preferably all the same size! While the nuns at St. Mary's arrived wearing work aprons and carrying large tarpaulins, they cleared the small orchard. Each week when the roses were in bloom, the Scots gardener would trim and pick roses for his church.

Although Bis was home only three nights a fortnight, the children and I had lunch with him on the Sundays that he worked.

Enver quipped, "Sunday lunch with father at hospital consisted of three kinds of veggies, large quantities of mashed potatoes, boiled potatoes, and not enough roast potatoes." There was the Australian doctor who filled his plate with most of the sliced roast meat, not in the least concerned about other diners.

I could not have been happier, and I took Nisha everywhere in a carry-cot, sometimes stopping at a lay-by on the road to bottle-feed and change her. Our friends visited and there was so much activity in London: the galleries, the theatre, and concerts. Hyde Park with the children and Nisha in a stroller, on a Sunday afternoon, was a special treat. Other favourite places were Hampstead Heath, where we went for long rambles when we visited friends who lived in the area, and Kenwood House Art Gallery, where tea was served in summer.

Bis had more free time at home. Weekends when he was on call, young Nisha and I spent the time at the hospital, where nurses were only too happy to babysit while I enjoyed a social life, playing Bridge and meeting people at the hospital pub, which was frequented by artists and journalists.

Quite unexpectedly and by sheer coincidence, or so it appeared, Rex popped up again and was a frequent visitor to our home.

"I have a job at Moorefield's Eye Hospital in London, and I also work at a clinic."

"You seem to follow us around," I said.

"It's pure coincidence," Rex said. "Do you mind if I bring an American friend who is dying to meet you? I told him we knew each other from Bara. I must warn you, he is not short like this. Rex bent his left arm at the elbow and tucked it tightly against his waist, then pointed the right-hand fingers upward. "He is nearly seven foot tall." He stooped forward as he explained, still holding the akimbo position.

I was bewildered. "Why are you holding your arm and hand like that? Are you in pain?"

"No, I'm okay. It's a habit when you have such a tall friend—it's a custom from my tribe that I believe in. If you hold your hand flat, and he straightens his hand, it means you will stunt the person's growth. In his case, it means wishing for his death, since he is already full-grown, and I can't do that to him."

This made absolutely no sense to me, especially as he was a doctor, but I did not know enough about African lore. What surprised me was his attention to it at this time, especially having known him since our Bara days, when he'd appeared quite worldly. Now he was ill at ease and superstitious, blinking his eyes, and he actually made the sign of the cross several times as he performed the peculiar stunt again. I honestly did not know what to make of his strange behaviour. All his worldliness seemed to have been lost and replaced by ignorance and superstition. I could not imagine what had caused him to change.

One evening, without warning the American accompanied Rex, and as Rex had mentioned, the man was well over six feet tall. He had to bend his head to enter through the doorway. But soon after his arrival and introduction, he asked to be excused, as he had to urgently return to his office. Rex apologised more than once for his friend's sudden departure. Rex seemed uneasy and subdued and was brooding, but he continued to bemoan the friend's departure. Then he began playing and tickling Nisha, who squealed with delight. He remarked, "Babies are so innocent."

Weeks later, I had an urgent dental appointment. Rex had offered to babysit Nadya and eighteen-month old Nisha, and he had not shown up. I phoned his clinic, only to be told that it was not a clinic but a book-maker's bucket shop. I was surprised, but knowing Rex, I shouldn't have been.

"Well, may I please speak to Dr. Rex?"

"Do you mean the tea boy? He's working to pay some of the money he owes us. His American friend had promised to get money from some friends of Rex, but that did not happen."

I was flabbergasted but I recalled Bis's earlier warning: "Please be careful. I don't trust him or his friend. There's something odd about the American as well."

CHAPTER 40
A Highland Fling

Toward the end of 1963, we sold the house in Surbiton and made a tidy profit, as the new owners wanted most of the furniture, and they loved the central heating and the Bendix washing machine. We moved into a ground-floor flat in a converted old manor house in Hampstead Heath. It fulfilled my dream to live in that part of London, where I had many friends. We were surrounded by fellow South Africans, who had fled the rigours that Apartheid imposed. Expatriates referred to Hampstead as the "Golden Ghetto," for most were professionals or business people and had little trouble settling in. Their only grudge was the dreaded English winter, but even that was easily overcome by the warmth and hospitality of a community who supported each other in times of need, particularly through the bleak winter months.

The Heath was one of our favourite places, where we took long walks, and the children revelled in the changing of the seasons. The red and orange-hued autumn leaves were a harbinger of winter, which momentarily was easily forgotten as the children gambolled and kicked through the rustling mounds of leaves that exploded into colourful bits, drifting and settling back into untidy heaps.

Bis was a senior registrar in obstetrics and gynaecology at St. Mary Abbot's Hospital in Kensington. The hospital was located in west-central London, where the residents enjoyed an active social life. The onsite pub attracted the wives and friends, as well as journalists and artists, and weekends when Bis was on call, I spent time at the hospital. I was fortunate to have the nurses babysit Nisha, who was almost three. This allowed me to participate in Bridge games and social activities. One night a month, a gala dinner was held and the proceeds went to a charitable organisation.

Nadya and Enver, who remained a weekly boarder at his school, spent the weekends with our friends, Dr. Abram and his wife Yasmina, who had four children. Three of them were slightly older than mine. They lived in a Georgian house in Stanley Gardens. All the houses along four streets backed onto a large, square quadrangle that formed the common gardens and playground. There were tall old oaks, horse-chestnut, elms, and evergreen trees, begonia and holly bushes, and large tracts of lawns. It was an endless source of delight for the children of the neighbourhood, and it was ideally suited to stage cricket games, Rounders', or to play Hide and Seek and Blind Man's Bluff, games that continued well into the long twilight summer evenings. Their joyful shouts could be heard well beyond the square and it did not end until dark when they were ordered indoors. It was a wonderful way to spend their holidays. In addition, they were introduced to the arts; they went to the theatre and one of their favourite pastimes was to visit the Victoria and Albert and the British Museums, where they were permitted to roam around at will, meeting up later for tea.

London was exciting, and like most South African expatriates, I was politically active, attending anti-Apartheid meetings without fear of reprisals. Although it was brought to our attention to be careful, for amongst us there were informants who reported directly to BOSS, the South African secret police. Happily, I found it more rewarding to join the Campaign for Nuclear Disarmament and I assisted in painting signs with "Ban the Bomb" slogans. Bis supported my pastimes, but my young family prevented me taking part in the Aldermaston Marches with Canon Collins. With Nisha in a stroller, eagerly I joined the hundreds of protesters who squatted in Trafalgar Square with Bertrand Russell, who lectured on the evils of nuclear armaments.

South Africa House overlooked Trafalgar Square, and unbeknownst to the anti-Apartheid protesters, cameras were trained on the site. The television pictures were displayed in the large lounge, where coffee and *koeksusters* were served to expats who gathered there to chat and read the South African newspapers. After one such visit, quite unexpectedly Rex showed up and warned me to be wary.

"Joan, be careful. The pictures are taken by BOSS and are used to identify all dissidents."

"What does it matter, we're not going back." *Why worry?* I thought. *We've left the country.* "Anyway, how do you know?"

"My cousin is in the police force, and he is worried that I will get into trouble with the authorities and lose my scholarship."

"Is he in London? I thought you were sponsored by the American Church."

"I never know where he is, but what news I get is from my father."

I too began to be suspicious of Rex; his statements did not add up. Perhaps Bis was right to be wary of him. We didn't see him or the American again, and suddenly, as if we had waved a wand, Rex disappeared from our life and we did not see nor hear from him until many years later. In 1994, when the Truth and Reconciliation board took place in South Africa, it was learned that Rex's debts had forced him to work for BOSS, the South African secret spy agency. He and an American had narrowly escaped a murder attempt. There were news reports that their landlord, who owned the house in Regent's Park, was a retired colonel, and apparently the house and its occupants at that time were under surveillance by MI5, the British Spy Agency! I cannot verify if any of this was true, but several acquaintances told the same tale. The last I heard of Rex was that he had been spotted at the Ascot races wearing a top hat and tails.

While I was blissfully happy, once again I became aware of my husband's restless mood. He was accustomed to a heavy work load, and now he was not as busy as he would have liked. The hospital catered to a different class of people and operated more like a private clinic, and it differed from a teaching hospital.

Through the medical journal, Bis had learnt of the doctors' strike in Canada and the general lack of doctors in that country. Information came through the Scottish Medical Association, but deliberately Bis refrained from sharing the news with me. He knew I would not want to leave London, especially now that we were living in Hampstead and appeared to be well settled. Typical of Bis, a very private individual, he was careful to ensure that whatever plans he had would come to fruition, and only confided in me when he was certain of their success. In fact, he was quite devious! He seldom banked on chance, aware that in this instance the suggestion of a Scottish holiday would be welcomed by me without question.

Part One

"Joan, how would you like a holiday in Scotland before the children return to school?" Bis asked casually.

"The children will be delighted; it will be their first real holiday as a family in three years." I thought that it would be lovely for them to meet Uncle Darren, who was not a relative, but a close friend. Out of respect, it was customary to address elders as uncles and aunts. I packed our bags, unaware my life was about to take another drastic turn.

Dr. Darren, whose family hailed from Durban, had done his medical training in Edinburgh, where he had married a young Scots lady, and he had not returned to the country. A surprise visit would be welcomed. Aunt Helen, as we called her, had invited us many times, and their only child Fiona would be happy to see us. Driving to Edinburgh, we stopped off at places of interest. The weather was balmy and one of the places everyone was keen to see was Loch Ness. Enver and Nadya swore they spotted the monster. They thought it great fun to live in bed and breakfast homes and be spoilt by little old ladies with sweets and ice cream treats.

Tired but happy, we arrived at Uncle Darren's house. He was standing on the doorstep on his way out. After a brief greeting he said, "Joan, take the children inside. Auntie Helen and Fiona will take care of you. Bis, you may as well come with me, I'm off to chair a meeting. We'll dine when we get back."

Bis followed meekly, and I was unaware how serendipitous the impact of that meeting would turn out to be.

Fourteen-year-old Fiona took great pleasure in our company. It was a special holiday now that they had house guests, and all rules were relaxed. Enver and Nadya were overjoyed to have her enlighten them in the way only a pseudo-sophisticated pubescent girl could. They played Monopoly, Scrabble, and Hide and Seek in the large old house with its nooks and crannies, where good natured Nadya was forever on a fruitless quest to find Fiona and Enver, who were too well hidden.

"You're awfully quiet Joan," Aunt Helen said.

"No, I'm just tired. I should put Nisha to bed." I was troubled, but I could not account for the odd feeling that was clouding my usual optimistic disposition.

"Mummy, Mummy look! I've got a hickey." Enver burst in excitedly pointing to his neck.

"What's that?"

"It's a love bite. Fiona gave it to me."

Before I could answer, Darren and Bis got back. Bis was waving an envelope in the air. "Guess what! I'm off to Canada," he exclaimed excitedly.

I was perplexed. "When? Why, what for?" I asked hesitantly.

"They're airline tickets," Darren explained. "The meeting was an invitation from the Rotarian Chapter in the town of Fergus, Ontario, Canada. The doctors are on strike, and there is a shortage of doctors, and they are desperate for medical help. The invitation is for a doctor to fill that need. Fergus is essentially a Scots settlement. It is billed as the home of the Highland Games, which are held annually. Hence, they appealed to us. Basically, they need a doctor who will have *carte blanche* to assess the situation, and guess who volunteered to go for ten days?"

The children thought it a great adventure. I felt a horrible sense of foreboding along with sudden cramps in my abdomen, but I remained silent.

Helen said, "Bis, you're so lucky, and you're the right age. It would be foolish to turn it down. What an opportunity!"

Later when we were alone, I said, "Did you have to volunteer for the assignment?"

"You're unhappy. I saw your reaction. Joan, look what better way to check it out? And all expenses paid. We'll drive back to London in a few days' time, and then I'm off."

Now I was convinced our Scots holiday was turning into a huge mistake.

Once again, Bis had his way and left for Canada a few weeks later. He was overwhelmed by the welcome he received upon his arrival in Fergus, and eagerly he completed the assessment of Groves Memorial Hospital.

A South African colleague practising in Fergus was in Ottawa preparing to write the Canadian medical exam. He was the assistant to a Fergus doctor, who had died while he was away and would not return until he qualified, which could still take some time. Of the two doctors who serviced the town, one, the doyen, had broken his leg, and the other had suffered a severe heart attack, thus leaving the small town without a doctor.

Groves Memorial Hospital was quaint and served the population of just under four thousand people. It was surrounded by a large farming community.

Bis took stock, and he made suggestions for the improvement of the hospital that were approved by the board. He was offered a position and urged to stay on.

Bis accepted their offer on condition he return to London to discuss it with his wife and to inform and resign from St. Mary Abbots, which would have no trouble finding a suitable replacement at short notice. He promised to be back as soon as he had settled his affairs.

Back in London, Bis faced the difficult task of trying to convince me of his decision to immigrate to Canada. It was all so sudden, and as he feared, his argument regarding a new start to life fell on deaf ears.

"For the first time in years," I argued, "we've settled down as a family."

"Yes, but here is an opportunity I can't refuse, and we'll have more time together in Canada. The experience alone will be invaluable."

"The children attend good schools. Why do we have to go tearing off to God knows where? I suppose you've pledged to return. Whatever happened to consultation?"

"Joan, you're being unreasonable. It's a chance to start afresh."

"No, be honest, it's your chance to be a big fish in a small pond. And further, we're always starting afresh."

"That small pond can swallow the whole of England! It will be an opportunity for me to practise without the headache of administrative duties, and I'll be able to concentrate solely on medicine without worrying about financial matters."

"You're infuriating and a self-centred prig. I almost hate you."

"You don't really mean that!" Bis said, taken aback by my outburst.

"What am I going to do in a place named Fergus that no-one has ever heard of? Have you ever met a Canadian? The only one I've ever met was dull as dishwater."

Bis was not prepared for any further argument and said deliberately: "Well in two days' time, you will meet several. We have an appointment at the Canadian Consulate, where we'll receive our papers. Do you realise how fortunate we are that everything's been arranged for us, including our medicals? And I'm assured of a good position, and furthermore I'll be on equal footing with all my peers."

I was livid. "You're devious and self-centred, and I'm not impressed—you invariably put your needs before all else."

"I'm leaving in a week after we've been processed. You will follow as soon as you've packed up."

"Now I'm being ordered. You certainly are taking my chattel status seriously. Whatever happened to your promise of our partnership?"

"I'm acting in our best interest. Ultimately, darling, you'll thank me."

"Never!"

Bis returned to Canada. I phoned my mother-in-law to inform her of his plans.

"Tell Abdul Haq that you won't go. You'll see, he'll come back. Tell him I said to stay. Canada is so far away!"

I thought, *So far away. Why did it matter? London too is far away, and it may as well be Timbuktu!* Bis phoned daily to ensure that I was packing up. Invariably, I had an excuse why I had not finished. I relayed his mother's message.

"Please ask Ma to support you in the style you're accustomed to. Also, see if she is prepared to take care of the children's school fees, which will be due when school re-opens after the holidays. I'm not returning to London."

I was fighting a losing battle, but I intended to drag it out for as long as I could. Just maybe Bis would relent. Deep down I knew my intransigent husband did not believe in losing. I was convinced he had planned the Scottish holiday relying on my gullibility, as he was wont to remind me.

That summer, London was filled with relatives and visitors from South Africa—all were eager to be entertained. It kept me busy and provided me with an excuse to delay the inevitable. I could not begin to pack up and to finalise the sale of the house without offending so many guests.

Nisha had a miniscule part in a movie, *Bunny Lake is Missing,* which was being filmed at her nursery school, "The House on the Hill." This provided another excuse to delay our departure. Nadya and Enver were fully occupied, going on field trips and to tennis lessons. They were enjoying life with the Abram children. London had never been more rewarding, but it could not last. Bis was impatient and entreated me to get on with closing the sale of our house and packing up. He missed his family. I was unsympathetic. The children kept asking, "When will we see Papa? And Mummy, when are we going to Canada?"

One morning I went to the bank and the cashier said, "Mrs. Bismillah, the bank manager would like to have a word with you."

Now what? I thought. I'd just settled the sale of the house.

"Good morning, Mrs. Bismillah. Please be seated. Your husband telephoned me yesterday. He has instructed me to close your joint account, to pay any outstanding bills, and to purchase your tickets to Canada. But before you leave, I will need you to sign the affidavit once the sale is finalised, and all money is to be deposited in the joint account."

I stood transfixed. I was speechless.

The manager continued, "Of course, there are currency restrictions, transferring sterling to dollars. However, you will be permitted to take the maximum family allowance."

I felt weak. I clenched my fist and without uttering a word or looking at the messenger, I took my leave. My eyes brimmed with tears as I drove home to phone Bis in Canada. "How could you humiliate me like that?" It was the age-old question of male domination over their female partners.

"Joan, it's four o'clock in the morning and I've been up all night. You're making no attempt to leave London. We can't continue this way. Let us compromise. Darling, please come, please try it out, I miss you, and I promise if after a year you haven't settled in, we'll return to London." Bis appeared solicitous, and with his usual guile, he managed to hoodwink me and have his way.

There was a lengthy silence. *Why and how does he always manage to make me feel guilty, and also ashamed?*

"Darling, in an imperfect world, Canada is a refuge from the indignity and terror of Apartheid."

There was a moment of silence. Neither of us spoke, and finally I answered, "Okay." I put the phone to rest in its cradle.

Part Two

CHAPTER 41
Woodlawn Memorial Garden Cemetery

I HAVE PASSED MANY MILESTONES ON MY JOURNEY THROUGH LIFE. NOW I have reached a bend in the road, and probably there are other milestones that I am bound to encounter. As I continue, I reminisce about the past, and I'm reminded of the numerous occasions I told Bis jokingly: "The moment you die, I will board the first flight bound for London! But of course you'll out-live me, merely to thwart any plans I may have so that you may continue to orchestrate my life until the very end."

"No, you will continue muddling through on your journey without me!" Bis prophesized.

My husband's death, when it occurred, devastated me, and I did not have the time to worry how I would fare. Overwhelmed as I was by grief, my survival depended on making sense of a life without the maestro who had orchestrated it for the best part of fifty years. There was little time to dwell on my loss, and ultimately, I had to answer the question he had asked out of concern for me: "What will you do here all alone?" I had no answer then, but now I know I have to continue to live and run the golf course we built. It was his passion, and it is a memorial to him.

It is seventeen years since his demise, and I'm still here, muddling through as he had predicted. Those who have loved and lost appreciate the anguish of travelling alone, and constantly I evoke poignant moments of the past that help to sustain me.

On the drive to the graveyard, I recalled the warm autumnal day and the sun-drenched road as we approached the tall, wrought-iron gates of the Woodlawn

Memorial Garden Cemetery in Guelph. It opened to permit our limousines into the tree-lined avenue streaked with glimmering light, which led into the parking lot. The family alighted and we were greeted by the splendour of the verdant gardens with their magnolia bushes, dogwood, and bougainvillea. The occasion was solemn, but the tranquil scene mitigated our grief at the loss of a beloved husband and father. Bis, a keen arborist and gardener, would have approved the aesthetics of the venue and the simplicity of the occasion.

We walked slowly towards the Belmont Chapel with the backdrop of native evergreens and unusual tree species, whose foliage was clad in colourful fall regalia. I welcomed the serenity that was punctuated by intermittent birdsong, and a lone hawk's screech. Under the marble mausoleum with its plastered dome, hand-painted in spring shades of gold, green, pink, and grey stood a bier supporting the plain wooden coffin covered by a kilim rug.

We gathered around the casket. The occasional stifled sob interrupted the silence. Bis, who had lived according to the dictates of his heart, had prescribed the final act for me to carry out. He had been specific about his burial. "Joan, I don't want a fuss," he beseeched me, and he had arranged to be cremated in a private family ceremony. This was contrary to his Islamic upbringing.

Enver read the "Prayer for the Dead" from the Baha'i Prayer Book, and Fazel, a nephew, read an Arabic prayer from the Holy Koran. Family members offered their silent prayers to honour their father and uncle. Bis may not have approved of the ritual prayers, but they comforted the mourners.

I was overcome with sadness and the nostalgia of the moment, and it rendered me speechless. I gazed up at the Tiffany stained-glass windows to shield my emotions, as I struggled to maintain my composure. Thoughts of my beloved husband of fifty years overwhelmed me. Among the blurred jumble of my thoughts was Bis's declaration of love, *"And what I assume, you shall assume. And every atom that belongs to me as good belongs to you."* He had inscribed it on the fly-leaf of Whitman's *Leaves of Grass*, his first gift to me so many years ago. Now those atoms would have to sustain me on my solitary journey.

I wiped away a tear and whispered, *"My Heart, go gently into the light."*

I remembered my reluctance to emigrate to Canada, and the months that had elapsed before the children and I joined him. So much wasted time!

During the last weeks of his life, Bis's words echoed: "Joan, finally in Canada, I found the dignity and the respect I craved, and at last I am content."

I marvelled why it had taken me such a long time to accept and believe that Bis had finally found his nirvana.

In my reverie, I recalled it was almost thirty-six years ago that with our three children, I had left our favourite city of London for a small town in Ontario to join my husband. The taxi cab was waiting, and I recalled the last-minute phone call Bis had made from Fergus, a place somewhere on that vast Canadian landscape. I was indifferent—for all I cared, it may as well have been in Timbuktu.

I had allowed the telephone to ring while I ushered the children out to the waiting taxi, ready to transport us to Heathrow Airport. My first impulse was to ignore the call, but then I hurried to answer. An anxious husband was on the line. "Darling, please bring sheets and towels."

I had no wish to begin life in Canada with an argument, and so I agreed and thought as I banged the phone down, *Trust Bis to be so impractical concerning domestic issues. Calling at the very last minute. Don't they have those items in Canada? Did it not occur to him to purchase them himself?* All our essential household goods had been crated and sent ahead. To avoid our prized Persian carpets contracting mould on the long sea voyage, we had packed them in an antique naval cedar chest together with *The Survey of Persian Art*, and the canteen of sterling silver cutlery, and transported the chest by air. A few pieces of furniture were in storage. I decided that whatever else we required could be bought in Canada.

The taxi driver allowed me fifteen minutes to do my shopping. He insisted that he had no choice but to stop off at Harrods. It was the only place with street parking at that hour. Any more time or delay would cause us to miss our flight.

Canada 1965

Arriving on a late October afternoon, the BOAC aircraft circled, waiting for permission to land at Toronto's International Airport. It gave my family our first glimpse of our new country. I stared out of the airplane window and despite my resistance to join my husband, I was impressed by the rich October colours of the Ontario landscape.

The children were amazed by the volume of vehicular traffic, all travelling at great speed on the intersecting highways down below. They could barely conceal or contain their excitement. Their whoops of "OOH" and "AAH," amused the other passengers. "Look at the all those cars, and how fast they're travelling. You'll never see that in London," Enver said.

"From here they look like giant beetles scuttling about," echoed Nadya.

With trepidation, I awaited my reunion with Bis, who for the past four months had implored me to leave London and join him. He missed his family and he believed that immigrating to Canada was in our best interest. In hindsight, I realised that he was correct, but then Bis always had a vision and planned for our future.

The formality of immigration was expeditiously dealt with. Before the clerk stamped my passport, he asked me, "Madam, why do you not have a surname, and in place of it, is w/o. What does it mean?"

I grinned. "Because, in South Africa I was merely the 'wife of' my Indian husband, Abdul Hak Bismillah."

The officer shook his head and handed back my passport.

My first impression of Canadians was the courtesy with which we were processed and welcomed. I had few preconceived notions about the country, except that it was deadly dull. Another milestone had been left behind. This was to be a journey of discovery and the beginning of a quest in search of an identity. How could I predict what life held in store? The old refrain *the past is prologue,* came to mind, and I resolved to meet whatever challenges awaited me. A new chapter in my life was unfolding.

My reunion with my husband was warm, but to onlookers it could have appeared to be restrained and did not seem to express the joy and love we shared. The children clamoured around him. Bis was delighted to see them, but he was an extremely private man who scorned shows of affection in public. After brief hugs, he led us to his new car, a large green Pontiac, where the porter stowed our luggage in the trunk. The car did not impress Enver, who exclaimed that it was big and shiny. He, of course, was comparing it to the compact British cars he was accustomed to. We drove the seventy-odd miles amid chatter and noticed the village signposts every few miles along the way. They were reminiscent of our recent holiday in Scotland: for instance, there was Aberfoyle, a place where we had dined during our stay in the Highlands. All the signposts harkened back to their Scottish origins. It seemed as if we would never reach our destination.

At last, an oversized placard with a thistle and a Highland dancer at the roadside appeared: "Welcome to FERGUS, Home of the Highland Games. Population 4,000." What a shock. The actual number of inhabitants was two hundred fewer. Bis had led me to understand that it was a town, but in reality, it was a rural dot on the vast North American hinterland—barely a village. I found myself in a world very different from anything I had experienced. It was unlike the rabbit hole of Potchefstroom, where I had lived after cosmopolitan Johannesburg, and world-famous London. Fergus was the epitome of the hypothetical Podunk town of North America. A small, insignificant, rural place.

On my husband's arrival in Fergus, the hospital board had secured lodgings for Bis with the Fardellas, a prosperous Italian couple and their middle-aged son, Tony. Their home was a large, mock-Tudor-style house on Union Street that was two doors away from the hospital. The Fardellas owned the local cinema and the greengrocers. In the interim, Bis was expected to find lodgings for his family. Unbeknown to the good people of Fergus was the fact that Bis was domestically incompetent. He relied on his wife to take charge of such matters. He had grown up in a male-oriented culture where women were at the beck and call of men, and here he was too proud to ask for assistance.

There were few houses for rent or for sale. Bis had been fortunate to obtain a newly-built brick cottage, very small, but it would suffice until we were settled. It was unfurnished except for new twin beds with blankets in each of the two bedrooms. Worn bedspreads secured with nails curtained the windows and provided a modicum of privacy, shutting out inquisitive neighbours. *Bleak*, was my first reaction, but I applauded the central heating, which kept the rooms cozy. It was superior to the British system where central heating was a privilege rather than a necessity and constantly had to be adjusted and only turned on in very cold weather.

After my disappointment of leaving London, I resolved to make the best of my situation. I reasoned that at the very least, we would be living under one roof, and being together as a family was worth the effort. As immigrants, we were neither pioneers nor refugees, for Bis had been recruited by the Rotarians to run Groves Memorial Hospital. Our family was in the vanguard of the thousands of fortunate South Africans who would flee Apartheid for a better life in England, Canada, and Australia. Finally, I was forced to concede we were here to stay, and I hoped our life would turn out to be an exciting adventure. All that my husband promised, although I had my doubts!

Driving into Fergus in a spanking new Pontiac motor car did not impress Enver, who was at the age when cars were important to young lads. He complained to Nadya that it was an American tinny machine. His sentiment expressed his British bias towards things American. The children were fascinated as they passed many houses where the front porches sported gigantic golden pumpkins lit from inside with candles that turned them into lanterns at dusk. Bis explained that they were Halloween decorations. At that time, Halloween to non-North Americans was merely a word describing the macabre when ghosts and goblins roamed freely. The children were enchanted by the ghostly effigies of skeletons that dangled from windows, roofs, and trees tops. The pleasure they derived was beyond their wildest dreams. It was a festival where a carnival atmosphere prevailed.

We had arrived a week prior to Enver's twelfth birthday, and he would celebrate it on Halloween at the end of the month. Best of all was the thrill of dressing up in witch, vampire, and demon costumes, and going door to door to "Trick or Treat" and collect free candy. How it differed from Guy Fawkes Day in Britain, where only a few needy children politely begged for a penny for the Guy. Here they played games in the street with other children and ran wild, a completely novel experience.

The informality was precisely what the convent-educated Nadya and Enver liked. It contrasted with his formal boarding school training. Nadya said the town reminded her of the Wild West she had seen in movies, but where were the "Red Indians" in their buckskin regalia, beaded moccasins, and turkey-feathered headdresses that she had read about? Where were they hiding? She was anxious to see them, and she could not wait to explore their new environment.

Nisha was not old enough to accompany her older siblings on their Trick or Treat adventure. She clamoured to see Tatsu and Misu, her Japanese playmates at her former nursery school, in London, and she cried to be taken to Regent's

Part Two

Park to feed the swans. She tried everyone's patience. To pacify her, I drove her about and tried to explain that we were in a new country. I bargained with the soon to be four-year-old, promising her all sorts of little treats in exchange for her promise to be a good girl.

I was happy that my family were settling in. However, I recalled my first evening and our meeting with the Fardellas. They had welcomed the family with an invitation to dinner. During the course of the evening, I was informed that it was a privilege to live on that particular tree-lined street with its lovely old limestone houses. Gleefully and with pride, Mr. Fardella told me that the only Jewish family in the town, owners of the men's haberdashery, were unable to obtain a permit to live on Union Street, and that they were compelled to build their home on the edge of the town. I was shocked by his attitude, but it was a sentiment held by other notable townspeople I met later on. It reminded me that racial prejudice was one of the reasons we had fled Apartheid and segregation, but politeness as a guest prevented me from responding. My four-year-old expressed the disgust I too felt but for a different reason. The old man's spittoon was on his lap, and Nisha said, "He 'pits too much, I won't kiss him," when it was time to leave.

Mrs. Mamie Fardella, an American lady and devout Catholic, had married the widower and settled in Fergus. She was familiar with some of the problems I would encounter in this little town. She still ordered her Folgers coffee from Chicago! On the mantelpiece in her living room was a statue of Jesus wearing a red cape. Nisha fell in love with the "doll" and asked to play with it. "No," said Mamie, "it's not a toy."

"What is it then?" asked the inquisitive child.

"It's Baby Jesus."

Nisha's ignorance perturbed Mamie, who invited the children to church on Sunday. I could hardly refuse, after that amusing reply. Sunday arrived and Enver, Nadya, and Nisha dressed in their best went off with Auntie Mamie. As the choir started singing, the priest walked in wearing a red surplice, followed by the servers.

An excited Nisha said, "There goes Baby Jesus."

"Shush, he's dead," said Mamie.

"Who shot him?" from the irrepressible child—she had been allowed to watch television with her older siblings in London.

Bis had not mentioned the ultra-conservative nature of this small Canadian enclave. He knew that it would have been another excuse for me to prolong my stay in London, thereby hoping to lure him back. Whatever guilt I may have felt for my delayed departure vanished when I was informed of yet another incident that had occurred weeks prior to my arrival. A dark-skinned teacher and his family were made unwelcome and they were run out of town. I thought, *am I supposed to feel grateful that we have been welcomed simply because the town was in need of a doctor?*

Fergus, a rural, predominantly colonial Scottish outpost of the British Empire, replete with its own brand of systemic racial bias, was comprised of a white Anglo-Saxon Protestant majority, who barely tolerated their Irish-Catholic counterparts.

I was ambivalent and troubled, but for the sake of the children, who were enjoying the novelty of our new country, and Bis, who was absorbed in his work at the hospital, I refrained from complaining. I did not vent my anger. Necessity rendered it politic for the locals to accept the East Indian doctor and his family into their community, just as I found it expedient to remain silent. In frustration, I chided myself, *how convenient it is for me to be quiet and complacent in the face of prejudice.*

Unable to vent my emotions, I busied myself with the cottage, which was completely inadequate for our needs. It was too small. To open the clothes' closet, it was necessary to sit on a bed or move it out of the way. I realised that I could not rely on Bis. I was his domestic idiot savant, and it was my duty to seek out an estate agent, assuming there was such a person available! To myself I muttered, *you're thinking like a condescending snob.*

Camping was how I described life in the cottage that first month. The lack of formality and order suited the children, who had no organised routine other than school, and they had amassed large stacks of Halloween candy to enjoy at leisure. Fortunately, they had not yet acquired the North American habit of watching television. In London, it was limited and a privilege rationed to weekends. We did not own one at this time but they watched it at the Fardellas'.

I was surprised by the well-stocked grocery stores and the variety of fresh produce. The abundance of fruit at affordable prices was unlike Selfridges in London, where watermelons were cut into rounds, stacked, and displayed on shelves like dinner plates, and cost as much as a whole melon did here. There were hands of bananas, oranges, bunches of grapes, and a variety of apples, which reminded me of my early days in London after the war. I was pregnant then, and every week, I received a ration of a Canadian apple and an egg, courtesy of a relative who was a doctor at the Royal Canadian Hospital in Buckinghamshire.

Although there was a furniture and a hardware store, shopping in Fergus was mainly done through the Eaton's or Sears' catalogues; a practice I was unaccustomed to. Therefore, I decided to visit their main department stores in Toronto—a seventy-mile drive away.

Two days after our arrival, I dropped the children off at school and asked Bis to take them to the Fardellas, who had issued an open invitation for supper any time I did not get back in time. I was determined to explore the city of Toronto, if only to find my bearings. I was an alien in this isolated town. First, I would stop at the licencing office and obtain a Canadian driver's licence. Friends in London had urged me to apply for an international licence before I left for Canada.

"You must get it. North Americans are a litigious lot, and they will sue you over the slightest infraction," I was cautioned by several British friends. At that time, there was an anti-American attitude, and slogans appeared all over London: "Yankee Go Home."

"I'm told they drive like cowboys over there," said another.

At the office in Guelph, a much larger town ten miles to the south of Fergus, the instructor spoke with a broad Scottish accent, yet he had never been out of the country. On the test drive, he told me to reverse and start again. "Remember, this ain't England where *yous* drive on the wrong side, eh."

I was accustomed to my compact British car, and I had to adjust to the large Pontiac and drive on the right-hand side of the road, whereas I had been accustomed to "keep left," which was firmly etched in my brain. But I was determined to obtain the licence, and with Nisha screaming in the back seat, I passed with ease, after the first gaffe.

Bis had implored me to be careful. He instructed me to follow Highway 401 East, the main highway to Toronto, and to exit at Yonge Street, which would lead directly to the central shopping district. Shortly after the exit, I stopped off at a filling station, and the attendant kindly explained the way to Eaton's and gave me a road map.

Nisha had finally stopped yelling. I promised her chips and ice cream, but first she had to promise to be a good girl. "I promise," she said.

At Eaton's, the first order of business was to fulfil the promise to my child. I wasted little time selecting most of the household goods I needed. The store clerk said, "Madam, it will be delivered in two weeks when we service your area."

"Is there any way it can be sent out sooner?"

"I'll have to ask the manager."

Impatiently, I tapped my fingers waiting for a decision. Things moved at a snail's pace even in the city. I clutched Nisha firmly with my right hand—she was intent on exploring despite her promise to be obedient.

At last, the clerk returned. "Your purchases can be sent if you pay the delivery charge and it will go care of Eaton's, our local catalogue office in the town of Fergus."

Thankful, I agreed.

It was early evening and I made my way up Yonge Street and onto the 401. In my haste, I forgot to travel west and entered the road where I had exited earlier that day. Having travelled about a mile, to my horror I realised my error. I pulled over onto the centre median of the four-lane highway where workers were busy. Either they did not speak English, or they did not understand my predicament. I sat in the car contemplating my next move, as passing motorists honked and glared as they gesticulated pointing with rude finger signs. It occurred to me the only thing that moved fast was the traffic. Motorists, irrespective of where they were, became impatient and ill-mannered when their speed was impeded.

Just then, a police car drove up. "Madam, you're parked illegally."

"Officer, I'm lost, and not sure how to get to Fergus." I was quite anxious.

"What are you doing here?"

"I made a mistake, and I forgot which way to enter the highway."

"How long have you been driving?"

"For many years. And I do have an International and an Ontario Licence that I got this morning. I arrived from London two days ago."

The policeman shook his head. "Wait here, and when I motion, cross over the median, and I will direct you."

He walked across the road, stopped the westbound traffic, and beckoned to me to make a U-turn and park at the side of the road. Then he signalled the traffic to proceed. "Now Madam, tell me exactly where you wish to go."

"To Fergus, Ontario. I know it is north of Guelph."

The policeman grinned. "All I know of Fergus is that it has one traffic light, eh. Look, I'll call a mate and he'll meet you in Acton. I'm not familiar with that part of the world, but please be careful and watch out for the Acton sign. Do not pass it, and do not exceed more than fifty miles per hour. I'll stop the cars to allow you back onto the road. Please, be careful and good luck."

I appreciated the patience and kindness of the Canadians I had encountered, especially that of the good natured and caring police officer. How different from the South African police, where we trembled at the mere sight of them. It helped me feel a lot better about immigrating. "Thank you, Officer. I promise to be careful."

How many times had Bis stressed, "Don't miss the turnoff"? *Now I know how Columbus must have felt when he dared to sail around the African continent. What if I missed the turn-off? Where would I land?*

As I neared the Acton road sign, an officer flagged me down. "Good evening, Miss. Where exactly are you headed?"

"Good evening, Officer. I need to get to Fergus."

"I will lead you to Guelph and that will take you to Highway 6 North. Go straight and the road will take you right into Fergus. Will you find your way from there?"

"Yes, thank you, Officer. I'm most grateful for all your help."

"We're only doing our duty, miss. Please follow me."

I obeyed and cautiously followed him for approximately twenty-five miles before the officer signalled and pointed when we reached the turn-off to Highway 6 North, as he had promised. He waved, and I was on my way.

Bis was waiting. "I was becoming anxious. I see you found your way?"

"Yes, with a lot of help from two very efficient and helpful policemen. They restored my faith in the goodness of people in authority; something that is sadly lacking in South Africa."

I was struck by how different these Canadians were from the brutish South African police from whom we were forced to flee. Canadians were not only polite but genuinely concerned for my welfare. The care they took to ensure my safety went a long way in my appreciation and understanding of the civilised and under-appreciated country that had accepted us.

"By the way, we're having dinner with the Fardellas, who will be pleased to know that you're safe. They could not believe that I allowed you to go to Toronto."

"I hope you told them it is the twentieth century, and women are liberated," I scoffed.

Within days, it seemed as if the entire town knew that I had gone to Toronto on my own. The locals were flabbergasted, and several people turned up at Bis's office to verify if it was true.

Enver coined, "Only in Fergus, eh?" A refrain we would use again and again.

The Fardellas suggested an excellent furniture store in Baden forty miles away, adding that it was much safer than going to Toronto. The road meandered through picturesque villages. I found my way there without much ado. On my way back, the sun set and darkness arrived. I stopped off at a filling station, and suddenly, without any warning, the lights went out. Everything was engulfed in complete darkness. There was a power outage, something that I was unfamiliar with. I was frantic with worry; how would I find my way home? The blackout was widespread and anxiety prevailed. People left their cars hoping to find out the cause, and not knowing, they speculated. Rumours were rife. What was the reason for the outage? Talk of nuclear destruction was the current topic of discussion and concern at that time. Had "The Bomb" actually been dropped?

I was extremely anxious and continued to worry, but the sympathetic garage owner filled my tank from a can with sufficient gas for me to make it home. Fortunately, while my car was being filled, people gathered around exchanging ideas about what to do and how to manage if the blackout lasted much longer. A garage attendant heard my concern and offered to lead the way to Fergus, as he lived close by. "Miss, all yer have tedo is follow me closely."

I was beholden for the help from a complete stranger. Once again, I was overcome with conflicting emotion. Here was the kindness of strangers, as opposed to the petty attitude some held towards others who were different.

What's next? I wondered. It was a miracle that there were no major accidents.

In the emergency, concerned citizens left their vehicles and directed the traffic with flashlights. I admired the resilience and practical thoughtfulness of the Canadian public, with the exception of the few road-hogs who were hooting and trying to edge ahead.

Part Two

The hydro outage of 1965 was a calamity—it lasted for over twenty-four hours. The things in life that people were accustomed to had come to a standstill. For me, it was an important lesson in neighbourliness. The entire south-eastern area of the United States and Canada had been blacked out. Later, news filtered through that the cause of the outage was discovered: a mouse had gnawed through a vital hydro line at the Niagara Falls Generating Power Station.

Nine months later, in the aftermath of the blackout, there was a significant increase in the birth rate both in the Eastern United States and Canada.

CHAPTER 42
Life in Fergus

BIS HAD ARRIVED IN CANADA IN JUNE 1965, AND THE CHILDREN AND I did not join him until October of the same year. A general election scheduled for November 8, 1965, was a pleasant surprise that awaited us. As immigrants, we discovered that we were eligible to vote in the election. Citizens of the British Commonwealth (1910 Union within Commonwealth. Verwoerd walked out in1960) were entitled to participate, and South Africa was a charter member. Voting in an election was beyond Bis's wildest dreams, something he was denied in the land of his birth, where Indians and non-whites were deprived of the franchise. But strangely, the vote did not extend to Black South Africans; this had to do with the fact that in South Africa, the Bantu did not enjoy the franchise, thus they were not included in the South African Charter. Bis was surprised by the discrepancy, for he was East Indian, and was also denied voting rights in his home country. However, he was not about to make a federal case, and joyfully accepted the privilege. A Black South African acquaintance who had lived in Canada for a number of years corroborated this fact. We knew nothing or very little about Canadian politics and being new immigrants, it amazed us. In gratitude, we set about learning as much as we could in the short time before the election.

A Liberal government was in power, and Bis and I cast our votes. On leaving the polling station, we encountered a hawk-eyed, hostile Fergus resident wearing a blue Conservative button, who glared at us as we were leaving. In a very loud voice the lady said, "I wonder if they know who to vote for."

The Liberal Party under Lester Pearson won by a narrow margin, but the Conservative candidate in Fergus won his seat with a hefty majority.

Part Two

Fergus was a town steeped in its own insular traditions, and it had the reputation of being the safest Conservative seat in the country. Later, when the charismatic Pierre Trudeau ran for the Liberals in the general election in 1968, many women in the town canvassed on his behalf. Despite this, they stated that they could not personally cast a vote for him, as it would go against their family tradition of being loyal Conservatives. Such was the incongruity of this ultra-Tory town.

The majority of the town's people were employed at the prosperous Beatty Brothers' Factory, a farm-implement supply company, which had been started in the late-1800s. It was the mainstay of the Fergus economy. The irony was, the Beatty Brothers were Irish in a Scots town, but that was a fact that was easily pushed aside due to their economic importance to the town. Yet there was antipathy between the Scots and the Irish residents. It was common to hear members of one group deride the other. Orange Parades on the twelfth of June were still championed in parts of Ontario in the mid-sixties.

The Beatty Brothers not only provided economic stability, they had an enormous impact on the social mores of the Fergus community, which persisted well into the twentieth century. During the war years, it was said that Beatty's ensured that at least one member of every family was employed, and the people were forever grateful. In order to maintain their jobs, the workers were compelled to abide by the stringent rules that Beatty's imposed.[6] Although Fergus had a licenced liquor store and a Legion Hall, which served alcohol, drinking publicly was forbidden in the town, and a licence was required when serving alcohol at private parties. Smoking too was frowned upon. Dancing was strictly taboo and fraternising of the sexes was considered wanton. These were some of the outdated conditions that existed when we settled in Fergus. However, as new immigrants, we were considered different, and as my husband provided an important service, we were not really expected to conform. Bis and I seldom, if ever, drank or smoked, and thus it did not affect us, but I railed against the medieval concept of being dictated to.

After we'd been living in a cramped cottage and a rented house that was barely adequate, a modern, five-bedroom house on an acre of land at the east

---

[6] *A Scottish Town* by Pat Maittaini Mestern.

end of Elora Street was for sale. Bis did not hesitate to purchase it from the businessman who had made his money in real estate. The house was airy and beautiful, with pegged oak floors, large windows, and a stone fireplace in the lounge. The dining room was a surprise. The light from the windows that flanked two sides towered over a two-foot-wide copper-lined trough filled with potted plants, and beneath were storage cabinets. A standard kitchen, study, master bedroom, and ensuite bathroom completed the ground floor. A wide oak staircase led to the upstairs landing and to the four spacious bedrooms, den, and bathroom. The garden was in need of work, but there was a wonderful old willow tree at the edge of the property where the neighbourhood children congregated to play. It was sheer luxury after the cramped cottage, and we revelled in our good fortune.

Bis was determined for me to settle and be happy and he gave into my numerous requests to improve our living conditions. I accepted that we were there to stay, yet I still needed to find my own way.

I was busy coping as housewife, mother, and office assistant. At night, I filled out sensitive medical forms for Bis, including insurance claims. Bis had decided that some were too sensitive and better kept out of the office. The local culture of gossip undermined all attempts to maintain a patient's privacy. The impression was that everyone was related in one form or another.

The children were at school all day and after classes, they participated in clubs and sporting activities—ice skating and skiing during the winter months, and tennis in summer. Enver, who had celebrated his twelfth birthday, was placed in grade eight, the final year of junior high school. Ten-year-old Nadya started in grade six. Enver was very small for his age, with a shock of curly brown hair. What he lacked in stature, he made up with a sharp mind and quick tongue. He was a typical product of the British public-school system, where he had been a weekly boarder from the age of seven years old. Self-assured, he insisted on wearing his school tie and blazer until he outgrew the latter. He was not about to give up his tie, which he wore daily, despite the fact that all the other pupils were casually dressed.

Nadya, by contrast, was taller than Enver then, and she possessed a sweet, quiet, charming personality and had large, luminous dark eyes and long, dark-brown hair. She quickly made friends and fitted into school without much difficulty. Except one day, her teacher called me to discuss the fact that Nadya, although a voracious reader, was failing at spelling. When I saw Nadya's papers, it was apparent that the teacher's accent was the root of the problem. Nadya could not decipher the words with the long-sounding Canadian "a" and consequently, she spelled phonetically. She was artistically inclined and a staunch defender of her argumentative brother. Many years later when she was at university, she discovered that she was mildly dyslexic. Bis had kept it a secret, believing that she would outgrow it. He feared that she would have to attend a special school, which would not further her education. Her adult success has proved his point.

Nisha, a pretty little girl, was about to start kindergarten, but Bis thought it a good idea to send one of his patients to be Nisha's nanny and companion. Edith was a slow learner, whose mother treated the forty-six-year old women as a child. She was delighted and could attend to Nisha's needs in my absence and walk Nisha to school and back. She was an adequate substitute for the South African maids.

Miss Edith, as the children addressed her, was a large-boned woman with a very small head, out of all proportion to her size, which was emphasised by her tom-boy haircut. Edith had a peculiar gait. She galumphed and waddled along, moving from side to side, one foot firmly planted before putting the other down. Poor Edith: she was the butt of many unkind and cruel jokes. However, she was happy to have a fulltime job.

Enver and Nadya respected her, as she kept Nisha, whom they found to be a nuisance, at bay. Nisha was a precocious child and taught Miss Edith to play her favourite card games: Crazy Eights, Go Fish, and Gin Rummy, which she had learned from her elder siblings and always expected to win. Edith had a few minor household chores and the cleaning woman too found her an irritant, preferring her out of the way. It was amusing when on arrival each morning Edith would ask, "What's for lunch?" in her baritone voice, before greeting.

Miss Edith complained that when they were within several blocks of school, Nisha would run ahead, and she could not keep up with her. Nisha explained, "Mum, the kids make fun of her, and I don't want them to tease me." To resolve the problem, Miss Edith was told to leave her charge before they reached the school, but to watch out and ensure that Nisha entered the grounds safely.

On one occasion and completely out of character, I found the stolid Miss Edith sitting on the first rung of the staircase, her skimpy dress exposing her thighs. She clutched a dishtowel to her face and was sobbing and visibly upset. Enver entered just then and said, "Sexy beast!" For a second, she stopped crying and grinned stupidly at him, and then started bawling again.

"Miss Edith, what's wrong?" I asked.

"Nadya told me to push up daisies," sobbed Miss Edith.

Nadya, normally placid and happy-go-lucky, leaned over the banister and shouted, "Don't lie. I told you to drop dead. You were nasty to my friends and then you made them leave."

After Nadya's outburst, Edith howled like a dog baying at the moon. "There, she said it again." A fresh outburst followed Edith's wailing.

I tried to pacify her and made Nadya apologise.

"I'm sorry, Miss Edith, but you were very rude to my friends."

After a good cry and much coaxing from me, it transpired that Edith had a twin sister who had "dropped dead" as a child. Edith was over-sensitive to that particular phrase. "To drop dead" conveyed a curse that called for her own death. She could not even bear to hear it repeated.

The incident smoothed over and one day at the post office, I was accosted by a hawkish woman who said, "My Edith likes to work for yous, but you must give me her pay."

"I can't do that. You'll have to ask the doctor. Edith is an adult."

"Well, I won't speak to no witch doctor. I used to put a dime in the church box for yous in Africa and now look, yous are here, richer than us, eh." Bystanders who witnessed the exchange were embarrassed.

I merely smiled. "Good afternoon and thank you," I said, and made for the exit. *Poor, poor Edith. Little wonder she's a ninny,* I thought.

The naivety and ignorance of some locals astounded me—there appeared to be a number of simple-minded people, and I marvelled how Bis contended with them. "What do you say to them?" I asked.

"They don't come for advice. All they want is someone to listen to them. Anyway, even if I gave them advice, they wouldn't act on it. Basically, this is still an isolated farming community, steeped in old lore and superstition."

"Doesn't it bother you? The domestic and sexual abuse? The incestuous relationships? And worst of all the odd cases of bestiality?" I asked, looking for understanding of how these behaviours even developed.

"Of course it does. All I do is to warn them of the dangers of infection. I'm not a priest passing judgement or doling out absolution. Why do you think I bring home so many letters for you to type and charts to file away? Initially I thought that I would not let you type these case histories, my prudish wife," Bis said grinning.

"Bis, this is no joking matter. This is serious misbehaviour."

"Yes, but it's human nature. And it's a small town where half the people are related and many are ignorant. Many of them have never been farther afield than Guelph. Despite my cautioning them, the office staff gossip, so it's only you I trust with doctor-patient privileged information."

"Don't you find it strange that this sort of behaviour was rare amongst Africans?"

"Yes, in many ways we despised the Africans, and we rarely mixed socially. But their social and cultural structure in many respects was more open and permissive than ours."

In spite of the rapid changes that were happening during the sixties, social conditions in Fergus were slow to adjust. Although never overt, in reaction to the apparent acceptance of foreigners, an undercurrent of racialism existed and was fostered by ignorance, which persisted mainly through distrust. It was never open, but periodically it reared its ugly head. The only obvious foreigners in many Ontario small towns were the local Chinese family who owned restaurants, and apparently, they did not engage socially. They went about their business, their children attending the local schools without any problems.

A few years after our arrival in Fergus, a Japanese family became Bis's patients. They had moved from Guelph to Ennotville, a tiny hamlet four miles north of Fergus. The father was employed by the Agricultural College as a "Chick-sexor." I was curious and wanted to know what he did. I was astonished to learn that he determined the sex inside an egg by touch and feel.

Bis encouraged many provocative topics at our family over dinner. It was to instruct the children, and it allowed them to learn the art of discourse. Dinner time was sacrosanct, and regardless of the hour, they had to wait until Bis had completed his long day before they could sit down to the meal I had prepared.

One day, Bis related how a twelve-year-old farm girl who had come to have an inoculation rushed out of the office before he could tell her about the possible side effects. An hour later, she was back with her mother in tow. "I must see the doctor." At that moment, Bis came out of the examination room.

The girl dashed over to him and grabbed and pushed up the sleeve of his lab coat. "Look Ma, look all them black hairs on his arm. Why, eh?"

Bis smiled and the mother apologized. "It's quite all right," Bis said to the mother, pulling his sleeve down. He handed the girl a lollipop from a jar on the desk.

Nadya informed the family about her friend Rachel, who happened to be the only Jewish girl in school. She was bullied by some of the nasty farm kids, who referred to her as a Christ killer. They said that all Jews had long noses and were money grubbers, just like her father. Prejudice was so deeply ingrained that it was difficult to ignore and even harder to make the people aware of the effect. Often the racial epithets were seemingly inflicted without malice, as simply another part of speech, and culprits were quite inured to and oblivious of the hurt it caused.

Coming from an all-girls convent school, Nadya was disturbed by incidents involving two brothers in her class, and she flinched each time the older one suffered a severe caning from their teacher for the slightest offense when he was unable to compete at the required level. They were obviously very poor, and the younger brother, who seemed quite intelligent, hung his head in shame when his older brother was beaten. Nadya was averse to any form of violence, and she told her father that she was upset each time one or the other was caned, for it amounted to a severe beating. Bis spoke to the principal, who promised that he would speak to the teacher involved.

"What can you expect? They're Metis, half-breed hill-billies and their father is the town drunkard," said the principal.

In England, Enver and Nadya had been exposed to the Indigenous Canadian and American Indians through movies and comic books, and they were romanticised as fearless "Red Indians," and not the pathetic boys in her class. However, they discovered that in Fergus, these people were spoken of with disrespect and even loathing and were not the heroes of the silver screen. Nadya's complaints bothered me, and I was overcome with a sense of guilt. I explained that racialism was part of the reason how things had become so complicated in South Africa, forcing us to leave.

The children were taught that when such offences occurred, they were not to be influenced by them and should not to be afraid to speak out, but to try to correct the insult. "Remember, we've told you many times that the reason we left South Africa was because of racial hatred and prejudice and the suffering it caused. The incongruity was that in many ways, we lived a privileged life, but we were stripped of our dignity. You will probably lose some friends for speaking out, but then they are not worth keeping."

CHAPTER 43
Guelph University 1966–1970

I WAS NOT TO BE THE THESPIAN MY LATE MOTHER HAD ENVISAGED, BUT instead, I would chalk up another milestone. House-wifely duties and life in Fergus had become a monotonous round of playing Bridge with the kind ladies who welcomed me into their midst. But it was stifling—there was a limit to how often I was prepared to play Bridge, and once again, I had become a confidential secretary to my husband. I realised that I had to find an activity to occupy myself and to accept and fulfil my needs in this rural environment.

A chance encounter with the dean of the recently opened Wellington Art College, a division of Guelph University, resolved my problem and reawakened my love of learning. I enrolled as a mature art student, and the pleasure I derived from study was secondary to academic results, but my effort was rewarded with excellent grades. I set an example for my children and for the younger students, who regarded me as a mentor. A busy schedule occupied me, and there was little time to brood over leaving London. Often, I scrambled for time to finish projects.

I majored in fine art, which included art history, drawing, painting, and sculpture. English literature, philosophy, and history were also subjects that appealed to me. A whole new way of life had opened up. I was content living in the small Canadian town. The life of an art student filled my time. Bis encouraged me in all my pursuits, and I took care that the children and housekeeping were not neglected. Nisha was permitted to stay up late in the evening so that she had dinner with the family and she was allowed to sleep in. In the afternoon, Miss Edith escorted her to her afternoon kindergarten class.

I realised how insulated some Canadian students in small towns were. It appeared that there was little for them to rebel against. By contrast, students all over North America were protesting the Vietnam War, and in Western Europe they were protesting against the establishment. The counterculture of the sixties, as it became known, barely affected Canada. There were few if any riots or demonstrations, except in larger centres, in Quebec where the FLQ crisis was brewing, and at McGill University in Montreal, where students were destroying university and civic property.

During the mid-1960s, youth in Europe and the United States were in turmoil. Their motto, PEACE, LOVE, and FREEDOM, was emulated. By 1967, Flower Power and pop-culture flourished and became the byword for the peace-loving young, pot-smoking students, and it was one aspect of the counter-culture that reached the art college. However, Guelph students limited their participation and adopted the social mores of the hippie culture by wearing wide, flowing garments and wild hairdos. Otherwise, they were law abiding and laissez-faire. As a mother with young impressionable children who needed my guidance, I could not ascribe to the free-spirited ways.

I recalled my own activist-student days in the Forties in South Africa, where student protests were quickly brought under control by the constant police surveillance of the vigilant, repressive Nationalist Government. Even then, I never quite fit the mold, but I adapted as an observer and distributed pamphlets, and on one occasion, I was bundled into a police van with a several older people. Due to my young age, and because I was wearing a nurse's uniform, I was dismissed with a warning. Age always appeared a factor in my life. I was either too young or too old for the time, but as a conscientious objector, I had to find other means of helping the cause by helping to educate the less fortunate and lending my service wherever I could.

In the United States, students were being drafted to fight in the Vietnam War. There was opposition to this, and on university campuses, there was rioting and discord and strong police interference, which caused the death of students in the struggle. Young blacks had formed the Black Panther Movement that encouraged civil disobedience and to protest racism and their unjust treatment, and they too were brought to heel by force of the police.

The sub-culture in the United States and the Vietnam War produced many draft dodgers who fled their country. A small number of Canadian students who sympathised with their plight, including me, drove to the border cities of Windsor, Detroit, and Buffalo to pick them up. It demonstrated our solidarity with the conscientious objectors. I believed that they were setting an example, hoping to induce other students to join the cause. Their destination ended in Toronto's Yorkville, then a haven for artists and pot smokers, or at Rochdale College on Bloor Street. I was reminded that students were the catalyst for revolutions against oppressive regimes and social injustice.

Many of the Guelph art students were complacent, and they remained disinterested in student affairs abroad. Their main interest was hockey and the on-site pub, the *Bullring*, which harkened back to its agricultural background. It was reported that the pub cliental was the largest consumer of beer in Ontario at that time. I recalled the old adage, *I'm all right, Jack*. There was so much to interest me that all thoughts of London lay dormant.

In my third semester, I discovered that within an approximate radius of five hundred miles were many renowned art galleries. I proceeded to explore them. A few hours' drive away was the Albright Knox Art Gallery in Buffalo, with its large collection of Picasso's Cubist works. I purchased a linen-printed limited edition of his Guernica and hung it in Bis's office above the stone fireplace. An art teacher at Fergus High School saw it and in all earnestness said, "Doctor, nice to see you display your wife's work."

"Yes, it's quite good. Don't you think?" Bis said, tongue in cheek! He was not surprised; her remark demonstrated the isolation and the lack of exposure.

The Detroit Museum of Art possessed murals and works by Diego Riviera. In addition, they had a large gallery of Islamic Art. My interest was roused by the collection of Persian miniatures, and I treasured one Bis had given me as a birthday gift. On another anniversary, he presented me with a complete set of a rare edition of Arthur Pope's *Survey of Persian Art*. I cherished these gifts, and despite the over-sized volumes, they travelled with me from Africa to England and finally to Canada, where fifty years later in 2016, I presented them to the Aga Khan Museum in Toronto.

Flushed with excitement and egged on by students, I organised tours. Best of all was the bonus of excursions to New York City, with its bountiful treasures.

Enver and Nadya were always included on these trips to further their art education, which had begun years before in London.

On a visit to Boston, I was intrigued with the number of art galleries and exhibitions at the Busch Reisinger and the Harvard Art Museum. At an exhibition, a painting by Jean-Louis David, *The Dying of Marat Sade,* gripped my attention. I was mesmerized by the image on the canvas. The dangling arm and the bandaged forehead recalled a tableau I had witnessed as a seven-year-old. I shut my eyes, and the stuffy camphor fumes of a sick room came flooding back.

We were travelling on Route 97, through Rochester in New York State. My friend Holly Middleton, a painting instructor at the university, and I were travelling with a party of students to an exhibition at the Metropolitan Museum in New York City. Holly drove a large station wagon and I drove a Mercedes sedan. Suddenly, a motorcycle policeman bore down and ordered the two vehicles to stop. One hand on his hip clutching a firearm, the officer approached the cars with a menacing glare, and said, all the while clutching his weapon, "Ontarians, yous are speeding. And where yous long hairs get them fancy cars?"

I was terrified; suddenly I was back in Johannesburg! "Sorry, Officer, I thought we were well inside the speed limit," I offered, and before he could respond, a student giggled.

That enraged the New York State traffic cop. "I can put yous all in jail now and take them cars and lock 'em up." His words frightened us into silence.

It was 1967 and violence was erupting in the neighbouring cities of Detroit and Buffalo. American citizens and students were rebelling against authority and racism. It was, therefore, with apprehension that we awaited his next move.

"I tell yous what, I take yous to the judge and he tell yous what to do. Follow me."

There was no choice but to obey. We followed nervously behind, not knowing what to expect. At the first turn off the highway, he led us into a seedy side street where he stopped at an ordinary, shabby, suburban house. I shivered with apprehension. The policeman ordered us out. We noticed the unkempt garden as we were lined up in front of a chain link fence that surrounded a swimming pool. Frolicking about were several young screaming children and a scrawny man who swam up to the edge of the pool. He did not bother to get out, and he did not say a word.

"Judge, I bring them long-hairs speeding. What to do?"

"Here come the judge," whispered the student who had giggled.

"The fine for speeding is twenty dollars' cash for each person. If you don't pay now you can go to court or to jail," the judge said.

The entire episode appeared to be a hoax. Were we part of an elaborate charade? We were in unknown territory. Our only option was to comply. Each paid the fine, happy to be on our way from a potentially dangerous situation. There was no receipt.

"Judge, I go bring some more long hairs." The officer revved his motor cycle and waved in triumph as he scooted away. He certainly had earned his keep.

So much for the American justice system! I thought, or was it? We had no paper proof, and was that a bona fide judge?

The incident did not affect the students' morale. Our visit was to view the sculpture exhibition of the *San Marco Horses* on display before they were to be returned to their permanent home in Venice. Meanwhile, I thought how lucky I was to be living in peaceful, innocent Canada. However, the officer's behaviour reminded me of the South African police and the casualness with which they flaunted the law and instilled fear. My young companions had no idea of what it meant to be afraid and to live in a police state. Everything was relative. We had bought our way out of trouble. While the loss of money appeared more important to the students, for me it was the loss of dignity, and a reminder of the police subjugation suffered in my homeland, with the scars firmly implanted in my mind.

The art college at Guelph was still in its infancy and attracted its share of instructors, many of whom resented adult students. It testified to their insecurity, as the majority of mature students were teachers upgrading their diplomas to bachelor of arts degrees, which up until now had not been a requirement; a diploma from the teachers' college had sufficed. But many professors found it refreshing to deal with mature students, who invariably handed their work in on time and contributed to the discussions.

One day, an instructor of sociology entered the eleven o'clock class and read out the names of several people, all mature students, to inform us that on the dean's orders, we were to attend the eight o'clock morning class. This was highly unfair as most of us were married and had children to see off to school before attending class. I was elected spokesperson to represent the students, and I approached the dean, who denied giving any such order. "Can you handle the matter?" the dean asked.

I returned to the instructor's office, so as not to embarrass her in front of the class, and I confronted her. "Madam, I'm afraid we adults with families find it inconvenient to attend the eight o'clock morning class, and the dean said the eleven o'clock was specifically designed to accommodate us."

The instructor was obviously annoyed by my audacity, and she had her revenge. She awarded the adults low grades as if she were dealing with naughty school kids. I felt sympathetic towards her—her lack of confidence had resulted in pettiness and got the better of her. Ultimately, word of her bias spread and she had difficulty attracting students to her classes.

The Royal Ontario Museum (the ROM) has one of the finest collections of Chinese art, including furniture and architecture. The university engaged the notable Dr. Hsio-Yen Shih, a specialist fresh from Harvard, to teach two three-hour courses on the appreciation of Chinese art history. She taught one day a week at Guelph, and once-a-week classes were held at the ROM in Toronto from six to nine p.m.

Dr. Shih was a brilliant lecturer and made use of the museum's collection to illustrate her lectures. One day, a Kenyan student went missing from the lecture and Dr. Shih sent me to find him. After scouting around the darkened museum, I located him snoring loudly, sound asleep on an antique Chinese four-poster-bed. He had climbed, boots and all, over the protective ropes and had passed out. He was stoned and could not be roused. To avoid damaging the precious bed, several security guards were summoned to remove the big man.

Dr. Yen Shih was livid. "What can you expect from savages?" she said disdainfully.

Her comment was an echo from across a continent two decades ago. That particular sentiment had been expressed by a young, Chinese female doctor who had objected to living in the non-European doctors' residence at Baragwanath Hospital, due to her fear of being molested! I pondered: *Do things ever change?* Most prejudice is endemic, but to encounter it here in a place of learning was quite surprising.

Toronto boasted a lively art scene, and there was a surfeit of cultural stimuli where Bis and I could indulge our passion. We introduced our children to art early on, and we took them to the galleries. The ROM was renowned for its collection of dinosaur bones and its programs for children.

The Art Gallery of Ontario possessed impressive sculptures from Henry Moore, a gift from the great sculptor. In addition, the Canadian "Group of Seven" painters, whose works were exhibited at the McMichael Gallery in Kleinberg, offered a pleasant country outing and a day off from school. We introduced the children to Shakespeare at the burgeoning live theatres in Stratford and the Royal Alexandra Theatre in Toronto, which attracted prominent stars from England and America. Other treats were the Toronto Symphony Orchestra and the Toronto Ballet. It all added to their cultural education, and for us adults it was a pleasant break away from the mundane town. These excursions were something Bis had been denied in the land of his birth. He was deeply gratified to witness his children enjoying the advantages Canada offered.

Gradually, I stopped making comparisons to my life before, and no longer did I lament having left London. The change in my attitude was gradual but was spurred on by South African expatriates from London who made it their annual pilgrimage to visit with us in Fergus, and to lord over me all that I was missing in London. They criticized all aspects of Canadian life and belittled the fact that the children had lost their plummy English accents and that they were running around like hooligans. Yet, every year, our house guests came to enjoy the Canadian summer sun and continued to denounce the Canadian educational system they contended was inferior. Despite the onslaught, I desisted from making excuses and apologies to visitors for having immigrated. I ignored their disparaging remarks and dismissed it as petty jealousy. In fact, it helped me to see the merit of having left London. Here in Canada, Bis felt equal—he had found himself and was proud of who he was, and we were privileged to afford the kind of lifestyle we chose.

"Now I understand why you were intent on leaving England," I said to Bis. "I was being infected with British snobbishness—something you despised." Finally, I had embraced my new country and all it had to offer with pride and gratefulness.

The turnaround delighted Bis, who could not help but gleefully refrain, "I told you so."

To which I responded, "And I simply hate you for being right."

I furthered my education and in so doing found within myself a strength of purpose. No longer did I question my identity, and I do not mean racial but rather my id, my internal energy, and I especially owe a debt of gratitude to the educators in the philosophy department. Above all, I had accepted what Canada had to offer. I speculated that I was fortunate to have studied in an age of Canadian innocence, where we were insulated from the turmoil that beset the sixties. From 1965-1969, it had been relatively easy and a pleasure. Despite the unrest in the United States, I had travelled there freely, except for speeding and paying the fine, taking many students back and forth by car, bus, and air without a worry or a care during those troubled times.

The question of safety and insurance never arose, giving lie to the notion that one could be sued for the slightest infraction, as my London friends had warned me. Sadly, that is no longer the case. It has all changed, and there has been a loss of innocence. Today, I could not go on a day's shopping trip to Buffalo without insurance.

I completed my honours degree in 1969, but the graduation ceremony was not until summer 1970. The same year we became *bone fide* Canadian citizens. Bis could not have been happier for my success. It absolved him from worrying about my disposition. He always believed that I had to be fully occupied doing the things I enjoyed. Now it was time to concentrate on our home and the children. In fact, Bis felt another child would be welcome, but he would wait for the right moment before broaching that subject.

I had adapted well to my new environment. All talk of going back to London ceased. We went there on holiday though, and for us it had changed—we now observed it in a new light. Bis and I were determined that the children know, understand, and appreciate their new adoptive country. Canada offered them the freedom and opportunity to become anything they chose without being relegated to second-class status.

Our home was filled with young people. Often, I had other students home to dinner and many times, I would come home to find a student waiting or playing with the children. After they had gone to bed, I would work late into the night to finish my assignments.

Early one morning while the household slept, the phone rang. Bis answered. It was the friend who had invited himself to dinner earlier that evening. He had left a manila envelope in Bis's study. "Doc, it's very urgent. Can you hide it for me? It's grass."

"What do you mean hide it? And why?" Bis recognised him as the landscape architectural student and assumed that it was some grass seed project he was working on.

"Don't they know that I work? Phoning here at this hour," he chastised me.

I was wide awake as Bis related the call, and I burst out laughing. I gave the envelope with the newspapers to Edith to burn before she left.

Brian was waiting for me when I arrived at university. "Did you bring the envelope?"

"No, it's in the incinerator."

"Oh, my God! It wasn't grass seed. It was the stuff you smoke," he said indignantly.

"How was I to know? Don't ever bring that into my home again. Incidentally, Bis was furious that you called at that hour of the morning."

Later I told Bis, who shook his head and scolded me. "Serves him right! What types you mix with. Joan, you accept people too easily. You should be more discriminating; remember that it sets a bad example."

"Bis, I find it difficult to avoid or ignore certain students. Have you forgotten what you experienced in Africa?"

"No. Keep in mind that the circumstances differ from those in Africa, but balance and integrity are what matter. I question some of the hippies you bring home."

"Yes, they're not my friends, but mere acquaintances. As usual, you're right. I have become too complacent, but I do warn our kids."

In my first semester, I had made a true friend with a wonderful girl named Kitty. She did not fit the mould of the average student. *She's every mother's dream child!* I thought. She was always simply but immaculately groomed and stood out in that wild era. My grandmother would have approved. Kitty was my alter ego and Bis too enjoyed her company and encouraged her visits. She was a good influence for the children, unlike some of the hippie students I befriended.

In short, Kitty was lady-like. She was pretty and brilliant and conscientious and we shared several art classes. Her art was also neat and dainty and not reflective of the time, nor of the turbulence that affected most students' work. Kitty was virtuous though there was nothing prudish about her, but her taste in music marked her as a product of the hippie culture. Philosophically, Kitty and I had much in common. I thought her an old soul. She too was the eldest of four sisters. She adored her father, an Eastern European businessman, who had influenced and encouraged her quest for self-improvement.

Kitty went on all the tours that I organised. She visited our home frequently, and we spent time into the wee hours discussing religious philosophy, medieval history, and literature. She had a handsome boyfriend whom she married after graduation. They went abroad and apart from the odd post card, Kitty and I lost contact for three years.

Our friendship was resumed when Kitty returned to live in Cambridge, the prosperous, growing town less than half an hour's drive away, where she was appointed art director of a Catholic school. She was divorced by now and had two sons, and she shared joint custody with her ex. Their relationship remained amicable, as he was an excellent father. "He was unfaithful, and I could not accept it," was all Kitty said.

Kitty would visit and stay over on weekends when the boys were with their father. She was restrained in all her habits and our bond had grown closer.

"Is she happy? I have the feeling that she carries the weight of the world," Bis had said to me the first time he met her.

"I think she is. She is gentle and very spiritual by nature."

"Actually, she reminds me of a young prude I once knew," Bis said.

I rolled my eyes and shook my head.

— ⚜ —

Boxing Day. Bis was dead and I was grief stricken, living on my own. My children had left earlier that morning.

The phone rang—it was Kitty. "I'd like to spend the day with you and go cross-country skiing, if that's okay. I hope there's lots of snow at the farm."

"Of course there is, and I'd love that."

Kitty arrived, glowing as usual. We skied, and we ventured farther afield than we had intended. Later we returned to a lunch of cold turkey leftovers, plum pudding, and champagne. Kitty and I sat up 'til dawn in front of a blazing fire, to which Kitty kept adding logs. How happy I felt. It was the first time since Bis had died that I had a brief respite from my grief and loneliness. The cycle of life and death was a topic we had discussed ad-nauseam in and out of the lecture room. Our discussions had been academic. Now the reality of death was personal, and this knowledge did not assuage my aching heart.

"Why don't you spend what's left of the night," I suggested, but I was unable to persuade my friend to stay.

"I've loved every minute of today. I'm so glad we had this time, but I need to meditate in my special place."

"Suddenly, you seem earnest. Is everything okay, Kitty?"

"Why shouldn't it be? It's been such a lovely outing. Though I'm sure my neighbours think that I'm a woman of the night."

"We both are, but not in the way they think," I said, and we laughed.

Four months passed and there was no contact between us. That was not unusual; our friendship transcended ordinary time, and there was a deep bond of cognition that existed between us. Invariably we picked up where we had left off.

Early one morning I was woken by the incessant ringing of the phone.

As I lifted the receiver and before I answered, a voice said, "Is that Joan?"

"Yes, this is she."

"I'm Kitty's mother. We've never met, but I promised Kit that I would call you personally."

Involuntarily, I shivered. *Was Kitty ill? What was the message Kitty's mother had to impart?*

"Kitty died this morning. She was stricken with a virulent form of breast cancer. Few people knew. That was so like Kitty. She wanted all of us who loved her to remember her as she was. That Boxing Day that she spent with you, just two days before she had learnt the horrible news. But she did not want to interfere and ruin her visit, or add to your grief. Spending time with you was her way of consoling you."

With this news coming so soon after Bis's passing, once again I was consumed with emotion that rendered me speechless. I stood holding the phone, unable to think, let alone ask questions or offer condolences. I dropped the phone and went into the garden. The bright morning sun drew my attention to the pure-white star magnolia tree blossoms, herald of spring, which were in full bloom, but already beginning to drop their flowers, soon to be replaced by lush, green foliage. The eternal cycle continues. I stooped and picked up a handful of the fallen petals. They were not withered, but merely fallen, their time, like Kitty's had come. In the rustling breeze under a mackerel sky that drifted overhead, I blew the petals into the zepherous wind. This reminded me of my sibylline grandmother, who claimed the rows of tiny clouds were angel wings come to ferry the blessed to the Promised Land.

CHAPTER 44
A Canadian Education

Our first Canadian winter was a total surprise. The dazzling sunshine after a snowstorm contrasted with the dreary, grey London fog we had left behind, where the pallid English sun was a sorry replica of a dull moon that emitted no light nor heat. Enver and Nadya claimed the sun was an imposter, a pale disc posing as the sun. Despite the brilliant sunshine, we gradually accustomed ourselves to the bitter cold, where the temperatures dropped well below freezing point. But the heated homes adequately compensated for any discomfort.

Enver chimed, "Good show! We've left all that damp greyness and exchanged it for bright-blue Canadian sky."

The storm had dropped a minimum of six inches of fluffy snow, and it shimmered in the golden sunlight and beckoned the children to play. Nadya invited Nisha to make snow angels, and with their arms and legs spread out lying in the soft snow, they revelled in it.

"How is it possible that the sun shines so brightly and yet it is so unbelievably colder than anything we've experienced?" Enver asked.

Nadya added, "We're so lucky to have central-heating and proper waterproof suits that allow us to enjoy the outdoors." She was standing in the open doorway watching her breath freeze, and she sang, "Look out, look out, Jack Frost is about, he's after our fingers and toes." She had to be cautioned about the danger of icicles that resembled popsicles, dropping from eaves troughs, and about sticking her tongue on the enticing, ice-covered metal railings. Winter could be perilous for the uninitiated and sunglasses against the glare of the brilliant snow were a necessity. The frigid temperatures demanded warm clothing and bundling up against the icy blast of winter to ward off colds and particularly frostbite.

Arctic temperatures did not faze the salubrious young Canadians, who embraced winter. The lengthy period of sub-zero weather was ideal for a variety of sporting activities: skiing, ice skating, and the Canadian national pastime of ice hockey, a game played by young and old in the streets, backyards, or on frozen ponds. Some hardy souls indulged in strange pursuits like ice fishing or jumping into a freezing lake in the heart of winter to raise money for charity.

On weekends when Bis was free, we joined the children in skiing lessons, and in a short time the children were better than average.

"Mum, adults are retarded," five-year-old Nisha scolded her parents. "You don't listen to what the teacher says."

The little minx was called out by the instructor to show her parents how to perform stem turns. We alas, would never become good skiers or skaters like our children, who delighted and excelled at winter sports.

James McQueen Public School was adequate. It differed from the British public schools that were private and to which the children were accustomed. Enver and Nadya made a pleasant discovery: school was not regimented nor as formal as the schools they had attended in London. Although the absence of school uniforms was a nuisance for Nadya, who had to think about what to wear, Enver continued to wear his blazer until high school. As parents, we demurred at the lack of discipline and regretted the loss of respect for elders, where children called adults by their first names, but all the basic subjects were taught. Much to our surprise and disappointment, French, the other official language, was not a compulsory part of the curriculum.

To our relief, Fergus possessed a well-stocked public library and Bis and I had inculcated the habit of reading in our children encouraging them to read more Canadian literature. Since coming to Canada, they had discovered the works of Margaret Lawrence and Robertson Davies, among many others, which gave them a sense of the country's origin and development. Hugh MacLennan's *Two Solitudes* highlighted the friction that existed between the English and French.

Nadya, who'd been labelled a Trojan for her diligence at the Rudolph Steiner School in England, continued to work hard and completed all her assignments on time. She was awarded the Citizens Certificate and voted the nicest girl in school, and she was presented with a cut-out silhouette of herself. She was in her final year of junior school. Her small stature did not preclude her from being a star athlete and gymnast. She held the Ontario Girls' Bantam Hurdles Record and played basketball on the first team, and like Enver, she excelled at tennis.

Bis and I were relieved when Enver entered high school, where he would be forced to work. He was younger and much smaller than his class-mates. He stood up to would-be bullies with clever repartee. Sports was an aspect of school life that Enver enjoyed and so was debating, where he won most of the speech competitions. In his last year at high school, an announcement over the school intercom applauded him as the winner of the speech contest earlier that day. An hour later, the stentorian voice of the principal rescinded the result. In his speech, Enver had questioned the school's educational raison d'être. His speech was deemed offensive and critical of some of the staff. In it he'd said, "We are here to be educated and taught how to become useful citizens. We beg for values, but instead, we are given prices." This was barely original, but it was the current sentiment of youth throughout the Western world.

There were daily reports of student dissent over the air waves and in newspapers. These young people believed that the establishment was more concerned with economics and the status quo, which was riddled with false values and hypocrisy. Internationally, barriers were being broken down, but in small town Fergus, this teenager got pilloried by the school hierarchy, and the punishment that followed was unduly harsh. Teachers penalised him by subtracting marks for minor infractions because of his insolence.

He argued that he was making a general observation. "If I don't stand up and air my views, I'll be bullied by everyone."

"Do not treat the matter lightly," Bis was warned by the new general manager of General Steel Wares, formerly Beatty Bros. The manager had recently moved into Fergus and had become friendly with our family. "Small towns in general will not tolerate any sort of criticism, nor change. There is a bias toward outsiders who hold some status in these insulated rural communities and who dare to question it."

Bis agreed. "It's time to transfer Enver to another school."

"Yes, it's the kids who bear the brunt," the manager added. "To enter university, they are better served by transferring to boarding or city schools, where they are anonymous. To date, as far as we know, very few students from rural schools get into university."

"I expect you're right," said Bis. "My observation is that people here are complacent. There is little to aspire to other than guaranteed jobs at Beatty's, which sets the standard and ensures them a future."

"It is no accident that there are two Canadian high schools in Switzerland, offering grade thirteen and guaranteeing university entrance," the manager said.

Sending Enver to Switzerland solved the problem. He was very small for his age and the year abroad allowed him time to catch up. He had left Canada a preppy schoolboy and a year later, he returned a grown-up, teenaged hippie replete with outrageous hairdo. He attributed his growth spurt to good European beer. Enver had averaged decent grades and was accepted to a university in London, Ontario.

The negative experience that Enver had faced at school was something that Bis and I decided we did not want Nadya exposed to. She was enrolled as a boarder in grade 13 at Havergal College in Toronto. We reasoned that the city school would be better preparation for her entrance to university.

Nisha boarded the school bus daily to Elora senior school, the adjacent town approximately four miles away. Nisha was a competitive and industrious student, whose report card testified to her A-plus status. She was popular, and her friends considered her a leader. Toward the end of her final term in grade eight, I received a message from her class teacher, requesting a meeting.

Upon arrival at the school, I found Nisha, her classmates, and the teacher squatted on the floor in the corridor. I thought, *What are they doing? And why is the teacher crouched on the floor with her charges?* They were playing a game of Rock-Paper-Scissors. No one made any attempt to get up until Nisha said, "Hello Mummy."

The teacher stood up and led the way into the classroom. "Mrs. Bismillah, I sent for you because I have been instructed to tell you that Nisha is a top student. The kids look up to her, and she influences their behaviour." The teacher appeared ill at ease and did not make eye contact with me.

"Is she a bad influence? Is that why you sent for me?"

"Not really. We only wanted you to know," she trailed off.

"What is it you wish me know? Is Nisha misbehaving?" I noticed that the teacher was quite flustered, even confused, and still not prepared to face me. *Something's amiss. But what?*

"It is nothing that we cannot handle. She will pass into high school. Thank you for coming."

I thought, *surely there is something wrong?* I was perplexed and felt uneasy. I had been invited and summarily dismissed. To what purpose? What was the teacher not telling me?

The teacher showed me out, and she re-joined the students and resumed playing on the floor.

Nisha came running after me, "What did she want, Mum?"

"I'm not sure. We'll talk when you get home."

A week later, I attended eighth-grade graduation at James McQueen Public School. Nisha was very excited, as a dance was to follow the ceremony in the school gymnasium.

To her graduation, Nisha wore a dress that Nadya had worn to her high school graduation. I considered the quaint Canadian ritual of a formal graduation even at the kindergarten level amusing.

The buzz and noise of the eighth graders was deafening as I waited for the proceedings to begin. As the honours and winners were announced, students audibly whispered Nisha's name, only to be disappointed as yet another name was called. This occurred throughout prize giving.

Nisha sat in stunned silence, as did many of her friends. I was confused. The ceremony was over. Despite her sterling report card, Nisha had not received a single prize or mention. I was proud of my daughter, who congratulated the winners after the ceremony. A girl came up to Nisha and said, "This is yours by right." Nisha shook her head, and her eyes brimming with tears, she embraced the girl and said, "No, you keep it, it's yours." Students were asking questions. I offered to take Nisha home. The stoic girl refused. "I'll stay for the dance, Mum."

I was too upset and recalled my unusual meeting with the class teacher. If Nisha had done something wrong, then as a parent I had a right to know. I discussed the matter with Bis.

"We'll take it up with the principal on Monday," Bis said.

Saturday, the morning after the graduation, I was at the supermarket line-up waiting to pay when a woman approached me. "Oh, Mrs. Bismillah, did you notice how we dealt with Nisha?" I was aghast as she continued. "We stripped her of her prizes." This woman was the school secretary.

I was astonished, tongue-tied, hurt, and angry all at once, more than I would publicly admit. I had no response. And without asking why, or paying for my groceries, I left empty handed. I rushed home.

Bis was in the garden. "What's the hurry? You drove in like a maniac."

"I'm mad." And I related the encounter at the supermarket.

"On Monday, we'll ask the principal for an explanation. I'm off to the hospital, but I'll be back later, and we'll discuss it then."

A nurse who had witnessed the incident at the supermarket, told Bis as soon as he arrived, "Doctor, the school secretary really upset your wife."

"Yes, it was very unfortunate. The secretary's lack of discretion was out of order."

In the small, incestuous town, very little was private and pettiness prevailed. Bis gleaned from the hospital gossip that Nisha's transfer to a private school did not sit well with the principal because he had not been consulted. He felt that his authority had been undermined. He had not been asked for a reference for a student under his tutelage. *And denying their daughter her prizes would somehow even the score?*

Enver trotted out his favourite saying: "Only in Fungus, eh!"

Nisha assured us that although she was disappointed and hurt, she would cope, and she begged us not to pursue the matter, especially as she would be leaving Fergus. She did not want to appear a spoil-sport to her friends. She would put the whole unfair business behind her.

CHAPTER 45
Fergus Medical Centre

THE OLD FESSENDEN LIMESTONE HOUSE WHERE BIS HAD HIS OFFICE had become too small to operate efficiently. His practice had grown and many people from neighbouring areas consulted him. A local architect said that it would be more practical to start afresh, as the cost of renovating the old building would be prohibitive and take double the time to restore. Bis could not afford the time, as he was expecting two doctors to join the practice. Reluctantly, he agreed to have the old house demolished. There was a slight problem, as my sister Jean and her four children resided in the main part of the house.

Bis had sponsored them after Jean's divorce in South Africa. She had been at her wits' end and extremely unhappy, so she agreed to come and work for Bis, as she had been an executive assistant for a medical firm in Johannesburg. Within a year in Canada, she had met a wonderful man, Bent Christiansen, and they were contemplating marriage. The demolition of the house meant moving the date forward. We approached Jean and Bent and explained, and they were quite happy to comply.

The proposed new premises would be built in sections to accommodate four doctors. Parking facilities were in the backyard facing the Grand River. I never quite understood why the people who had settled the towns of Fergus and Elora used the river at their backdoor to dispose of their refuse. I put it down to the fact that they were thrifty Scotsmen who refused to pay for garbage disposal when the river would suffice free of charge.

Fergus Medical Centre operated all day, but usually the doctors did not arrive until after lunch. Surgery and hospital rounds filled their mornings. The early years were difficult due to the lack of doctors. Bis worked long hours but he was extremely happy.

"Joan, I love the hospital. It is part of my practice but without the headache of administration, and we are able to perform surgery as well."

The small town was surrounded by a widespread farming community and Bis made calls to several housebound patients before returning to the office in the afternoon. There was a number of odd, insane, and asocial people. It was more apparent in the small, isolated rural areas. Domestic abuse and incest were a problem. Ignorance, superstition, and religious fanatics added to the workload, and a doctor's duty was not without danger. Born-again Christians placed Bibles with specially marked texts and threatening notes on the office doorstep. The anti-abortion argument had existed for years but had escalated in the past decade, and it raged both in Canada and the United States, where the first murder of a doctor occurred in 1994. From then on, Bis referred all his patients who were requesting an abortion to a Hamilton hospital for their own safety.

One day, the police summoned Bis to a house where an ex-serviceman with a rifle was taking pot shots at passers-by. The police were powerless to stop him. He had barricaded himself in behind his front window and threatened to throw a grenade and blow up the semi-detached cottage if anyone attempted to enter. He demanded that the police call his doctor.

Bis arrived at the scene. The police aggravated the situation by refusing to allow Bis access to the cottage. The stand-off lasted for some time. All the while, Bis talked to the man through a loudspeaker, trying to persuade him to hand the gun over.

"Doc, not 'til 'em bastards go away, eh," he said.

Several anxious hours passed before Bis was able to convince the police to make a big show of going away. Then calmly, Bis went into the house and the troubled man handed him the gun.

"Doc, 'em bastards was sleeping with the wife, eh." The disturbed man ended up in the asylum.

Domestic abuse was often provoked by infidelity and in some cases, daughters were the victims of sexual abuse. It was not uncommon for a mother to blame the young girl for enticing her father, or to accuse her of seducing her brothers. Other male relatives took advantage of vulnerable girls. One newlywed woman pleaded with Bis to have her father-in-law arrested for forcing her husband to have sex with his older, unmarried sister. The father-in-law also expected to have sex with the new bride. Bis was compelled to report the case to Social Services, but sadly the complaint produced more abuse, as the young husband retaliated by beating his wife! It reminded Bis of a similar case that had landed up in court in London, where he'd given evidence against the culprit, and the mother had denied any wrongdoing by the father and blamed her daughter.

Bis had a knack for dealing with violent and disturbed patients. He attributed this to years of experience working at Baragwanath Hospital and his general practice in Potchefstroom, where violence was a factor in the oppressed black community, and where Indian wives would suffer in silence, not daring to expose the culprits.

— ⚜ —

It was my birthday, and we were on our way to celebrate at a symphony concert in Toronto. "I have to stop on the way and make an urgent farm call first," Bis said. He switched off the car, got out, and pocketed the keys.

"Don't be long. We don't want to be late," I called.

Bis left, whistling in the pale moonlight as he trudged up the snow-covered path.

I waited patiently, but as time passed from minutes to hours, my sandaled feet began to freeze. I was dressed in a flimsy sari. Thankfully, I was wearing a fur coat. *Whatever is keeping him? It's too late now,* I sighed, irritated by the delay. Without the car keys, I could neither turn on the heat nor the radio. I dallied with the idea of fetching the keys, but my frozen feet would not allow me to tramp through the snow. I tried tucking them under me on the seat but that too failed, and then... *Bang... Bang...* two rifle shots rang out in the eerie stillness and shattered the tranquillity. Simultaneously, dogs barked and birds squawked as they flew from the barn roof, adding to my fear. Locked in the car, I was obliged to wait. Startled by the rifle report, I knocked my head against the dashboard, wondering what had happened. I had not hurt myself, but I was slightly dazed. I shivered more from fear and the unknown rather than the cold. With trembling hand, I reached for the horn, but I was petrified and unable to perform the simple act. I did not wish to intensify what appeared to be a perilous situation at this isolated and desolate farm house.

An overwhelming dread consumed me. I was reminded of another tragedy that had occurred so long ago. *Please* not *another memorable birthday!* I prayed.

My thoughts were a jumble: *Why were my birthdays tinged with tragedy? What was happening inside that rundown farmhouse? Was Bis all right? When and how would this nightmare end?* Outside, a tethered horse was champing in this ghostly night, and the emaciated dogs continued howling and yapping around, scratching at the door. Quivering with fright and chilled to my fingertips and toes, I wondered what madness the night had wrought.

Then, by the languid light of the full winter moon, I saw his shadow silhouetted against the snow. He hesitated and looked back, and then I saw him stride purposefully towards the car carrying a small child. Lagging behind him was a scrawny shadow of a woman with hair askew, dragging a whimpering child. A sigh of relief escaped me, and the tears flowed freely.

Bis shooed the yapping dogs away. He unlocked the car and settled the distraught mother and the frightened children into the back seat.

"Sorry," was all Bis said, conscious of my heavy breathing and the stifled sobs of his three passengers. He inserted the ignition key and in the half-light, I saw his blood-stained cuffs. Bis drove in silence to the police station, and I once again was left alone in the car, but thankful that my husband was alive. More time elapsed before he came back. He leaned over and kissed me, wiped my tears, and took my ice-cold hands, and rubbed them between his. "I had to ring for an ambulance and report the man's self-inflicted injuries," he explained. "Happy birthday, darling. Let's go home and enjoy that hot cup of tea."

Weeks later, a news item in the local newspaper reported the attempted suicide of a deranged man, who had threatened to shoot his wife and children. A doctor had persuaded the father to spare their lives.

CHAPTER 46
Bigotry

On the surface, it appeared that life in Fergus unfolded at a slow and easy pace, and though the residents found much to celebrate, there was an undercurrent of discontent and prejudice inherent in the apparently peaceful town.

One cause for revelry was the well-publicised annual Highland Games. That was the highlight of the year. It added a welcome source of revenue that flowed into the town's coffers from thousands of people, including many from the United States, who descended on Fergus for the annual Highland pilgrimage. Visits to the hospital kept the doctors busy setting the broken bones of boisterous youth who had tried to prove their prowess by arm wrestling and tossing the caber. Although permits were required for the consumption of alcohol, the games provided an excuse for the over-indulgence in drinking, so the eruption of domestic violence and the rivalry between the bigoted Scots and the maligned Irish increased.

Conservative Fergus was a dry town, but it had a government-licensed liquor store that was well patronized. The society ladies called it the "den of iniquity that would only lead to perdition." They espoused sobriety in their crusade against drinking. Yet, if I happened to be there, it was not unusual to encounter one or another of the blue-haired doyennes in the liquor store, who ducked behind counters hoping they had not been spotted, and if they were, they felt the urgent need to explain their presence to me.

Thanksgiving was celebrated with a bountiful harvest and feasting on turkey, butter tarts, and pumpkin pies. The end of October ushered in Halloween,

Part Two

signalling the end of summer and the last of the festivities before the Christmas parade down St. Andrew Street. Everyone prayed for a white Christmas. The town folk vied with each other in decorating their homes and gardens with colourful bunting and lights for all occasions.

Suddenly, change came to Fergus. *Take Thirty,* a CBC television documentary series by Paul Soles featured "Fergus: An Ideal Canadian Town," which brought new industries into the town and attracted many people to the area. Gradually, the town was changing and catching up with modern times. Canada Wire and Cable Company and Bell Telephone created much-needed employment opportunities. The chain stores and large supermarkets slowly followed, also offering jobs and a greater variety of shopping, and new ideas.

However, Fergus residents were firmly entrenched in the past. Stuck in another era, the town limped gingerly into a rapidly changing world that some people viewed as a corruption of their values. But transformation could not come fast enough for me. I had graduated from university and needed a new challenge. Volunteering and tutoring students did not satisfy nor fulfil my needs. I was restless and overcome with nostalgia. Thoughts of London that had lain dormant and buried deep inside my subconscious now resurfaced. I pondered—what to do next?

Without warning, fate intervened, and my dull, staid world was disrupted as Bis's career and his reputation were in danger of ending in infamy!

Three Canadian doctors had moved into town and opened a medical clinic. Bis's practice had grown and he was relieved, for his workload was onerous and the Guelph doctors who assisted him at surgery would be spared the trip to Fergus. Bis reckoned that he would have more family time and he could indulge his passion for gardening. Bis welcomed the new doctors and invited them and their spouses to dinner. I was an accomplished hostess and my love of entertaining had not diminished despite the lack of domestic help. I now relied on Enver and Nadya to help out.

Whispered rumours began to circulate in the insular town: "Now we have our own doctors to treat us. We don't need foreigners attending to us." A few of Bis's patients left, which was to be expected, but then one of Bis's staff also left to join the new group. What neither Bis nor I foresaw was the jealousy and pettiness that followed. It was a difficult time as the family, after so many years being a part of the community, now came under negative scrutiny. A local cartage contractor spread the rumour that he had delivered a single carpet that was insured for thousands of dollars to the doctor's home and that the doctor's uppity son had signed for it. His parting salvo: "Yous have got rich on us, eh?"

Bis and I chose to ignore the gossip and cautioned our children to do the same. I thought perhaps here was an opportunity to leave Canada. Bis believed that things would settle down in time, but he was wrong and it became much worse.

One blustery winter morning with temperatures well below zero after a heavy snowfall the night before, a man was found lying face-down, frozen to death in a snow bank a few blocks away from Bis's office. He had not been Bis's patient, and a few weeks had passed when Bis was summoned to attend an inquest into the death. Bis assumed that the inquest was a routine enquiry, but he was puzzled as to why, so many weeks after the man's death.

Unbeknown to Bis, a woman had lodged a formal complaint to the local police, accusing Bis of neglect, hence forcing the inquest. She stated that she had observed the man knocking on Dr. Bis's office door earlier that afternoon. Her assumption was that he had not been admitted and attended to but had been left to die in the snow storm.

The police investigation took six weeks to collect evidence and examine the witnesses. In the interim, the incident turned ugly. Mischief-makers blamed Dr. Bismillah for negligence. Others accused him of manslaughter. Those who knew the doctor believed he was innocent. Unfortunately, in this small community, innuendo spread and the spectre of racial bias cropped up. It dawned on some people that Dr. Bis was not one of them, and they encouraged others to come forward with complaints.

Waiting for the inquest put a strain on our family, and it was reported that a teacher had remarked loudly in the supermarket that foreigners and Jews could never be trusted. I had never seen my husband more distressed. Bis was devastated by the false accusation, yet he refused to defend himself against public opinion, and he showed no outward emotion. He was stoic and appeared aloof, drawing more unwelcomed criticism. His cool disposition was mistaken for arrogance. My thoughts of returning to London now surfaced. Here was an opportunity for me to encourage Bis to leave Canada. However, my sense of honour prevailed. I thought about how easily people were influenced by gossip and innuendo. Shelving my own desires, I decided that it was more important that we stay and clear my husband's good name.

It was difficult facing the mob, who believed the worst. Bis ordered our family to ignore the gossip and to remain silent. In the meantime, rumours for and against were rife. I thought of how typical it was of some people in a dull, small town to find credence in gossip.

The day of the inquisition arrived, reminding Bis of one in South Africa. It differed only in that here it was the locals creating a great deal of mischievous excitement in the town. Some people took the day off from work to attend the hearing, which was held in a large hall. The coroner, an eminent Guelph physician, officiated and read the charge of negligence that had resulted in the man's death. A taxi driver testified that he had dropped a drunk man off in front of Dr. Bismillah's office on Wednesday at approximately five p.m. The office lights had been on.

In her testimony, the office cleaner stated that she had been cleaning the office at that time. The door was locked, and she had let herself into the office earlier, as she usually did, with her own key. It was an established fact there were no office hours at any of the doctors' offices—all were closed. The doctors and staff went off at lunch time on Wednesday afternoons, and any person requiring a doctor had to go to the hospital, where the doctor on call attended.

The coroner was aghast. "What a mischievous falsehood, and where was their loyalty?" he said. He decreed that the case against Dr. Bismillah was a complete farce and a waste of time and money. This case should never have been reported, for it was not the first time that a person had been trapped in a snow bank and died from exposure.

The public scandal was not only a disservice to the doctor, but it did not show the townspeople in a good light. Surely, the local police had been negligent and should have ascertained the facts. The coroner pointed out that their lack of a proper investigation had almost ruined the reputation of a good doctor. Further, the coroner admonished and chastised the complainant. He stated that her report was unconscionable. Rather than causing malicious gossip that deliberately besmirched the sterling character of a doctor, it was her duty as a citizen to have offered assistance to the unfortunate man. The jury found Dr.

Bismillah not guilty and several prominent townspeople, including two church ministers, thanked Bis for his years of dedicated service to the community.

"Isn't it strange that when things go awry, how the dark side surfaces and we forget the good?" I said, relieved.

"Yes, it's human nature. But the truth eventually prevails. Faith and courage are what's important. Fear of dire consequences drives people to hide until conscience gets the better of them," a grateful Bis answered.

I instructed my children that the moral of the unfortunate episode was a lesson that demonstrated how petty jealousy and gossip could destroy a person's reputation. I warned them that as outsiders they were vulnerable to systemic prejudice, and that they had to be vigilant and always seek to tell the truth and rise above the pettiness.

CHAPTER 47
Menopause

After the stress of the past few weeks and the aftermath, life should have been back to normal. I ought to have been elated, yet I felt listless and out of sorts.

One night, I was startled when Bis woke me. I sat up. Clearly, I wasn't dreaming when I heard Bis say, "Joan, did you see Bawa? He was standing right here, next to the bed, and I distinctly heard him say, 'Abdul Hak, I forgive you for running away.'"

I tugged at Bis's shoulder. He lifted his head and appeared somewhat dazed, as if he was lost and unsure of his bearings. I was curious to hear more. "Bis, were you dreaming? You said that you spoke to your father."

Now fully awake, Bis denied it. "No! No. You're imagining things. I don't subscribe to dreams and those superstitions and all that nonsense you inherited from your grandmother."

"All I know is that you woke me from a deep sleep and asked whether I'd seen Bawa. Were you dreaming?"

For an answer, Bis laughed, but he appeared somewhat embarrassed.

"Why do you always make fun of me?" I said.

"Because you're gullible, you thrive on mystery, and you've kicked all the bed covers off. Most likely you're hallucinating and you're feverish."

"And you think that's funny?"

"My darling, you're experiencing the first symptoms of menopause. So, I'm not surprised you're hearing voices."

"Oh, no," I sighed, not bothering to contradict him, because I was more interested in his reference to menopause.

"You know there's a way to stop it. Another baby will trick your hormones."

"Bis, for weeks now you've been hinting at having another child. Mentioning menopause is a devious ploy to encourage me to have a baby. Incidentally, I distinctly heard you ask me about Bawa. Was there a problem with him?"

"No, but he begged me to stay. He was fond of you and the children, and he said I was making a big mistake by taking you away. I was aware that they were displeased, for Mother too had pleaded with me. Naturally, I blamed you. I told her you were unhappy."

"You've just proved how devious you are by not owning up to the truth."

Bis ignored my accusation and any further mention of his parents. He continued, "It's a fact that there's no documented research on hormonal activity preventing menopause, but let's test it." Bis had no desire to defend himself, but he knew that this was an opportunity to convince me.

"No, now you're using reverse psychology to influence me."

"Try it. Prove me wrong. It will prolong your youth," he laughed.

"Why is it you always have the final word and manage to outwit me? Is it because my vanity trumps common sense?"

"Remember, you said that, not me."

Not too long after that conversation, I was pregnant with our fourth child when Nisha, my youngest, was nine years old. My dilemma was how to impart the news to my teenage children. One day, when I was writing to my mother-in-law about the coming event, Nadya happened to peer over my shoulder. "Mum, you're pregnant? How lovely. We'll have a baby." That was the ice-breaker I needed. I was healthy and usually suffered few ill effects of pregnancy. However, I had an irritable uterus, which meant that I had painless contractions that occurred at intervals, which had been the cause of all three of my children being born prematurely.

I consulted a friend, an expatriate South African obstetrician at Kitchener-Waterloo hospital. It would save Bis the embarrassment of treating his wife at the local hospital. Also, if my pregnancy was at all like my previous ones, then the baby would be premature, and the local Fergus hospital had no premature unit. Premature babies were sent to Hamilton or the Kitchener-Waterloo hospital.

Part Two

At the consultation, my friend the obstetrician said, "Are you mad to have another baby now that we're all having fun? Do you really want to be bothered with nappies, et cetera?" He did not wait for my answer but picked up the phone and dialled. "George, I have a colleague's wife here. Will you do a termination? I'm Catholic and I can't do it."

I was horrified. I leaned over and pressed the off button on his phone. "I consulted you professionally and even before I had a chance to finish, you humiliated me. I did not come for an abortion. And you lectured me on the inconvenience of having another child. Worse, you call yourself a Catholic."

"I thought that I was doing you a favour."

"You weren't. This baby, unlike my other children, was planned."

"I assumed you wanted an abortion and that's the reason you consulted me."

"I did not consult you about an abortion! I am surprised that you practise a double standard, advocating a termination though you're not prepared to perform one. Some Catholic! How insulting!" I was fuming and did not wait for an answer but left his office.

Fortunately, I had several other options. Even without a referral or an appointment, I could consult another specialist.

"Come," said a voice as I knocked on his door. "Joan, lovely to see you. What brings you here, an invitation to dinner?"

"No. I'm here to seek your professional advice." He was an English expatriate, a friend, as well as an obstetrician.

"With pleasure, my dear. You'll have to wait half an hour if that's okay."

"It's more than okay. It will give me time to recover my equilibrium."

"Sounds serious."

"No, I'm just annoyed." I related the earlier incident. "What a nerve, advocating abortion, yet his principles won't allow him to perform it."

"Do you want an abortion?"

"Certainly not! His presumption and hypocrisy irked me."

Later, on examination, the doctor confirmed that I was almost five months pregnant but in good health. "Take it easy though. We don't need you to deliver too soon. And continue to do what you're doing. You'll have the baby here?"

"Yes. Am I fit to travel to Europe? Enver's eighteenth birthday is coming up."

"With my blessing, but don't overdo it. You're barely showing."

Enver was at school in Switzerland. He had extracted a promise from us that we would visit and celebrate his eighteenth birthday with him.

Back in Canada, life continued apace when I started having very strong contractions. With another nine weeks to my due date, I was admitted to hospital and remained there for three weeks before I went into labour. A premature, underweight baby boy was born. He was named Sergei and was placed in the premature unit. Eighteen years later, modern conditions were very different from the primitive ward Enver had inhabited for the first four months of his life. Sergei spent a month in the special premature unit. Bis assured me that our baby would receive the best possible care, and he took me home. Nevertheless, I was unhappy to leave hospital once again without my baby. My day began with a call to the nursery ward to learn that the baby was doing well and had gained two or three ounces. I had experienced this routine when Enver was a baby, but now they had made great strides in premature baby care. Being a midwife, I understood only too clearly the risk of early discharge, but that only made the waiting so much harder before I could actually cradle the tiny person.

As a young boy later, Sergei was curious about his birth. I related the story.

He was visibly upset. "You mean you left your baby and went home?"

"Yes, just like with Enver, you were tiny and premature and you were put into an incubator for three weeks. It was the only way you could survive. I had no choice but to obey doctors' orders if I wanted you to be healthy. Enver was in hospital for five months before he was discharged. It was a sacrifice I was compelled to make for both you and Enver to grow into the healthy children you turned out to be." My explanation did not appease Sergei!

Contrary to what is speculated about premature babies, I was fortunate that my four children had no birth defects. Like other children born at term, mine thrived and grew into healthy, normal children.

CHAPTER 48
The Farm at Ennotville

A DERELICT 210-ACRE FARM IN ENNOTVILLE, FOUR MILES SOUTH OF Fergus, was for sale. Amina, my mother-in-law, was visiting the family and she encouraged Bis to purchase it. Owning land would be the fulfilment of a dream denied him under the segregated policy of Apartheid in his native South Africa. Indians were considered non-citizens and were prohibited from owning property in the Transvaal. Many Indian men subverted the law by marriage to non-Indian women and purchased property in the wife's name. The problem with this solution was that invariably the man already had an Indian wife, and thus he had to support two separate homes with all the problems that it caused. My father-in-law constantly berated this act, as it was one of the difficulties of inheritance he was asked to resolve.

Bis, the prospective farmer, bought the fallow farm from the childless elderly couple who owned it. He got a mortgage from the bank and was intent on turning the farm into a paying venture. To manage and advise him in the maintenance of the land, he employed an experienced, retired Czechoslovakian farmer, who had been interned by the Germans during the war. This farmer and his wife set about clearing the mountains of garbage that had accumulated over decades before the land could be utilised. More than two months passed before the land was fit to be used. The enthusiastic couple began to harrow and till the land in preparation for cultivation of crops that would feed the steers that Bis was intent on raising. He was advised to import two hundred and fifty grass-fed steers from Alberta, as they produced the highest quality beef and fetched the best prices.

A new silo and barns were built to replace the crumbling, dilapidated ones. During the harsh winters, the doors to the silo froze and Enver, by then a university student, had to climb the sixty-foot tower each morning to dislodge the frozen door to release the cattle feed. Three years later, Bis realised that the profit was marginal, and the added upkeep and responsibility of maintaining the steers did not warrant the expenditure. He sold the herd and soon after, the market in livestock hit an all-time low. Bis was lucky to escape, and with this, his dream of becoming a gentleman farmer evaporated.

Bis considered other options. He divided the land into two parcels. The existing farm house and buildings that faced the noisy highway were his portion. The other 110 acres was mine, where we intended to build a home. I, the reluctant immigrant, ultimately conceded that it was in our best interest to set down roots.

Bis had visions of settling down at the end of a long and busy day, where he could enjoy the solace of a country retreat and pursue his out-door interests. We explored the property and found an ideal spot on an elevated slope. A contractor was commissioned to build the house on a knoll one mile from the side road, to ensure the privacy we sought. We occupied the old farm house until the new house was completed.

Bis had ambitious plans for the land, and he was anxious to get the garden planted before the onset of winter. A lush, twenty-six-acre forest of maples, conifers, and deciduous trees formed a screen and shielded the south-facing house from the onslaught of the icy northern wind.

Most of the land was rented out to a farmer, an arrangement that would change the following season, as Bis intended to plant trees on the property. However, he would continue to rent forty acres close to the bush. On the advice of the local agricultural advisors, the farmer was restricted from planting corn or soy beans; they claimed the genetically-treated seed and herbicide now in common use depleted the nutrients in the soil, and it would take about three years to replenish and rehabilitate the land.

Bis decided our best bet was to plant trees. The Conservative premier, William Davis, was in office and had introduced a programme that allowed persons who owned four or more acres of land to buy seedlings at a penny a tree. The only restriction was that the trees had to be seven years old before they could be cut. Failure to observe the rule would result in a penalty of seven times the original cost. Bis took full advantage of the offer and bought hundreds of tree seedlings, sufficient to cover fifty acres. Thirty students from the University of Guelph's agricultural department descended on the farm to plant the trees. They worked for a month to complete the task, a labour that would have taken us much longer. I joined the Grand River Conservation Authority, who supervised and advised me on the proper maintenance of the land.

During winter, the farm resembled an Artic landscape. The fierce ice storms and blowing snow blanketed the laneway, making it impassable. One solution was a snow fence to run parallel to the laneway, but we disliked the omnipresent slatted wooden snow fencing used in rural areas, it lent a pedestrian shabbiness to the windswept fields. The alternative was to plant a screen of four-foot tall evergreens. Bis was impatient, for it would take years before the tiny seedlings grew. The problem was easily solved by purchasing four-foot evergreens trees from a tree farm. To save the expense of contracting a company to plant the young trees, we embarked on the project ourselves with the help of our teenaged children, as the hired man had retired.

I remarked, "It's all right for you to be the boss and make plans because Enver and I are the labourers who implement them."

The task was daunting and maintaining the land was onerous, and we did much of the work ourselves. It surprised me how we had developed from urban city dwellers to farming caretakers.

The following spring, we set out together with the six-month-old Sergei asleep in the truck to purchase the evergreen trees from a farm in Delhi (pronounced Delhigh), sixty miles away. The owner was a delightful Scot who advised us on the selection of the trees and effortlessly loaded them onto the truck.

"Your vehicle is adequate to transport them but be sure to water them thoroughly as soon as you reach home. To do so now would add weight to the truck."

"Are you sure it's all right to transport them the way they are?" a concerned Bis asked.

"I wouldn't suggest it if I did not think so," responded the practical Scot.

We were on our way with the heavy load and had almost reached the gate when the truck ground to a halt. Bis, who had absolutely no knowledge of mechanics other than driving a motor car, blurted, "We're stuck!"

The owner of the tree farm was nowhere in sight, but I was sure that he was somewhere in the forest, for we had left him inspecting some new growth. But how to attract his attention? Would he even see us in the dense forest?

I climbed onto the roof of the truck and was perched in a precarious position, but I started shouting out, hoping that the sound would carry beyond the tall trees. Waving my brightly coloured scarf, I stamped my feet on the roof and continued shouting until I was hoarse. I was desperate to attract attention, while Bis tried to pacify our squalling baby, who had been roused by the racket I was creating.

The light was fading and it appeared that we would be stranded overnight. I was concerned for the baby and determined to spare us the ordeal of spending the night marooned on a tree farm with naught but what we were wearing. Frantically, I continued waving and screaming while Bis tended to the howling infant and started honking the horn with his free arm. Darkness was descending—we were desperate. Then I spotted a flashlight in the distance. I was hopeful that the owner had heard the hullabaloo, and I redoubled my effort and gave a last desperate shout. A few anxious moments went by, and then a huge truck came barrelling down and stopped in the clearing. Suddenly, I felt limp and cold. What a relief. The owner had arrived and he helped me down from the truck.

"You're lucky I came back to fetch the cheque I'd left in the shed," he said. He inspected the trouble. "Sounds like a broken axle." He fetched the tools from his truck and ordered Bis to hold the flashlight as he applied first aid. "It will hold until you get onto the highway, but you cannot exceed ten miles an hour," he warned us, and bidding us Godspeed as we left. We followed his instructions. Sergei finished the only bottle we had brought and dropped off to sleep in the safety of my arms, probably from sheer exhaustion. The sound of the engine with its slow, continuous whirr had a hypnotic effect, and the tedium almost put me to sleep. We travelled in silence. Mercifully, there was no policeman to order us off the highway, but passing cars honked and hooted making rude signs as they raced by the disabled truck that crawled along a main highway. An interminable time passed before we entered the final stretch of our journey.

After what seemed forever, we reached our farm, and Bis was too exhausted to unload the trees. But if they were to survive, it was necessary to water them, particularly after all the trouble we had experienced. I was too weary to assist him. I settled Sergei, then I relented and together we completed the arduous task.

The trees that replaced the snow fence did well with a minimum of care and added to the landscape. But Bis was still dissatisfied and he sought other means of improving the site. "I'm going to take that field out of service and plant grass."

"Surely you're joking. It's almost a mile long, and who will plant it?"

"We will. It will improve the approach to the house."

I had no answer. I knew the futility of arguing once Bis had fixed on an idea. It had to be accomplished post haste.

The majority of the evergreen seedlings and maple trees thrived but a few black walnuts did not fare as well. Scattered about the farm were some very old oak and beech trees that nature had sown eons before. All the elm trees had succumbed to Dutch elm disease and were in the process of becoming organic mulch and nests for birds and squirrels.

A magnificent cherry tree at the edge of the forest close to the house was admired by several prospective wood buyers, but Bis refused all offers to sell. One weekend we were away, and on our return the tree had been rudely cut down—only the sorry stump remained. It was a mystery. Neighbours said a helicopter had hovered over the farm for hours. I complained to the police, but in order to file the report a name for the farm was required, and there was no time to consult with Bis. For a minute, I contemplated while the impatient clerk drummed his fingers. I filled in Senjan Farm, a corruption of St. John. When I was still at the convent I had adopted him as my patron saint, but that too was a long time ago. St. John (pronounced "Sinjin" as a surname in England) was an acronym made up of the initials of our family's first names.

Swan Creek, a boundary that separated Senjan from our neighbour's farm, was home to many beavers. On the bank were a couple of five-hundred-year-old cedars that the university's horticultural department had authenticated. One of the trees had been struck by lightning. It leaned to one side and had continued to grow in that direction. The heavy branches formed a natural protection over a large beaver dam that grew into the creek. The pesky rodents blocked the free flow of water, and to permit drainage the local highway crew flushed them out from time to time.

I had settled into country living and, like Bis, was always eager to improve the property. Constantly, we added more ornamental trees and shrubs. We loved the deep, maroon-hued colours of the *prunus negra* species that were planted to offset the verdant conifers. In the garden, our favourite Japanese maples varied from light orange to pale shades of red and vermillion and were juxtaposed to catch the light. Magnolia trees, including the star variety with its translucent white blooms that confirmed the arrival of spring, added to the landscape. Bis planted an avenue of maple trees along both sides of the laneway, which formed a canopy and provided shade during the hot summer months.

Our family were keen tennis players and Bis built a grass tennis court and added a hard court. Enver commented that his father invariably found more work before one project was completed. Soon after, Bis suggested a putting green.

He employed the services of the greens-keeper at the Cutten Club in Guelph.

"Doctor, on that piece of land, you have sufficient land to build five holes."

"And what will that cost?"

"Not any more than it would cost to build a swimming pool."

"Well then, let's get started."

First, the land had to be cleared and all stones and rocks removed in preparation for the Kentucky Blue grass for the fairways and Bent grass for the greens.

The husband of Bis's secretary was unemployed and was engaged to help on the land. Jim Quarrie had developed multiple sclerosis, and as a result had lost his job at the local co-operative store that dealt in farm equipment. Mr. Jim, as the children addressed him, was an asset. I could not accept the North American habit of children calling adults by their first names, I had been brought up in a different era, and politeness demanded respect for elders.

Mr. Jim had been born and raised on a farm and his knowledge of the weather, farming, and machinery was invaluable. He was conscientious and hardworking. A Presbyterian Scot, and an elder in the church, he was thrifty and resourceful. He never ordered any new implements but improvised and invented things as they were needed, or else he knew how and where to obtain things at bargain prices.

The preparation of the once-fallow field seemed endless and the work was strenuous after a day spent under the supervision of Mr. Jim, who encouraged everyone to work hard. Despite his sclerosis, Jim was strong as an ox, and I admired the man for his diligent work—he set a good example for the occasional labourers we were compelled to hire. Jim expounded, *"An itsy weeny bit o' work is good for yous, eh."* Jim was tall and lanky and his shoulders stooped slightly, which exaggerated his loping gate. His watery blue eyes looked directly at one when he spoke, and he was a good judge of character and tolerated no nonsense. "What a fool thing to go chase after a silly ball," he said when he learnt that Bis intended to add a few putting greens. He snorted and shook his head. Years later, when the course was established, he joined in the fun, and on his retirement due to ill health after thirty-five years of devoted service, he managed to play almost daily, applying the same dedication in trying to improve his game.

Jim's attention to detail often amused the family. In 1981, Enver opened up a restaurant, and I did much of his shopping for fresh produce and supplies that were unavailable in Fergus or Guelph. This entailed me going to Toronto. One day, I hurried home before stopping at Enver's restaurant to deliver his supplies. Once there, I placed a tray of raspberries on the roof of my car to get at some fruit for our home. My intention was to put them back. However, I hurried into the kitchen with the fruit, and in my haste, I forgot the raspberries atop the car and drove off. Not until I got to the restaurant did I remember the berries. When I returned later in the evening, I found the box on the doorstep with each raspberry meticulously wiped, though some were squished and embedded with grains of sand. An irate Jim drove up. "Yer sure took yer time to come back," he scolded.

"I'm sorry Mr. Jim. Enver needed some help. Did you need something?"

"If yer wanted me to have 'em berries, why did yer throw em at me?"

I had difficulty concealing my amusement. "I'm sorry. I was in a hurry and I forgot them, I had put them on the roof of the car, and they fell off as I drove away. Enver was very cross because I had lost them." I hoped that the explanation would mollify him. He put a handful in his mouth but spat them out, possibly because of the sand.

"I'll take 'em home. Yer've no need of 'em now. I don't believe in waste."

I envisaged him meticulously picking each grain of sand out of each raspberry.

Regardless of the weather, Mr. Jim patrolled the grounds daily. One year, a violent winter storm deposited more than six feet of snow around the house.

Jim declared that it was the worst he had seen since he was a boy. He had a rough time ploughing the lane, which was essential if Bis was to get to the hospital. A few days later, brilliant sunshine presented a winter wonderland of pristine beauty.

"The snow's good for tobogganing and clearing the eaves troughs," Jim said, as he set about the task.

"Oh God, Mum! Mr. Jim just fell off the roof," said Nisha, who had been facing the dining room window talking to me as we heard a thump. We went rushing outside. Jim was lying in a huge snow-drift, his legs stuck up in the air, his felt hat stuck on a branch, and his head and neck buried in the soft white powder.

"Have yer never played in the snow? An itty bit canna hurt yer." None the worse, he avoided our out-stretched arms to help him up.

"I dinna need yer help. But I could do with a wee drink, eh."

Living on the farm was a constant learning experience, and it was hard work. I would not go so far to say I enjoyed it, but I did it to the best of my ability. With Jim's help, we did all the manual labour. In Africa, we would have given orders, and even in London we employed a gardener. But Bis derived pleasure from the voluntary labour. He said it helped to restore his dignity as a free man. The nightmares he had once suffered had since diminished.

At the beginning of spring, rocks would push up through the frozen earth as the ground thawed. Jim said rocks grew like weeds. Picking rocks in spring was a chore that was required before the fields could be ploughed and planted. Bis organised work parties to clear the land of the stones. Enver and the staff from his restaurant spent several Saturday mornings and Sunday afternoons picking rocks. Even four-year-old Sergei helped by carrying little stones to add to the piles that Bis and Jim later carted away in a front-end loader attached to a tractor.

A construction company was engaged to dig ponds and install the drainage system. In the beginning, Senjan Golf Course started with five holes. Family and friends derived much pleasure, and on weekends, relatives joined the fun. Soon after that, Bis decided to add another four holes, which meant clearing large tracts of conifers from the proposed site. He offered the trees to the neighbours, who eagerly accepted them. The entire street and surrounding area had benefitted from his generosity. Eighteen months later saw the completion of the regulation nine-hole golf course, replete with bunkers and several ponds.

An open invitation to friends to play caused a problem, as they expected Bis or me to accompany them each time they chose to play. To maintain the course was expensive. Bis decided to charge a nominal fee to offset the cost, thus encouraging people to play on their own. He introduced an honour system, and in the club house he installed an English, sloped wooden desk with a letterbox in which to post the fees. Each evening after a round of golf, Bis emptied the box and the fees were deposited in a golf account.

Due to the number of active participants, Bis decided to open up the membership. It was a great success. Members paid a one-time fee at the beginning of the year and they were eligible to play for the rest of the season simply by signing the register at the time. They were entitled to invite non-members, for which they paid a greens fee. The honour system allowed members to play at their convenience, doing away with designated time slots, a feature of most golf courses. It worked to the convenience of the golfers. People arrived to play and never had to wait too long before starting. Tuesday evening was men's night and seniors played Wednesdays between nine a.m. and one p.m.

Members regarded their participation as a privilege, and several players approached Bis to act as wardens to keep things running smoothly, which they took seriously.

Medical pharmaceutical representatives gained permission from Bis to hold tournaments for doctors on Wednesday afternoons. Their one request was that a tutorial or an address by a medical specialist be given prior to playing. It was a means of advertising their particular brand, and it spared them visiting individual doctors at their offices. The company also provided a catered supper or a barbeque. The doctors' meetings on Wednesday afternoons were popular and well patronised by the doctors from the area. Bis encouraged this, and it was an added source of revenue, which helped to defray some of the expense involved in maintaining the high standard of course maintenance as set up by the Turf Grass Institute in Guelph.

Things were running smoothly, and the golf course was on the threshold of beginning to pay for its upkeep. Bis and I could not have been happier with the success of our golfing enterprise. Then, a calamity! One day, during a usual tour of the course, I found a pink slip pinned to a tree, ordering the closure of the course!

The local town council was accusing me of running an illegal business. The property was registered in my name, and I did not have the necessary licence to operate a business, nor had I obtained the express permission of the local town council. We called our lawyer, who incidentally was a member. Play was permitted to continue provided I applied for a retro-active business licence and paid the arrears and a fine. The huge fine was the relatively easy part, though the course had never made a profit, and the money had to come from our private funds. In addition, I had to satisfy the town council's inspection and demands, which appeared to be in a constant state of flux. The inspectors, such as they were, had been appointed by the town council and had no training. One town councillor who inspected the land could only identify maples and grass. I had expected that they would at the very least have called in someone from the Turf Grass Institute.

The Town Council declared that the business licence I had obtained was in fact an admission of my guilt. They demanded an investigation of all farming and sewage and water facilities. I was outraged. I had all the necessary permits before any project was started. In addition, no legitimate contractor would begin any work, however minor, without first obtaining the requisite permit from the town council.

My admission of guilt and the enormous fines I had paid should have ended the matter. However, it was insufficient to let me off. My lawyer consulted two high-priced Queen's Councillors from Toronto to defend me. The cost was prohibitive. Fortunately, I had subscribed to the Grand River Conservation Authority for years, and they brought in an environmentalist to support my cause. I relied on the Horticultural Department at the University of Guelph to explain that I had improved a derelict wasteland. The Turf Grass institute sent a specialist as a bona fide witness. A youth councillor and several prominent people testified that the original farm had been a blight and that it had improved under the Bismillah stewardship.

Bis and I and our three lawyers were summoned to attend the local town council meetings scheduled for seven p.m. The local agenda had first to be dealt with, and invariably we were kept waiting in the corridor until nine p.m.

before we were called in. After each meeting, I received a bill for five hundred dollars. The invoice stated that the meeting had been convened on my behalf. The cost to us was excessive and we felt harassed and thought it unfair. It took two years at great cost before the issue was resolved in our favour. Since we'd paid the initial fine and formally applied for a licence, the investigation made little sense. In a small town, little remains confidential. The entire unpleasant episode stemmed from a complaint lodged by another would-be golf-course developer in the Fergus area, who incidentally was reported to be related to a member on the town council, or so the story goes. I said that it illustrated the petty nature of the "small town" mentality. Ignorance is not an excuse, but our initial purpose was not to build a golf course. It had happened in degrees, and not once when I'd applied for permits for wells and sewage tanks had I been questioned or informed of any rules regarding the property.

To maintain the course and the garden became a labour of love. Both Bis and I were environmentally conscious, and there was a limited use of pesticides. Working with soil was therapeutic but costly. The little beasts that inhabited the bush did not help —rabbits wreaked havoc in the vegetable patch. I discovered that they disliked daffodils, so I planted them among the tulips, where they remained untouched. Raccoons were a major problem. They were cheeky pests, and they used the patio and sundecks as toilets and scratched for grubs on the fairways, where they dug up whole sections of land. Traps were set and one of the workers drove forty miles away to let them out, only for them to find their way back. One day, two raccoons were trapped by the greens-keeper and he suspended the trap in the pond for hours. At the end of the day, he assumed they were dead, and he was about to bury them when they started breathing. He was a superstitious man and threw shovel and empty trap into the pond, allowing the raccoons to escape.

I called on the services of the Wild Life Conservation to remove the troublesome beasts. They charged sixty dollars per raccoon, and fifty for a groundhog. A month's haul amounted to tidy sums. I was convinced that people from other neighbourhoods released their coons onto the course at night, as cars were often seen parked along the quiet side road.

One day, a conservationist who had come to remove the traps was asked by Rafik, our grandson, who worked on the course, "Where do you release them?"

"I don't. I shoot 'em buggers in the cage," was his response.

I was approached by a fisherman for permission to collect some grubs. Gladly, I agreed. One night returning very late from Toronto, we were astounded to find dozens of lights moving around on a putting green. On inspection, we found it was a few dozen Asian men with flashlights strapped to their heads, picking grubs. None spoke English. No one appeared to be in charge. Bis ordered them off, or he would call the police. Gesticulating and protesting they left. The fisherman who employed them was conveniently absent and later claimed ignorance. Two weeks later during the night, a truck was driven over a green and destroyed it. Bis laid a complaint with the local police but to no avail. The mystery remains!

Canada geese were another nuisance and chose to use the greens to leave their poop behind. A good hosing discouraged them. Other birds were welcomed and encouraged by providing feeding posts. However, a pesky and persistent red cardinal repeatedly bashed its beak into a front window pane of the house. I pasted a black-paper cut-out of a hawk in the window to deter the stubborn bird, and waited for the bird to knock itself unconscious, but it never happened. Other annoying visitors were the occasional woodpeckers, who seemed to take great pleasure in visiting at all hours and rat-a-tatting on the garage door.

I would be amiss not to mention an irritating feature of a typical Canadian summer in the country; the bugs, giant horseflies and zither-buzzing mosquitoes that despite spraying manage to annoy and sting exposed flesh. In sharp contrast, many years later when my grandchildren came along, they were enchanted by the fields of fireflies flickering and fluttering, emitting their light in the summer dusk. They named it "fairy dust."

There was an elegant, solitary wild turkey that visited the farm regularly for eleven consecutive years and always made its way to the downstairs glass patio door and stared undisturbed for long periods at its reflection. Turkeys mate for life and Mr. Jim assured me that it was a male who thought his reflection was that of his partner! "Unlike us, they're faithful, eh."

On occasion, a white owl squatted on the barn roof, looking like a weathervane as it hooted at the moon. Black crows that circled over a particular spot meant that they had found a meal. Other beasts not to be outdone were the howling coyotes. At least they kept some of the raccoons at bay.

The advantage of living in the country on one's own land allowed our family to enjoy the privilege, and it fostered a love of the outdoors and an appreciation of the need to care for the environment. Once, I saw a solitary silver fox perfectly poised, its nose in the air. Afraid of disturbing it, I kept dead still and thought, *How graceful.*

Squirrels were lovable and no threat to the golf course. A pair of giant turtles inhabited one of the many ponds Bis had created to ensure water during dry spells. Often one or the other could be seen sidling across the path. One day I was out playing golf, and my ball came to rest on what I thought was a pebble. To my surprise, it turned out to be the tiniest baby turtle, no bigger than my thumb. I was stunned by its size, and wondered how it had gotten half a mile away from the nearest pond and onto the fairway. I picked it up, placed it in a plastic mug, and took it to the vet school. There I learned that it was impossible for it to have travelled that far. Most likely, I was told that a bird had picked it up and dropped it in flight. I left the minute creature for observation. Each day there was a new learning experience.

My favourite animals were the svelte white-tailed deer who often came right up to the house, their heads held high as they nosed around sniffing the air without turning their sleek bodies, then with disdainful shrugs, thundered off. It was a reminder of our visit to the Kruger Game Reserve.

Mr. Jim seemed to delight in trapping mice; "They dirty little critters." He kept as many as a dozen barn cats, whom he fed sparingly to whet their appetites in order to combat the rodent population.

Frogs abounded and their nocturnal mating calls were a reminder of my native home in the Transvaal, where together with the chirping cicadas, they formed a duet that ushered in the night, reminiscent of the starry night sky, the one thing of Africa I missed.

CHAPTER 49
Our Home in Ennottville

WE HAD BEEN IN CANADA FOR FIVE YEARS AND I, THE RELUCTANT immigrant, together with my family, embraced the country and became proud Canadians in 1970. I was delighted my Canadian passport was issued in my name, and I could dispense with the stigma of being my husband's chattel. For the first time, I admitted to Bis that he had made the right choice of immigrating to Canada.

"I'm infallible," he smirked.

"You sound like the cat that swallowed the canary."

"I know how you hate to be wrong."

"As always, you're insufferable!" I responded. "The day after you die, I'll board a plane bound for London, but by sheer vindictiveness you'll outlive me and marry again."

To celebrate our citizenship, we visited Quebec. There we fell in love with Montreal. The beauty of Mount Royal and the St. Lawrence River added a picturesque charm to the modern, cosmopolitan city. The hotels and restaurants were a reminder of the cities we had left. What a treat it was to enjoy the culture and luxury that was so different from mundane Fergus.

Other visits to Quebec were skiing in winter, and summer holidays were equally rewarding. We had fun. We sought out hotels that offered golf and tennis, and we enjoyed the wonderful cuisine. Visiting historic sites was an opportunity to brush up on the country's history, and an attempt to learn some French. Another highlight was touring the provinces en route to Vancouver. It compensated for living in a small rural town and was the perfect excuse to get out and explore our new country.

Our new home was under construction. The project ran over budget and well over time. We were furious and dismissed the initial contractor and replaced him with another, who also came highly recommended but at a considerable cost.

"Let's get the place finished and settle down without further ado," Bis pleaded.

My task was to oversee the completion of the work. The house was unlike any of our previous homes, and we wanted it to reflect our new country. A maple bush formed a backdrop to the house, which was built on a knoll that overlooked a wide expanse of fields that led down to the road. We envisaged the land with conifers and ponds, but that would come later.

Our house was spacious and airy. The floor to ceiling windows were designed to let the sun in and provide a view that changed with the four seasons. The children joked that London had only one and a half seasons—a long dismal winter and a short, often wet, summer. The split-level house with its high, sloped ceilings in the kitchen, master bedroom, and living room were clad in clear cedar that gave the rooms a lovely country finish. By contrast, the pegged-oak living room floor added a perfect foil for our Persian rugs, some of which we had purchased on a visit to the Iranian Pavilion at Expo '67 in Montreal. The arabesque designs and colours of the rugs were echoed in the clerestory stained-glass windows of the entrance hall. I had commissioned them from a local artist in the neighbouring village of Elora, where recently a colony of artists had settled.

The fireplace in the breakfast room and the hood above the kitchen stove were copper clad. An Elmira wood stove in the kitchen, and a free-standing iron fire pit in the downstairs family room were practical additions in times of hydro-electrical outages, which assured some heating during the cold Canadian winters.

Bis was thankful that at last he lived in a country that allowed him to be all that he aspired to. "Thanks to Canada, I have the best of all worlds. I enjoy the luxury of owning land, and in my work, I'm not limited to my speciality. I have access to a hospital where I am respected and can treat my patients with all the facilities that are available. A far cry from Bara, where I learnt a great deal, but where I was subservient to a racially-biased European chief," he said.

The farm in Ennotville was a place of contentment—all was working out to our satisfaction. Bis and I could not have been happier and we settled into the comforts of our home. We had built a tennis and a grass court, and most weekends during the summer we entertained our nephew and his wife, both teachers, and their young friends who had immigrated to Toronto and enjoyed a country outing.

Our home was an open house. We welcomed other South African and British doctors and their families who were contemplating immigrating. Bis hoped to introduce them to the benefits of practiing in this benign society. He invited several doctors to join him in his busy practice and sponsored many young people. Usually, nought came of it. The visitors, having spent a month or two as our house guests, were not prepared to live in the rural town of Fergus, which they found unsophisticated and remote, particularly during the icy winter months. They all came from cities and the wives objected and were unprepared to stay. They did not, nor could not, understand how and why Bis and I chose to stay in such a bland place. Perhaps as an aside I should have mentioned that it provided a welcome retreat for them to enjoy country living without the expense other than air fare. Bis was not prepared to defend nor to justify his choice. Our visitors were aware of my initial reluctance to join Bis, and I attempted to explain the advantages and also the freedom of living in a society that was all-embracing. Naturally, I conceded it had taken some time for me to become acclimatised. It is no secret, I explained—one had to be gainfully occupied. Living in Fergus had taught me a valuable lesson; it was not where one lived, but how that was important.

Bis had found the dignity that had been denied him—finally he was the equal of his peers. He could relax without fear of the humiliation and shame of being castigated non-European, which had dogged him throughout his life in South Africa. The need to prove his worth was no longer there, nor did he feel the need to compare or compete. He was free from the tyranny of Apartheid, and he was happy to practise medicine as a general practitioner and offer hospitality to friends and family.

Now that the family had settled and Canada had become our home, we were free from the indignity suffered under the brutal police state in South Africa. My first encounter with the policemen on Highway 401 was an example of how helpful the policemen treated people here. It was a sharp contrast to the American traffic cop who exercised his superiority while stopping me on Route 67 in New York State, and to the brutality of their South African counterparts. It proved that Canada was truly a safe haven, and if I thought of Canada as ordinary that was all to the good, for now I appreciated how truly fortunate we were to be living in a sane, safe, empathetic, and well-run country.

Another example of the kind of police employed in Canada is borne out by how seriously they took responsibility and carried out their duty. One blustery winter's day, Nisha phoned from the Ponsonby School six miles away, saying the school bus had dropped her and three other pupils off at the wrong school. She asked if I could fetch them and drive them to their school in Elora.

First, I had to check on Sergei, who was sound asleep. It was freezing with sub-zero temperatures. A fierce storm was raging with blowing snow and white-outs and I pondered whether I could risk leaving him. I would have to wake and dress my sleeping child, which would take away valuable time. I reasoned he was safe and that I should rush to protect Nisha and her schoolmates, who were caught in a blizzard.

When I got to them, the four stranded young girls were frozen. They bundled into the car, and I drove them to school.

On my return, I found three-year-old Sergei seated on the doorstep in pyjamas. He was shivering. "I'm sitting tight," he said. But the phone was ringing, and I straddled him to answer it.

"No Officer, I do not have a little girl called *Verney Miller*."

"We received a call from your home. You do know that it is an offence to leave a child under twelve," he warned.

"I assure you, Officer, my twelve-year-old girl is at school."

"Well, a *Verney Miller* called and said she saw her mother drive away."

Sergei was tugging at my coat, trying to attract my attention while I tried to stifle the persistent child, well aware of the penalty for leaving an underage child alone.

"I'll just drive out there and check it out. One cannot be too careful."

"Most certainly, Officer. You're welcome."

I was frantic but managed to keep calm and played for time, trying to dissuade the officer. "Please, do be careful. The driveway is a mile long and there are heavy snow-drifts in places, and the side road is impassable. It will not be blown out until the storm dies down." I hoped that I had thwarted him. Then I heard the click. Either the policeman was on his way, or he had believed me. I put the phone down.

All the while Sergei continued tugging on my coat. "The policeman told me when I phoned to 'sit tight' until he came."

"Yes darling, you did the right thing." It turned out the policeman had decided not to come, but for the rest of the day, I waited and silently gave thanks that three-year-old Sergei had the confidence to phone the police for help. As a Canadian, the child had trust in the police. This was something his father still could not entirely feel comfortable with, as Apartheid had left its scars. Any time Bis was approached by a policeman, the hackles on his neck flared.

Another year had ended, and a party at Enver's restaurant ushered in the New Year. We toasted Canada, thankful for the many blessings the country had afforded us. Our three older children had left home and were making lives of their own. Only Sergei was still at home.

Sergei was akin to an only child. His older siblings could have been his parents. They adored him, but like all only children, he spent much time on his own. Living on a farm, he was forced to amuse himself. Bis taught him the alphabet, and at the age of three, he could read and he knew the capitals of most of the countries. He was a lonely child who took comfort in books, but Bis spent time with him that previously he could not afford our other children.

French immersion was being introduced in Ontario schools. Fergus needed twenty pupils to start the programme. I helped to recruit pupils but encountered opposition from some of the locals, who tended to despise the French. They expostulated, "We don't need our children to speak the 'Froggy' language." This sentiment was repeated by many people. Fortunately, enough parents were convinced of the advantages of a second language. The French immersion teacher was highly qualified, and the children adored her. Unfortunately, when they reached grade four, they would be transferred to the local public school, and French would become just another subject.

The time had come to transfer Sergei to St. John's, a private school for boys that had recently opened in Elora. It was not surprising that he headed his class, but he was small for his age and could not participate in the robust hockey games. However, he was a very good tennis player, who from the age of twelve spent all his summer holidays teaching and playing the game. He made the high school team and went to Australia and New Zealand to represent his school.

New Year's Day dawned to brilliant sunshine. The snow on the fields glistened and beckoned skiers; an invitation neither Bis nor I could resist. As Bis donned his skis, he noted, "Oh, Joan how lucky we are. Our children are in good health and doing well."

"Yes, we have so much to be grateful for, especially your foresight of migrating."

Bis was already out the door, and I followed. We cross-country skied around the perimeter of our property, noting all the changes we had made. Tired but happy, we called it time to stop for lunch and to listen to a recording of the Queen's speech.

I was unstrapping my skis when the phone began to ring incessantly, and I rushed to answer it. "A call from Kuala Lumpur for Dr. Bismillah," the voice said.

"Yes, Bis here," Bis said, taking the phone from me.

"Doctor, we need permission to do a lumbar puncture on your daughter Nisha, who is in a coma at our hospital."

Bis was stunned and asked the speaker to repeat what he had said. Shocked at the response, Bis replied in the affirmative. "Please let me speak to the doctor in charge," he added.

"Doctor, I'll call you back in an hour when we have the result," the speaker said.

Bis and I were speechless. There was little to do but wait for the call. We were aware that Nisha and her fiancée Gary were on holiday, but we were perplexed and worried.

"I thought that they were still in South Africa. What are they doing in Kuala Lumpur?" Bis queried.

"I'm as mystified as you are."

The hour seemed more like years. Waiting was unbearable, and to hasten the time we called Nadya and Enver. There was little to do but wait for the call about Nisha.

At last, the phone rang, but it was the wrong number, which only increased our anxiety.

We waited indefinitely, and then the call came. "Nisha has falciparum malaria," the doctor informed Bis, and then explained the treatment.

Gary phoned to inform us that Nisha had contracted it from a mosquito bite on a visit to the game reserve in the Transvaal. They had been flying back to Hong Kong, and she had collapsed on the plane. Gary had taken charge. The pilot was forced to land in Kuala Lumpur, which was the closest hospital, as she needed treatment immediately and there was no time to fly on to Hong Kong. Nisha worked for the British civil service in Hong Kong, and Gary informed her superiors as well.

Once apprised of Nisha's condition, I called a travel agent. I was not able to leave until a day later, when there was a flight via Alaska and Hong Kong that would get me to Kuala Lumpur. Due to poor weather conditions, the flight was held up in both places, and it took thirty-six hours before I reached my destination.

Gary and his friend Mark were at the airport to meet me. Gary informed me that Nisha was worse and that Bis was on his way and would be there the following day. That alerted me to how serious her condition was, and I learned she was on life support. I was comforted knowing that Bis was on his way.

At the hospital, seeing my daughter so close to death shocked me, and all I could do was hold my child's hand. The doctor urged me to speak to her and just maybe she would snap out of the coma.

For weeks, Nisha remained in a coma, though her condition remained stable. The hospital was well equipped to deal with her, but the time came when it was suggested that they turn off the life support. Gary went to the hospital at six a.m. on the appointed morning to dissuade any such measures. I too could not bring myself to agree and I refused to the sign the order. It was pointed out that Nisha's condition had deteriorated, and that even if she woke up, the chances of being normal were slim. It was decided that nothing more could be done, and under the circumstances, the doctors wanted her transferred to Hong Kong. Bis was non-committal and abided by the decision made by Gary and me.

Part Two

Singapore Airlines were extremely helpful and could not have been more supportive. They would transport her to Hong Kong. Mark travelled between Hong Kong and Kuala Lumpur throughout the ordeal, to fetch cash to pay the hospital expenses. The airlines provided first-class service free of charge for Bis, Gary, Mark, and me, and we travelled on a separate plane, courtesy of the airlines.

All the time, Nisha was in critical condition and she had two seizures. Friends and relatives from around the world were praying for her recovery and sending telegrams and email letters to support the family. This was my introduction to the wonders of computers and modern technology.

Each day, Bis attended the doctors' ward rounds, and Nisha's condition remained the same. Weeks later, on a bright, sunny morning, we arrived to much activity surrounding Nisha's bedside—she was awake! One by one, we went in to see her.

Gary came out laughing, and I was perturbed. I approached him. "Gary, what's so funny?"

He replied, "There's nothing wrong with her brain! The doctors' prediction is all wrong."

"How do you know?" I enquired.

"When you entered, Nisha put her hand on her shoulder to hide the tattoo of a butterfly she had done. 'My mother will freak out if she sees it,' she said."

Bis returned to Canada and Nisha remained in hospital. After another month's stay, she was discharged and we flew directly to Canada. Happily, after months of recuperation on the farm and playing golf, she regained her strength.

Nisha made a full recovery. She went back to Hong Kong and married Gary. She had defied the all odds, and the many medical prognoses, including that she would be sterile. I recalled her birth in the old converted church and the belief that children born there were protected under a lucky star. Eight years later, she gave birth to a beautiful, healthy, baby girl.

The anguish a parent suffers when a child's life is at stake is beyond description, and I could only give thanks for the recovery of my daughter. It was beyond me to imagine how parents coped with the loss of a child. I counted my good fortune once again, grateful that I had passed another milestone.

CHAPTER 50
A Return to Johannesburg 1982

My distraught sister Peggy telephoned to inform me of our father's sudden death, and she requested I return to help sort his affairs. Our father's death came as a shock, for he had not been ill. Father had gone for his daily five-mile hike. On his return, he did not go to lunch; instead, he went to lie down. When he did not show up, an orderly was sent to fetch him. He thought that Father was resting peacefully, but he was unable to rouse him. The doctor pronounced a heart attack as the cause of death.

Too many years had elapsed since Bis and I had been to South Africa, and we had no desire to visit our country of origin, but duty called. As Canadian citizens, we were required to apply for visas like all foreigners. After much haggling with the authorities at the South African Embassy in Canada, we were granted visas and flew to Johannesburg to attend the memorial for my father.

On arrival at Jan Smuts Airport, Bis and I were sequestered in an office and kept waiting for over two hours without any explanation. We were anxious and could not fathom the reason for the delay, or for being detained, but Apartheid overlords were at the zenith of power and were taking no chances with expats who suddenly returned. We became paranoid, waiting alone in the bare room. At last, we were interrogated by a surly official as to the nature of our visit. Bis explained that we were there to attend a memorial service for my father and to see his ailing mother.

"Why did you make a stop in Vienna?" the official asked.

"It was a stopover on our long flight to Johannesburg, and our daughter is married to an Austrian. They reside in Vienna and it was an opportunity to meet with his family."

"Do you have contact with any notable South Africans?"

We were stumped, not fully understanding the question. Before either of us could answer, he continued, "Like important people; professors, leaders—you know."

"Yes, my old friend Professor Phillip Tobias visited us last summer. He had been invited by the University of Western Ontario to accept an honour, and to give the inaugural address to the graduating medical class. He was keen to visit the theatre at Stratford in Ontario, where we picnicked after a matinee performance."

Without another word, the official scribbled a few notes, and left the room.

We had left South Africa seventeen years earlier in 1965, yet the old insecure feelings returned. The questions bothered us. We wondered why we were being detained, questioned, and then stranded in a bare room for another hour before we were allowed to clear immigration and have our Canadian passports returned. I supposed the veracity of our statements was being checked. Bis and I definitely had misgivings about our return.

Bis decided not to waste any time and to leave as soon as we had met with our relatives. He arranged with the driver to drop me off at my Aunt Leah's house in Jeppe, then to drive him on to the medical school to meet with his old friend.

My aunt was surprised but delighted to see me. "How lovely to see you, my dear," she said, hugging me. "You've come in time. I'm finally preparing to join my children in Australia."

"How the country has changed," I said. "Auntie, Bis and I are here for a short visit to attend Father's memorial, and I came to help Peg sort his affairs. I think she needed emotional support."

"Yes, Peggy told me. I am sorry," said Aunt Leah. "Now that you're here, could you please take the dog for a walk? I usually let him out in the garden, but he doesn't get much exercise with me. He's a good guard dog. But do be careful, it is no longer the place of your childhood. Violence and unrest have increased. Police presence is still much in evidence, and restrictions on freedom are more stringent. Most of the people we knew have left the neighbourhood; either they've migrated or they've moved to the affluent northern suburbs of Houghton and Sandton. And the place has been taken over by natives and other undesirables."

Signs with "Europeans Only" were more prevalent than I had remembered, and people appeared unfriendly and were less helpful. I was struck by the vast difference in the attitude of people here. I had become accustomed to the helpful and polite citizens of Canada.

Walking the dog, I recalled my childhood growing up in Jeppe. It was named after a mining magnate, Jules Jeppe, who had settled in Johannesburg following the discovery of gold. He owned a large mansion in the town and had attracted many other entrepreneurs to the area because of its proximity to the gold-bearing reef of the Witwatersrand. Jeppe had developed into a flourishing neighbourhood quite close to the city centre, but now it had deteriorated and was shabby.

As I ventured through the streets, I was astonished to see the destruction of the once picturesque suburb with its many old mansions and beautiful churches that I remembered. St. Mary's Anglican Church, where my sisters had been married, still stood, but it was in a state of disrepair. The library was no more, and Juta's bookstore had become a seedy convenience shop.

Hyland's Chemist had been a lavish building out of all proportion to the surrounding buildings, and it was equally dilapidated. The indigo ceramic tiles that covered the exterior walls were chipped, and many had been removed. Zinc and wooden boards replaced the stained-glass windows. The beautiful garden that fronted the building, which once had been the pride of the town, was now littered with beer bottles, cans, and old newspapers. A jalopy stood abandoned on what had been the front lawn. The adjacent mansion now housed squatters and drug dealers. The grand house was of historic importance because the Prince of Wales, later King Edward VII, had stopped there in 1934 for afternoon tea on his way to open a new gold mine.

I had been a little girl, but I still remembered my mother taking me—there were hundreds of people to welcome His Royal Highness. I recalled the excitement of the crowds waving Union Jacks to the strains of the brass band that played "Rule Britannia, Britannia rules the waves." Impatiently, we waited for hours to see him. Pandemonium had broken out when the motorcade bearing the dapper prince finally appeared. Dozens of policemen were needed to keep the crowds at bay.

Revisiting the old familiar park, my nostalgia was soon blighted by the squalor, seeing the well-tended gardens of yesteryear reduced to a jungle of

Part Two

weeds, which crept over the disintegrating cobblestone walkway. I remembered the days I'd spent in the park in happier times. It had been our playground and a child's paradise. In my mind's eye, I saw and heard lopsided Parky, caretaker and head gardener, as he trundled along with his one short leg attached to a boot with a platform. A cigarette would hang loosely from the side of his mouth, and once in a while he removed it with his rust-stained fingers, which were the same colour as his hair. I recalled that he was friendly in an odd way. He chased black kids away who loitered outside the wrought-iron fence, peering in at the delights offered to white children but excluding them. His behaviour had been a mystery to me then. Now, black kids were kicking a football on what had been the tennis courts. What would he have said?

It was a time of innocence and I had found it confusing. I did not understand why Parky allowed our black nannies to sit on the benches marked "Europeans Only." Was it because they wore uniforms of striped dresses with white aprons and caps? I smiled as I remembered my nanny, Marta, whose words went unquestioned.

The nannies loved their charges, and the children returned their love. Nannies settled all our quarrels and kept the bullies away. They were surrogate parents. But what delighted the children most was the ice cream vendor who sold cones at a penny each, and little packets of pink sugar lollipops that we licked from sticky fingers. All gone now. Those were happy days, certainly for me, but what of those black kids Parky had threatened? Where and why had it all vanished?

Wistfully wandering around the grounds, tightly holding the obedient dog's leash, I approached the centrepiece of the park. Water no longer gushed from the iron water fountain, where once a statue of Peter Pan had stood. The bust, minus a head, was roughly sawn off and lay face down in the dirt. Also missing were the three iron mugs that were attached by chains from which we children quenched our thirst without any regard for germs or cleanliness. Now all that remained were the chains that dangled idly to and fro.

The ornate octagonal bandstand was a tumbledown wreck. I shut my eyes and thought about those care-free Sunday evenings. Occasionally, as a reward for being a good girl, Nanny would take me, dressed in night-gown and slippers, to hear the band. And in my mind, I heard the echo of the popular tunes from Gilbert and Sullivan.

The swings from which I had fallen were now broken and held together by rusted chains. I touched the scar on my forehead, a testament to my wilful childhood. Some unkempt black children were attempting to climb the steps of the brass slide, half of which were missing. The slide had lost its sheen and looked unsafe, and the merry-go-round was stationary and falling to pieces. I recalled the organ grinder begging for a penny, and his sad-looking monkey, which peered with great dark eyes. Added to our amusement was the circus that visited Jeppe annually.

Squatters and drug dealers were now the inhabitants of Jeppe, which during my childhood had mainly been the habitat of proud English subjects and second-generation European immigrants.

My childhood home was situated between those of an Afrikaner family, whose father was the pastor of the Dutch Reform Church, and the Goldsteins, who owned a delicatessen. At that time, Jeppe was a cultured, cosmopolitan suburban town. A French family owned *Bon Marche Bazaar*, which stocked imported goods—a special treat for children was the delectable packets of jujubes and bonbons. On display in one of their windows was a miniature porcelain tea set I had coveted for my dolls' house. It was the last present I'd received from my mother on my sixth birthday.

Chinese and Indian grocery shop-keepers were located on side street corners. The Indian merchants stocked haberdashery and fine fabrics, shoes and accessories, and they operated the Bombay Emporium. Collectively, these stores were referred to by the derogatory term of "koolie shops" and Chinese and koolies were not given residential permits. However, many lived behind their premises. Native domestic workers resided in servants' quarters in the backyards of their employers' homes. Often, these were mere shanties. On arrival in Canada, the absence of servants' quarters in suburban homes and outbuildings was the first thing that I found odd.

Native men were required to carry special passes at all times, and a curfew existed that forbade them to be on the streets after eight o'clock at night. It was a law that applied equally to the Gypsies (a collective term applied to the Romani, vagabonds who visited Jeppe several times a year). Gypsies were accused of stealing and kidnapping—a threat that nannies used to frighten disobedient children. They parked their brightly painted, horse-drawn caravans at the edge of town, where after a time they were ordered by the police to move on. They were tinkers and knife sharpeners, and servants queued to have pots and pans mended.

I could not forget the enchanting Gypsy women who wore beautiful, rainbow-coloured head scarves and long dangling earrings that accentuated their dark eyes. Their arms were covered in bangles that jingled, and their long, full skirts swayed as they moved about, calling to the townspeople to sample their wares and have their fortunes read. They foretold the future, and my sceptical Gran said, "They're no match for my Ouija board."

At night, the Gypsy songs and tambourines could be heard, and nannies would plead, "Don't listen. It's the devil calling to naughty *chilluns*. So go to sleep."

The Gypsies offered the children sweets, but parents and nannies warned, "Don't take it. You'll never be seen again." Nonetheless, we children were bewitched, and we loved to spy on the Gypsies from behind barbed-wire barricades that the police erected to keep them out of the town.

Garbage and rubble were covered in fine yellow dust that wafted in from the mines, reminding me how the maids always dusted the living and sitting rooms every afternoon before tea. The litter and the pot-holed streets underlined the neglect and poverty of the present inhabitants. Some of the old houses were still standing derelict and badly in need of restoration. I recognised what was left of my childhood home by the veranda pillars that had been stripped of their iron railings. The Goldstein's delicatessen was now a grungy fish-and-chip shop where Tsotsi Boys lounged against the dirty windows smoking *dagga* and intimidating passersby.

I was saddened by all the destruction as I returned to my aunt's house and unleashed the dog into the backyard. My thoughts were interrupted by Bis, who had returned to fetch me. He was not prepared to spend the night at Aunt Leah's or at Peggy and Monty's. "We have to leave for Potch immediately," he ordered.

We left Johannesburg for Potch to visit Bis's mother, who was frail. His older sister Maryam was there on a visit from Ireland. On the third day, Bis declared that it was time to leave. His mother tried to persuade us to stay but to no avail.

Privately, he told me, "We've done our duty. Stay if you must. I'm leaving as soon as I can change our tickets." Bis knew I would not stay on without him.

It was a Sunday morning and Jan Smuts Airport was strangely empty. We were checking in at the desk, when quite unexpectedly a head popped over our shoulders. Bis was taken aback. I said, "Sam?"

"Yes. I thought it was you. You were easy to spot in this empty hall."

"Bis, this is Sam Hurwitz. He was a PF fellow traveller."

"Hello," Bis said. "I've heard about you, but we never met. Are you going to London as well?"

"Yes. Our mutual friend Rex told me you were here."

"I didn't know that you knew Rex," I said.

"That's strange, we've only been here a few days. We haven't seen him since London," Bis remarked.

"So, you're off to London. Will you be staying there?"

"Yes, just visiting friends," I interrupted, conscious that my husband was irritated by this acquaintance, but more concerned about the reference to Rex.

The steward was becoming impatient. "Please move on."

"Hope to see you later," I said. "What a coincidence."

When we were far enough away to speak without being overheard, Bis said, "I don't think it is a coincidence. Our trip here was spur of the moment, and the long delay before we were admitted does not make sense. It's suspicious—his mentioning Rex does not add up. Who else knew we were here, and that I had decided to leave suddenly?"

Bis and I were travelling in business class, unaware of where Sam was seated, possibly in first class. I had heard that he was a successful lawyer. The flight was uneventful until an announcement informing us that we would not be landing in London. The plane was being diverted to Brussels. All passengers would be accommodated overnight. No reason was given for the change. It was surprising that there were so few people on the flight, except for first and business class, which was full.

Later that evening, Sam burst in on us in the hotel dining room with a bottle of wine. "Let's celebrate and catch-up on old times," he said.

"I'm too tired. You stay if you want," said Bis, and I sensed his displeasure.

"There's an important delegation on board who are remaining in Belgium, hence the change. But I'd rather hear what you've been up to," Sam said.

Part Two

As usual, I felt obliged when I was left with an unwelcome guest. The conversation, if one could call it that, became an interrogation where I fended off questions regarding our friends, and whether I had joined any political movement.

After a while, I said, "I'm tired. Goodnight Sam."

The flight would depart early the next morning and we did not see Sam again, although I looked for him when we reached London. Bis was convinced that Sam was not as innocent as he appeared. Too many things did not add up.

"Do you really think it was pure chance that we were on the same flight? No one knew that we were leaving after only three days. And the odd way he spotted us, as if he expected us to be on that flight. Remember all the questions we faced on arrival? And remember my flight to London when the plane landed in Khartoum, and their personnel ordered me to another hotel? Joan, when I saw Phillip today, he cautioned me to be wary. BOSS have eyes and ears everywhere, and the airlines play ball with them."

"I'm sure you're right. Is that what prompted you to leave now?"

"I didn't tell you that Phillip saw Rex at med school two days ago, and Rex specifically asked Phillip whether he had seen me yet."

It was common knowledge that widespread unrest was causing more fear and speculation as more and more dissidents and informants were disappearing. There was a revolution in the offing, and who knew what form it would take. The government was leaving no stone unturned, and everyone was under suspicion. There were rumours that under a certain minister, the government was spending millions abroad hoping to uncover any subversive activity.

CHAPTER 51
Secrets

Among my late father's papers, I found a birth certificate for Ivor Hugo, born March 3, 1935, in Johannesburg. That was the day before my birthday, and a day before my mother died. What did it all mean? I trembled as I recalled how Barney had informed me of our mother's death. Slowly, it all came flooding back. That last time I had seen my mother, she made me promise: "Take care of your little sisters." There had been no mention of a baby brother. I was shocked, confused, and hurt. I felt guilty and unable to account for the distress I felt. What had happened to the baby? Why did Father not acknowledge him, though he had kept the birth certificate? The entire family had harboured and guarded the secret. Why the mystery?

I told no one of the birth certificate. I needed time to think and to understand why the secret had been locked away for so long. Whatever the reason, did I have a right to disclose it?

The mystery had to be solved. My mother's only living sibling, Aunt Leah, was quite old and still living in Jeppe, where I had visited her only two weeks ago. My aunt was not on speaking terms with any of her children because they intended to put her in a retirement home as soon as she reached Australia. I determined to discover the secret and decided to phone her. Why had she not mentioned it when I last saw her? I had to make an urgent phone call to her.

"Auntie Leah, how are you? I need some information, and only you, as far as I know, may have the answer."

Although she was happy to hear from me so soon after my visit, Aunt Leah said, "I dreaded this day would come. Is it regarding a family secret?"

Part Two

"Yes Auntie. Among Father's papers, I found a birth certificate. I did not check Father's papers while I was in Johannesburg; I only looked at them on my return to Canada."

"I'm surprised he kept it all these years. Your father was devastated by your mother's death. She gave birth to a baby in the ambulance on the way to the hospital, a day before she died. The baby was premature and was hospitalised. The birth was not announced. Your father could not bear to even look at the child. In his grief, he blamed your mother's death on the baby. When the baby was well enough to be discharged, your father, with your grandmother's consent and against the advice of your grandfather, decided to give the baby up to a distant relative of your father, who was childless. We lost touch with them. They went back to Italy and took the baby with them. Years later, they returned, but they had no contact with our side of the family. We learnt that the husband had been killed in an accident. That was the last we heard, until a few years later we were informed that the young boy, Ivor, had died of tuberculosis. Your father and grandmother felt guilty and ashamed that they had given the baby up. You must understand, you were all so young, and your grandmother could not look after another baby.

"In any case, what they had done was illegal, and everyone was sworn to secrecy and forbidden to talk about it by the lawyer who handled the case and the childless relatives who returned to Italy with the baby. It was the most painful thing to have to deal with. There was no point in letting you children know. The burden my mother and your father carried lay hidden and buried all these years. It took its toll. I must warn you there is little to be done now, and it is not our secret to divulge. It will cause more heartache. I'm sorry that you found out the way you did. You're strong, and I hope you will continue to keep their secret. Don't tell your sisters. What good can come of it? All families have secrets, and ours is no different. Our family, and you as a young person in particular, have seen much sorrow. Your father was mortified, but he made sure that you girls were well provided for. I think it was his form of penance to compensate for having abandoned his baby. May they all rest in peace? And now my dear, a weight has been lifted. Do not let the knowledge weigh you down. Let the secret remain buried. Good bye, Joan."

Now, on every birthday, I would not only think of my mother, but of Ivor, the brother I never knew. Another milestone had passed.

CHAPTER 52
A Routine Check-Up 1997

Bis had the ability to snatch cat-naps wherever and whenever time permitted him to replenish much-needed energy he required to perform his work. Of late, he appeared to be in a contemplative mood, and all my prodding was met with negative replies. One day he ordered me to accompany him to visit his doctor for his annual check-up, something he neglected or ignored most years.

The doctor pronounced him fit. "There's nothing to worry about," Dr. Eric assured him. "Your blood report is all we're waiting for."

"As one colleague to another, Eric, I admire your nonchalance—that's usually my stance," Bis said.

"I don't believe in crossing bridges until I have to."

"That's okay for you," Bis replied. He was concerned about the constant cramps and the varicose veins in his legs, which until now had never bothered him. Two days later, he was requested to revisit the doctor's office.

"Joan, I'm glad you're here," said Dr. Eric. "There is a problem. Bis, your blood test confirmed that it was more serious than I thought."

"Doctor, what are you implying?" I asked.

He ignored my question and continued. "Bis you'll need to have all the routine tests, scans, etc. You know the drill."

Bis nodded in assent. He did not want to alarm me and casually agreed, but he was certain that all was not well. A second opinion was obtained, and Bis consented to undergo further investigation. He reflected how different it was to be on the receiving end and to subject oneself to all that was demanded of a patient. For the practical doctor it was a role reversal, but he refused to speculate.

Bis and I were familiar with the sterile odour of disinfectant that greeted our arrival at the hospital clinic. Bis was calm. He held my hand. I trembled as we were ushered into a waiting room and Bis was led to the X-ray and MRI departments of the Henderson hospital in Hamilton. With trepidation, I waited and worried, dreading the outcome. My pulse beat rapidly, in contrast to the calmness my husband displayed. Bis appeared resigned and showed no emotion, but I knew it belied what he really felt, otherwise he would never have consented to the examinations. He had practised medicine for such a long time that he'd surmised all was not right.

For the next two weeks, we spent much time at the hospital. Bis was afraid of exacerbating my fear. I looked into his eyes and marvelled at his stoicism and his courage. He did not flinch but looked straight ahead as he submitted to being prodded and poked, as interns tried to take blood from his flattened veins. Finally, they resorted to a "cut-down," which meant using a scalpel to get at the vein in order to extract a sample of blood.

The efficient nurses and technicians scurried about, eager to ensure that Bis was comfortable. I was shown into the doctors' lounge, where tea and sandwiches were served. I had never been so nervous. The ordeal of the unknown weighed heavily.

"Please, help yourself and ring if there is anything you need."

"Thank you, Nurse. Please let me know when my husband is done."

An abdominal scope revealed stomach cancer. I was shocked and for once, I was tongue-tied. The worry and anxiety of the past few days was worse than either of us were prepared for. Bis retained his composure but appeared to be lost in thought. I wondered, *what is he thinking?* He tried to make light of the dire situation. There was so much that was unspoken between us on the drive back home, as I watched his tense expression, fearing the worst.

Two days later, we were back at the clinic, where the oncologist monitored all the prescribed examinations and tests to ensure the diagnosis was correct. "I'm sorry. Bis, we'll do all we can to make you comfortable." He handed Bis the report, but he did not look at his patient.

Bis hesitated before reading the diagnosis. "It's a death sentence!" he said, deliberately looking at me. He wanted to inform me of the inevitable and to gauge my reaction. I was non-committal but stared as if I had not heard what he had just said, hoping that the diagnosis was incorrect.

The doctor interrupted my thoughts. "Bis, you realise that remission from this particular cancer is rare."

"What do you suggest?" Bis asked in a modulated tone.

"Well, drastic surgery of the stomach. You'll be fitted with a bag and then undergo chemotherapy.

"Fine, then let's get on with it."

"Okay. We'll operate in the next few days. I'll make the arrangements."

Bis showed no emotion, but by the slight pursing of his lips, I knew otherwise.

All options were examined and the surgery was scheduled for the following Friday. His entire stomach would be removed. The prognosis was depressing.

The dreaded day arrived and the operation was in progress while I waited anxiously, checking the time with Nisha, who had flown in from Jersey on the Channel Islands to support me. For once, I did not speculate on the outcome but hoped for a favourable result. Conversation between my daughter and me was stilted. To pass the time, Nisha went off to phone her siblings.

The hours ticked away—it proved to be an endurance test that left me limp with concern. Six hours later, the surgeon emerged from the operating theatre, his slumped shoulders a harbinger of bad news. He approached us. "Mrs. Bismillah, it was infinitely worse than I thought. I suspect your husband has adenoma carcinoma, but I will wait for confirmation from the lab report. I decided against the radical operation and did not remove the entire stomach, as that would have entailed repeated surgery over a period of months. I've left sufficient skin in place to form a pouch that will allow Bis to consume modest morsels of food. It will be more comfortable for him, so there is no need for a bag."

A lengthy silence ensued. The doctor fiddled with his stethoscope. What more could he say? Anything else would seem trite.

Nisha was in tears, but I was dry eyed, trying to process the doctor's report. Eventually, I asked, "How much time does he have?"

"Very little. I'm surprised he's lasted this long. I hate to speculate or predict, but in this instance, given his condition and the size of the tumour, I'd guess three months."

"May I see him?"

"He's still out of it. The anaesthetic hasn't worn off yet. Come and have some tea," the surgeon said wearily.

As the tea was being poured, an alarm sounded. Code blue. Over the intercom, it called for the surgeon to return to the operating theatre. More anxious moments. What was happening?

His patient was in trouble. Nisha squeezed my hand.

A young doctor came out of the operating theatre and explained that Bis had suffered a cardiac shock resulting in the depletion of oxygen to the brain, and that had caused a rapid increase in his blood pressure. Three hours passed before Bis was stabilized. The deprivation of oxygen over that lengthy period resulted in severe damage to his brain. Bis would never again be the same.

One week later, a stubborn Bis signed himself out of hospital against the advice of his doctors. He rejected any other form of treatment. He felt that being in hospital for an extended length of time was not only an invasion of his privacy, but left him open to infection. Privately, he told me as I sat at his bedside, "All my life I fought to uphold my dignity, and it has come to this."

I had no answer but stroked his cheek. He knew that the cancer was lethal.

A week later, Bis was quite lucid as he addressed the assembled medical team, who had gathered around his bedside to persuade him to reconsider treatment, and to remain in hospital.

Bis was defiant. "Despite the insidious cancer that has invaded my body, I refuse to subject myself to chemotherapy. I intend to live what's left of my life, however short, as normally as possible. In my experience during all the years of practice, I observed few patients with stomach cancer who benefited, or whose quality of life was improved with chemotherapy. In my opinion, the treatment was more drastic than the disease, because it compromised the quality of what life there was. Joan, please take me home." From past experience, I knew that trying to argue or to persuade my intractable husband was futile.

Bis appeared to ignore his condition. After a three-week convalescence at home, where he had spent the time reading and listening to music and poetry, he acted as if nothing had changed. He was inspired by Dylan Thomas, *"Do not go gentle into that good night. Rage, rage against the dying of the light"*—a precept by which Bis intended to live on his terms. He would focus all his strength on living with purpose and he returned to work. Colleagues and staff treated him with deference. The cardiac shock that had deprived his brain of oxygen had impaired his short-term memory, but Bis believed that he was normal. He was defiant and intended to prove that he had made the right decision. His privacy was paramount and his feelings would remain hidden from the outside world.

Doctors deal in life and death situations all the time, and Bis believed that at least for a time he was exempt. He intended to live according to the dictates of his will. From that moment our life became a battle; it was a test of wills with a cantankerous husband. I was reminded of a cricket match so long ago, when I had first discovered that Bis was capable of rage. In the privacy of our home, a brilliant, courtly gentleman had reverted to adolescent tantrums. He was wilfully childish, but there was nothing childlike about him now. Like the schoolyard bully, Bis had become petty and cruel, and I bore the brunt of his anger. I accepted his irrational behaviour without retaliating because I could not bear to see him humiliated. I knew his outbursts were simply expressions of frustration and anger. In all our time together, he had been the conductor who had orchestrated our every move, but now I had become the authoritarian figure who had to contend with a wilful, disobedient child. The role reversal was damaging to our relationship, but I could not allow it to affect me in a negative way.

Bis was determined to prove his doctors wrong, if not incompetent. He believed that he knew better! I thought his arrogant attitude was akin to hubris and that it tempted fate.

A year passed and despite the gravity of his weakened condition, Bis continued to work. His practice sustained him. Patients flocked to him for counselling. To them, he remained the genial, compassionate doctor of old, but now they revered his wise council, for he spoke from personal experience. He could no longer practise obstetrics and gynaecology, and all-night calls and surgery ended.

I begged his partners to prevent him from working and to stop him from driving, but to no avail. "Bis drives like a maniac. Stop him before he has an accident and kills someone," I pleaded repeatedly, but in vain.

"How can we stop him?" his partners said to me. "Provided he doesn't operate, and we can monitor any prescriptions he writes, that's all we can do. His patients trust him implicitly—that keeps him going."

"At what cost? You do not have to live with his temper tantrums and his suffering, which is something that I witness daily."

I feared for his safety, and all my pleas with him to slow down and to stop at stop signs fell on deaf ears. "Bis, please allow one of the men to drive you," I said, but my pleading only enraged him.

Meanwhile, Bis was losing weight, and he was worn out at day's end.

Mealtimes had become a contentious issue. Always a fussy eater, Bis subsisted on abstemious portions of food, seeming to exist on sheer will power and anger. His complaints regarding food were numerous, and each day I racked my brain trying to make his small meals attractive. Although my patience was tried, I refused to succumb to his quarrelsome behaviour and forced myself to be upbeat by gaining the support from my children, who telephoned daily.

Thankful that circumstances had forced me to accept the wonder of modern technology, I bought a computer to keep in touch with my children via e-mail. We were in daily contact with those who lived abroad, except for Nadya, who lived close by. She supported and nourished my anguished soul, which helped me to cope in the belligerent atmosphere. Bis did not use a computer and threatened to break mine for spending time on it and reporting nonsense. I told my children that it was their father's fighting spirit that kept him alive. He would not hear of any of them returning home. I think it was a question of his pride, for he could not bear to allow them to witness his suffering, or any sort of pity or even to have help, apart from the cleaning lady, who had to be out of the house before he returned from the office.

I questioned how much longer our torture could continue. I scanned his face looking for the man I loved and wondered how much longer we could endure life in what had become purgatory. Already Bis had proven his doctors wrong by outliving the prescribed three months.

He continued to keep appointments with his doctors, but he rejected all their advice. He perked up when they told him how miraculous it was that he was still able to perform the way he did. Their remarks bolstered his ego. I was surprised by the strength of his character and his vanity. The sole purpose of visits to his doctors was to prove that he was still alive and in control. Bis believed he was the supreme commander of his destiny, and he affirmed that he suffered no physical pain. He certainly did not complain of any.

In the infrequent tender moments, he would ask, "Joan, what will you do here all alone?"

"It's possible that I could go before you," I ventured, as I could not conceive of a life without him. Unlike Bis, I seldom planned ahead and often he accused me of muddling through.

"You're like an ostrich with your head in the sand, refusing to accept the inevitable. I'm dying," he spat at me.

I was incapable of an answer. How did one reply to a tormented soul that was intimately twinned with one's own? We had been together for so many years, and we were mirror images, who before his illness had known each other's thoughts. So much was left unsaid due to the bitterness that gnawed at him. Our once-happy home had become our prison. I acquiesced to all his demands. However, after the interminable questions about my future without him, I resolved to enrol in the Turf Grass Management Course at the university. I was resolved to continue to run his beloved golf course. Bis endorsed my decision and I detected a glint of the old Bis in his bloodshot eyes. At last, he saw a sign that I had a plan and was coming to terms with my future. I had to balance the onerous tasks of attending to his needs and to my studies. I ensured that I was home in time to have dinner with him. His lunch was a light snack, which I prepared before leaving for class. The course, scheduled from nine a.m. to five p.m., was a distraction, as it forced me to concentrate on something other than my ailing husband. More importantly, it renewed the energy I needed to deal with my difficult domestic situation. Sadly, I felt that the end could not be far off.

Visitors, mainly doctors and his colleagues who came to pay their respects, were astonished by his resilience and his determination to carry on.

"How are you?" they queried.

"What has Joan been saying? Can't you tell that I'm fine?" he replied contemptuously, then straightened his ascot that kept slipping from his scrawny neck as he steered the conversation to other topics. His discussions, and the clarity of his arguments, amazed our visitors. For Bis, it was a brief respite from the underlying thoughts that beset him, but more importantly, it was to demonstrate that he was still in charge.

Often, after the guests had left, Bis would ask, "Who just visited us?" He was unable to recall, and he would be in a state of collapse and at his most virulent.

It was a strain on both of us. The effort of putting up a brave front took its toll and weakened him. I was hurt, but I accepted his taunts without comment, not wanting to inflame an awkward and delicate situation. How could I even contemplate blaming him? *Do I wish for the end?* In all honesty, there were moments of extreme heartache and anguish in which I did, and then I would rationalize that it was only to deliver him from his suffering. I became ashamed and guilty for harbouring any such thoughts. In reality, he had lost control, but he still held the power to make me feel guilty. My wish for him was to be at peace. On reflection, I realised that publicly, Bis minimized his condition. He still needed to prove that he alone was in charge of his destiny. He had conducted our lives and could always make me see things his way. I loved and cherished my companion, friend, and lover, but the frustration… We were soul mates, and fifty-one years of marriage was not that easily erased—our love was intact.

It had been three and a half years since his operation, and the only medication was half a sleeping tablet each night. So much more time than his doctors had predicted. Bis was jubilant. Triumphant in victory! He had out-witted them and their prognosis, and he had proved his point. Life had been prolonged without their treatment. Although he had won a major battle, he was losing the war. He attempted to play golf but his wraith-like body prevented him from finishing a round. After a few holes, he was exhausted and forced to retire. Too proud to admit that he was weak, he made excuses and claimed that he needed to supervise the tees that had to be changed, and restructure bunkers, and that there were trees that had to be removed and transplanted to make way for the construction of a new pond.

"Joan, this is where I want my ashes buried!"

The Sword of Damocles hovered.

One of the course workers, an ex-policeman, complained to me that he'd seen Bis driving erratically on the wrong side of the road. He was sure that Bis would have an accident. I had little choice but to plead to his partners to stop him from driving. They understood that Bis was nearing the end, but they lacked the courage to tell him to stop driving. I was left to impart their instructions.

"What if you killed someone on the road?" I asked.

Disgusted, Bis threw his car keys at me. He was furious, accusing me of discussing our private matters with outsiders. And suddenly, the fight was over.

He stopped driving and working, and he did not set foot in the office again. Everything would be dictated according to his terms. That was his final day of work, precisely one week before he succumbed. I was not aware how close the end was.

A surreal peace descended that week. I did not realise that it was to be our last. We settled into a comfortable companionship. We listened to music and recalled our discussions of times passed when we were young. Both of us believed that energy was the essence of being, and at the end it passed back to the source in that mysterious and unknown void.

Bis now applauded Nadya's visits, and her bubbling personality had a soothing effect and eased what tension remained. She too joined us in listening to music, and Bis ordered her to purchase his final gift for me, a recording of Rodrigo's *Aranjues Concerto*. I held his hand as we listened, and I reminded him, "Bis, do you recall that night at the Royal Festival Hall where we were introduced to Segovia, and his classic guitar? The patrons were unwilling for Segovia to stop playing, and he performed one encore after another."

Bis smiled. "The London County Council ordered the tube and busses to run for an extra hour because the concert went over-time."

I read aloud our favourite Rumi passages, recalling a happier time when we had first met. Bis even managed to laugh. "You were such a prude!" Intuitively, we both acknowledged that the end was in sight. Bis had made his peace. He was rational, calm, and loving. There was no need for words or apologies.

We had endured the greatest ordeal, or rather, our love had sustained us, and I knew then that it would always be with me.

My sadness was inexpressible. We spoke tenderly to each other.

I pondered, *How is it possible that in his weakened condition, and having renounced all that modern medicine had to offer, he has survived this long?*

I attributed his will to live to his indomitable spirit and his fierce, competitive drive. He had always played to win—his victory was that he had proved his doctors wrong.

It was ironic that he developed stomach cancer. Until then, Bis had been extremely fit, a model of abstemious eating habits, who eschewed junk food or any other excess. He drank rarely and in moderation and certainly he never smoked. At no time throughout the ordeal had Bis taken to bed. He woke at six a.m., as was his habit, and still took pride in his dress, asking me each morning, "Joan, does this tie match?"

Doctors commented on his resilience and the fact that he had lived so many years without treatment, defying all the odds. In the last year of his illness, we attended Enver and Leslie's marriage in San Francisco, and later the celebration in New York. Enver joked, "Papa you should have abused your body and developed some immunity like the rest of us." The remark went unchallenged.

I recalled the surprise Bis had in store for our family six months before he succumbed. He had organized a golfing holiday in Southern Ireland. We were to play at several major golf courses. He called it, "The last round." It was his parting gift to me and our children. "Deliberately, I have not invited your spouses," he said. "Only our immediate family is to enjoy this time together. Forget that I'm not in the best of health."

We played, or rather we competed against each other, as we toured Ireland's famed golf courses: Ballybunion, La Hinch, Kilarney, Watervale, and Portmarnoch. The latter did not permit females. Bis quietly insisted that when he had made the reservation six months ago, they had omitted to inform him that females were prohibited and as this was his last round, he insisted that Nisha was the fourth member of the team. The manager was apologetic and relented.

"The three-thirty p.m. starting time at the end of the day is available. You will be the final group. Your daughter will be allowed to play, but she must hide her hair under a man's cap."

At dinner that evening, Bis called his family to attention, and revealed the purpose of the Last Round. "I have left everything to your mother, my partner for more than fifty years. You were educated at the best schools and I'm proud of you. However, if there are any complaints, now is the time to air them. Always remember this time. I'm happy that we're here together as a family. As immigrants, we have been extremely fortunate. We've worked hard to make Canada our home and it is my hope that you will continue to love and to look after one another."

Every evening, after a day on the links, we dined at notable restaurants, accompanied by our nephew, Dr. Rashid, who practised medicine in Dublin. He was not a golfer, but observed the fun the family had being together, and how competitive we were, not conceding any allowances to the ailing father. He determined then and there to take golf lessons.

We stayed in quaint bed-and-breakfast places. At night, Bis and I retired early, as he was worn out but happy at the end of the day. Our children's *joie de vivre* was infectious. And after visiting a local pub, of which there were quite a few in every small Irish town, the children returned to play cards well into the wee hours. Their merriment and laughter brought a rare smile of contentment as it reached us in the next suite.

After the children left, Bis and I stayed on in Dublin to visit the gravesite of Rashid's mother Maryam, Bis's oldest sister. We went on to London to visit old friends, and some of our favourite haunts.

Finally, we returned to Canada, where Bis worked up until the week before he succumbed. A day before the end, he took me to our lawyer to ensure that our affairs were in order. The lawyer was amazed by his resignation and how calmly he took charge of business.

I continue to relive that fateful last day and in the stillness, I hear Bis's quiet, rational voice: "Joan, take me to the hospital. I have a problem. I'm in pain." It was the only time he had admitted to having pain. I did his bidding.

Bis spoke to a young doctor whom we met at the door about to go off-duty. "I need to be catheterized now," he ordered. The doctor turned back and attended to Bis. Two hours later, I was called back to the hospital.

"Bis has dismantled all the intravenous drips and wants you to fetch him immediately," the doctor said.

Back home in his own bed as he was writhing in pain, I attached the Wagenstein and the vacolitre, which was laced with morphine. Bis seemed a little more comfortable.

"Good, the morphine's taking effect," he said. He slept fitfully for about an hour, and then suddenly his restlessness increased. Enver, who had arrived that morning from San Francisco, got onto the bed beside his father and put his arm under Bis's shoulders to support him. Rafik, our grandson, held the Wagenstein drip that collected his urine while I changed and bathed him. I wiped his brow and held his hand, and it appeared that some colour had returned—or was I imagining it? Bis looked up and I met his appealing gaze as a solitary tear spilled from under the long eyelashes that had attracted my attention on our first encounter. The tear dribbled down his emaciated cheek. I wiped it away. It was a simple gesture that I had performed once before on a loved one, a very long time ago. I bent lower and my voice barely audible, I whispered very slowly, "I love you." I'm unsure that he heard me. Momentarily, our eyes locked, and Bis looked beyond me, and from his throat a slow rattle emitted. He gurgled and we thought he was choking, and then he exhaled and all was quiet. Enver, Rafik, and I were unaware that it was his last breath. At that precise moment, all was deathly still. The three of us were transfixed like statues as if in a state of suspended animation. We could not estimate how long the moment lasted—a second, a minute, or an hour? Silence prevailed. Bis's marathon ordeal was over.

"Mum, what just happened?" Enver, who still supported his father, queried as he checked his pulse. Rafik was pale and trembled, but held on to the IV, and I let go of his hand while the clock ticked away. It read twenty to seven. The date was the 27th of September, 2001.

Bis was a sportsman and a gentleman. He had lived his life according to the dictates of his heart. He was a fierce competitor who thrived on challenge. The final battle had been fought with dignity with me at his side, witnessed by his son Enver and his grandson Rafik.

Bis was agnostic. He was also a stoic who adhered to the principle that one was capable of exercising control and influencing the course of one's destiny. Competition was a vital part of his character. Therefore, the duel was between him and his peers with their flawed prognoses.

"Doctors are not God!" A dictum he was fond of quoting.

He could not win the war, but he had derived immense pleasure by outwitting them. That was his salvation, and his example of how to conduct one's life.

"Strive for excellence" was the mantra that had guided him throughout his adult life.

His public persona presented a private, gentle man, but it concealed the man of steel. He was dispassionate and calm, and said little and accepted praise with quiet charm, even modesty. But in those intimate moments lovers share, he relished his triumph. Love was the anchor that had sustained us.

In the aftermath, I reviewed those fateful three and a half years of pain and torment—they had taught me self-reliance and patience. More importantly, Bis knew that the staid and tranquil Canadian country, which I had been reluctant to emigrate to, offered equal opportunity to those who chose to settle on its shores. It is now my home, and the place where I fit in.

Given time, my pain would heal. I am resilient and I had reached another milestone. In his wisdom, Bis knew my strength and certainly my weakness. *Was his aberrant behaviour deliberately calculated to toughen my mettle for the journey that lay ahead?* I could not help but muse.

CHAPTER 53
Life as a Widow

Six months had passed and I was still overcome with sadness and possessed by monophobia in the large, isolated house. Overcome with nostalgia, I relived over and over again that first brief encounter and the spark that had been ignited those many years ago. I recalled how it had flamed into a beacon that lit my path, and that now only a flicker remained, reminding me of the uncertainty of the future.

Dawn interrupted my thoughts and presented me with a fairy-tale world of frosted icicles that hung from every tree. I welcomed the grey light that banished the darkness of the dreaded night, and finally, I hoped to snatch some much-needed sleep. Alas, that was not to be, as I continued to be overwhelmed by thoughts of happier times, and by fond memories of a beloved one, now no more.

Bis had been concerned for my welfare. He had catered to most of my whims, and he had tried to encourage me to talk about his encroaching demise and how I intended to manage once he was not there. Time and again, he had asked me, "What will you do here all alone?"

I had no answer and resisted the painful topic, for I could not contemplate life without him. I could not articulate that somewhere, deeply imbedded inside my mind was the knowledge that I would survive, and some unseen hand would guide me. Yet, after his death, I sorely regretted and reproached myself for not having tried to satisfy his concern.

Bis had been the maestro who had conducted my adult life. I realised what had prompted that particular question. I reminisced how Bis had lost his patience with my inability to budget, or to plan ahead. I recalled each month how I was overdrawn at the bank, and that I would raid the mailbox and extract my bank statement before Bis had a chance to see it. By the end of three months, I was compelled to ask for a cheque to cover the overdraft. At first, he scolded, but then he gave me the amount I needed. Soon it became a habit. And later, as if I were a naughty child, he deliberately kept me waiting while I fidgeted and listened to him lecture me about my lack of thrift and the need to budget, all the while I was thinking, *Please just sign the cheque.*

I mused, *Fifty-one-years as partners.* Togetherness was firmly wired in my brain and that could not easily be erased. But the time had arrived for each to tread our unknowable different paths. Our solo journeys would lead who knew where? Bis's went back to the source and mine into an uncharted domain. When we were very young, Bis had pledged, "*Every atom that belongs to me as good belongs to you.*" His gift of love became a part of my psyche. Now those atoms would have to sustain me, and I would have to find the strength in my solitude to continue on my journey, or "muddle through," as he was wont to say.

Soon after his passing, I was overwhelmed with grief, and I could not reconcile the splendour and warmth of autumn slowly inching toward winter with its cold and bleak demeanour. I strolled in the garden that Bis and I had planted, and I watched the many-hued crimson leaves flutter from the parent trees, sinking into heaps below. It set me thinking of my children, who only weeks ago had left to continue their separate lives. My existence was tormented—how would I overcome the grief that possessed my being? At night I dreaded being alone in the rambling house, where the floor boards squeaked, the ceilings creaked, and the raccoons rampaged on the roof and balcony, all adding to my insecurity. I shivered. My loneliness could not be assuaged.

My late-afternoon routine was to trudge up and down the passage checking and securing that every door and window was firmly bolted before dark. The security and comfort of home was lost. Even the burglar alarm did little to allay my fear. Slight movements tripped the sensitive motion detectors, which alerted the police and brought them to investigate. The long, sleepless nights added to my morbid fear.

I was rudderless, floating in a sea of despair and unable to steer to a safe harbour. During the day, working and managing the golf course provided temporary relief. But the dreaded night loomed. There had to be a solution. I rallied to find the strength to act. "Oh Bis," I sobbed, "How am I to manage without you?" I was reminded how my grandmother had communed with her late husband. At last, I understood.

I called an agency for a housekeeper, and Nadya drove me to pick her up at the office in Hamilton. Delia impressed me when we arrived home; she insisted on watering the plants and preparing our lunch. She spent the rest of the afternoon fixing her walk-out basement apartment. I was determined to make her feel comfortable and provided her with her own phone, radio, and television.

For the first time in weeks, I was relaxed as I watched television that evening, but suddenly I was interrupted by Delia, who appeared to have been crying.

"Please, I can tell you something?"

"Of course, please sit down."

"My daughter has friend-boy, but now he's mine," she said in pidgin English.

I was at a loss but checked myself. "Why are you telling me?"

"Because I afraid to stay here without man. It is too far and all alone."

"What would you like me to do?"

"I bring my friend-boy and he look after us. I phone him. He say he can come now. Please only you tell him the way to come."

That was unexpected. I was shocked but my common sense prevailed. I tried to act normally. "Look, it is too late tonight, and I can't direct him to find his way from Hamilton. Nadya will give him directions tomorrow. We'll wait until morning and I'll ask her."

I was petrified. My fear returned—was I to be the victim of a greedy caregiver? I did not want to alarm Nadya, who lived twenty miles away, but I sat up all night watching television in a somnambulist state, sleeping in fits and starts until the television announcer read the six o'clock news. Hurriedly, I showered and dressed. When I entered the dining room, Delia was seated at the breakfast table, sobbing.

"Good morning. What's wrong?" I asked.

"I must give you two weeks' notice. My friend-boy will give me some work. He say he can't live by himself, or he take my daughter back again."

I determined that it was prudent to be rid of Delia, and I was relieved. If she could so easily deprive her daughter of a boyfriend, what were her plans for me?

"You do not need to give notice. I will pay you for the two weeks and you may leave now. I will drive you to Guelph to get the early bus to Hamilton. If we leave now, you will be in time to catch it."

Delia sobbed even louder.

"I will write you a cheque."

"No, no. I must have only cash."

"I do not keep any cash in the house, but on the way to the bus terminal, I will stop at the bank and you can cash the cheque. Please, fetch all your things."

I drove to the bank in Guelph deliberately via a circuitous back route as a precaution to confuse Delia in the event she returned with her boyfriend. *Was I being paranoid?*

I withdrew the cash from the bank for Delia. Then I dropped her off at the bus stop. In a contemplative mood, I sat in the car trying to marshal my thoughts. *Did I have a lucky escape?* I pondered my next move.

Ultimately, I pulled myself together and phoned Nadya. "I'll spend the night with you. I need time to take stock."

I had no option; I had to manage the golf course. I used every ruse to get friends to stay. I even sent them prepaid airline tickets to visit me for weeks at a time. I knew that this behaviour could not continue indefinitely. Winter months were the worst when the golf course closed, snow and ice lay heavy on the ground, and the roads became impassable. I would be stranded.

My solution was to move into an apartment in Toronto for the duration of winter. It was a temporary respite from fear. Spring time returned all too soon, and the routine began afresh. For ten years I continued this part-time existence, at the beginning of spring-time onwards, and after a winter break in the city, the cycle would begin anew. I was becoming more restless and my fear of being alone in the house had increased. In addition, the upkeep of the golf course was becoming more expensive and began to erode my inheritance. The only option was to sell, which would liberate me from the dreaded seasonal commute, and isolation. Further, it would provide for my retirement. I was eighty years old. I had survived; another milestone had been reached.

CHAPTER 54
News from Zimbabwe

A PHONE CALL FROM MY SISTER BERYL, WHO LIVED IN RHODESIA, NOW Zimbabwe, informed me she was in trouble. It was spring, April 2002, barely seven months since Bis's death. My world was in turmoil. I had barely recovered or reconciled to the fact that he was no longer there to lean on, or to seek his advice. Beryl informed me that she and her husband George, a retired civil servant, were *persona non gratia* in Zimbabwe, and had to leave, and seek asylum in South Africa. My problems paled beside her need for immediate assistance.

Their country was in a state of anarchy, people were being murdered, and life in general was unsafe. In Beryl's name, I made an airline reservation in Toronto and purchased a single ticket for her to Johannesburg. All Beryl had to do was to show up at the airport in Zimbabwe. However, the rules for traveling out of Zimbabwe were stringent: a valid excuse was required. Beryl was going for a medical check-up following breast cancer surgery that had been performed in Johannesburg. George would sneak out once Beryl was safely aboard the plane. Their African retainer, Tabu, whom they trusted and who had been employed by them for more than thirty years, was sworn to secrecy, and agreed to drive George to the border and to safety.

In exchange, Tabu was offered the car and the contents of their home on condition that he did not divulge their plans. He would receive another fifty pounds in cash when they reached the border. George salvaged a few personal items that he could take in the car and Tabu proceeded to drive him and see him safely across the border into South Africa. At a prearranged spot, George would rendezvous with his son, who lived in Natal. The danger was the possibility of being robbed and murdered along the dusty dirt roads. Hundreds of white people were fleeing the country, and a black driver would attract little or no attention.

George had been a civil servant in the Ian Smith government. However, when Robert Mugabe took power, the country changed not only leadership, but also its name. People's lives, especially those of British descent, were rudely disrupted.

Rhodesia, which had been the bread basket of Africa, now became the new country of Zimbabwe, and many of its people were starving. New laws were imposed that affected the lives of all who lived within its borders. All "Old White Men," that is, civil servants from the Ian Smith government, were compelled to retire, and white South Africans were no longer welcome—they did not belong. Beryl, who had worked as a bookkeeper for Shell Oil for decades, would also lose her job. Later, they were deprived of their pensions as the regime became a dictatorship.

Inflation now added to the problems of poverty and ignorance. Economic hardship was borne by the masses of blacks. Poor black people began squatting on the property of whites, and they could not be evicted. Life was fraught with danger for those fleeing; they were being murdered and their possessions stolen on the journey to South Africa. The solution for them, including George and Beryl, was to find refuge back in South Africa. Leaving was difficult, for as soon as it was known that they were about to leave, their property was targeted by vandals, and murders were commonplace. Thus, secrecy for their protection was imperative.

Their journey was uneventful, but on reaching the border, Tabu ordered George out of the car. "*Basie,* I'm sorry. And you are safe now. Walk. And I keep car and everything."

Tabu had demanded the fifty pounds earlier. George had little choice but to oblige and surrender everything. He was devastated, realising that in their present society, it was each man for himself.

After hours of walking, luckily George liaised with his son, who was about to take off, assuming there had been a change in plans. George was exhausted and slept fitfully as they drove the five hundred odd miles in silence to the

Transvaal, only stopping for petrol. He was emotionally drained, but thankful to have escaped the physical brutality so many of their compatriots had endured when attempting to leave the country.

Beryl had managed to secure a small amount of money in South Africa. Life was bleak. Together with fellow expatriate Rhodesians, as they preferred to be known, they pooled their meagre resources and formed a co-operative on the outskirts of Johannesburg. Their humble houses or flats, such as they were, provided them with shelter and relative safety.

The ordeal had rendered George frail, and after three months in South Africa, he suffered a heart attack. Beryl used all of her limited resources to pay for a private ward, but George passed away. Grief-stricken and reduced to poverty, Beryl now depended on her sisters. Peggy supplied groceries and all the necessities for her well-being. I was thankful that I was in a position to keep the promise I had made to help my sisters by giving Beryl a modest annual allowance.

CHAPTER 55
Requiem for a Departed Sister

Four years had elapsed since Bis's passing in 2001. Once again, I had to attend the funeral of a loved one. The day was hazy, and an overcast sky matched my melancholy mood. My sister Jean's ashes were to be interred at the Danish Urn Cemetery later in the afternoon.

I arrived early at the Danish Centre and was greeted by a gracious host. The occasion was sombre and permitted me to eschew the schnapps he served. I offered my assistance, but I was assured that Bent, Jean's husband, had made all the arrangements to commemorate and celebrate his late wife's life.

To while away the time until the ceremony began, I asked for permission to tour the grounds. The gardeners informed me that they were volunteers and for a small donation, they would plant a red oak tree in her memory. Gladly I agreed and selected a sturdy specimen.

The property and gardens were immaculately maintained. The cemetery was beautiful, set in a glade surrounded by towering spruce and pine trees, maples, interspersed with larches, alders, firs, and majestic beech trees that hearkened back to the verdant Danish forests.

Grey mist had settled and added to the sublime atmosphere, which did little to relieve my grief. The leaden sky emitted a fine drizzle that diffused the light and had the effect of other-worldliness. It was breath-taking and serene in an ethereal and surreal way. All that loveliness provided some solace. I could not imagine a more exquisite setting to inter one's ashes. The lofty scene was in keeping with the reverent mood.

A gardener remarked, "It's a perfect Danish day, ordained by Thor."

Part Two

If one believed in the afterlife, then Jean's spirit would finally be at peace in this earthly Valhalla.

A large amphitheatre with a low granite wall surrounded the perimeter. Built into the wall at regular intervals were locker-like crypts to house the ashes of the deceased. Each was covered by a black marble plaque inscribed with the name and date. Jean's read: Eugenie Christiansen.13th September, 1932 –14th February, 2005. The centrepiece of the amphitheatre was an ingenious sculpture. The construction was composed of three large, pink granite rocks imported from Denmark. The polished stones were stacked together and met at the centre where the hollow formed a cruciform shape. The neat clean lines were implicit, iconic Scandinavian art.

Mourners and guests began to gather, awaiting the arrival of the minister who would officiate. Whispers of condolences and hushed voices all added to the gloominess and sanctity of the occasion. Now and then, the silence was pierced by muffled sobs and the odd screech of birds.

I was saddened and reflected on our relationship. Jean was a serious practising Christian, and my lack of formal religion, since I had abandoned it ages ago, added to the friction between us. Of the four sisters, Jean was third in line and was considered delicate, which was reinforced by our Victorian grandmother, who'd made allowances for Jean's capriciousness and showered her with treats. Yet, Jean clung to the notion that she was unlucky, and that I, her older sister, was blessed with good fortune. It was a belief I was unable to dispel.

As the eldest, I had assumed the responsibility of caring for my little sisters, an obligation my dying mother had imposed. From my grandmother, I had inherited a sense of duty. Years passed, and each sister chose her own path. Jean was headstrong and after the breakdown of two marriages was struggling in Johannesburg with four children, three of whom were teenagers. Bis sponsored their entry to Canada, where she met Bent Christiansen, the "Great Dane," as her sons dubbed him. Bent, a bachelor, was a well-to-do farmer who embraced her family as his own. In turn, her children adored him.

My other two sisters, Beryl and Peggy, agreed with me: "How lucky can one get?" Jean's marriage to Bent had endured for thirty years, and she claimed that Bent was the ideal loving husband. Jean had contracted rheumatoid-arthritis and was confined to a wheelchair, and she was in constant pain. Bent nursed her with the utmost patience and care. He built a new home with stairs and an escalator seat. He installed pulleys that could be lowered into a hot-tub, and they had a winter home in Florida.

Despite having the good fortune of having escaped from the rigours of South Africa, she still believed that life had treated her unfairly. Invariably, something intruded to mar our relationship. She felt that I did not conform to her version of sisterhood, as I did not agree with her on religion. But more often, Jean quarrelled with her oldest teenage daughter, something most mothers can understand.

I believe that there was something of the manic-depressive in Jean's nature, unwittingly fostered by our over-protective grandmother, who treated her differently from my sisters and me. Constantly we were reminded of her delicate nature, which worsened with age as her health deteriorated. I surmised that this was the reason for her distemper.

The last years of Jean's life were fraught with severe pain. Bent, the caregiver, must be commended for everything he did to alleviate his wife's suffering. I could only imagine the bleakness of their existence in the later years. Bent forfeited all his activities and sold his farm to care for Jean—a testament to his love.

A bell rang. It roused me from my reverie. Mass was about to begin. I had been oblivious to the lengthy tributes of condolences that were expressed, and paid attention to the service.

The Anglican priest, wearing his surplice, asked for silence, and he began the simple but eloquent ceremony in this beautiful setting. He bestowed his blessing, as he gently wafted the thurible, filling the air with fragrant incense. He had been Jean's constant friend and counsellor throughout her long ordeal. As he intoned the prayer for the dead, I felt that my sister Jean at last had found peace, and a weight had been lifted. I joined in the Lord's Prayer... Amen!

CHAPTER 56
Tribute to Peggy

Early one morning I was roused from a troubled sleep by the insistent ringing of the phone call. It was from Johannesburg.

"Hello," I answered. It was my niece Brigitte, Peggy's eldest daughter.

"Auntie Joan, Mummy is in hospital in a coma. The doctors have pronounced her brain dead, and they want to turn off all life supports. Please help me make a decision."

Now fully awake and very concerned, I asked, "What happened?"

"Aubrey, Mummy's partner, had gone to pick her up to go to lunch. They had played tennis earlier, and she went home to change. He found her lying on the bathroom floor. The doctors have diagnosed a brain aneurism."

"Oh Brigitte, I'm so sorry not to be there. I suggest you get in touch with her priest so that he can administer the last rites before you agree."

"I've called him. However, I'm waiting for my sisters. Natalie is in London. She will stop off in Dubai and meet up with Bernice, and they will arrive tomorrow."

"It is tragic, but we cannot prolong her life. Being brain dead is an indication that your mother is already on her way to another realm. I grieve for you and the family. Your mother was the sweetest and loveliest person. She never lost her childhood innocence. How is Auntie Beryl coping? And convey my sympathy to her as well. Let me know when the girls arrive. I will call each of them."

"Thank you, Auntie Joan. I'll be in touch."

Peggy was cremated on the April 11, 2013, two days after her passing. Her sudden death had a profound effect on me. She was closer to me than my other sisters. I had tried to shower her with love to compensate for the mother's love, of which she had been deprived. Pegs was barely two years old when we lost our mother. I could hardly comprehend my own loss, and my concern for my younger siblings had always troubled me. Had I done enough to ensure that Peggy's wellbeing came before anything else? At least I had not failed, and I'd tried to keep that promise to look after them.

Reminiscing, I saw the beautiful bride decked out in the ballerina-length wedding dress, of white guipure lace and tulle, made by a dressmaker who had been my mother's friend. A short, diaphanous veil covered Peg's light-brown hair, and her hazel eyes sparkled. Peggy's favourite nun from the convent, who had attended the ceremony, remarked, "She is as beautiful as the roses in her bouquet."

Peggy possessed a charming, naïve, child-like quality. She was generous of spirit and easy to like with a casual wit that was spontaneous. I was reminded of her first day at college. The lecturer had asked, "Are you as smart as your other sisters? Where did you come in class?"

"By the door, sir."

The students guffawed. He had spoken in Afrikaans and Pegs had misunderstood the question. He was quite annoyed with her, because he thought that she was trying to be clever. She, of course, was unaware until later when it was explained to her that he had been alluding to her rank in class.

Three days after Brigitte's phone call, I received the news that a memorial service, a tribute to Peggy, was held. The church was perfumed with beautiful floral bouquets and crowded with people who came to pay their respects. Two priests officiated at the ceremony where countless members of her various clubs and organizations eulogized her. Her daughters had been unaware of the extent of their mother's volunteer work and the number of charitable organisations she had supported.

A lady who did not know Peggy but lived in the same neighbourhood related a story about Peggy's kindness. Peggy regularly stopped in front of her house and picked the flowers that grew alongside the outer protective wall that all South African homes in affluent suburbs have. She then proceeded on her way with the bouquet. The neighbour was curious about the woman who stole her flowers. One day, she sent her maid to follow her. The maid reported that the woman visited a retirement home, where she presented the flowers to an elderly resident. Peggy's visits had brightened the lonely woman's day, as she never had any visitors. The neighbour concluded that she would continue in Peggy's footsteps and would visit the old lady in the retirement home.

Peggy's daughter Brigitte has accepted the responsibility of continuing the aid to her impoverished Aunt Beryl, a practice her mother had so generously started.

My own two fond recollections were of the two visits Peggy and Monty had made to Canada. On the first one, they'd brought their three daughters, and Bis had tried to persuade them to immigrate. Peggy responded, "Bis, I came especially to see a "White Christmas" rather than people, but I cannot imagine living in this cold climate." On their second visit, Monty spent a few days making a bench for the golf course, before going off to the Cayman Islands to visit Gary and Nisha.

CHAPTER 57
Verity Remembrance

The impact of Peggy's sudden death added to my grief. So many loved ones had departed, and their passing distressed me, adding to my sorrow. Grief had become my constant companion. As usual, I was all alone; three of my children lived abroad, but fortunately Nadya, who was employed in the city, could be relied on in an emergency. I realised that a drastic change was needed if I were to retain my sanity.

During the long summer days, I maintained my composure by working alongside the greens-keeper and the attendants on the golf course. But then dreaded nightfall loomed, and when darkness descended I was overcome with sadness that added to my fear. Out of sheer desperation and to while away the sleepless nights, I attempted to relive my conversations and intimate moments with Bis, but all eluded me. It occurred to me then that one cannot go back, but that I had to latch on to the memories and the gist of what remained and go on from there. Bis had already entered that other mysterious world beyond mortal comprehension, and my solace in the long, lonely nights was to have faith in the belief that at some point there had to be a reunion of souls. But that belief did not protect me from the frantic fear of burglars or intruders. My home was isolated from the street and the town, and it was a target for trespassers.

An incident heightened my terror; one afternoon I was startled to find a strange man standing in my living room. "I'm looking for the club house," he said.

"It is down near the entrance," I answered, and I showed him out. Trembling with fear, I called Mr. Jim and made him search the house. And each day, I began the ritual of securing all doors and windows well before sundown.

I was unable to articulate precisely how fear affected me, I only knew that it differed from the fear that I had experienced those many years ago under the brutal South African regime. Momentarily, I trembled and acknowledged that fear now stemmed from deep within, and it appeared to physically affect me. I wondered if perhaps I was confusing fear with grief. Night after night, I lay awake in the foreboding darkness, listening in the stillness and waiting, I knew not what for. At intervals I was startled by squeaking sounds and the odd night noises houses emit once the sun sets. Even the crickets and frogs hibernated and all critters went to sleep, but I could not. Neither did the coyote, whose shrill, nocturnal yipping sent shivers through my being. Once in a while, an owl hooted, reminding me of my childhood fear instilled by my grandmother, who claimed that a lone owl hooting and likewise, a dog baying at the moon, presaged death. But that superstition no longer held any terror for me. Grief had amputated a vital part of my being that was akin to a severed phantom limb with its recurring excruciating pain, which increased my fear. My survival depended on a change of attitude.

An item in the *Globe and Mail* caught my attention. It mentioned a newly opened women's club in Toronto. On impulse, I dialled the number and met with the owner, and without hesitation, I became a member and decided to relocate to Toronto during the frightful winter months.

Verity was a place for business women to mingle and network in a convivial atmosphere. The club became a refuge. It was a winter interlude, and I joked: "Old people winter in the Florida sunshine, but I go to Verity to enjoy the sunny warmth of congenial company."

The club proved lifesaving, and I made friends with many wonderful and accomplished women. The camaraderie helped to offset my grief. I owed a debt of gratitude to the late June, and also to Jan and Jane, who always ensured that I had a ride home. There was Jacqui, the engineer, who taught me how to operate the computer more efficiently—she rectified my errors and became a trusted companion.

Lucille, a travel agent and member, organised a tour of Egypt promising a special and exciting time. Twenty-two club members signed up. Her travel agency was responsible for a large percentage of English-speaking tourists to the Land of the Pharaohs. Under her patronage and influence, the Verity party was royally received by the minister for tourism, who assigned special guides to our group. As honoured guests, we received exceptional service. However, a way of life in Egypt, something I recalled from a previous visit with my late husband, was "Baksheesh," that is huge tips are encouraged and expected at all levels and at all times.

In Aswan, we admired the preserved rock temples of Abu Simbel built by Ramesses ll, which depicted the marvellous craftsmen of Ancient Egypt. The smaller temple cut into the rock was erected in honour of his beloved first wife, Nefartari. Our party was accommodated at the Old Cataract Hotel, and I slept in the room reputed to be where Agatha Christie had written *Death on the Nile*. I wondered how many other guests had been told that bit of local tourist lore. High tea was served in the beautiful garden overlooking the river and it was asserted that was where Ms. Christie had edited her bestseller and entertained guests.

While cruising down the Nile, I was woken at sunrise by the muezzin's ethereal call to prayers, which echoed from the turret of a mosque and reverberated across the shimmering water; what a poignant moment. I was overcome with nostalgia. The early morning call to prayer was reminiscent of my life with Bis in Potchefstroom. It resonated with the other exotic places and times; of sojourns to other lands where the Muslim call to prayer five times a day was an integral part of the raucous and bustling cities. I was joined on deck by a member I had not met before. Instantly we became friends, and I discovered that we were kindred souls. As we were cruising down the ancient river, Nancy wanted to know all about my life under Apartheid. What better place than here for a discussion, just as we were passing the remote Nubian village where the present inhabitants still lived in humble dwellings much as they did eons ago, exactly like the poor rural Africans who live in *kraals* to this day.

In the bazaars, the members purchased souvenirs. Some members bought expensive gold jewellery, and following local custom, we were encouraged to leave it overnight in the pyramid, a practice that was said to bring good luck and good health to the wearer. We sceptics thought it was a ploy by scheming merchants to replace the original items with fakes. In fact, several members, including me, had our jewels appraised on our return to London. Shortly after, I lost the gold bracelets in a taxi cab!

Part Two

One day, our chartered bus reached its destination of Luxor, where a caravan of camels chomped, and before we could alight, a camel lumbered up, lowered its haunches, and squatted directly in front of the entrance to the bus, preventing anyone exiting. The stubborn animal refused to move. I happened to be at the head of the queue and it so happened to be my seventy-ninth birthday. I decided to climb over the camel. At that precise moment, as if on cue, the beast stood up, and my only option was to hang on tightly until a drover came to my aid. Amid much laughter and many photo opportunities, the rest of the group mounted camels and we rode off into the desert.

The sighting of the enigmatic sphinx was awe-inspiring. Reclining on the desert sand, the magnificent, monumental stone behemoth appeared to be on guard, protecting the Great Pyramid of Giza. One of the many privileges we Verity tourists enjoyed was being escorted by runners carrying flaming torches that led into the Great Pyramid, which had been lit up for the occasion that night, and where we were served dinner.

We trekked into the Valley of the Kings to visit the tombs inscribed with hieroglyphs that detailed the pictorial history of the Pharaohs. The grandiose architecture of the vast temple sites of Karnack and Hatshepsut are mausoleums that speak and honour the dead rulers and is a tribute to the grandeur of Egypt's past. Their obsession with death was not confined but was pervasive and was a constant reminder to the present inhabitants, who are surrounded by monuments to the dead. Incidentally, they are a great tourist attraction appreciated by all who view them.

Our group were amazed by the awe-inspiring, gold-covered sarcophagus of Tutankhamen and the numerous tombs filled with hieroglyphics and magnificent treasures honouring the dead. But more importantly, they are also a reminder of the preparation for the transmigration to the afterlife.

Cairo began on the sands of the desert a thousand years ago, and one is aware that life and death in Egypt still co-exist as it did then. There are probably few other places where the presence of death is as prevalent in everyday living. There are constant reminders as the signs are everywhere, and they contrast with the lively garish sights of the streets and the market squares. Garrulous sounds of the traders and the masses assault the senses, punctuated five times a day by the call to prayer beckoning the faithful to honour their Maker, emphasising that life and death are part of being, and a mere stepping-stone to the hereafter.

I ruminated and marvelled at how Cairo, a modern metropolitan city that pulsed with life embraced death, and accommodated it so naturally. The Egyptian obsession with death altered my impression of death, and of grief in particular. It occurred to me that so much of the Egyptians' attention and time was taken up erecting and building monuments to their dead that it left less time to grieve, and much of their focus was in preparing for the afterlife.

The interlude away from Canada served to energise me and mitigate my loss. On my return, the first signs of spring were evident, the pure white star magnolia were in bloom, signalling the end of winter, and with it my old fears began to resurface. My trip to Egypt and my brief urban reprieve had deadened some of my pain and tempered my grief. I accepted that my life had changed. My recovery as a widow would be a slow process, but with patience, passion, and a zest for life, I would succeed.

Summer arrived all too soon, and I was forced back to an empty and forsaken home haunted by memories. The mundane routine of managing the golf club and checking my home for safety began all over again. Dutifully, my children visited from abroad during their brief summer vacations, but with their departures, I was saddened.

My seasonal commute between the farm and the city was a situation that continued until I reached my eighty-fourth birthday. Each year the demand on my physical ability to function became more onerous. Nonetheless, I managed to run the golf club until a harrowing year of adversity, including a near-fatal viral allergy and hip replacement surgery, meant that I was unable to continue, and that only by selling my home and my company could I move on.

Through it all, I tried to maintain a sense of humour. An end to my peripatetic life was in sight; I could not afford to fail, nor to become discouraged. The real estate agents and prospective buyers all wanted the property at bargain price. I stood firm.

"They know that I'm widowed and an old woman, and I'm expected to let it go for a song." I could not accept their low offers. I believed that however muddled my life appeared, things always righted themselves in the end.

Finally, a benefactor, my son-in-law, Gary Linford, bought me out. I could not have been happier with the arrangement. The barren field that Bis, I, and our children had built from scratch into a golf course and tennis courts was now in competent hands. Gary took the trouble, as I had done before, to enrol at Guelph University's Turf Management Course, to learn the art of golf course maintenance.

Senjan Golf Course would be preserved and kept in the family. I mused that somewhere, my husband was smiling. It would be a homage to him, and although he is absent, I feel a surreal presence close by, for Bis occupies my thoughts constantly. In an unexplained way we are together on another level, he in some far, far off Ruritanian world, and through mindfulness I am aware of his ever-present energy, and it is some consolation. But that does not end my longing for his physical presence.

At last I was relieved of the responsibility of maintaining a large home and a golf operation, and being free from domestic duties, I was at a loose end. Perchance I learned about a meditation course at Challis Wells in Glastonbury, England. Purely on a whim, I decided to go on a retreat, for it rang a bell of another time when I was a young, expectant mother. I remembered the excitement and the thrill that the ancient Druid stones had on me. I considered the trip a pilgrimage worth making again, hoping that perhaps I would recover the equilibrium I sorely craved. A visit to Stonehenge, I hoped, would induce the peace of mind I so desperately needed to appease my loneliness. Most of the people in our party extolled the merit of their surreal visions and out-of-body experiences (I should add that in some instances they were enhanced by cannabis). I had no such experience. All I saw was the back of a solitary blackbird perched on the farthest stone, ready to fly away. It evoked a memory from my childhood of a song my mother used to sing, "Bye, Bye Blackbird." Later it occurred to me that sighting the blackbird was simply a reminder to motivate me to live in the present and not to dwell in the past.

Life inexorably moves apace. I had benefited from my sojourn to Egypt, and I embraced that death was juxtaposed with life. It was the vital link between the land, the people, and whatever was to follow. The visit to Stonehenge once again captured some of the magical essence of life, and motivated me to move on.

I had just reached another important milestone in understanding, and accepting the importance of living in the moment.

An urgent call awaited me on my return to the city; my colleague, friend, and mentor, Dr. Bunny Tabb, had passed away. I recalled how Bunny had shepherded me through my first pregnancy and was always a phone call away. I was reminded of the time we spent in New York with our mutual friend, Phillip Tobias, doctor, archaeologist, and scholar at the launch of his book, *Into the Past*. In Bunny's address and tribute at the launch, he lauded Phillip's achievements, which left one humbled, and he stated what we his friends who had migrated believed to be true.

"Phillip, while many of your contemporaries and friends left South Africa, you stayed to fight for all the causes we espoused, but did not have the courage to face."

Phillip had responded, "I am touched to see you and Joan present today. It reminds me of our lost youth and our struggle against Apartheid. I've no doubt that between the two of you a record will be left of the struggles we faced."

Unfortunately, I have lost both of them, and recently a third friend Ahmed Kathrada, who figured largely in my youth, had succumbed. He had been Bis's roommate for nigh on six years, and prior to his imprisonment on Robben Island had willingly chauffeured me when Bis was not available. Ahmed was a Communist, a political activist, and despite our different political affiliation, we had been comrades. We'd shared true friendship. A treasured gift, and he had set an example of how to live in harmony with friend and foe alike.

My contemporaries are no more, and Apartheid too is extinct as the quagga.

Although the political pendulum has shifted, and white domination is no longer an issue in South Africa, unfortunately it remains a troubled country. Inequality and dire poverty exist, along with violent crime.

I am inspired to muddle on, for there is still a way to go, and like my icon the chameleon, I have to adjust to change. It is my aim to make each moment count. Ultimately, a passion for life is the one travelling companion essential for the road that lies ahead. In my quest to set an example, I must document the details I still remember as a reminder to my progeny and descendants to understand that duty, integrity, and a generous spirit are vitally important. Dreams do come true, and anything is possible in this land that is all embracing, and where one may live a contented and privileged life.

Are there other milestones? Who knows, and how will it all end?

I was married on my birthday, under the sign of Pisces, those twin fishes that swim in opposite directions, an example for co-existence in a restricted world. Bis and I personified them. Now he too is no more!

The loss of Bis impelled me to grow stronger, and yet again I had to chart a course in unknown waters. I was predisposed to find the courage that enabled me to confront and slay my dragons. The differences that bothered me throughout my life have diminished with age. But senescence is unavoidable, and I have found my niche that was waiting to be discovered, and it is proof that there are diverse choices. Unlike my namesake, the martyr whose choice was limited and burnt at the stake, I simply had to select which way to swim. I am confident that what will be, will be!

Recently I sustained a nasty fall, which unnerved me, and it alarmed my daughters, who were out of the country. They feared for my safety. With trepidation, I agreed to a residential retirement home. Entering it hearkened back to my first day at the convent. But then I was young and had my entire future ahead of me; now at ninety years old, this felt like a death sentence. In the first weeks, I knew it was not for me. I attempted to fit in. I failed miserably to adjust to that environment, and realised it was hopeless. After months of mild depression, I escaped to my own apartment. It was an immediate cure for what ailed me. I am fortunate to have the gift of all my senses, and privileged to enjoy in freedom what is left of my life. But I have another important duty to perform.

A new hospital in Fergus, Ontario, is currently under construction and I am grateful for the opportunity to sponsor the atrium in honour of my husband.

Dr. Abdul Haq Bismillah. MbBch; MRCOG(London) It is my tribute to him for all he had accomplished, and his foresight in choosing Canada to raise and educate our family, where we resided with dignity in this tranquil and beautiful country. I look forward to another milestone: my attendance at the new hospital scheduled to open in 2020.

Unlike me, Bis was sceptical when it came to horoscopes, and during his life I steered clear of the subject. Now, ever the optimist, I take pleasure and comfort in reading mine, discarding anything that sounds vaguely unpleasant, and delighting in any good fortune that is predicted.

My horoscope for my ninetieth birthday, on the 4th of March, 2018.

"You will be inspired by new challenges rather than frightened by them this year. At last you have realised that life is too short to dwell on the possibility of failure and that trying by itself is a measure of success. Go all out for glory, and you'll get it."

The End

ACKNOWLEDGEMENTS

I OWE A DEBT OF GRATITUDE TO MY DAUGHTERS, NADYA, THE FIRST reader, and Nisha, who read the original script written in third person and suggested I change and write it in first person.

I'm forever indebted to my friends and personal team of Jacqui d'Eon and Nancy Coldham, without whom this book would not have been possible.

Jacqui helped me with my computer skills. She saved my manuscript from destruction on innumerable occasions.

Nancy introduced me and my story to FriesenPress, and visited them on my behalf to ensure that it was the right decision.

Lastly, to my team at FriesenPress, without whose encouragement I could not have been published.

Printed in Canada